SOCIAL PROBLEMS

Social Problems

ENDURING MAJOR ISSUES

AND SOCIAL CHANGE

by F. James Davis

PROFESSOR OF SOCIOLOGY, CALIFORNIA STATE COLLEGE, FULLERTON

 THE FREE PRESS, NEW YORK

COLLIER-MACMILLAN LIMITED, LONDON

T O *Lucile*

A N D *Elinor, Miriam, and Sarah*

300
D261a
1970

The Free Press
A Division of The Macmillan Company
866 Third Avenue, New York, New York   10022

Collier-Macmillan Canada Ltd., Toronto, Ontario

Library of Congress Catalog Card Number: 76-111934

Printed in the United States of America

printing number
2   3   4   5   6   7   8   9   10

Contents

88868

LIST OF TABLES

LIST OF FIGURES

Preface

This book provides a meaningful sociological framework for the analysis of social problems. The approach is developed from collective behavior theory, with particular reference to the public opinion process. The conflict of values approach is incorporated into the treatment, but the framework also makes room for the discussion of conflicting beliefs of fact. Norms are supported by beliefs of fact as well as by beliefs of value. Issues are seen as controversies over emergent norms, which arise when traditional and bureaucratic norms fail to provide adequate guides for conduct. The issues that persist and become of major concern to substantial numbers of people in the society are social problems. (See Chapter 1 for a more precise definition.) The approach provides a useful way of relating social problems to the processes of social change.

This framework is used to analyze relevant data about a limited number of social problems. The book has been kept to a modest size in the belief that courses in social problems are more likely to be worthwhile and interesting if the textbook is supplemented by material in paperbacks and in books of readings. The hope is that the theoretical framework will prove useful in the discussion of other reading materials. The assumption in writing the book has been that students who have already had a course in introductory sociology, as well as those who have not, will profit from it, although each teacher must gauge his own situation.

My debt to many researchers and scholars, mostly sociologists, is at least partly apparent in the footnotes and the chapter bibliographies. Anyone who attempts a work of this scope becomes aware of the difficulties and the variety of the efforts to develop dependable knowledge about the dilemmas of human societies. I am grateful to a number of colleagues for their help, and for the interest of many other friends. Professor Harold W. Saunders has had much influence on all my thinking, and the late Manford H. Kuhn would recognize some of his handiwork in my treatment of the processes of public discussion. My thanks to my patient family and to all those who have encouraged me in this effort.

F.J.D.

I

A Framework for
Sociological Analysis

. . . the most learned of sociologists is not competent to go among the lowest of Australian tribesmen and point out to them that they have such and such social problems—for example, improper child feeding, sexual immorality, or poor housing. One guilty of such impertinence would arouse astonishment and ridicule, if not resentment, and might very properly be informed that no such problems existed in that group.[1]

1. Social Change, Collective Behavior, and Major Issues

Peoples whose traditional cultures endure without major disruption have few if any social problems. They experience hardship and pain, even war and natural disaster, but such trials are expected and traditional answers for them are plentiful. Not until the whole shared way of life is under great pressure to change is there serious confusion about what to do and why. Then, unequipped and disenchanted with the old ways, these people must somehow learn to wrestle with the dilemmas that accompany change. In more complex societies social change knows no end, and fresh problems spring up for every one that is brought under control or outmoded. Many a "modern man" falters in the face of such threatening confusion. "Is nothing sacred?" he often asks.

The view that the people of a society are competent to identify their social problems—whatever terms they may use—obviously rests on a particular definition of a social problem. It implies that the members of a community know what is bothering them; they know "where it hurts." Sociologists and other social scientists enter the scene as

---

[1] Clarence M. Case, *Outlines of Introductory Sociology: A Textbook of Readings in Social Science* (New York: Harcourt, Brace & Co., 1924), 627.

systematic observers, seeking explanations of the conditions involved and of why the complaints are being made. But before we can understand clearly the definition of social problems set forth in this book, we must gain some perspective on that complex phenomenon so intimately associated with social problems—social change.

First, are social change and cultural change the same thing? A social pattern or system is a network, large or small, in which persons have mutual expectations and in which they influence one another's actions. *Social change*, then, is a *modification in patterns of human expectations and interaction.*[2] *Culture* is a relatively integrated and comprehensive *pattern of social life* that members of a group learn, share, and pass on; it is *a social product that lasts through generations.*[3] Thus cultural change involves modified social patterns, but *not all social change produces cultural change.* Changes may occur in patterns of social relationships that have not been transmitted as guides to conduct from generation to generation. Much of the social change to which we now turn, however, does result in cultural modifications.

COMPREHENSIVE SOCIAL CHANGE

Many of the broadest sociological theories have centered on the theme that human societies have been going through a long-range transformation from one type to another. Opposite types have come to be thought of as falling at opposite ends of a continuum so that given societies can be placed at appropriate points along the scale.[4] Some writers have defined three or more types, and some have created subtypes. There have been cycle theories, too, and still other approaches, but analysis in terms of two polar types of society has predominated. The basic changes thus illuminated often have been identified as causes, or at least concomitants, of social problems.

American sociologists have emphasized the transition from pri-

[2] George A. Lundberg, Clarence C. Schrag, and Otto N. Larsen, *Sociology* (3rd ed.; New York: Harper & Row, 1963), 675.
[3] *Ibid.*, 105. Culture includes standards of conduct, ways of behaving, symbols, and (in some definitions) material products.
[4] John C. McKinney and Charles P. Loomis, "The Typological Tradition," in Joseph S. Roucek (ed.), *Readings in Contemporary Sociology* (Paterson, N.J.: Littlefield, Adams & Co., 1961), 557–82; Weber is master of what he called the "Ideal Type"; see Max Weber (trans. by A. M. Henderson and Talcott Parsons), *The Theory of Social and Economic Organization* (New York: Oxford University Press, 1947).

mary to secondary social relationships that accompany the shift from rural to urban life. *Charles H. Cooley depicted the primary group as small, intimate, usually face-to-face, a group in which the members know one another as "whole persons."* In a society in which most or all social relationships are of a primary group nature, such *informal social control* as praise, gossip, ridicule, and avoidance effectively *sustain feelings of personal loyalty to the group.*[5] Cooley also implied the existence of an opposite kind of group and social organization,[6] and many sociologists responded by defining this *secondary group as impersonal, unsentimental, specialized, contractual, and usually large.*[7] Informal social controls, it was held, lose their effectiveness in secondary group situations and must be supplemented by law and other *formal social controls,* which involve *explicit rules, planned sanctions, and appointed officials to interpret and enforce the rules.*[8]

The reason why American sociologists were so prompt in supplying their supplement to Cooley's analysis was their familiarity with a number of paired societal types used by European writers. One of the most relevant treatments was by Ferdinand Tönnies, a German, whose *Gemeinschaft,* or "communal society," is clearly a "primary community,"[9] one in which there is *interaction among "whole persons," unlimited loyalty to the group, and a feeling of belonging together based on homogeneity of* kinship, habitat, work, and traditions. Tönnies' *Gesellschaft,* or "associational society," is one of *rational self-interest, voluntary group memberships, segmental and contractual interaction, a complex division of labor, and heterogeneity of experience.*[10]

Central to Tönnies' thinking was the idea that social unity rests on different foundations in different types of society. It rests on traditionally assigned obligations in a *status society,* but on voluntary agreements in a *contractual society.*[11] It depends on cultural similarity

---

[5] Charles H. Cooley, *Social Organization* (New York: Scribners, 1909), 23–31.
[6] McKinney and Loomis, *op. cit.*, 362.
[7] Kingsley Davis, *Human Society* (New York: Macmillan, 1949), 303–06.
[8] John W. Bennett and Melvin M. Tumin, *Social Life* (New York: Alfred A. Knopf, 1948), 525; F. James Davis *et al., Society and the Law* (New York: The Free Press, 1962), 43; Richard R. Korn and Lloyd W. McCorkle, *Criminology and Penology* (New York: Holt, Rinehart & Winston, 1959), 75–83.
[9] Leonard Broom and Philip Selznick, *Sociology* (3rd ed.; New York: Harper & Row, 1963).
[10] Ferdinand Tönnies, *Gemeinschaft und Gesellschaft* (1st ed., 1887); trans. and ed. by Charles P. Loomis as *Fundamental Concepts of Sociology* (New York: American Book Co., 1940).
[11] Sir Henry Sumner Maine, *Ancient Law* (New York: Henry Holt & Co., 1930, first publ. in 1861), 54–57, 180–82.

in societies with *mechanical solidarity,* where people do what they are expected to do without question, but on the interdependence required by a complex division of labor in societies with *organic solidarity*.[12] It is based on the authority and common culture of the kinship group in the *folk society,* but presumably on extra-familial formal authority in the *urban society*.[13]

Although sociologists often focus on one or two aspects of social organization when using these societal types, the types are defined as consisting of a number of characteristics that seem to cluster together. One must consider the different aspects separately in order to compare different treatments carefully or to use the types for field research. The sacred-secular typology includes many traits, but its name points to one that is particularly important in the approach to social problems we use in this book—attitudes toward social change. In the *sacred society, people take a worshipful and unquestioning attitude toward the total tradition;* it is reinforced by religious belief and practice, but the family, economic practices, and all other customs also are considered sacred. Thus social change is unthinkable; a dissenter on any aspect of community life is a heretic. In the *secular society, people* continually *question their own practices* because they *seek more efficient* ways of doing things; nothing seems too sacred to question, and all institutions are under constant criticism. Churches may flourish in secular societies, then, but they face unrelenting pressure to change. Howard Becker uses these as abstract, analytical types and invites us to think in terms of a sacred-secular continuum.[14]

Straight-line evolution has often been assumed by those who have made use of these typologies. Some thinkers, in effect, have believed in the reality of progress and have tilted the continuum upward toward a shining zenith;[15] others have slanted it downward toward ultimate doom. Some, then, have characterized the evolving urban community as a delightfully sophisticated and rational place, while others have seen it as chaotic, lonely, and wicked. Becker, for one, used his types in a scientific way, to aid in the discovery of the conditions and conse-

[12] Emile Durkheim, *On the Division of Labor in Society* (New York: Macmillan, 1933), Chapters 1–3.
[13] Robert Redfield, "The Folk Society," *American Journal of Sociology,* 52 (January, 1947), 293–308; Horace Miner, "The Folk-Urban Continuum," *American Sociological Review,* 17 (October, 1952), 529–37.
[14] Howard Becker, *Through Values to Social Interpretation* (Durham, N.C.: Duke University Press, 1950), 248–80.
[15] Don Martindale, *Social Life and Cultural Change* (Princeton, N.J.: D. Van Nostrand Co., 1962), 13–15.

quences of given types of social organization. He investigated the process of *sacrilization* as well as *secularization,* pointing out that both occur in industrial-urban communities. Hitler and other dictators, for instance, have enforced a prescribed sacred way of life in complex societies.[16]

In proposing to correct and test rather than abandon the hypothesis of evolutionary growth of human societies, Wilbert Moore argues that demonstrably effective technology survives and accumulates, but norms and values are "optional" and therefore noncumulative.[17] As man has increased his ability to adapt to his environment and control it, he reasons, four extremely long-range trends have been occurring: (1) Man's numbers have increased, (2) "objective knowledge and rational technique" have been additive, (3) increasing attention has been given to matters other than material needs and comforts, and (4) all human beings are increasingly part of a single social and cultural system.[18] Clearly, Moore refers to mankind as a whole over a period of many thousands of years, because negative instances can be cited for given periods in the histories of particular peoples. But let us narrow our focus somewhat in time and space for further clues to the how of social change.

SOME KEY DIMENSIONS OF MODERN SOCIAL CHANGE

A list of the major axes of social change in our time must include growth in technology, urbanization, and formal organizations. The interrelatedness of these major dimensions of change is inescapable.

Technological Growth

A little over two centuries ago in Western Europe, steam power was wedded to a large number of new inventions to begin a startling revolution in industry and agriculture. Societies around the world have been profoundly affected ever since, and this technological revolution is still accelerating and spreading. In a time of space exploration and

---

[16] Becker, *op. cit.,* 249.
[17] Wilbert E. Moore, "A Reconsideration of Theories of Social Change," *American Sociological Review,* 25 (December, 1960), 810–18; see also Pitirim Sorokin, *Social and Cultural Dynamics* (4 volumes; New York: American Book Co., 1937–41), 667.
[18] Wilbert E. Moore, *Social Change* (Englewood Cliffs, N.J.: Prentice-Hall, 1963), 116–17.

computerization, it is hard to realize that much dramatic technological change had already occurred before the horse culture began to subside in the United States half a century ago. The "population explosion" began long before this century. (See Chapter 11.) In 1850 more than four-fifths of the nation's work was performed by animal power and only about 7 per cent by the power from mineral resources, then coal and waterpower only. By 1940 the situation was reversed, with but 10 per cent of the work being done by animal and human labor and 90 per cent by mineral power. During this same period output per man-hour increased more than fourfold. Compact and inexpensive, mineral power has evidently been a major reason for our current material well-being. Very likely our technological growth will continue to accelerate, but an important variable is the conservation of minerals used for motive power and the development of new sources.[19] Atomic power is apparently extending the changes already in process by World War II.[20]

In the early 1960's the typical American worker produced about three times as much as he had in 1910, and his income would buy three times as much.[21] From 1947 to 1958, with only a slight increase in the total labor force and a decrease in workers engaged in production, the output of America's manufacturing concerns increased by one-fourth.[22] The tractor, electricity, related improvements in machinery, hybrid strains, and other *innovations enabled the farmer to increase his output per man-hour nearly four times from 1930 to 1961.[23] Such rapid development requires that people swiftly accept, learn about, and invest in new technology.*

As agricultural production has increased, the proportion of persons in farming has declined sharply, more than fourfold from 1910 to 1960 (Table 1.1). The table also shows a marked decline in the percentage of unskilled workers, a modest increase in skilled and semiskilled laborers, and heavy increases in the proportions of professionals, proprietors and managerial officials, salesmen, and clerical workers. A great many new occupations were created during this period as the trend toward greater specialization proceeded.

---

[19] J. Frederic Dewhurst, *America's Needs and Resources* (New York: Twentieth Century Fund, 1947), 680–87.

[20] Vincent H. Whitney, "Some Sociological Consequences of Atomic Power," *The Annals*, 290 (November, 1953), 67–75.

[21] U.S. Bureau of the Census, *Statistical Abstract of the United States, 1961* (Washington, D.C.: U.S. Government Printing Office, 1961), 218–21.

[22] *Ibid.*, 777.

[23] Statistical Abstract of the United States, 1962, *op. cit.*, 644.

TABLE 1.1

CHANGING COMPOSITION OF U.S. LABOR FORCE,
1910–1960

Occupation	Percentage in 1910	Percentage in 1960
Farmers	16.5	4.4
Farm laborers	14.5	2.9
Professionals	4.4	12.2
Proprietors and officials	6.5	11.5
Clerks, sales, and kindred workers	10.2	22.8
Skilled and semiskilled workers	26.4	31.6
Laborers	14.7	4.4

SOURCE: *U.S. Bureau of Census,* Statistical Abstract of the United States: 1960 (*Washington, D.C.: U.S. Government Printing Office, 1960*), 217.

Although output has increased continuously during the past century, the work week in both agriculture and industry has shrunk considerably (Table 1.2). Many professional and managerial occupations have not been affected by this trend, but for the great majority of the employed the increase in leisure time has radically changed their way of life. Countless new activities, associations, and businesses have emerged, and to many people work is a means of support for leisure time preoccupations. Some people work at more than one job because the short work week gives them more leisure time than they want or feel they can afford. Some observers regard the use of leisure time as a social problem.[24]

The almost continuous introduction of more efficient machinery also has created unemployment—enforced leisure—a problem we leave for Chapter 4. Furthermore, it has resulted in much monotonous manual work, especially on assembly lines, frequently resulting in feelings of meaninglessness and powerlessness. There is evidence that these feelings of "alienation from work" are much less common in

[24] Erwin O. Smigel, *Work and Leisure: A Contemporary Social Problem* (New Haven: College & University Press, 1963).

TABLE 1.2

LENGTH OF AVERAGE WORK WEEK (IN HOURS) IN AGRICULTURE AND
IN NONAGRICULTURAL INDUSTRIES IN THE U.S., 1850–1960

	All Industries	Agri- culture	Nonagricultural Industries
1850	69.7	72.0	65.7
1870	65.3	70.0	60.0
1890	61.7	68.0	57.1
1910	54.9	65.0	50.3
1930	45.7	55.0	43.2
1940	43.8	54.6	41.1
1950	39.9	47.2	38.8
1960	38.5	44.0	38.0

SOURCE: Sebastian DeGrazia, Of Time, Work and Leisure (New York: The Twentieth Century Fund, 1962), Table 1, 441.

more highly automated, continuous-flow, plants. Highly skilled technical workers apparently derive meaning and a sense of responsibility from their work.[25]

TECHNOLOGY, SCIENCE, AND SECULARISM. Although a great many inventors are not scientists, they usually devise applications of scientific principles and often use the scientific method. Scientific contributions to the development of new sources of power and to new techniques such as data-processing are widely recognized. Scientific knowledge continues to mount, to be disseminated in schools and through the mass media and in technological pursuits in industry and government.

Science probably has been the major secularizing force in modern times. That is, science encourages people to be curious, open-minded, and to question existing explanations of everything, including how a society is arranged. Those who would maintain a sacred society, in

[25] Robert Blauner, *Alienation and Freedom: The Factory Worker and His Industry* (Chicago: University of Chicago Press, 1964).

Becker's sense, usually reject science or try to keep it in rather strict compartments.

Urbanization

With industrial technology came the factory, and in turn the shift of people from farm to city. In 1790 only about 5 per cent of Americans lived in places with a population of 2,500 or more; by 1960 the percentage had grown to 70. From 1850 to 1960 the number of American cities with a population in excess of 250,000 increased from 1 to 51.[26] After many decades, the pattern of population growth was shifted from the central cities to the suburbs by the streetcar, the electric train, and later the automobile.[27] Since World War II, suburban areas have grown much faster than the central cities, so that perhaps half of America's urban dwellers now live in suburbs. The nation's major industrial and commercial areas have become huge urban agglomerations—the "megalopolis"—that often spread across state lines.

Immigration has made our central cities the homes of heterogeneous national, racial, and religious groups, although most of our central cities today have fewer foreign born, more descendants of the foreign born, and a much higher proportion of Negroes than they did some decades ago. The rural-urban migration continues as more machinery and other improvements reduce the amount of labor needed to produce a given farm output. There is also considerable movement from one urban place of residence to another. Migration to a new city, state, or region is usually prompted by better economic opportunities, which often facilitate upward movement in the class system. The automobile and airplane move hundreds of thousands of Americans daily. Heterogeneity and increasing mobility continue to be hallmarks of the American city.

Although the proportion of secondary contacts increases with urbanization, and many people have limited contact with those who live or work close to them, primary group relationships are much in evidence and are essential to the maintenance of urban society.[28]

[26] *Statistical Abstract of the United States,* 1961, *op. cit.,* 21–23.

[27] Donald J. Bogue, *Population Growth in Standard Metropolitan Areas, 1900–1950* (Washington, D.C.: Housing Home and Finance Agency, 1953), Table 1; William F. Ogburn, "Inventions of Local Transportation and the Pattern of Cities," *Social Forces,* 24 (May, 1946), 373–79.

[28] Broom and Selznick, *op. cit.,* 145–67; Lundberg, Schrag, and Larsen, *op. cit.,* 67–76; William F. Whyte, *Street Corner Society* (Chicago: University of Chicago Press, 1943), 3–25, 255–68.

There are families, primary neighborhoods, friendship groups, and primary groups that are crucial to the operation of such formal structures as the factory, the insurance company, and the school system. Sociologists for some time assumed that urbanites were heavy joiners and suggested that the great diversity of special interest groups was a response to urban social differentiation.[29] Some reasoned further that the voluntary association was the urban replacement for the primary group. Evidence now indicates that most Americans, rural and urban, belong to no or to very few voluntary associations, and the typical member is not active. Membership is especially infrequent in the urban lower class,[30] and less common in large heterogeneous cities than in small ones.[31] Interaction in the voluntary association is segmental; it does not involve "whole persons," because it exists for special interests. A further explanation is suggested by the following statement:

> Voluntary associations are an important mechanism for implementing the specialized interests of people, but many of our interests can be satisfied in secondary interaction that does not involve *joining* an organization. It is not necessary to "join" a chain store, a movie theater, or a professional baseball team in order to patronize it.[32]

Studies in other countries indicate that the emergence and functioning of voluntary associations, urban and rural, is influenced by the cultural pattern.[33]

Criticisms of the rural-urban continuum include the suggestion that cultural and population variables must be separated. Cultural traits such as secular outlook and literacy may be found in both rural and urban communities, and so may sacred outlook and illiteracy. Richard Dewey suggests that increasing size and density of population

---

[29] Herbert Goldhamer, "Voluntary Associations in the United States," in Paul K. Hatt and Albert J. Reiss, Jr. (eds.), *Cities and Society: The Revised Reader in Urban Sociology* (New York: The Free Press, 1957), 592.

[30] Morris Axelrod, "Urban Structure and Social Participation," *American Sociological Review*, 21 (February, 1956), 13–18; Charles R. Wright and Herbert H. Hyman, "Voluntary Association Membership of American Adults," *American Sociological Review*, 23 (June, 1958), 284–94; Bartolomeo J. Palisi, "Ethnic Generation and Social Participation," *Sociological Inquiry*, 35 (Spring, 1965), 225.

[31] Murray Hausknecht, *The Joiners* (Bedminster Press, 1962), 9, 39.

[32] Lundberg, Schrag, and Larsen, *op. cit.*, 313–14.

[33] Robert T. Anderson and Gallatin Anderson, "Voluntary Associations and Urbanization: A Diachronic Analysis," *American Journal of Sociology*, 65 (November, 1959), 265–73.

cause the following five social changes independent of cultural patterns:

1. Anonymity
2. Division of labor
3. Heterogeneity, induced and maintained by (1) and (2)
4. Impersonal and formally prescribed relationships
5. Symbols of status which are independent of personal acquaintance.[34]

Growth of Formal Organizations

A *formal organization* is one that is *planned to achieve certain goals* through a *division of labor,* a *pyramid of authority,* and *explicit rules.*[35] It makes it possible to coordinate the specialized activities of large numbers of people. Although bureaucracies are not a modern invention, their rise has facilitated the technological revolution. Without them the vast networks of production, distribution, and finance that characterize the modern economy, capitalist or communist, could not be coordinated. The industrial plant, the railroad corporation, the savings and loan company, the department store, the labor union, the professional association, the farm organization, and the Chamber of Commerce are but a few of the new bureaucratic economic organizations that have appeared during the past century.

Today an increasing proportion of people work within the framework of formal organizations in government, education, the military, police and correctional work, religion, the professions, and voluntary associations. Relations between organization and individual are contractual, so the individual is expendable from the larger, impersonal organization view that places efficiency first. If an employee fails to follow the time schedule and to meet all the other obligations of his assigned role, he is seen as endangering organizational goals and must face appropriate sanctions, perhaps loss of his job. Thus an individual may well feel powerless, especially in *complex organizations,* those vast networks that consist *of units* which are themselves *formal organizations.* Primary groups do exist within formal organizations, as we have seen, and they often shield a person from formal

---

[34] Richard Dewey, "The Rural-Urban Continuum: Real but Relatively Unimportant," *American Journal of Sociology,* 66 (July, 1960), 65; see also Louis Wirth, "Urbanism as a Way of Life," *American Journal of Sociology,* 44 (July, 1938), 18.
[35] Most sociological analysis of formal organizations stems from Weber, *op. cit.*

sanctions. Informal groups may hinder efficiency under certain conditions, as managers often suspect, but without them formal organizations could not function.

The need for coordinating formal organizations has given rise to a new type of career, that of manager or administrator. *The administrative part of the formal organization is the bureaucracy.*[36] The higher up in the pyramid of authority, the more a manager must be able to think rationally and act decisively in terms of the *general goals* of the organization. The general expectation is that the administrator will identify closely with the organization and compete for the highly rewarding positions at the top. Some observers think that the organizational demands imposed on those in positions of middle management are excessive. They say this "organization man"[37] and his family must live in the prescribed, "other-directed" fashion,[38] in the proper type of suburb. Then, as an interchangeable cog in the impersonal machine, he may be required on sudden notice to move across country and fit quickly into another presumably identical suburb. At any rate, the manager, like others in the labor force, moves to enhance his economic opportunities.

Government, at all levels, is one of the areas in which the growth of formal organizations is most conspicuous. More governmental coordination is sought as population grows, society becomes more complex, and new services are demanded. There would be no Atomic Energy Commission if scientists had not released energy from radioactive minerals, and no Federal Bureau of Investigation without the demand and public support for a federal detective agency. At the state level we would have no motor vehicle and highway departments without the automobile and the demand for a mass system of public highways. Cities would have no fire departments or urban renewal authorities if it were not considered desirable to control fires and eliminate slums. Leaders of the many new emerging nations in the world quickly appreciate the value of public administration, since they must manage complex organizations. The division of powers is especially perplexing to them, but authority must be allocated in all types of formal organizations. Where and how the administrators are to

---

[36] Broom and Selznick, *op. cit.*, 224.
[37] William H. Whyte, Jr., *The Organization Man* (New York: Simon & Schuster, 1956).
[38] David Riesman, in collaboration with Reuel Denney and Nathan Glazer, *The Lonely Crowd* (New Haven: Yale University Press, 1950).

function along the democratic-authoritarian continuum must be related to culture and situation.

Coordinating a formal organization also requires effective communications, and methods of recruiting new personnel and assigning and training them. It requires efficient record-keeping; no formal organization, whether it be a college or university, a credit company or a football league, can operate without some "red tape." In many instances consultants and researchers are sought to help with these matters, and with production or other primary tasks of the organization. Increasingly, organizations are conducting their own research, sometimes seeking sociological knowledge of the organization itself. Research is increasingly being accomplished through formally organized effort. Man is no longer leaving the development of new technology and the acquisition of basic knowledge so much to chance and private motivation as he did in the past. There is indeed a striving for rationality in the formal organization.

COLLECTIVE BEHAVIOR

Looking back on such significant developments as secularization and bureaucratization, we may be tempted to conclude that changes have been quite orderly, and perhaps inevitable. If we examine closely a historical period, however, or a given aspect of current change, we find more sound and fury than is at first apparent. The Founding Fathers disagreed with one another, sometimes violently, before they adopted the Constitution. And just *how* is current change in American race relations taking place? Is technology advanced without any disagreements? Urbanization? Sociologists have developed a perspective on social change-in-the-making that can illuminate the dynamics of the group contests involved in processes of change. This approach, "collective behavior," provides an effective way of defining and analyzing social problems, and other helpful perspectives may be incorporated into it, or related to it.

Basic Perspective on Collective Behavior

Collective behavior must be understood in relation to *norms*, which are *rules of conduct.* They facilitate predictability of actions by indicating correct and incorrect behavior for persons in given situations. *Traditional guides for behavior are cultural norms; those prescribed by formal organizations are formal or bureaucratic norms.*

Collective behavior is evidently a response to the lack of sufficient cultural and formal norms to guide group behavior. Despite the appearance of complete normlessness of some collective behavior, it is evidently guided by shared expectations which emerge either spontaneously or gradually. *Collective behavior may thus be defined as conduct guided by emergent norms rather than by cultural or formal norms.*[39]

Although such diverse forms of collective behavior as panics, riots, fads, social epidemics, public discussions, and social movements are all guided by emergent norms, do all of them promote social change? By definition, they all result in at least a fleeting departure from established social patterns, but often they effect no lasting modification. Many crowds and many rumors, many fads, fashions, and crazes come and go, and not all public discussions and social movements result in lasting change either. Many emotional expressions of unrest do presumably contribute at least indirectly to social change, however, and many crowd actions, discussions, and social movements clearly modify existing social arrangements. Our interest in collective behavior will be primarily in how it implements social change.

Norms are based on beliefs of two kinds: (1) value judgments, beliefs that certain things are desirable; and (2) judgments of fact, beliefs that certain things are possible.[40] A (positive) value is an affirmation that a certain state or condition is desirable, although to a given person or group, some values are more important than others. Among the values underlying the norm that final examinations are to be taken when scheduled except for accident or serious illness, for example, are convictions that a person should accept the consequences of his own actions, the conditions of the contest should be equal, and efficient operation of a formal educational system should take priority over personal convenience. Among the judgments of fact that underlie the same norm are beliefs that a clear and firm rule will deter students from procrastinating, it will prevent complaints about disappointing performances, it will motivate students to study more consistently, and thus they will learn more. These are cause-and-effect

---

[39] Ralph H. Turner, and Lewis M. Killian, *Collective Behavior*, (Englewood Cliffs, N.J.: Prentice-Hall, 1957), 12–13.
[40] Max Weber, (trans. and ed. by Edward A. Shils and Henry A. Finch), *Methodology of the Social Sciences* (New York: The Free Press, 1949), 49–112. The fact-value distinction is discussed in Chapters 2 and 20.

beliefs; there are also "simple" judgments that certain things in fact exist. Obviously the underlying support for social norms is complex; complete agreement is difficult to obtain in a relatively secular society on either underlying value priorities or factual assumptions.

Traditional and formal behavior are guided by norms, but so is collective behavior. A great deal has been learned about the collective beliefs that underlie emergent norms,[41] but it is difficult to separate judgments of fact from value judgments. Sometimes one is crucial, sometimes the other. Sometimes traditional or formal values are combined with emergent factual beliefs; sometimes the reverse occurs. Changes in one can influence changes in the other, so they obviously are not identical (see Chapter 2).

An otherwise puzzling phenomenon—that groups often intensify their demands at the very time when the conditions they complained about are improving—is understandable in terms of changing beliefs. New vistas from higher ground may lead to new factual beliefs about the probability of achieving certain values. Assertions that new steps now *should* be taken bespeak emergent norms, but not necessarily new values. This interpretation in terms of the "revolution of rising expectations" was applied to the French Revolution by Alexis de Tocqueville.[42] The Marxian view, that the struggle between the "haves" and the "have-nots" causes revolution, goes against the observation that the historical outcome of extreme inequality has been apathy.[43] Perhaps revolutionary protest is most likely when a lengthy period of improvement is followed by a sudden reversal.[44]

Whether conditions are improving, deteriorating, or whatever, determined collective action for change depends on a mood of dissatisfaction. This mood requires that people believe that certain things are in fact true and that certain values are so important that a marked discrepancy between desired and actual conditions is intolerable.[45]

---

[41] For a provocative and thorough treatment, see Neil J. Smelser, *Theory of Collective Behavior* (New York: The Free Press, 1963), Chapter V, "The Creation of Generalized Beliefs." (For instance, he says panic rests on the simplest form of generalized belief, hysteria, which is a "belief empowering an ambiguous element in the environment with a generalized power to threaten or destroy."), 84.

[42] Alexis de Tocqueville, (trans. by John Bonner) *The Old Regime and the French Revolution* (New York: Harper & Bros., 1856), 214.

[43] Turner and Killian, *op. cit.*, 519–23.

[44] James C. Davies, "Toward a Theory of Revolution," *American Sociological Review*, 27 (February, 1962), 5–19.

[45] *Ibid.*, 6.

When this combination of beliefs results in *marked social unrest, the necessary general foundation for change-oriented collective behavior has been laid.*[46] What form the action will take depends in considerable part on the judgments of fact and value that undergird the emergent norms.

The Public Opinion Process

In modern democratic societies, a very important form of response to social unrest is the discussion of issues by publics. *An issue is a matter on which there is disagreement; a public is a dispersed collectivity that includes everyone who is interested in discussing and trying to influence the resolution of an issue.*[47] The public opinion *process consists of* (1) *defining the issue,* (2) *discussing the issue, and* (3) *expressing views concerning what action to take to resolve the issue.* Except for a binding direct vote on an issue, the process implies a division of labor between the public and those who have formal responsibility to make and implement decisions.

Public discussion is more rational than such responses to unrest as riots and panics because it involves searching for and weighing *alternatives.* It is quite like a person's thought processes, except that a system of communications is required and authority must be delegated with an eye toward action.[48] But various factors work against the rationality of public discussion, including propaganda, lack of information, and failure to include all possible alternatives. The quality of public discussion varies a good deal, so it is only *relatively rational* as compared with other forms of collective behavior.

Despite this qualification, public discussion is an attempt to meet the challenge of group crises peacefully and with reason. Because he conceived of democracy as government responsive to enlightened public discussion, Thomas Jefferson valued newspapers and mass education. This emphasis that all citizens be informed, that they discuss issues and influence their leaders, is a highly secular view, unlike the mood of the folk society and the "prescribed sacred" outlook in the

---

[46] Herbert Blumer, Part IV, "Collective Behavior," in Alfred M. Lee (ed.), *Principles of Sociology* (Rev. 2nd ed.; New York: Barnes & Noble, College Outline Series, 1951), 172–73.

[47] *Ibid.,* 189; Turner and Killian, *op. cit.,* 219; Kurt Lang and Gladys Lang, *Collective Dynamics* (New York: Thomas Y. Crowell Co., 1961), 371.

[48] Cf. Elliott Friedson, "A Prerequisite for Participation in the Public Opinion Process," *Public Opinion Quarterly* (Spring, 1955), 105–11.

dictatorship. Their sensitivity to the consent of the governed causes men of power carefully to assess public opinion before they take action.[49] Even totalitarian rulers can be swayed by the will of an informed people.

The *basic norm that initiates public discussion* appears to be that *people concerned* about a given condition *ought to seek a sound diagnosis of the difficulty and participate in an informed discussion of alternative actions.* The norm is emergent in a given situation, though in general form it is readily available in a secular society. Other collective responses to crisis are violent outbursts, collective flight (panic), social movements, or resignation[50]—depending on what type of norm emerges to define the situation. A given form of collective behavior depends on a group's adopting a particular type of emergent norm. Which type will be adopted depends, in turn, on the collective beliefs that prevail in the situation.

Judgments of fact that support the general norm of public discussion are (1) that people can meet the problem with reason, (2) that a range of actions is possible, (3) that adequate information can be obtained about various alternatives, and (4) that responsible leaders will take expressions of public views into account. Among the underlying value judgments are (1) that rational discussion is desirable, (2) that peaceful change by the resolution of issues as they arise is better than violent revolution, and (3) that active interest in public affairs is a good thing. The general framework of such beliefs often comes from tradition and formal arrangements, but new norms may emerge at any stage in the public opinion process.

A distinction between the "proposal phase" and the "policy phase" of public discussion is sometimes helpful. The former means considering and choosing from general alternatives; the latter, the discussion of means of implementing the preferred alternative.[51] However, these phases need not follow each other in a neat time sequence; very frequently people anticipate the "policies" while they are considering the "proposals." Contending interest groups are ever

---

[49] Lang and Lang, *op. cit.*, 25–26, 372–85, 407.
[50] Robert E. Forman, "Resignation as a Collective Behavior Response," *American Journal of Sociology*, 69 (November, 1963), 285–90.
[51] Nelson N. Foote and Clyde W. Hart, "Public Opinion and Collective Behavior," in, Muzafer Sherif and M. O. Wilson (eds.), *Group Relations at the Crossroads* (New York: Harper Bros., 1953), 308–31. They also include the "program" or action phase in the public opinion process, as well as subsequent "appraisal."

alert to point out the policy implications of proposals of all sorts. Means and ends become entangled, especially when it is charged that proposals are being advanced for ulterior motives. The group dimensions of public discussion will be dealt with in Chapter 3.

Only those persons who become interested and who discuss an issue are members of that particular public. Often but a small proportion of a population are actively concerned with issues of broad significance. *A special public consists of persons discussing an issue of concern only to a special interest group.* Such a discussion, as among a group of chemists at a convention, is conducted at least to some degree in terms of a special "universe of discourse," or language. *A general public is all those discussing an issue of concern to the general community.* The community of reference may be local, state, national, or international; the important thing about a *community* is that it is *identified by its members with their general welfare.*[52] When members of special publics try to persuade other people to be concerned about certain issues, they appeal to the felt needs and hopes of the community at large. Agitation to create or enlarge a general public is crucial to an understanding of public discussion.[53]

More than one form of collective response to unrest often occurs, and one form may influence another. Sociologist Neil Smelser, while contending that public discussion is "on a different conceptual level" from collective behavior, remarks that it may contribute to the onset of panics, crazes, hostile outbursts, and social movements.[54] We have seen that it is guided by its own brand of emergent norms, and it is brought to bear on those who must act.[55] In any case, in conjunction with other forms of response, the public opinion process is a major way of bringing about social changes, as Ralph Turner and Lewis Killian make clear in the following:

Thus it is hardly possible to speak of the consequence of crowd behavior taken by itself. Its significance depends first upon whether it springs out of a well-established public, and second upon how the publics conceive the crowd after it has subsided. . . .[56] This development in which crowds and social movements operate within the context of changing publics may be

---

[52] Martindale, *op. cit.*, 44–48.
[53] Turner and Killian, *op. cit.*, 285–87.
[54] Smelser, *op. cit.*, 76. Perhaps his position rests on his emphasis on (1) the single episode, or (2) mobilization for direct action, or both.
[55] Herbert Blumer, "Public Opinion and Social Organization," *American Sociological Review*, 13 (October, 1948), 542–49.
[56] Turner and Killian, *op. cit.*, 524.

regarded as the tentative process within which new directions of culture and social organization are worked out.[57]

Social Movements

Our analysis of social problems will be primarily in terms of the public opinion process, but we will often have to take account of social movements. A *social movement is collective behavior in which people organize formally to promote or resist a change in social arrangements.*[58] It may emerge from a crowd or other ephemeral activity, or from public discussion. Movements frequently compete with one another, and they may succeed or fail at any stage. Although movements are often quite emotional, they are more rational than the fleeting forms of collective behavior because they embody (1) sustained effort toward a goal, and (2) the rational requirements of formal organization. They frequently are strongly emotional in their early phases, and they continue to be less rational than much of public discussion because the "believers" commit themselves quickly to one alternative and then stop discussing the original issue.

DEFINITION OF A SOCIAL PROBLEM

We can now relate social problems to social change and collective behavior, particularly to the public opinion process. Defined succinctly, *a social problem is an enduring, major community issue.* Some issues are considered to be of major significance for community (societal) welfare, some minor. Some are resolved fairly easily, but others persist for many years, some of them for decades, even centuries. Subsidiary issues often emerge to be fervently debated while the central dilemma lives on. These "persistent challenges"[59] to community life are social problems. *Defined in more detail, a social problem is:*

1. A condition, real or imagined,
2. Judged undesirable by a considerable proportion of the members of a community,
3. Judged by them to be a major threat to community life,
4. Considered beyond the scope of, or uncontrollable by, traditional and formal norms.
5. Considered capable of improvement through community action,

[57] *Ibid.*, 525.
[58] *Ibid.*, 308.
[59] Edward C. McDonagh and Jon E. Simpson (eds.), *Social Problems: Persistent Challenges* (New York: Holt, Rinehart & Winston, 1965), v–vi.

6. Which becomes a general public issue and receives community-wide attention, and
7. About which there is enduring major controversy over what new norms to adopt.

Imbedded in this definition is the "conflict of values" view that a social problem is not just a societal condition.[60] Many persons may deplore a situation, while others may judge it less critical. Both values and beliefs of fact are involved in judgments that the condition is a major threat, that it is outside the control of preexisting norms, that improvement through collective action is possible and desirable, and that it should be the subject of general public discussion. Continuing disagreement about what corrective action to take also reflects both conflicting values and conflicting factual beliefs.

Actually, as our definition indicates, an imagined condition can become the basis for a social problem. Most social problem conditions are indeed real, but issues based on mass delusions do arise, sometimes major ones. We now agree that the New Englanders were deluded in the seventeenth century when they attributed powers of witchcraft to certain persons; but many of the accused were put to death to solve the social problem. Nowadays endless statistics are cited to prove that certain conditions are getting worse, yet often the figures are unwittingly false or misleading. Newspapers keep reporting "all-time highs" by comparing numbers of something with numbers in past years. To use some meaningful type of *rate* is more difficult, and it often produces unexciting results, such as the disclosure that automobile accident *rates* were lower on a certain Labor Day weekend than they were the year before. A social problem requires a mood of concern, but it need not be based on an objectively correct view of situations.

Even if people are not deluded about the existence of conditions, they may worry about matters that can harm the community little and ignore others that may undermine it seriously. It has been argued that we should therefore concentrate on the "latent" social problems as well as on the manifest ones in order to emphasize matters relevant

[60] See especially the definitions in Paul H. Horton and Gerald R. Leslie, *The Sociology of Social Problems* (3rd ed., New York: Appleton-Century-Crofts, 1965), 4; John F. Cuber, William F. Kenkel, and Robert A. Harper, *Problems of American Society* (4th ed.; New York: Holt, Rinehart & Winston, 1964), 26–39; T. Lynn Smith *et al.*, *Social Problems* (New York: Thomas Y. Crowell Co., 1955), 4; John J. Kane, *Social Problems* (Englewood Cliffs, N.J.: Prentice-Hall, 1962), 4–8.

to sociological theory and to hold up an adequate mirror to society.[61] This topical choice has the potential of enlarging the general public on some issues and contracting it on others. When this result is deliberately sought, the social scientist can play such roles as consultant, applied researcher, and public speaker. Latent problems can be studied from various appropriate theoretical perspectives; and issues that arouse little interest or do not endure still are part of the study of collective behavior.

There are, however, at least three good reasons for concentrating on the enduring, major community issues. (1) Students and others are enlightened about matters of greatest public concern, including the role of values and perspective on distorted beliefs of fact. (2) Problems to be included are determined by the current value (and factual) beliefs in the community, not those of the analyst. (3) Like the lawyer who studies the "trouble case,"[62] we can learn basic things about human society by observing communities as they wrestle with their thorniest dilemmas.

Social problems, as defined here, are relative to time and place, which complicates the task of measurement. Americans once wrestled with such social problems as slavery, hostile Indians, and contagious diseases;[63] and the developing nations today have social problems different from our own. How are we to determine when a "considerable proportion" of the people is aroused? We need not seek a given percentage, but the proportion must be large enough to activate a general public that arouses community-wide attention. Relevant public opinion polls are helpful, if interpreted with caution; we might also analyze the content of the mass media to see what issues receive major emphasis over time; and we might consult such indications of public debate as the *Congressional Record*. We have not attempted such systematic measurement in writing this book, but the procedures suggested may be used to see whether the problems treated here are indeed the enduring, major public issues of our time. Some other issues would likely approximate being both "enduring" and "major" today, including use of leisure time, conservation of natural resources,

---

[61] Robert K. Merton and Robert A. Nisbet, *Contemporary Social Problems* (2nd ed.; New York: Harcourt, Brace & World, 1966), 788–95; Kane, *op. cit.*, 7–10, uses the terms "overt" and "covert" social problems.
[62] Karl N. Llewellyn and E. Adamson Hoebel, *The Cheyenne Way* (Norman: University of Oklahoma Press, 1941), 29–40; Preface, viii–ix.
[63] Smith, *et al.*, *op. cit.*, 12–13.

control of atomic energy, civil liberties, sexual deviations, abortion, and suicide.

Briefly, let us consider reactions to disaster in relation to our approach to social problems. Both man-made and natural catastrophes disrupt social arrangements, causing new norms and structures to be developed within the general framework of the social organization.[64] Major social disruptions often result from floods, tornadoes, and fires, and many preexisting norms are of little use in the face of such catastrophes. But there is evidence that consensus on emergent norms tends to be achieved quickly and with less conflict in these than in other crisis situations, mainly because of the urgency and immediacy of the emergency and the effectiveness of direct physical action. Other reasons apparently are that an outside threat welds people together so that they minimize subgroup differences, primary group solidarity takes over, and the drama of the event facilitates social understanding. [65] At any rate, it is evidently possible for people in certain circumstances to meet a crisis and implement new norms fairly quickly and rationally. Then the remaining difficulties are purely technical. Comparisons with such episodes help us see how social problems come to be, and why they pose such dilemmas for us.

THEORY OF SOCIAL PROBLEMS

Sound theoretical explanation is required if the study of social problems is to make the maximum contribution to basic knowledge of society and to attempts to control problem conditions. It is not easy to be uniformly logical and objective in treating a variety of social problems, but both logicality and objectivity are facilitated by a clear conceptual scheme, explicit assumptions, and general propositions. The answer in this book to the view that sound, objective theories of social problems are impossible[66] is that social problems are here defined and analyzed within a conceptual framework of collective

[64] Gideon Sjoberg, "Disasters and Social Change," Chapter 3 in George W. Baker and Dwight W. Chapman (eds.), *Man and Society in Disaster* (New York: Basic Books, 1962).
[65] Charles E. Fritz, "Disaster," Chapter 14 in Merton and Nisbet, *op. cit.*, 683–92; Irwin Deutscher and Peter Kong-Ming New, "A Functional Analysis of Collective Behavior in a Disaster," *Sociological Quarterly* (January, 1961), 21–36.
[66] Don Martindale, "Social Disorganization: The Conflict of Normative and Empirical Approaches," in Howard Becker and Alvin Boskoff (eds.), *Modern Sociological Theory in Continuity and Change* (New York: The Dryden Press, 1957), 340–67.

behavior theory. The hope is that the reader will find the effort both objective and enlightening.

The sociological framework for this book is an especially effective way to relate social problems to social change. While disagreements on values are emphasized, so are different beliefs of fact, and both are related to the dynamics of the public opinion process and collective behavior in general. The conflict of values approach has yielded many insights, but it has lacked an effective link with social change. In their concept of the natural history of a social problem, involving the stages of awareness, policy determination, and reform,[67] Richard Fuller and Richard Myers hinted strongly at the public opinion process a generation and more ago. The explicit development of the public discussion framework for analyzing social problems can contribute to knowledge of collective behavior, and therefore to our knowledge of social change.

In Chapter 2, beliefs of value and fact that underlie normative disagreement are examined further, and the approach is related to the perspectives of social disorganization and deviance, and cultural lag. In Chapter 3, the major dimensions of the public opinion process are applied to the analysis of social problems.

QUESTIONS FOR DISCUSSION AND STUDY

1. Would you assume that social relationships in a city area with a high incidence of social problems are entirely secondary? Why?

2. Can you think of examples of "sacred" attitudes toward social change in a large, metropolitan area? Explain.

3. What are some ways in which technological change has increased the proportion of contractual relationships among people?

4. What is the significance of the seemingly paradoxical statement that, "Science helps solve social problems but it keeps creating now ones all the time"?

5. Why do you think cities are such "hotbeds" of social problems? Are there significant variations in the incidence of problems in different

---

[67] Richard C. Fuller and Richard R. Myers, "The Natural History of a Social Problem," *American Sociological Review*, 6 (June. 1941), 320–28.

parts of a metropolitan area? Do suburban communities have social problems? Do rural communities?

6. In what ways is the following statement true? "Formal organizations help bring some problems under control and they often bring other problems into being."

7. In what ways are social mobility and social problems connected?

8. Are the norms that govern relationships among "surfers" traditional, formal, or emergent? What are some of the value judgments that underlie one of these norms? Some of the beliefs of fact?

9. Can some forms of collective behavior, in themselves, become social issues?

10. "Taking no action toward a problem condition is a very definite type of action." What does this comment mean?

SELECTED READING

Bernard, Jessie, *Social Problems at Midcentury* (New York: The Dryden Press, 1957), Chapter 5, "The Criteria of Social Problems."

Blumer, Herbert G., Chapter 5, "Collective Behavior," in Joseph B. Gittler (ed.), *Review of Sociology* (New York: John Wiley & Sons, 1957), 127–58.

Cottrell, Fred, *Energy and Society* (New York: McGraw-Hill, 1955).

Fellin, Phillip, and Litwak, Eugene, "Neighborhood Cohesion Under Conditions of Mobility," *American Sociological Review*, 28 (June, 1963), 364–76.

Kahl, Joseph A., "Some Social Concomitants of Industrialization and Urbanization," *Human Organization*, 18 (Summer, 1959), 53–74.

Lang, Kurt, and Lang, Gladys E., *Collective Dynamics* (New York: Thomas Y. Crowell Co., 1961), Part IV, "Collective Processes in the Mass Society."

Lee, Elizabeth B., and Lee, Alfred M., *Social Problems in America* (Rev. ed.; New York: Henry Holt & Co., 1955), Part I, "Frames of Reference." (A book of readings.)

McDonagh, Edward C., and Simpson, Jon E., *Social Problems: Persistent Challenges* (New York: Holt, Rinehart & Winston, 1965), Part I, "Contemporary Societal Orientations." (A book of readings.)

Meadows, Paul, "City, Technology, and History," *Social Forces*, 36 (December, 1957), 141–47.

Miner, Horace, *The Primitive City of Timbuctoo* (Princeton, N. J.: Princeton University Press, 1953). A test of Redfield's folk-urban continuum.

Nordskog, John E., McDonagh, Edward C., and Vincent, Melvin J., *Analyzing Social Problems* (Rev. ed.; New York: The Dryden Press, 1956), Chapter 1, "Approaches to Social Problems." (A book of readings.)

Smelser, Neil J., *Theory of Collective Behavior* (New York: The Free Press, 1963), Chapter I, "Analyzing Collective Behavior"; Chapter IX, "The Norm-Oriented Movement"; Chapter X, "The Value-Oriented Movement."

Turner, Ralph H., and Killian, Lewis M., *Collective Behavior* (Englewood Cliffs, N.J.: Prentice-Hall, 1957), Part I, "The Nature and Emergence of Collective Behavior"; Part V, "Social Consequences of Collective Behavior."

If this visitor [from Mars] possessed the usual Martian keenness and penetration, he would probably interrupt our recital [of social problems] to say: If it is not indelicate of me to remark, every social problem you describe seems to have the same characteristics as every other social problem, namely, the crux of the problem is to find some way of avoiding the undesirable consequences of your established laws, institutions, and social practices, without changing those established laws, etc. In other words, you appear to be seeking a way to cultivate the flower without the fruit, which in a world of cause and effect is somewhat difficult, to say the least.[1]

2. Conflicting Norms, Beliefs, and Social Disorganization

Even if there is no intelligent life on Mars after all, imagining what the perspective of a hypothetical man from that planet is like helps us to see activities of man on earth with more detachment. In effect, Lawrence Frank, author of the above excerpt, thought the man from Mars would see that we cannot eliminate social problem conditions because many people consider the cost too great. Put another way, there are dilemmas about desired social arrangements. In Chapter 1, such disagreement was related to social change, in terms of continuing public difficulty in resolving major issues concerning what new norms to support. Perhaps our Man from Mars would agree that this "normative dissensus"[2] rests on differences in beliefs of fact and value. It is the latter type of disagreement that has been emphasized in the "conflict of values" approach to social problems.

---

[1] Lawrence K. Frank, *Society as the Patient* (New Brunswick: Rutgers University Press, 1948), 14–15.
[2] Russell R. Dynes *et al.*, *Social Problems: Dissensus and Deviation in an Industrial Society* (New York: Oxford University Press, 1964), 4–10.

LACK OF VALUE CONSENSUS

Disagreements over values may be involved in defining an issue, enlarging a public, and continuing the discussion of the issue so that it becomes a social problem. At each phase the values taken into

TABLE 2.1

POTENTIAL FOR PUBLIC ISSUES AND SOCIAL PROBLEMS IN COMBINATIONS OF PERCEIVED CONDITIONS AND EFFECTIVELY REPRESENTED PRIORITIES OF VALUE

Priorities of Value Effectively Represented	*Perception of Objective Conditions*			
	No Change	*Worse*	*Improved*	*Entirely New*
No Change	No	Yes	Yes	Yes
Changed Priority Old Priority Reshuffled	Yes	Yes	Yes	Yes
New Values Included	Yes	Yes	Yes	Yes

LEGEND: *"Yes" indicates the possibility of issues and of their prolongation into social problems.*

account may be preexisting ones entirely, or they may be partly new. The important consideration, as suggested in Table 2.1, is their *rank order*. People relate their actions to a pyramid of values, not always with rigorous logic; and in heterogeneous societies different persons and groups have different priorities. Even when conflict within a group and within a person over how to reorder priorities of value is resolved, the issue endures as long as different groups disagree. The outcome is affected, of course, by any shifts that may occur in the degree of influence over public discussion wielded by different groups.

A further factor influencing the definition and discussion of issues is disagreement over what values are pertinent. Two people who begin with similar rank orders may not agree on what values are relevant to a given situation; they apply abstract values differently to specific instances. Even when there is agreement on priorities and relevance, different beliefs of fact about which values are affected may influence consensus on the issue. Accurate communication under such circumstances is not easy, even when people are calm. The statement, "Privacy just doesn't apply here," may mean: (1) I don't think privacy is very important compared to some of the other values, (2) this situation does not illustrate any invasion of privacy, or (3) privacy is not actually threatened by the condition. Those who play key roles in defining and redefining public issues, like editorialists, often attempt to clarify the implications for value priorities as they see them.

New issues and social problems may emerge and old ones may cease to be of concern without any change in objective conditions. This may be due solely to changed priorities of value. An increased valuation of efficiency may create anxiety over an ancient transportation system; a lessened valuation of thrift and saving may cause less concern over gambling. Societies may indeed create new problems for themselves and "solve" others by changing only their value systems.[3] Very frequently, however, shifting hierarchies of value are associated with changing beliefs of fact, including the perception that given conditions are worse, better, or new.

Fuller and Myers distinguished those social problems that are concerned with *means* for dealing with conditions from those involving *ends*, calling the former "ameliorative" and the latter "moral" problems. The latter involve fundamental or more ultimate values, including those concerned with whether the condition is a problem or not. Ameliorative problems involve conflicting values over what means to adopt to attain generally accepted ends.[4] If people in a community agree on the ends and cease to debate the means, leaving the choice of means entirely to the technical experts, there is no longer a social problem of either type in the Fuller-Myers scheme.

Some sociologists who have used the Fuller-Myers approach, have contended that conflicting values are the "root cause"[5] and the

---

[3] Neil J. Smelser, *Theory of Collective Behavior* (New York: The Free Press, 1963), 289–90.
[4] Richard C. Fuller and Richard R. Myers, "Some Aspects of a Theory of Social Problems," *American Sociological Review*, 6, (1941), 24–32.
[5] *Ibid.*, 27.

"source"[6] of social problems; but others have taken the view that conflicts of value "help" produce social problems.[7] Willard Waller suggested that "value judgments are the formal causes of social problems, just as the law is the formal cause of crime."[8] Such value judgments reflect the ideals of the "humanitarian mores," and social problems consist of conflicts between these mores and the norms of existing social organization, the "organizational mores."[9] In these terms, Waller then made the following suggestions about long-range social change and the rise of social problems:

> Probably the humanitarian impulse has always existed, but it has apparently attained group-wide expression at a relatively late period in our history, following the breakdown of primary group society. Social problems in the modern sense did not exist when every primary group cared for its own helpless and unfortunate. Social problems as we know them are a phenomenon of secondary group society, in which the primary group is no longer willing and able to take care of its members.[10]

To the extent that this is true, many new problems in our century have arisen from the public application of very old humanitarian values to changed conditions of life. Moreover, many specific new values were developed from general, latent ones, and rank orders of values have therefore been under constant reconsideration.

It is not hard to see why the conflict of values approach has been classified as conflict theory,[11] particularly when conflicting values have been considered sufficient or at least necessary causes of social problems. The *conflict theorist assumes that stability and order are always tenuous and at a minimum, that conflict among groups* as they compete for scarce values is *the correct image of society*. When disagreement on values is treated more as a contributing cause, however, it may become an important part of both the conflict theorist's and *integration theorist's* analysis of social problems. The latter *assumes that society is relatively stable* most of the time, its *institutions and values* at least fairly well *integrated*.

---

[6] John Cuber, William F. Kenkel, and Robert A. Harper, *Problems of American Society* (4th ed.; New York: Holt, Rinehart & Winston, 1964), 35.
[7] Paul H. Horton, and Gerald R. Leslie, *The Sociology of Social Problems* (3rd ed.; Appleton-Century-Crofts, 1965), 38.
[8] Willard Waller, "Social Problems and the Mores," *American Sociological Review*, 1 (December, 1936), 925.
[9] *Ibid.*, 922–33. Mores are those customary norms of conduct regarded as essential to group welfare and enforced by strong informal social controls.
[10] *Ibid.*, 125.
[11] Arnold M. Rose, "Theory for the Study of Social Problems," *Social Problems*, 4 (January, 1957), 190; Dynes *et al.*, *op. cit.*, vi.

Public discussion and other collective behavior phenomena may be analyzed from both the conflict and integration starting points, depending on the emphasis. What is ours? The definition of a social problem as an enduring major issue may seem like a conflict approach; yet public discussion cannot continue without some basic agreements, and some difficult issues do get resolved. The presentation of the public opinion process as a way of restoring consensus on norms implies an equilibrium-maintaining view of social change, a hallmark of much integration theory; but conflict theory has its own version of equilibrium. Let us assume that societies are relatively cohesive and stable much of the time, but that marked breakdowns occur under certain conditions, and that complete integration is never possible in a complex, relatively secular society. If this is integration theory, so be it, so long as the necessary attention can be given to contending groups and their conflicting beliefs.

DIFFERENCES IN BELIEFS OF FACT

A crucial judgment of fact in the development of a social problem is whether the condition complained about exists or not; and, if it does, whether it is becoming more frequent or less. Endless barrages of descriptive statistics are publicized, often to be criticized as biased to fit the values of those putting them forth. As we saw in Table 2.1, different perceptions of conditions may influence the rise and discussion of issues and their "elevation" to social problems. There may be great concern when people believe that unwanted conditions have arisen or worsened, and also considerable concern when they are seen as improved, because this may influence beliefs about what is possible. Since new issues may emerge, expand, or subside with shifts in value priorities, changes in beliefs about conditions are contributory, not necessary or sufficient, causes of issues and social problems.

Awareness of the existence or frequency of other conditions in society also enter into the discussion of a social problem. Someone commenting on juvenile delinquency may allege that it is increasing, and that school drop-outs, family instability, and teen-age automobile driving also are increasing. There are four "simple" factual beliefs here, each involving difficult problems of definition and measurement. The person may believe that these things are occurring together, which may in fact be true or not, and then proceed to the judgment that one causes the other. Such beliefs of fact are *explanations* of causes and are therefore *cause-and-effect* assumptions. The "revolution of rising expectations" phenomenon mentioned in Chapter 1 involves the belief that certain conditions are in fact improving, but it also indicates modified assumptions about the probable *effects* of various actions.

The theories of the social sciences provide the most systematic cause-and-effect explanations of human actions. The scientist strives for the best theory in two senses: (1) the most logically consistent concepts and explanatory ideas, and (2) ideas that stand when tested against factual observations. In our society, theory is often compared unfavorably with practical experience, so its crucial role in the drama of science is not well understood. The typical member of a public discussing an issue would deny that he has theories, though he probably will claim some knowledge of facts through practical experience and ability to think in a good common-sense manner. Actually, he cannot live and discuss issues without beliefs of fact, including cause-and-effect assumptions, though he probably considers his own to be "just plain facts." Despite the uncritical way many people hold to their own explanations, beliefs of fact do change. In a relatively secular society the pressure to consider new states of affairs and new explanations is unrelenting.

Essential to the rise of an issue and a social problem is the belief that something can be done about a deplored condition by collective action.[12] The definition of an issue by a public includes specifying alternative means to certain ends, each resting on particular causal explanations. Each also rests on certain priorities of value; but an editorialist, or whoever would define an issue clearly, takes care to separate questions of value from fact. If his values appear unduly to influence his judgments of factual existence, frequency, association, and explanation, it will probably be noticed, especially by those with different value priorities.

CAUSES OF SOCIAL PROBLEMS

Now we can improve on the general suggestion that social problems are caused, or at least aggravated, by social change. Issues, remember, are concerned with the development of new norms. *Neces-*

---

[12] The conflict of values writers include this in the definition of a social problem. See Horton and Leslie, *op. cit.*, 5, who also use other approaches.

*sary to the rise of an issue and its development into a social problem
is a change in either beliefs of value or of fact.* Since either may be
missing, changes in hierarchies of values are contributing causes
rather than necessary or sufficient causes, and the same is true of
changes in factual beliefs. Very often, changing beliefs of both fact
and value are present in some degree in a public as a whole, although
a given segment might be experiencing change in only one. There
must be enough change in one type of belief or the other, or both, to
arouse a general public and to attract community-wide attention.

Are general social changes such as technological growth and
urbanization, or more specific ones like the invention of television
and the freeway, causes of social problems? Yes, they are, because
they are connected with changes in belief, including peoples' perceptions that certain situations require new norms. In this sense, are
societal changes indirect causes of social problems? Are they necessary or contributing causes of changes in belief? There are many un-
answered questions in the "sociology of knowledge," but let us adopt
the general thesis that *beliefs are related, in various ways, to their
social contexts.* Some aspects of this position are illuminated in the
discussion of the public opinion process in Chapter 3, but first let us
consider some of the main attempts that have been made to relate
problem conditions directly to social contexts.

SOCIAL DISORGANIZATION

Much sociological theorizing about social problems has been of
the social disorganization type,[13] though often under other labels.
Social problems are seen in this approach as *indexes of social disorganization,* as indications of the breakdown of an earlier state of at
least relative social organization. So this is a type of *integration
theory,* implying that the elimination or control of social problems
restores the equilibrium of society. When not clearly related to a conception of social organization, the approach becomes sterile. It also
stresses agreement on norms of conduct, with the *breakdown in influence of established norms* on individual behavior being *defined as
social disorganization,*[14] or a measure of it. Aspects of disorganization

---

[13] Rose, *op. cit.,* 193–99, says disorganization and conflict theories can be har-
monized only to a limited extent.

[14] Florian Znaniecki and William I. Thomas, *The Polish Peasant in Europe and
America* (2nd ed.; New York: Alfred A. Knopf, 1927), 1127–30; Mabel A. Elliott

varying from the institutional to the personal have been included, and the approach involves an effort to relate particular problem conditions to underlying social changes.

Deviant Behavior

Perhaps the adaptability of the concept of social disorganization to both the group and personal levels of analysis has been largely responsible for its wide use. Some now prefer to limit the definition to the level of social structure, and to develop *social deviation* as an approach in its own right.[15] Systematic study of the deviant person, however, still falls within the general scheme of social disorganization. The problem is conceptualized as frequent departures from traditional and formal norms, so alleviation of the problem requires *social controls* that will bring individual behavior into line with desired norms. This orientation is useful, but it loses its advantages and its relevance when attempts are made to expand it to include problems of social organization (like issues in education or population growth) that do not inhere in deviant persons.

Some studies of why children in high delinquency neighborhoods do not become offenders resulted in a more general effort to identify the conditions under which social controls prevent deviance. This *containment theory* then was extended to adult criminality,[16] and later to social problems in general.[17] In this approach the concept of the social role is used to analyze those control processes that prevent deviant conduct. The analysis of containment falls within the general framework of social disorganization theory and of social deviation in particular. Although socio-psychological perspectives have been used before in the analysis of disorganization, this particular use of them is an important development in the study of deviant behavior.

and Francis E. Merrill, *Social Disorganization* (4th ed.; New York: Harper Bros., 1961), 23–24.

[15] Marshall B. Clinard, *Sociology of Deviant Behavior* (Rev. ed.; New York: Holt, Rinehart & Winston, 1963); Robert K. Merton, and Robert A. Nisbet, *Contemporary Social Problems* (New York: Harcourt, Brace & World, 1961), 718–29; Horton and Leslie, *op. cit.*, 29–35.

[16] Walter C. Reckless, "A New Theory of Delinquency and Crime," *Federal Probation*, 25 (December, 1961), 42–46; W. C. Reckless and Shlomo Shoham, "Norm Containment Theory as Applied to Delinquency and Crime," *Exerpta Criminologica*, 30 (1963), 1–8.

[17] William E. Cole, and Charles H. Miller, *Social Problems: A Sociological Interpretation* (New York: David McKay Co., 1965), Chap. 2, "Theoretical Orientation."

Personal Disorganization

Some deviant persons, like the professional criminal, are problems to society but not to themselves. Others, like the mentally ill, the addicts, and compulsive gamblers, become personally disorganized. Collectively, they are defined as a social problem, but they suffer whether or not their conduct becomes a persistent, major issue in the community. Demoralized behavior has been included in treatments of social deviation and of disorganization generally, but some special perspectives have also been developed for the presumed personal victims of societal disturbances. These approaches have usually stressed personal maladjustment, a key idea being that the disorganized person regards himself as a failure.

One such approach has been *social pathology,* in which *both society and the person are considered sick,* or pathological. The social problems emphasized are those personified in disorganized individuals, and analysis has often included use of the personality theories of psychology and psychiatry.[18] A basic assumption of the approach is that the way to solve problems of social disorganization is to rehabilitate the individual. Responding to the view that society is in such a state of confused transition that it cannot be made "well" by coercing individuals into line with outmoded or ambiguous norms,[19] a social pathologist has said that the sick society must be cured by treating the sick individual, since person and society are inseparable.[20] One line of development of this approach has been *social participation,* part of the diagnosis of personal disorganization being that the individual is isolated, and the suggested cure being active involvement in group activities.[21]

---

[18] John L. Gillin, *Social Pathology* (3rd ed.; New York: Appleton-Century-Crofts, 1946); and Edwin M. Lemert, *Social Pathology: A Systematic Approach to the Study of Sociopathic Behavior* (New York: McGraw-Hill, 1951).

[19] Lawrence K. Frank, "Society as the Patient," *American Journal of Sociology,* 42, (1936–37), 335–44.

[20] L. Guy Brown, "Society as the Patient" (communication), *American Journal of Sociology,* 42 (1936–37), 717–18; see also his *Social Pathology: Personal and Social Disorganization* (New York: Appleton-Century-Crofts, 1942).

[21] Stuart A. Queen, "Social Participation in Relation to Social Disorganization," *American Sociological Review,* 14 (1949), 251–57; see Elliott and Merrill, *op. cit.,* 24, 56–60, for the same view within a "regular" framework of social disorganization.

Anomie

Another orientation stressing isolation and personal disorganization, and often classed as a social disorganization approach,[22] has become important in the sociology of deviant behavior.[23] Under Robert Merton's influence, Durkheim's attempt to explain suicide in terms of the concept of anomie[24] eventually was applied to other forms of deviance.[25] *Anomie is normlessness, a condition in which adequate norms to inform people how to act are lacking.* There is either a confusing clash of norms or an awareness that appropriate ones are missing. This condition goes well beyond the failure of controls to support norms still generally perceived as dominant; so anomie is either extreme social disorganization or lack of any organization at all. Durkheim reasoned that the frequency of this condition in certain urban areas causes many people to lose all sense of purpose in living, thus the higher suicide rates in those areas.

Although anomie may result in personal disorganization, the concept refers to a marked breakdown in the social structure or to gaps in it. Sociologists have used the term *anomia* to refer to *the person's sense of lack of social cohesion,*[26] and they have usually assumed that anomia is the subjective response to the objective conditions of anomie. Using Srole's scale,[27] researchers have found anomia to be associated with social isolation, lack of participation in both informal and formal groups, and with low economic status,[28]

---

[22] Reece McGee, *Social Disorganization in America* (San Francisco: Chandler Publishing Co., 1962), 20, 34–36.

[23] Marshall B. Clinard, "The Theoretical Implications of Anomie and Deviant Behavior," in Clinard *et al., Anomie and Deviant Behavior* (New York: The Free Press, 1964), 2, 10–11.

[24] Emile Durkheim (trans. by John A. Spaulding and George Simpson), *Suicide* (New York: The Free Press, 1951); Marvin E. Olsen, "Durkheim's Two Concepts of Anomie," *Sociological Quarterly*, 6 (Winter, 1965), 41.

[25] Robert K. Merton, "Social Structure and Anomie," *American Sociological Review*, 3 (October, 1938), 672–82; *Social Theory and Social Structure* (New York: The Free Press, 1949), 125–49, and (Rev. ed., 1957), 161–94.

[26] Clinard, *op. cit.*, 34. "Anomy" is the term used by Robert M. MacIver in *The Ramparts We Guard* (New York: The Macmillan Co., 1950), 84.

[27] Leo Srole, "Social Integration and Certain Corollaries: An Exploratory Study," *American Sociological Review*, 21 (December, 1956) 709–16.

[28] Wendell Bell, "Anomie, Social Isolation, and the Class Structure," *Sociometry*, 20 (June, 1957), 105–16. Wendell Bell and Dorothy L. Meier, "Anomia and Differential Access to the Achievement of Life Goals," *American Sociological Review*, 24 (April, 1959), 189–208.

although one study found a negligible relationship between anomia and income.[29]

The condition emphasized by Merton as a major cause of anomie, and thus of anomia, is the disparity between cultural goals and the opportunities available in the social structure for people to achieve these goals.[30] People in all social classes learn to share the same general goals, yet not all have equal opportunity to attain them, so groups with the poorest avenues to success are most likely to become highly discouraged. The city is the place of extremes, of great opportunities and dramatic failures, thus the place of great frustration for many.[31] Merton stresses a condition in which norms of achievement are explicit, then, but in which many persons come to feel that such norms are meaningless. There is some evidence that anomia is related to the lack of certain group supports for the person,[32] and to personality factors,[33] as well as to lack of access to means of reaching life goals.

One possible outcome of anomia is *alienation, the feeling of not being a part of the community or other group of reference.* The alienated person need not be hostile, or disorganized. Since anomia may evidently be a cause of alienation, the two are not the same.[34] If X may cause Y, X is not Y. Yet some of the attempts to clarify the concept of alienation, and to measure it, seem to point to anomia, anomie, or both. Seeman has identified alienation with: (1) feelings of powerlessness, (2) feelings of meaninglessness, (3) normlessness, (4) feelings of social isolation, and (5) self-estrangement.[35] Only the fourth seems to pertain to alienation, as defined above, although in

[29] Alan H. Roberts and Milton Rokeach, "Anomie, Authoritarianism, and Prejudice: a Replication," *American Sociological Review*, 61 (January, 1956), 355–58.
[30] *Social Theory and Social Structure* (Rev. ed.), *op. cit.*, 162.
[31] Robert K. Merton, "Anomie, Anomia, and Social Interaction: Contexts of Deviant Behavior," in, Clinard *et al.*, *op cit.*, 222–25.
[32] Ephraim H. Mizruchi, "Social Structure and Anomia in a Small City," *American Sociological Review*, 25 (October, 1960), 645–54; also his *Success and Opportunity: A Critical Examination of Class Structure and Anomie in American Society* (New York: The Free Press, 1964).
[33] Herbert McClosky and John H. Scharr, "Psychological Dimensions of Anomy," *American Sociological Review*, 30 (February, 1965), 14–40.
[34] Gwynn Nettler, "A Measure of Alienation," *American Sociological Review*, 22 (December, 1957), 672; J. L. Simmons, "Liberalism, Alienation, and Personal Disturbance," *Sociology and Social Research*, 49 (July, 1965), 456–64; J. L. Simmons, "Some Intercorrelations Among 'Alienation' Measures," *Social Forces*, 44 (March, 1966), 370–72.
[35] Melvin Seeman, "On the Meaning of Alienation," *American Sociological Review*, 24 (December, 1959), 783–91; McGee, *op. cit.*, 66–78, uses four of these

his proposed interpretation Seeman does not draw such a definite line as this. The first and second meanings appear to be aspects of anomia; the third is either anomie, or, if subjective response is stressed, anomia; the fifth refers to departure from a social philosophical ideal or "true" self, or to failure to be one's own ideal self, neither of which is alienation from a community. Nettler's scale, which measures the feeling of separation from the common culture of the community,[36] seems to be a valid, direct measure of social alienation and not of anomia, anomie, or maladjustment.

Development of the Durkheimian thesis is one of the major efforts in sociology to connect social problems (of deviance) with the growth of urbanization, formal organizations, and technology. Much remains to be discovered. For instance, why do many people "exposed" to anomie not develop feelings of anomia? Why do some who experience anomia become disorganized, or feel alienated, while others do not? Why do some resign themselves to a conflict or absence of norms? Why do others respond by cleaving to a particular subgroup, by becoming aggressive, or by destroying themselves? Why do still others join a social movement or a public discussion? We return to anomie as it affects juvenile delinquency and other topics in Part III, and in Chapter 3 we relate it to the public opinion process.

Perspective on the Social Disorganization Approach

Whether the person or the social structure is emphasized, the social disorganization approach has the potential of relating social problems to the whole of society. This goal has often been achieved reasonably well during the half-century that varied attempts have been made within this general framework. One criticism has been that the researcher or writer, consciously or not, emphasizes those situations he most deplores. He may argue that certain conditions are indexes of disorganization whether there is much public concern about them or not. He may describe them as harmful, morale-destroying,

---

meanings as types of alienation in a brief treatment of the "beats" and the "beatniks"; see also, Dwight G. Dean, "Alienation: Its Meaning and Measurement," *American Sociological Review*, 26 (October, 1961), 753–58.
[36] Nettler, *op. cit.*, 675. McClosky and Scharr, *op. cit.*, 30–40, use separate scales for anomy (anomia) and alienation, treating the latter as a measure of low ego strength; see also, Elmer L. Struening and Arthur H. Richardson, "A Factor Analytic Exploration of the Alienation, Anomia and Authoritarianism Domain," *American Sociological Review*, 30 (October, 1965), 768–76.

corrosive, or by the intentionally neutral concept, "dysfunctional,"[37] but the burden is on the analyst to demonstrate that the condition really has the alleged effects and is not just a threat to his personal values. This criticism would seem most apt when social change is slighted in favor of moralistic labeling and description of "bad" conditions.[38]

Another charge is that the approach is implicitly conservative, suggesting that the way to solve social problems is to enforce the preexisting norms. Certain new conditions have disturbed the social organization, in other words, so the logical procedure is to bring them under control, perhaps to stop or even reverse them. Thus, if the horseless carriage frightens horses and otherwise disturbs the community, let us outlaw it, or limit its numbers, or rigidly control its operation. Or if more women are working away from home, and if this seems to have undesired consequences, doesn't the concept of social disorganization suggest that the problem can be solved by getting these women back in the home? The implication, however, has not been followed through in many treatments; in fact some writers on social disorganization have been charged with an opposite bias, of favoring the ways of the changing city.[39]

Although such criticisms have sometimes been deserved, they nevertheless have helped minimize the difficulties discussed above. The fact that a given approach can be, and has been, used in a biased manner does not prove that it must be. The social disorganization orientation has shed much light on social problems and has been related explicitly to a good deal of sociological thought and research.

Matters that arise involving social disorganization are relevant at a number of points to the public discussion approach to social problems. However, we must note that the emphasis in the latter approach is on developing support for emergent norms, not preexisting ones. In the treatment of problems involving deviance in Part III, beliefs about social control that underlie the discussion of norms by various groups

---

[37] Merton and Nisbet, *op. cit.*, 731–37; Merton, *Social Theory and Social Structure* (Rev. ed.), *op. cit.*, 37–51, 182–84; Alvin Boskoff, "Social Indecision: A Dysfunctional Focus of Transitional Society," *Social Forces*, 37 (1959), 305–11.
[38] C. Wright Mills, "The Professional Ideology of Social Pathologists," *American Journal of Sociology*, 49 (1943–44), 165–80.
[39] Don Martindale, "Social Disorganization: The Conflict of Normative and Empirical Approaches," In Howard Becker and Alvin Boskoff (eds.), *Modern Sociological Theory in Continuity and Change* (New York: Dryden Press, 1957), 349.

in a public are emphasized. Comparing public beliefs of fact with tentative conclusions of sociologists and other social scientists opens the door to perspectives of the social disorganization type. Also, knowledge of social disorganization may be related to attempts to analyze the building of consensus on emergent norms through the public opinion process.

CULTURAL LAG

Ogburn noted that different parts of culture change at unequal rates of speed, and he defined *cultural lag* as the *delay in the adaptation of one part of culture to a change in some correlated trait.*[40] While some adjustments are quick and easy, *slower adaptations create strains* or maladjustments in the cultural pattern. Ogburn devoted his career to demonstrating the far-reaching effects of technological change, his *major hypothesis* being that the *typical modern cultural lag* consists of *incomplete adaptations of social arrangements to mechanical inventions.*[41] This idea has been borrowed widely to explain a variety of situations faced by modern man.

Because cultural lags make it difficult to apply and enforce norms, and involve tensions that reflect a disturbed cultural equilibrium, the lag concept sometimes has been classed within the social disorganization fold.[42] However, as Figure 2.1 indicates, the application of the concept implies that the way to solve a social problem is to promote adaptive changes as rapidly as possible. If the change is not considered good it is at least irrevocable, so the cultural lag concept has an implicit liberal bias.[43] It is too bad if automobiles frighten horses, but people will have to put blinders on their animals and learn how to control them when a car passes. If women's working away from home is regarded as a cultural lead, or as an adaptation to earlier leads, the lag concept suggests that people need to change their attitudes and the family must adjust to mother's work schedule.

Cultural lag often has been used quite objectively, but it also has seemed an apt weapon for those wishing to castigate society for not changing faster. It has facilitated much of our understanding of social

[40] William F. Ogburn, *Social Change* (Rev. ed.; New York: The Viking Press, 1950, originally published in 1922.)
[41] *Ibid.*, 200–13.
[42] Rose, *op. cit.*, 193.
[43] Martindale, *op. cit.*, 353.

FIGURE 2.1

THE OPPOSITE BIASES IMPLIED IN THE CULTURAL LAG AND SOCIAL
DISORGANIZATION APPROACHES TO SOCIAL PROBLEMS

Implicit Direction of Solutions of Social Problems Envisioned as, or Associated with, "Cultural Lags."

| Lagging Cultural Traits | ⟶ | Leading Cultural Traits |

Implied Diagnosis:

The problem is either the lag itself, or is caused by it.

Appropriate Slogans:

"Let's move it!"

"It's the Twentieth Century!"

"Horse and buggy methods won't do in the space age!"

Implicit Direction of Solutions of Social Problems Defined as "Indexes of Social Disorganization."

| Lagging Cultural Traits | ⟵ | Leading Cultural Traits |

Implied Diagnosis:

The problem is either the disturbing change itself, or is caused by it.

Appropriate Slogans:

"Not all change is for the better!"

"People just aren't ready for it yet!"

"If we can't turn back the clock, or stop it, let's slow it down!"

CAUTION: *These implications are followed through in some treatments, but not in others. See explanations in text.*

change, particularly where technology is concerned. The important thing is to see that even when one strives for objectivity, this particular pair of "glasses" regularly implies a certain type of solution to whatever social problem is considered. If one is aware of this implicit bias, he is more able to avoid it, or at least to correct for it, as he can also for the implications of the various formulations of social disorganization.

It is difficult to enforce formal norms that either have lagged far behind or have been enacted too far ahead of related changes in practices and public sentiment.[44] When dominant community opinion clearly opposes the norms, whether they are leading or lagging, a *"patterned evasion"* of them occurs.[45] When officials support public sentiment that favors evading old vice codes or legal grounds for divorce, or some "ridiculous" new building ordinance or military regulation, the pattern of evasion is actually the "law in force" in the situation.[46] The conduct is then not treated as deviance, or as a problem. When leads and lags of formal norms do become issues, public sentiment may divide into two general orientations: (1) the cultural lag outlook, suggesting either that (a) "blue laws" should be replaced in accordance with "enlightened practices," or (b) "backward practices" should be adapted to "forward-looking laws"; and (2) the social disorganization outlook, implying either that (a) "law and order" should prevail over "half-baked ideas," or (b) "responsible opinion" should be brought to bear on "hasty laws."

Ogburn made the implicit bias of his concept quite explicit in elaborating his major hypothesis. If mechanical inventions typically have been the leading traits of modern cultural change, and if we ought to take up the gaps rapidly to reduce the strains, material changes must be good, inevitable, or at least irrevocable. This has seemed to some critics to constitute economic determinism or at least a materialistic bias. Among other criticisms are: that the distinction between material and nonmaterial culture is unsatisfactory, that very often nonmaterial changes come first, and that rapid adaptations are not always the most effective.[47] Sociologists now concern

---

[44] Ronald Freedman *et al.*, *Principles of Sociology* (New York: Holt, Rinehart & Winston, 1952), 172; F. James Davis *et al.*, *Society and the Law* (New York: The Free Press, 1962), 75–76.
[45] Robin Williams, *American Society* (New York: Alfred A. Knopf, 1951), 215; Merton, *Social Theory and Social Structure* (Rev. ed.), *op. cit.*, 317–18, 343–45.
[46] N. S. Timasheff, *An Introduction to the Sociology of Law* (Cambridge: Harvard University Committee on Research in the Social Sciences, 1939), 140–61; R. M. MacIver, *Society* (New York: Holt, Rinehart & Winston, 1947), 76–77.
[47] Leonard Broom and Philip Selznick, *Sociology* (3rd ed.; New York: Harper & Row, 1963), 82–83.

themselves less with the typical direction of lag and more with the conditions and consequences of particular lags.

Adaptations to cultural leads involve working out new norms, so there are frequent occasions to relate this perspective to a collective behavior approach to social problems. Lagging cultural traits may be associated with social problem conditions, or they may themselves become major public issues. Beliefs of value and fact held by some of those discussing a public issue sometimes fit the cultural lag view of change, while those of others may suggest some type of social disorganization orientation. Focusing on the content and assumptions of the discussion of public issues may, in return, add depth to what otherwise can be a rather mechanical treatment of cultural leads and lags.

PERSPECTIVE

In this chapter, the ways in which beliefs of value and fact become involved in the rise, discussion, and perpetuation of public issues have been sketched. The relevance of the conflict of values approach to social problems, the many formulations of social disorganization and deviance, and of cultural lag also has been indicated. All these approaches include ways of dealing with disagreements over norms in relation to social problems, and the main features, strengths, and particular difficulties of each have been outlined. The purpose has been to show some of the points at which we might profitably borrow, not to attempt a synthesis. The collective behavior framework will remain the primary "glasses" through which we attempt to see social problems clearly.

QUESTIONS FOR DISCUSSION AND STUDY

1. How can a new social problem arise, or an old one be "solved," without any change in the objective condition itself? Can you illustrate each situation?
2. Can you think of some new value that has emerged in recent decades, or one that has been upgraded in importance? Has it been at least partly responsible for any new social problems?

3. Has there been any significant shift in the norms for the behavior of high school students in your community in recent years? If there has, does the change seem to be based on a change in value priorities? In beliefs of fact? Or both?

4. Many churches that once strongly disapproved of dancing, card-playing, and the movies, no longer do. Have their values changed, their factual beliefs, or what?

5. After the development of modern methods of dam-building, many people began to say that flood damage is a disgrace and should be prevented. Did their increased concern reflect changed beliefs of value, or of fact? Explain.

6. Can deviant behavior become a social problem if the persons involved are not maladjusted? Illustrate.

7. X says he is a practical man with a workable program for reducing the number of chronic welfare recipients in his city. It calls for intensive work with the individual heads of household. What sociological approach to social problems does this sound like? Does X have a theory?

8. L and M are children living in a deteriorating area of a large city. L develops feelings of anomia but M does not. What differences in their family experiences might account for their different responses?

9. Suppose someday widespread concern arises because more and more teenagers are spending their vacations on poorly supervised platforms in outer space. How might the situation be diagnosed from a social disorganization point of view?

10. How might the above situation be seen from the perspective of a cultural lag orientation? What solutions would logically follow?

SELECTED READING

Barnet, H. G., *Innovation: The Basis of Cultural Change* (New York: McGraw-Hill, 1953).

Cottrell, W. Fred, "Death by Dieselization: A Case Study in the Reaction to Technological Change," *American Sociological Review*, 16 (June, 1951), 358–65.

Clinard, Marshall B. *et al., Anomie and Deviant Behavior* (New York: The Free Press, 1964). Includes, "Appendix: Inventory of Empirical and Theoretical Studies of Anomie," by Stephen Cole and Harriet Zuckerman.

Durkheim, Emile (trans. by John A. Spaulding and George Simpson), *Suicide* (New York: The Free Press, 1951).

Fallding, Harold, "A Proposal for the Empirical Study of Values," *American Sociological Review*, 30 (April, 1965), 223–33.

Fuller, R. C., and Myers, R. R., "The Natural History of a Social Problem," *American Sociological Review*, 6 (1941), 320–38.

Himes, J. S., "Value Analysis in the Theory of Social Problems," *Social Forces* (March, 1965), 259–62.

Lemert, Edwin M., "Is There a Natural History of Social Problems?" *American Sociological Review*, 16 (April, 1951), 217–23.

McGee, Reece, *Social Disorganization in America* (San Francisco: Chandler Publishing Co., 1962).

Ogburn, William F., *On Culture and Social Change* (Chicago: University of Chicago Press, 1964). Edited and with an introduction by Otis D. Duncan.

Ogburn, William F., *The Social Effects of Aviation* (Boston: Houghton Mifflin, 1946).

Rose, Arnold M., "Theory for the Study of Social Problems," *Social Problems*, 4 (January, 1957), 189–99.

Turk, Herman, "Social Cohesion Through Variant Values," *American Sociological Review*, 28 (February, 1963), 28–37.

Turner, Ralph H., "Value Conflict in Social Disorganization," *Sociology and Social Research*, 38 (May, 1954), 301–08.

The existence of an issue means that the group has to act; yet there are no understandings, definitions, or rules prescribing what that action should be. If there were, there would be, of course, no issue. It is in this sense that we can speak of the public as having no culture—no traditions to dictate what its action shall be.[1]

3. Public Discussion of Social Problems

THERE ARE several forms of collective response to a situation perceived as being inadequately covered by existing norms, and as requiring some type of action. The public opinion process—defining and discussing an issue and expressing views to influence its resolution—is the relatively rational form. It is concerned with the working out of new norms—thus with social changes; but the process itself rests on the emergence of certain norms (see Chapter 1). Often a single episode of discussion facilitates a satisfactory resolution, but other issues prove to be community dilemmas. Social problems are defined in Chapter 1 as those major issues that persist over a considerable period of time.

One view in sociology is that enduring issues tend to destroy discussion, changing publics into organized movements and other forms of collective behavior. Persons converted to the views of committed groups no longer consider alternatives, presumably, so a power struggle replaces public discussion.[2] But we shall see that contending groups are involved in most issues from the beginning. The prolongation of an issue does tend to harden arguments and routinize the

---

[1] Herbert Blumer, Part Four, "Collective Behavior," in Alfred M. Lee (ed.), *Principles of Sociology* (Rev. 2nd ed.; New York: Barnes & Noble, College Outline Series, 1951), 172–73.
[2] Ralph H. Turner and Lewis M. Killian, *Collective Behavior* (Englewood Cliffs, N.J.: Prentice-Hall, 1957), 266.

struggle for influence, but a major arena of the contest for power is the public opinion process itself. Many people remain uncommitted on a given issue, including some of those who identify themselves with pressure groups, and a public may be greatly enlarged during any phase of the opinion process. So we need to follow public discussion as issues drag on, break up into subissues, and become foci in the struggle for men's minds.

COMMUNICATIONS ABOUT ISSUES

In all levels of community the mass media are now so involved in the public opinion process that it is difficult for us to imagine how an issue could be discussed without them. An important beginning in the study of mass communications is the analysis of content.

Content of Communications

ENLARGING THE PUBLIC. Because those persons not discussing an issue are not members of that particular public, and because their votes or other expressions of opinion are sought, many communications are designed to alert people to an issue and to arouse their active concern. This *agitation* to enlarge a public is prominent when the issue is being defined; but such efforts are also frequent during the phases of discussion and expression of opinion. Repeatedly calling attention to an issue often seems aimed as much at enlarging a public as it is at selling a program.

Many if not most issues within special publics never become items of general concern. General news about specialized discussions at national and regional conventions is often oriented toward social problems, usually to provide some pertinent information from experts. Sometimes either a specialist or a journalist makes a specific appeal to the general public to arouse its concern about something. This appeal may spring from a desire to gain adherents or to get people to do something about their own welfare. Members of a special public may then do one or more of the following: (1) attempt to help define the issue for a general public, (2) provide information and specialized interpretations, or (3) become partisans.

INTENT BEHIND COMMUNICATIONS. Mass communications about issues are intended to accomplish one or both of two general objectives: (1) to provide information, or (2) to get people to believe and act in desired ways. The latter may be attempted by (a) propaganda, or (b) persuasion. Efforts to enlarge a public usually involve persuasion or propaganda, but sometimes consist primarily of disseminating information. Mass communications produce the intended responses under the right conditions, but they may fail.

Let us consider first that information which is directed specifically toward a given issue. It may deal with the existence or frequency of conditions or with cause-and-effect relationships; but information also may involve positions taken on questions of value. *A statement of preference for one value over another is a judgment of value, but it is a judgment of fact that the choice has been expressed.* If Senator Q is quoted as saying that effective billboard advertising is more important than roadside scenery, it may be reported as a matter of fact that he has expressed this rank order of values. It is in this sense that *social scientists treat values as part of the data of society. Similarly, mass communicators often report on value judgments as part of the facts of situations.*

All three of the above kinds of information—"pure facts," explanations, and reports of value judgments—are sometimes simply asserted in mass communications, but supporting evidence is very often indicated. Members of an increasingly secular society are inclined to ask, "How do you know?" A reporter may describe events he has seen, or provide pictures of them; next best, he asks witnesses what they saw or he seeks out what has been officially recorded. Interviews with officials are used to obtain reports of their explanations of events and of the value priorities of persons in a position to affect the outcome. Information of all kinds also may be borrowed from some acknowledged source. For a complex issue, scientific writings, history, or other judgments of fact rendered by special observers may be cited. The "background" article or book applies a body of knowledge to a given situation.

Second, much information carried by the mass media is not pointed directly toward particular issues, although implications for some social problems may be touched upon. People vicariously experience numerous faraway daily events, or try to, and they also receive an unending flow of comment about medical discoveries, scientific findings, economic development, population growth, and other matters. The flow of general information through the mass media supplements the efforts in the schools and adult education programs to help people comprehend the changing, complex world in which they live.[3] The images of reality and the general explanations developed by persons over a period of time affect their responses when an issue arises.

Much of what is offered in the mass media consists of *propaganda, the use of one-way communications to get people to believe and act in desired ways without thinking.*[4] (This definition distinguishes propaganda from persuasion, defined below.) *Propaganda depends on* the psychological mechanism of *suggestion, the use of stimuli that bypass thought.* A person about to be hypnotized is in a state of suggestibility—he is about to accept the ideas and do the bidding of someone else. A person is more suggestible than usual in relatively unstructured situations, for he shares the task and the mood of working out a collective definition of the situation. Although this is more pronounced in crowds,[5] publics and audiences also may be influenced by suggestion under the right conditions. The mass advertiser, as well as the propagandist on public issues, seeks an uncritical, automatic response. Some propaganda is designed to gain attention, thus to enlarge a marketing audience or a public; the rest consists of suggestions to buy a product or accept an idea about some other action.

Propaganda involves the deliberate use of *techniques of suggestion.* Seven of the common devices are illustrated in Table 3.1 and defined in the following:[6]

1. *Name-calling:* the use of despised or unpopular words to get people to reject a belief or a person without evidence.
2. *Glittering generality:* the use of noble-sounding words and phrases with vague meanings, to obtain uncritical acceptance.
3. *Plain Folks:* identifying ideas and actions with those of common people.
4. *Testimonial:* connecting a highly regarded, or despised, person with an idea or action.
5. *Transfer:* connecting something highly regarded, or despised (not a person), with an idea or action.
6. *Card-stacking:* omitting some relevant facts and selecting and organizing others, both true and false, to build a convincing case.
7. *Bandwagon:* implying that almost everybody is supporting an idea or action, and that others should hurry or risk being left alone.

---

[3] Kurt Lang and Gladys E. Lang, *Collective Dynamics* (New York: Thomas Y. Crowell Co., 1961), 434–35.
[4] Robert K. Merton, *Mass Persuasion* (New York: Harper & Bros., 1945), 38–39.
[5] Turner and Killian, *op. cit.*, 51–57, 84.
[6] Alfred M. Lee, and Elizabeth B. Lee, *The Fine Art of Propaganda* (for the Institute for Propaganda Analysis; New York: Harcourt, Brace & Co., 1939), 23–24.

TABLE 3.1

ILLUSTRATIONS OF SEVEN COMMON PROPAGANDA DEVICES IN
ADVERTISING AND THE DISCUSSION ISSUES

Propaganda Device	Examples in Advertising	Examples in the Discussion of Issues
Name-calling	"ordinary brands" "old-fashioned kind" "cheap imitations"	"wild-eyed schemes" "political pay-off" "head-in-the-sand"
Glittering generality	"modern" "exclusive and luxurious" "the original"	"responsible leadership" "progress" "truly American"
Plain folks	"the working man's smoke" "a real sensible buy" "listen to ol' Uncle Ben"	"good common-sense program" "came up the hard way" "as my farmer friends say"
Testimonial	"preferred by (actress)" "why don't you try it?" (baseball hero, on TV)	"Churchill's great vision" "the mind of a Hitler" "in Shakespeare's words"
Transfer	"used in the movies" "that sagging look" "preferred for travel"	"as in medical practice" "to avoid violence" "among executives"
Card-stacking	presentation of selected statements by only those who use X product	publicizing only that portion of a graph which supports one's argument
Bandwagon	"get yours while they last" "really catching on big" "for a limited time only"	"most Americans now see . . ." "landslide victory ahead" "almost universal agreement"

SOURCE: *Based on definitions in Lee and Lee, op. cit., 23–24.*

NOTE: *See text for definitions, and for other propaganda devices.*

The same message may contain several suggestive words and other propaganda devices, so it is important to consider the communication as a whole. It is possible to convey an emotion or an idea subtly by *innuendoes,* "between the lines," or by tone of voice. Thus it is *important to understand the net import of a communication, within a given context.*

A propaganda device not dependent on verbalization is *propaganda-of-the-deed,*[7] *action which dramatically suggests an idea or mood.* Verbal messages, however, often are used to spread information about the deed, and to influence its interpretation. The earliest lightning conquests by Hitler's troops suggested great power and determination, but radio broadcasts spread the word and interpreted the deeds. The technique of the *big lie,* also employed by Hitler, rests at least partly on its dramatic suggestiveness. If someone repeats an absurdity loudly and often enough, many people may eventually conclude that there must be something to it.[8] Leveling strong charges against a person or group, whether false or true, may arouse attention and enlarge a public; and under favorable conditions it may produce desired beliefs and actions.

Another device is the *deliberate withholding of ideas about alternative actions.* As compared with card-stacking, in which facts about conditions or about the outcomes of given proposals are manipulated, this practice amounts to "issue-stacking." By carefully presenting two or three alternatives, the impression may be created that no others are possible. Community and professional leaders are often trusted to delineate "the" alternatives for the consideration of the uninformed. Perhaps only one proposal is outlined, suggesting that there are only two possible positions—for and against.

One reason for the success of techniques of suggestion is the existence *of stereotypes, false generalizations about people or events.* They are based on insufficient or distorted facts, and they may be developed from personal experience or learned from others. Oversimplification and distortion are inevitable as people attempt to understand their complex environment,[9] but the less accurate a general-

---

[7] Merton, *op. cit.,* 92.
[8] Raymond E. Murphy and associates, *National Socialism* (Washington, D.C.: Division of European Affairs, Department of State, 1943), 56–62; Adolph Hitler, *Mein Kampf* (New York: Reynal and Hitchcock, 1939), 252.
[9] Walter Lippmann, *Public Opinion* (New York: Penguin Books, 1946, first publ. in 1922), 77–85.

ization, the less rational it is. The grosser the errors and the less one corrects for them, the less successful one's predictions will be.

When stereotypes are reified, all contrary evidence is discounted because the *image has come to be thought of as reality.* When images are held this rigidly, a person's thinking is inflexible; he cannot readily consider alternative interpretations and programs. He is then susceptible to suggestions that fit his stereotypes, but inhospitable to others.

Techniques for making suggestions *via* the mass media to the subconscious were developed after World War II. "Motivational research," using "depth" techniques, became an important part of market research.[10] Calculated attempts were begun to sell everything from cars to toothpaste by appealing to subconscious drives for love, emotional security, social status, a sense of power, and so on. Vance Packard, author of a best-selling book about apparent invasions of privacy and appeals to the buyer's hidden fears, called for a general public discussion of these practices.[11] He recognized that depth suggestions do not always work, but that research goes on to find out more about what makes them succeed.[12] He noted that during the fifties both of our major political parties turned to these "hidden persuaders," and that television showmanship became important in politics. The Democrats at first had trouble getting an advertising agency to take their account for the 1956 presidential campaign, but eventually Adlai Stevenson was to complain that he was not a breakfast cereal and was not in a beauty contest.[13]

Persuasion is the use of appeals to get people to believe and act in desired ways by adjustments to feedback communications. The persuader varies his arguments as letters, telephone calls, or other reactions come in.[14] Unlike one-way propaganda thrusts, this procedure involves deliberate use of social interaction, although mass communication must be largely in one direction. Sometimes the feedbacks are reported in such a lively way on television or radio, or in newspapers or magazines, that people get the feeling that they are engaging in a face-to-face conversation. The interaction reinforces the initial interest, and it may catch the attention of others, thus enlarging the public. Kate Smith's appeals in World War II for pledges of bond purchases

---

[10] Vance Packard, *The Hidden Persuaders* (New York: Pocket Books, 1957), 1–47.
[11] *Ibid.*, 48–70, 219–29.
[12] *Ibid.*, 208–18.
[13] *Ibid.*, 155–72.
[14] Merton, *op. cit.*, 38–39.

involved a carefully planned use of persuasion in a series of "marathon" radio broadcasts.[15]

Because an exchange takes place, it is possible for persuasion to be quite rational. Raising questions may expose factual material to critical discussion and encourage comment about additional alternatives. It is also possible for persuasion to become highly emotional, characterized by marked suggestibility, similar to the pattern of circular response of a compact crowd. Thus, persuasion ranges all the way from earnest, informative appeals to accept certain views and actions to adept manipulations of moods and subconscious drives with techniques of suggestion.[16] Persuasion of all varieties can be very effective, but there are limits to its success,[17] just as there are to propaganda.

The Mass Media

Although the printed word has been influencing the discussion of issues for four centuries, new technology and mass advertising have greatly extended and modified its impact in recent generations. Together with the development of electronic media, these recent changes justifiably have been called the Communications Revolution. Some of the salient features of each of the major media must be noted, but they all have an important common foundation. They are, in the United States, operated as private businesses.[18]

NEWSPAPERS. The profits and losses of newspaper owners have become increasingly tied to advertising, thus to circulation. One consequence of the increase in capital requirements has been a marked increase in the concentration of ownership; There are now actually fewer daily newspapers in the United States than there were at the beginning of the century, and the number of cities with competitive ownership has declined steadily to less than 5 per cent in 1960.[19] Local ownership and the number of news services also have declined.

---

[15] *Ibid.*, Chapter 2, "The Marathon: A Temporal Pattern."
[16] *Ibid.*, 178–86.
[17] *Ibid.*, Chapter 5, "Guilt-Edged Bonds: The Climate of Decision."
[18] Charles V. Kinter, "Economic Problems in Private Ownership of Communications," in Wilbur Schramm (ed.), *Communications in Modern Society* (Urbana: University of Illinois Press, 1948), 16–41; J. T. Klapper, *The Effects of Mass Media*, (New York: Bureau of Applied Social Research, Columbia University, 1949), 23–24.
[19] Raymond B. Nixon and Jean Ward, "Trends in Newspaper Ownership and Inter-Media Competition," *Journalism Quarterly*, 38 (Winter, 1961) 3–14.

Another consequence has been the proliferation of special features —sports, fashions, comics, television guides, advice to parents—on any matter that might sustain or boost circulation. Feature writing provides a wealth of material for entertainment and for discussion of issues concerning the areas covered, but a great many people evidently read little else. This does not necessarily mean that the *proportion* of the population following matters of general community significance has been declining. Caution is necessary in generalizing about such trends.

The amount of news reported in the dailies is, in fact, very great; and the predominant approach since the era of "yellow journalism" earlier in the century[20] has been to try to limit expressions of opinion to the editorial pages. Some norms of "social responsibility" have evolved,[21] probably supported by the conviction that extremism or the appearance of any bias might alienate numerous subscribers, or advertisers. Probably a major motive for printing syndicated columnists' views that differ from those of the publisher is to provide "a little something for everybody." The desire to avoid antitrust prosecution and other governmental controls as ownership becomes more concentrated is also a factor. Freed from extreme competition, a publisher may emphasize social responsibility without financial loss; but one study indicates that bias is unrelated to the amount of local newspaper competition.[22]

Editorial writers attempt to clarify issues and information, and they often express strong preferences. Many readers evidently ignore editorials, especially the anonymous ones. The syndicated, by-line columnists apparently have large personal followings; people like to be advised on an issue by someone whose general stance they favor. Columnists often refer to responses from readers, maintaining an atmosphere of persuasive interaction, thus granting such writers considerable influence over the size of a public on a given issue. In considering alternatives, their influence probably lies mainly in reinforcing latent views, because people are not easily persuaded to go against what they consider their self-interests. Perhaps those who read but one commentator are more likely to be influenced, other things

---

[20] Frank L. Mott, *American Journalism* (New York: The Macmillan Co., 1950), Chapter 31. The greatest excesses evidently were committed in circulation wars.
[21] Commission on the Freedom of the Press, *A Free and Responsible Press* (Chicago: University of Chicago Press, 1947), 20–29.
[22] Raymond B. Nixon and Robert Jones, "The Content of Noncompetitive vs. Competitive Newspapers," *Journalism Quarterly*, 33 (Summer, 1956), 299–314.

being equal, because of the absence of competing suggestions and versions of fact.

After World War I, Walter Lippmann supported the view that newspapers cannot provide satisfactory information for the rational discussion of complex issues. Under the pressures of advertising, he declared, news coverage merely signalizes events and presents their stereotyped aspects. The newspaper does well with routine matters, especially those of clear public record; but it fails when there is a crisis.[23] He called for a government "Intelligence Bureau"[24] to enlighten the government and the public about crisis conditions. According to this view, the newspaper fails when an issue arises. The rational development of new norms requires sufficient information, readily available to the public.

Today, in competition with radio and television, the newspaper is the major medium for news *detail*. It provides a continuous flow of information about current events, and a considerable amount of background material. Whether all this is adequate for intelligent public discussion remains a puzzle, one requiring consideration of the other news media. Some intelligence services have been provided for governmental agencies, and "leaks" from these provide some of the daily news. Even at best, a further question remains: On *how many issues* can the average reader be reasonably competent?

MAGAZINES. Although magazines as a whole stress entertainment value and have fewer regular readers than newspapers,[25] they do add perspective to the consideration of issues. Concerned less with daily deadlines, they can emphasize background material on major issues. However, the highly competitive drive for increased circulation to sustain profitable advertising has resulted in the heavy use of interest-catching devices and special features, as well as in concentration of ownership. The many feature magazines created to appeal to special interest groups may influence the discussion of issues by their readers.

BOOKS. Of all the media the book is best suited for the educational function because of its length and its freedom from regular deadlines

---

[23] Lippmann, *op. cit.*, Part VII, "Newspapers."
[24] *Ibid.*, Part VIII, "Organized intelligence."
[25] Angus Campbell and Charles A. Metzner, "Books, Libraries and Other Media of Communication," *Public Use of the Library* (Ann Arbor: Survey Research Center, University of Michigan), 1–14.

and the pressures of advertising. Book readers are heavy users of the other media of communication,[26] suggesting that people who develop the greatest interest in public issues often tend to rely on books for enlightenment. A most significant development in recent years is the publication of large quantities of paperback books. Material of all types is available in this form, including treatments in depth of major public issues.

RADIO AND TELEVISION. The coming of radio greatly accelerated the speed of communication to the mass audience. For over a century the telegraph has sped information to newspaper editors, but it takes time to set type, print, and distribute the papers. The broadcasting station, by contrast, can transmit the news immediately. Radio and television can be used for propaganda and emotional persuasion, but their speed in transmitting information can facilitate the democratic discussion of issues. Democracy can be cumbersome, especially in a large and complex country, so the quick news bulletin can help integrate large publics. There are, of course, limits to the accuracy and fullness of such rapid communications. The brief news summaries over the air create and enlarge publics and often stimulate listeners to read newspapers and magazines to get more information. Background coverage by television and radio in the United States tends to be limited to those instances in which the demand seems to be very great.

The rapid diffusion of the radio in America took place from the late 1920's to World War II. The diffusion of television to nearly nine-tenths of all American homes required only about a decade, the fifties. Television has cut movie attendance and radio-listening to about one-half, and greatly reduced the reading of fiction. Reading for information has not decreased; in fact people often are stimulated to read by television presentations on public issues. The general magazine field has become extremely competitive since television, but the special interest magazines have prospered. The typical American now spends almost as many hours a week with the various mass media as he does earning a living.[27]

Although television and radio contribute to the definition of issues and provide some background information for their discussion, their

[26] *Ibid.*, 6–10.
[27] Leo Bogart, *The Age of Television* (New York: Frederick Ungar Publishing Co., 1958), 66, 147–48.

programs are designed primarily for mass entertainment. A large proportion of broadcast time is controlled by a few advertising agencies.[28] There are now very few national networks, and there is a good deal of interlocking in the control of radio, television, and newspapers. Although trends toward monopoly of the mass media are a potential threat to democratic processes, a more likely *hypothesis* is that the *pressures of advertising result in a catering to majority views rather than in a monolithic bias, in spite of concentrated access to the mass media.*[29] The effects of limited access deserve careful study,[30] however, including the conditions under which the presentation of material on highly sensitive issues is discouraged.[31]

GROUPS, PRESSURES, AND IDEOLOGY

Mass communications about public issues are usually on behalf of groups, even when the members are not in full agreement. The flow of information, propaganda, and persuasion is calculated to have the maximum effect in a community of contending groups; and it is this interaction among groups that renders mass communications meaningful to a person. The public opinion process is thus not a dialogue among disparate individuals, and persons do not share equally in it.[32] Groups do not share equally in it either, as an examination of pressure group activities will show.

Pressure Groups

Those interest groups that attempt to influence opinion and action on public issues are pressure groups. Members share the desire to achieve certain prized values, and some beliefs about how to achieve them. Many pressure groups continue to work toward general goals

---

[28] Llewellyn White, *The American Radio* (Chicago: University of Chicago Press, 1947), 94; Bernard Schwartz, "FCC and the Networks," *The Nation,* 188, (May 23, 1959), 473–75.

[29] George Lundberg, Clarence C. Schrag, and Otto N. Larsen, *Sociology* (3rd ed.; New York: Harper & Row, 1963), 236.

[30] R. M. MacIver, *The Web of Government* (New York: The Macmillan Co., 1948), 221; Morris Ernst, *The First Freedom* (New York: The Macmillan Co., 1946).

[31] Paul F. Lazarsfeld and Robert K. Merton, "Mass Communication, Popular Taste, and Organized Social Action," in Lyman Bryson (ed.), *Communication of Ideas* (New York: Harper & Bros., 1948).

[32] Herbert Blumer, "Public Opinion and Social Organization," *American Sociological Review,* 13 (October, 1948), 542–49.

over a considerable period of time, focusing on many specific issues, while others emerge to influence the discussion of but one controversy. The use of the mass media by pressure groups varies all the way from thoughtful, information-centered persuasion to highly emotional and misleading persuasion and propaganda.[33] To influence opinion they also use public meetings and campaigns to arouse public sympathy for their causes, such as getting lists of signatures on petitions. Often they attempt direct action, by such means as lobbying, letter-writing, or supporting persons sympathetic to their views for key appointments or elective office to influence decision-makers.

Why are there so many pressure groups in America today? An increasingly complex division of labor means that new interest groups keep emerging. Not only are voluntary groups allowed freedom to assemble and organize, they are encouraged to participate in the discussion of public issues and to expect a "fair hearing." Americans also share a widespread belief in progress, and many people are willing to search out the best alternative to achieve it.

POWER OF PRESSURE GROUPS. Pressure groups vary greatly in size and scope, and in the power they are able to wield over public opinion and action. The size and financial means of the group are not the only factors involved here, although concentrations of capital, technical knowledge, and administrative functioning are significant. The extent to which the group supports the basic value consensus of the society, the relation of the group to other pressure groups, and the connection of its established interest with the issue at hand also are important. Other variables are the solidarity of the group, its prestige, the articulateness and efficiency of its leaders, access to the mass media, and access to decision-makers.

A common assertion is that an all-powerful pressure group or a bloc such as "Big Business," "Big Labor," the "Militarists," or "Big Agriculture" is "taking over everything." The influence of a particular group or coalition has evidently varied with social conditions in America. It appears that now, at least, no group or bloc can control completely the outcome of national discussions. A coalition may have considerable influence on some matters and little on others, and on a given issue the *alignment* is important. The role of "Big Government" has been increasingly to act as a *balance wheel* on behalf of society,

---

[33] Herbert Blumer, in Lee (ed.), *Principles of Sociology, op. cit.*, 192.

as a referee to prevent any "me-first" grouping from gaining general power.[34] Government has continued to support well-established interest groups; but it has also regulated them in the general interest, and it has recognized and protected the emergence of *countervailing power groups*.[35]

For example, some powerful business combinations emerged during the rapid industrial development of the nineteenth century. As these giant economic interest groups fought among themselves, pressure group activities themselves became a public issue. From Roosevelt to Roosevelt, "trust-busting" efforts were only partly successful. Legislative highpoints were the Norris-LaGuardia Act of 1932 and the Wagner (National Labor Relations) Act of 1935, supporting labor's right to organize and bargain collectively. The U.S. Supreme Court, after a century of almost total rejection of the legitimacy of organized labor,[36] upheld these enactments.

But while these and other developments have reduced the relative power of "Big Business,"[37] labor's newfound strength has been curbed in its turn by the Taft-Hartley Act of 1947 and other laws. Evidently the majority in Congress (and the Court) believed that organized labor had become a well-established interest and that controls were needed to stabilize the balance of power, as well as to protect minority groups and insure peace and order, political security, and individual freedom.[38] The contest among these and many other economic groupings continues, with some interests poorly represented but none wielding unchecked influence.

PRESSURE GROUPS AND DEMOCRACY. The public issue concerning monopoly influence has apparently been largely resolved by adopting such controls as the regulation of lobbying, continued antitrust efforts, and the support of countervailing groups. What are the effects, however, of the more limited, more controlled activities of pressure groups on democratic processes? If suggestion techniques are used to produce

---

[34] Stuart Chase, *Democracy Under Pressure* (New York: Twentieth Century Fund, 1945).

[35] John K. Galbraith, *American Capitalism, The Concept of Countervailing Power* (Boston: Houghton Mifflin Co., 1952).

[36] Alfred W. Blumrosen, "Legal Process and Labor Law," in William M. Evan (ed.), *Law and Sociology* (New York: The Free Press, 1962), 191–208.

[37] Robert L. Heilbroner, "The Power of Big Business," *The Atlantic* (September, 1965), 89–93.

[38] Blumrosen, *op. cit.*, 208–20.

marked factual distortions, it would seem that rational discussion is defeated, although the existence of a contest at least indicates alternative paths. Suppose there were neither overwhelming influence nor extreme use of suggestion, would a "me-first" pressure still work against the representation of the interests of all the people?

One view is that pressure groups give the individual a needed voice. Just as the political party system was invented to supplement our territorial system of representation, so perhaps pressure groups help make the republican form of democracy work in a large, complex society with numerous interests. Also, some pressure group effort is educational, providing versions of fact as well as alternative programs of action. Some groups concentrate on the advancement of equal opportunity, some on the encouragement of political participation, and others on peaceful settlement of conflicts—all justified at least partly by reference to democratic values. Even so, the question of the representation of all interests and individuals remains, and it is difficult to determine the net effect of pressure group activities on the quality of democracy.

Ideologies and Groups

THE ROLE OF IDEOLOGIES. Positions taken by pressure groups on public issues are guided by *ideologies, those systems of ideas that provide justification for a group's support of (a) existing social arrangements, or (b) desired changes in them.* Ideologies support members' convictions that the group is right, and they may influence the thinking of others. A set of ideas that effectively supports action is thus very practical; it contributes to the power and influence of the group.

Realism calls for accurate knowledge of an opposing group's ideology, whether the goal be to counter the group or to reach an accommodation with it. Knowledge is also valuable concerning the group's deviations in practice from its ideology, and the ways these are handled and rationalized. It is common to impute false motives and to proceed from stereotyped notions about an opposing group. Realistic action also requires that the members of a group understand its own ideology, and deviations from it.

CONTENT OF IDEOLOGIES. The entire body of ideas in an ideology is designed to support the way certain things are done, or the way the group wants them done. To this end five interrelated kinds of content are developed: (1) The social arrangements desired by the group, including the supporting norms of conduct. (2) The means preferred for achieving the goals, varying from the specific program of a social movement to general ideas about ways of proceeding. (3) The priorities of value shared by the group members. Values most prized are strongly and frequently affirmed, and linked with the desired arrangements. Values are also identified or implied in choices of the means adopted to reach the ends sought. (4) The shared beliefs of fact. Some of these are related to the operation of norms in the desired state of affairs. Others concern the adoption of means, including beliefs about who the groups are that stand in the way and the means by which they may be countered. (5) A conception of society, often of its past and future as well as the present.[39] The hopes and various beliefs of fact and value are fitted together to form a general frame of reference to support group action. Some ideologies are highly systematic, but those with less coherence still present at least an implicit view of society, or a considerable part of it.

Some ideologies are quite involved, and attempts to defend them often add to their complexity. Others are brief and unsophisticated, but they may be convincing to many people. To specify clearly premises of fact and value and to develop an ideology with unswerving logic is no easy task, especially for an ardent partisan. Many if not most ideologies thus include (1) some reified stereotypes, (2) some other debatable beliefs of fact, (3) some unstated assumptions of fact and value, (4) some techniques of suggestion, and (5) rationalizations of what appear at least to outsiders to be inconsistencies.

A rationalization that may seem incredible to out-groups may become accepted as an unquestioned truth and taught to children in all sincerity. For example, the post-Emancipation laws and practices of racial segregation seemed contradictory to the norms of equal protection of the laws and full citizenship in the Thirteenth, Fourteenth, and Fifteenth Amendments to the Constitution—except to people who hold the factual belief that the Negroes are a biologically inferior race. A common argument in the ideology of segregation that evolved was that equal opportunity applies only to those of equal capacity, so it is wrong to encourage Negroes to compete with whites on equal terms.

TYPES OF IDEOLOGY: FROM MODERATION TO EXTREMISM. Although the terms must be qualified and refined for analytical use, the usual

[39] Turner and Killian, *op. cit.*, 331–32.

distinction is between *conservative ideologies, supporting a status quo, and liberal ones, favoring given changes.*[40] Ideologies are conspicuous in social movements, which are often classed as conservative, reform, and revolutionary. Smelser distinguishes between movements oriented toward modifying only the norms of a social system and the values underlying the norms.[41] Movements also have been classed as value-oriented, power-oriented, and participation-oriented.[42] Supporters of a movement often become a pressure group when the discussion of an issue seems connected with their goals; sometimes they manage to make their specific program a public issue. But those pressure groups that are not tied to specific movements also act on the basis of ideologies, indicating concern about the direction, speed, and the scope of social changes.

The analysis of social problems frequently requires consideration of *extremist pressure groups.* For this the simple *dichotomy of liberal and conservative is not adequate; it is necessary to think in terms of differences of degree.* Figure 3.1 identifies the major segments of a continuum running from extremely liberal to extremely conservative ideologies. Reformist positions are either moderately or strongly liberal, revolutionary ones usually more extreme. Conservative ideologies vary from the moderate tolerating and limiting of social change to extreme reactions against it. This scale may also be used to classify pressure group actions as well as ideologies, and to note gaps between beliefs and practices.

A major limitation of this continuum is that there are important similarities between the extremist beliefs (and actions) at its opposite

FIGURE 3.1

TYPES OF IDEOLOGY WITH RESPECT TO SOCIAL CHANGE

Extreme Strong Moderate	*"Center"*	*Moderate Strong Extreme*
LIBERAL IDEOLOGIES (those favoring change)		CONSERVATIVE IDEOLOGIES (those opposing change)

---

[40] Karl Mannheim called ideologies of change "Utopias" in his *Ideology and Utopia* (New York: Harcourt, Brace & Co., 1946).
[41] Neil J. Smelser, *Theory of Collective Behavior* (New York: The Free Press, 1963), 270–78, 313–19.
[42] Turner and Killian, *op. cit.*, 327.

ends,[43] as we might suggest by bending it into a circle. *The key idea in both liberal and conservative extremism is the belief of fact that there is a powerful conspiracy against the society.* The presumed conspirators are believed to be infiltrating all institutions of power and influence to prepare for an imminent "take-over." Extremist groups thus foster fear and hatred of the groups they believe to be plotting, and present themselves as the true patriots, the guardians of society. They believe their leaders already have the answers, so anyone who disagrees must be one of the "enemy," or a "dupe." Moderates are mistrusted by both liberal and conservative extremists. All scientists, teachers, and other "eggheads" are suspect, probably in part because they are prone to question such a simple black-and-white diagnosis. The extremist uses techniques of suggestion heavily, shaping "the facts" to fit his arguments. All extremists are expected to be "True Believers,"[44] giving unquestioning and all-encompassing loyalty to the cause.

The actions believed necessary are thus radical. Liberal and conservative extremists want sudden comprehensive changes in opposite directions—by violence if necessary. They believe that the underhanded methods of the enemy must be borrowed and used against him, or he will triumph. There is scorn for democratic discussion of alternatives, since quick and decisive action is thought necessary for survival. Extremist commentary on public issues consists largely of general moral judgments and suggestions about the motives of leaders and groups in the news, rather than a weighing of immediate alternatives. Society's manifestations of "moral decay" are attributed to the enemy, so that all-out attack, not a discussion of choices, is the only appropriate strategy.

However, militant action is not necessarily extremist. Political activities and strategic pushing of lawsuits may be vigorous yet lawful, and not based on a conspiratorial ideology. Public demonstrations reflect the conviction that unusual measures are necessary to enlarge the public on an issue and to bring pressure on decision-makers, but efforts may be made to avoid violence and to follow the laws governing public assembly. There is always the risk that a compact crowd

[43] One political scientist lists nine similarities. See, Julian Foster, "The Nature of Extremism," *Reason, A Review of Politics,* 1 (Nov., 1965), 6–8.
[44] Eric Hoffer, *The True Believer* (New York: Harper and Row, 1951); Egon Bittner, "Radicalism and the Organization of Radical Movements," *American Sociological Review,* 28 (December, 1963), 937–39.

will become an unlawful mob, under certain conditions, and the extremist often tries to exploit this. He is contemptuous of the controlled militancy sometimes exhibited by the strong liberal or conservative.

In recent years, probably most of the public demonstrators for civil rights and peace, and those against poverty, have rejected extremist ideologies and tactics. However, such demonstrations have been an effective training ground for some extreme New Left Groups, which emphasize action for change without articulating clearcut reasons.[45] The Old Left extremists—the Communist party and some socialist groups—have emphasized systematic ideology as the basis for action. A major Communist belief has been that liberal reforms outwardly must be supported but actually must be undermined in order to promote unrest. Revolution is believed likely if the government can be made to appear in violent reaction against reformers. The communist invites persecution and encourages violence—anything to foster revolution rather than gradual reform.[46] The ideologies of both the Old and New Left portray leaders of established institutions as reactionary conspirators against the people. Radical liberals seek influence and power to save society, especially from the radical conservatives.

Returning the compliment, the ultraconservatives strive for influence and power to preserve us from Far Left conspirators. In the late fifties, "McCarthyism" was based on the belief that large numbers of Communist Party members had infiltrated the United States Department of State, the Army, and other major agencies of government. Far Right groups in the sixties, such as the Rev. Billy Hargis' Christian Crusade and the John Birch Society, have contended that most leaders in government, politics, religion, and education are Communists, sympathizers, or dupes—traitors all.[47] They believe that government controls and public welfare programs promote socialism and eventually communism, and that the Communist conspiracy is forwarded by changes in education, religion, and inter-group and

[45] Amitai Etzioni, "The New Left: Act Now and Theorize Later," *Los Angeles Times*, August 15, 1965, G, 1–2

[46] J. Edgar Hoover, *Masters of Deceit* (New York: Henry Holt & Co., 1958), 100; Herbert A. Philbrick, *I Led Three Lives* (New York: McGraw-Hill, 1952), 186–87, 202–10, 292.

[47] Seymour Martin Lipset, "Three Decades of Radical Right: Coughlinites, McCarthyites and Birchers," in Daniel Bell (ed.), *The Radical Right* (Garden City, N.Y.: Doubleday & Co., 1963), 373–446; see also, Arnold Forster and Benjamin R. Epstein, *Danger on the Right* (New York: Random House, 1964).

international relations.[48] They do not want to conserve the *status quo;* they favor drastic change to return the society to the condition it was presumably in before the alleged traitors began their conspiracy.

Several times in American history extremist groups have had considerable influence, but their contempt for democratic processes has limited their appeal. They have sometimes swayed large numbers of people with appeals to fear, but the Anglo-American values of moderation and compromise are held strongly enough to prevent the development of extremist political parties. Public discussion is only relatively rational, but it limits extremist organizations to the role of pressure groups.[49]

On the local level extremist groups have often used intimidation to influence the operation of businesses, newspapers, radio stations, schools, churches, and other institutions. Sometimes they gain direct control of local P.T.A.'s, labor unions, school and library boards, political party organizations, and agencies of city government.[50] Such efforts are less likely to succeed when they are strongly denounced at the state, regional, and national levels by respected leaders.

Although extremists would silence all opposition, they themselves are protected by the democratic norm of toleration of dissent, and they provide a crucial test of it. Freedom of speech, assembly, and of the press mean that one may think what he will and also express his ideas freely. The Founding Fathers advocated peaceful social change; they valued constructive dissent and assumed in their ideology that revolution would be unnecessary so long as all groups enjoyed free expression. So attempts to curb the activities of an extremist group are likely to be challenged, even by those who loathe the group involved. If free expression and fair investigation are not guaranteed to all groups, perhaps they are safe for none. Thus even the outlawing of the generally detested Communist party by the Communist Control Act of 1954, based on the belief of fact that the party was overtly and continuously advocating the overthrow of the government of the United States, has been an issue.[51]

---

[48] G. B. Rush, "Toward a Definition of the Extreme Right," *Pacific Sociological Review,* 6 (Fall, 1963), 64–73; Richard Dudman, *Men of the Far Right* (New York: Pyramid Books, 1962), 9–10.

[49] Donald Janson and Bernard Eisman, *The Far Right* (New York: McGraw-Hill, 1963), 11–21, 237–46; Robert R. Alford, *Party and Society* (Chicago: Rand McNally & Co., 1963), 11–12.

[50] Gene Grove, *Inside the John Birch Society* (Greenwich, Conn.: Gold Medal Books, 1961), 158–73; Forster and Epstein, *op. cit.,* 3–5, 14–19; Dudman, *op. cit.,* 75; Carey McWilliams, "The Enemy in Pasadena," *The Christian Century,* 68 (January 3, 1951), 10–15, reprinted in Turner and Killian, *op. cit.,* 237–44.

[51] *New York Times,* August 29, 1954, IV, 6.

What motivates members of extremist groups? One explanation is *political alienation,* the conviction that their goals cannot be achieved by participation in existing political processes.[52] The Marxian view is that capitalists monopolize political power, excluding all workers from it. The "romantic" type of ultraconservative, if not other types, feels that all his cherished traditions and values are being crowded out by new ways. While some with anomic and alienated feelings (see Chapter 2) about modern changes become resigned or adjust in other ways, some believe they must replace the seeming normlessness with a "prescribed sacred" way of life before it is too late (see Chapter 1).[53] To them, evidently, secularization is the result of a conspiracy, so strong actions are called for. Some observers suggest that such conservative extremists are the "dispossessed," people who feel that a return to earlier institutions and simple virtues would restore their lost status and power.[54]

Another explanation in terms of status anxiety is that extremists have moved up the occupational ladder somewhat, from a lowly beginning, but are obsessed with the idea that any further rise is blocked by a conspiracy among the elites. This outlook may support either liberal or conservative extremism. It seems applicable to Senator Joseph McCarthy and his followers, who persistently charged that Communist conspirators were drawn from the wealthy, educated Eastern elites—the conservative, upper class, Anglo-Saxon Protestants.[55]

This interpretation was rejected after a 1962 study of 308 supporters of Dr. Fred Schwarz' Christian Anti-Communism Crusade, who were found mainly to be respectable, native-born Protestants, above average in education, income, and in participation in politics and other associations. There were no nonwhites, almost no Democrats, and few who had experienced upward or downward social mobility. While their views on specific areas of change varied considerably, nearly all shared the belief that subversion by American Communists, especially by professors and students, was a grave threat. Eschewing all "status politics" explanations, the researchers suggest that the

[52] Edward A. Shils, *The Torment of Secrecy* (New York: The Free Press, 1956), 231–34; Joseph R. Gusfield, "Mass Society and Extremist Politics," *American Sociological Review,* 27 (February, 1962), 20–23.
[53] Howard Becker, "Normative Reactions to Normlessness," *American Sociological Review,* 27 (December, 1962), 803–10.
[54] Daniel Bell, "The Dispossessed," in Bell, *op. cit.,* 1–45; Alford, *op. cit.,* 14; Mark Sherwin, *The Extremists* (New York: St. Martin's Press, 1963), 225–26.
[55] Seymour Martin Lipset, "The Sources of the 'Radical Right,'" in Bell, *op. cit.,* 360–65; Peter Viereck, "The Revolt Against the Elite," in Bell, *op. cit.,* 162–83.

Crusaders are Republicans who reject what they see as the "welfare state" position of their party.[56]

Perhaps extremism cannot be explained without taking personality processes into account. Many studies have found that liberal and conservative extremists have different views of the nature of man and of what social arrangements are desirable, but that both tend to think in stereotyped and authoritarian terms, and to be intolerant of ideas at all different from their own.[57] Seymour M. Lipset maintains that although extremists are found in all social classes, the person who is socialized in the working class will most probably support extremism, because his developmental experiences are most likely to produce authoritarian traits.[58] One study found that feelings of anomy (anomia, see Chapter 2) are associated with several aspects of personality, including political alienation and authoritarian attitudes,[59] but another found alienation, personal disturbance, and ideological position to vary independently.[60]

REFERENCE GROUPS AND THE PERSON

When a person receives a mass communication about an issue, he perceives it in the light of his *apperceptive background*, his organization of relevant past experiences. He connects the communication with those groups that seem pertinent to the issue. These *"reference groups" provide the person with a frame of reference for responding to the communication.*[61] He need not be a member of the group, but it must be meaningful to him, even if imaginary.[62] The more strongly he identifies with a group, the more likely its norms will guide his re-

[56] Raymond E. Wolfinger, Barbara K. Wolfinger, Kenneth Prewitt, and Sheilah Rosenhack, "America's Radical Right: Politics and Ideology," in David E. Apter (ed.), *Ideology and Discontent* (New York: The Free Press, 1964), 262–93.
[57] Earl R. Carlson, "The Extremist Personality," *Reason, A Review of Politics,* I (June–July, 1965), 1–2, 8; R. N. Barker, "Authoritarianism of the Political Right, Center and the Left," *Journal of Social Issues,* 19 (1963), 2; T. W. Adorno *et al., The Authoritarian Personality* (New York: Harper & Bros., 1950); Sherwin, *op. cit.,* 227–30.
[58] Seymour Martin Lipset, "Democracy and Working-Class Authoritarianism," *American Sociological Review,* 24 (August, 1959), 482–501.
[59] Herbert McClosky and John H. Scharr, "Psychological Dimensions of Anomy," *American Sociological Review,* 30 (February, 1965), 14–40.
[60] J. L. Simmons, "Liberalism, Alienation, and Personal Disturbance," *Sociology and Social Research,* 49 (July, 1965), 456–64.
[61] Tamotsu Shibutani, *Society and Personality* (Englewood Cliffs, N.J.: Prentice-Hall, 1961), 257.
[62] *Ibid.,* 258; Lang and Lang, *op. cit.,* 10.

sponses.[63] For the mass communicator, the unseen audience is a vast reference group or a complex of them, and he orients his messages to his imagined recipients. These images may be influenced by feedback communications such as telephone calls, letters to editors or congressmen, opinion polls, television ratings, or reactions of group spokesmen.[64]

Secondary Reference Groups

Secondary groups to which a person may relate mass communications include social class, racial and ethnic groups, occupation, nation and region, political party, church, and many other formal organizations. They need not be operating as pressure groups in order to be reference groups on an issue. When it is recalled that each group ideology contains a complex set of beliefs of fact and value, it can be seen that it is difficult to determine why people decide to vote as they do or make other responses to barrages of mass communications.[65] There is some evidence that the greater the cross-pressures felt by the person the less consistently liberal or conservative he will be from issue to issue.[66] A study of the failure of official appeals to Americans to build fallout shelters in 1961–62 suggests that a person can resist strong appeals when he cannot accept the proffered beliefs of fact. Those who believed in the safety and war-deterrent effects of the shelters seemed oriented toward the views of military groups; nonbelievers seemed to refer their thinking to secondary groups with other perspectives.[67]

The "mass politics" theorists might suggest that this general refusal to build fallout shelters was a mass protest against feelings of powerlessness, an explanation applied to findings that the politically alienated tend to vote "no" on school bond issues,[68] on consolidating

---

[63] Turner and Killian, *op. cit.*, 253; Herbert C. Kelman, "Processes of Opinion Change," *Public Opinion Quarterly* (Spring, 1961), 57–78, distinguishes three processes of influence—compliance, identification, and internalization.

[64] Lundberg, Schrag, and Larsen, *op. cit.*, 231–35.

[65] Leo A. Goodman, "Statistical Methods for Analyzing Process of Change," *American Journal of Sociology*, 68 (July, 1962), 57–78.

[66] Marvin E. Olsen, "Liberal-Conservative Attitude Crystallization," *The Sociological Quarterly*, 3 (January, 1962), 17–26; Paul F. Lazarsfeld, Bernard Berelson, and Hazel Gaudet, *The People's Choice* (New York: Columbia University Press, 1948), 52–61.

[67] F. K. Berrien, Carol Shulman, and Marianne Amarel, "The Fall-Out Shelter Owners: A Study of Attitude Formation," *Public Opinion Quarterly* (Summer, 1963), 206–16.

[68] John E. Horton and Wayne E. Thompson, "Powerlessness and Political Negativism: A Study of Defeated Local Referendums," *American Journal of Sociology*, 67 (March, 1962), 485–93.

local governments,[69] and other local referendums.[70] It should not be assumed that such a vote is the act of an isolated individual, not when there are groups (including extremist ones) opposing such actions on ideological grounds, and which may thus serve as salient reference groups for a person.[71]

Primary Reference Groups

Although a person receives many messages directly from the mass media, he gets some from other people, especially in primary groups, in a *two-step flow of communications*.[72] In either case, he usually does more than merely receive news about an issue. He participates in a *talking-over process*[73] through which he learns the responses of people in both those secondary and primary groups that are salient to him. He is influenced by these "significant others" and may in turn influence some of them. *Personal influence, in primary groups, becomes greater as the discussion proceeds toward decision,*[74] *and it may either reinforce or counteract mass communications.*[75] The effects may vary in different parts of the social structure.[76]

Mass communications may reinforce latent responses, but these may then be overcome by group influences. The person is thus not a puppet of the media, and mass communications only partly determine the quality of public discussion. Reference group influences may vary all the way from highly informative and logical persuasion to extreme use of techniques of suggestion, whether intentional or not. In a study of the discussion of flood control and water conservation in Kansas,

[69] Edward L. McDill and Jeanne Clare Ridley, "Status, Anomia, Political Alienation and Political Participation," *American Journal of Sociology*, 68 (September, 1962), 205–13.
[70] Walter C. Kaufman and Scott Greer, "Voting in a Metropolitan Community," *Social Forces*, 38 (March, 1960), 196–204.
[71] See Gusfield, *op. cit.*, 19–30, for a critique of mass politics theory, as illustrated by William Kornhauser, *The Politics of Mass Society* (New York: The Free Press, 1959).
[72] Elihu Katz, "The Two Step Flow of Communication," *Public Opinion Quarterly* (Spring, 1957), 61–78.
[73] Otto N. Larsen and Richard J. Hill, "Mass Media and Interpersonal Communication in the Diffusion of a News Event," *American Sociological Review*, 19 (August, 1954), 426–33; Joseph B. Ford, "The Primary Group in Mass Communications," *Sociology and Social Research*, 38 (1954), 152–58.
[74] Elihu Katz, "Communication Research and the Image of Society: Convergence of Two Traditions," *American Journal of Sociology*, 65 (March, 1960), 440.
[75] Elihu Katz and Paul Lazarsfeld, *Personal Influence*, (New York: The Free Press, 1955), 44–45, 131.
[76] Herbert F. Lionberger, *Adoption of New Ideas and Practices* (Ames: Iowa State University Press, 1960), 67–89; Otto N. Larsen and Richard J. Hill, "Social Structure and Interpersonal Communication," *American Journal of Sociology*, 63 (March, 1958), 497–505.

personal influences greatly distorted the information and proposals presented in a clear manner by formal organizations through the mass media.[77]

CRYSTALLIZATION AND EXPRESSION OF OPINION

At some point in the discussion of an issue, pressure groups and other reference groups take a stand and begin expressing it. Some persons involved in the talking-over process make up their minds early, some later, and some never do. Persons and groups with crystallized views express them in various ways in order to influence the outcome. The means of expression vary with the level of community and the type of decision-making concerned. Especially when the decision is by majority vote, or by some type of representative democracy, the result may be different from the initial crystallized views of any one group or person.[78]

Many decisions about issues in a democracy are made by government, at different levels. Expressions about issues are often made at the polls, and later an important means is writing letters to elected executive officers and legislators. Although they are influenced by the quantity of mail they receive, legislators usually pay more attention to spontaneous letters than to organized pressure campaigns. Sometimes the mail gives a very different picture of public views than is provided by representative opinion polls, so the latter have been increasingly relied on for balanced perspective. Elected officials are not bound by the views of their constituents; they may even try to change them,[79] although they thus run the risk of not being reelected. Appointed officials are not so directly responsive to public opinion, but they cannot ignore it. Even in dictatorships public opinion is heeded in order to manipulate it effectively. Opinion polls, by methods discarded in the United States a generation ago, are being used more and more in the Soviet Union.[80]

Decisions on issues made by all three branches of government—judicial, legislative and executive—become law. Laws are either pre-

---

[77] E. Jackson Baur, "Opinion Change in a Public Controversy," *Public Opinion Quarterly* (Summer, 1962), 212–26.
[78] Blumer, in Lee (ed.), *Principles of Sociology, op. cit.,* 191.
[79] Lang and Lang, *op. cit.,* 408.
[80] George Gallup, American Institute of Public Opinion, *Los Angeles Times,* August 13, 1965, Part I, 12.

existing or emergent norms, with the force of political authority behind them. Law provides an index of the values of a society, and of the nature of its unity.[81] But a single decision by a court or legislature often makes a mere dent in a broad, continuing issue. The same is true of nongovernmental decisions. *Each decision helps integrate the values of the community*[82] *and its beliefs of fact; but crystallization of opinion and adoption of a particular new norm may settle tentatively only a part of a complex dilemma.* Thus a dozen or a thousand separate decisions on issues within larger issues may leave a social problem as unsettled as ever, and decisions often raise more questions than they resolve.

PERSPECTIVE

The flow of mass communications brings information, persuasion, and propaganda to bear on ever new searches for norms that may resolve at least a small part of a social problem. Pressure groups, guided by the patterned beliefs of fact and value that make up their ideologies, use mass communications and other means to influence the members of a public. A person's responses, as he participates in the talking-over process, are influenced by those secondary and primary groups which are his own reference groups on the matter. At every stage in the public opinion process the influences on his thinking may vary from the highly rational to the extremely irrational. Personal and group opinions crystallize, are expressed, and decisions about new norms are often made. As long as disagreement about values or beliefs of fact concerning a broader issue in the community continues, however, a social problem persists and fosters seemingly endless rounds of discussion.

QUESTIONS FOR DISCUSSION AND STUDY

1. Can you think of a current example of an attempt to enlarge a public so that a matter will become a general public issue? Who is trying to enlarge the public, and by what means?

[81] F. James Davis *et al., Society and the Law* (New York: The Free Press, 1962), 56–59.
[82] *Ibid.,* 27–32, 66.

2. In today's newspaper can you identify at least one news story about each of the following: (a) an issue of very limited concern to the general public, (b) a major public issue which is not a social problem as defined in this book, and (c) a social problem?

3. In today's paper find examples of as many techniques of suggestion as you can. Why does each illustration fit?

4. Identify and explain an example of the use of persuasion (as defined in this chapter) by radio or television about a current public issue. What evidence is there of the process of persuasion?

5. Find a recent editorial dealing with a major public issue. Analyze the content by identifying attempts to (a) define the issue, (b) to inform, (c) to persuade, and (d) to propagandize.

6. In the area in which you live, how independent of each other are the various mass media of communication? What appear to be the results?

7. If a person is not a member of an interest group, and that group is not acting as a pressure group, can it function as a reference group for him? Explain, and illustrate.

8. Select an example and explain why the following statement applies to it: "When an issue arises, the person may be influenced by the mass media, and by various secondary and primary groups, but he cannot be completely controlled by any of these."

9. The norm in many state universities of admitting all high school graduates in the state who apply is being increasingly challenged as inappropriate. Briefly develop three different ideological positions with respect to this issue: (a) an extremely liberal one, (b) a "center" ideology, and (c) an extremely conservative one. Watch your reasoning.

10. What are the advantages of using the public opinion process as the theoretical frame of reference for the analysis of social problems? Are there disadvantages?

SELECTED READING

Baur, E. Jackson, "Public Opinion and the Primary Group," *American Sociological Review*, 25 (April, 1960), 208–19.

Bell, Daniel (ed.), *The Radical Right* (Garden City, New York: Doubleday & Co., 1963).

Berelson, Bernard, *Reader in Public Opinion and Communication*, (Rev. ed.; New York: The Free Press, 1966).

Blumer, Herbert, Part Four, "Collective Behavior," in Alfred M. Lee (ed.), *Principles of Sociology* (Rev. 2nd ed.; New York: Barnes & Noble, College Outline Series, 1951).

Carter, Roy E., Jr., and Clarke, Peter, "Opinion Leadership Among Educational Television Viewers," *American Sociological Review*, 27 (December, 1962), 792–99.

Hoffer, Eric, *The True Believer* (New York: Harper & Row, 1951).

Katz, Elihu, and Lazarsfeld, Paul, *Personal Influence* (New York: The Free Press, 1955).

Lang, Kurt, and Lang, Gladys E., *Collective Dynamics* (New York: Thomas Y. Crowell Co., 1961), Part IV, "Collective Processes in the Mass Society."

Lundberg, George, Schrag, Clarence C., and Larsen, Otto N., *Sociology* (3rd ed.; New York: Harper & Row, 1963), Chapter 9, "Mass Communication."

Merton, Robert K., *Mass Persuasion* (New York: Harper & Bros., 1946).

Neal, Arthur G., and Seeman, Melvin, "Organizations and Powerlessness: A Test of the Mediation Hypothesis," *American Sociological Review*, 29 (April, 1964), 216–26.

Schramm, Wilbur, *The Process and Effects of Mass Communication* (Urbana: University of Illinois Press, 1954).

Sussman, Leila, "Mass Political Letter Writing in America as the Growth of an Institution," *Public Opinion Quarterly*, (1959), 203–12.

Turner, Ralph H., and Killian, Lewis M., *Collective Behavior* (Englewood Cliffs, N.J.: Prentice-Hall, 1957), Part Three: "The Diffuse Collectivity."

Wirth, Louis, "Consensus and Mass Communications," *American Sociological Review*, 13 (February, 1948), 1–15.

II

Emergent Problems in
a Century of Change

What shall we tell the American poor, once we have seen them? Shall we say to them that they are better off than the Indian poor, the Italian poor, the Russian poor? That is one answer, but it is heartless. I should put it another way. I want to tell every well-fed and optimistic American that it is intolerable that so many millions should be maimed in body and spirit when it is not necessary that they should be. My standard of comparison is not how much worse things used to be. It is how much better they could be if only we were stirred.[1]

4. Economic Insecurity

THE BOOK in which this appeal appears signaled and accelerated a vastly enlarged public concern in the sixties with the problem of poverty. The emphasis in the fifties on the affluence of American society[2] was interpreted by many people to mean that poverty was largely a thing of the past, at least in the sense of physical suffering, a view echoed or implied by many sociologists.[3] This view gave way to a provocative discussion that has raised new controversies within the framework of the broad ongoing issue of economic insecurity. When it began, toward the end of the 19th century, this broader debate was centered on poverty.

ISSUES AMID RISING PLENTY

Early in the present century, as productivity continued to increase with the use of new machines, concern arose about the unemployment

[1] Michael Harrington, *The Other America* (New York: The Macmillan Co., 1962), 18.
[2] John K. Galbraith, *The Affluent Society* (Boston: Houghton Mifflin Co., 1958). Actually, Galbraith dealt with poverty within the framework of relative affluence.
[3] Jessie Bernard, *Social Problems at Midcentury* (New York: The Dryden Press, 1957), 23; Joseph A. Kahl, *The American Class Structure* (New York: Holt, Rinehart & Winston, 1957), 99; Harold Wilensky and Charles N. LeBeaux, *Industrial Society and Social Welfare* (New York: Russell Sage Foundation, 1958), 100.

resulting from technological innovations. This concern then broadened to include the hazards of industrial accidents, resulting in the debates over Workmen's Compensation laws. The second decade also witnessed a rising conviction that low-paid industrial workers should be protected by minimum wage laws.

Public concern for such matters abated during the twenties, but economic issues were urgently debated during the thirties as the nation struggled to recover from the mass unemployment and deprivation of the Great Depression. Public spokesmen, as if forced to see the whole elephant, portrayed particular difficulties as aspects of the larger issue of economic insecurity. This elicited ideologies in support of broad programs of cure and prevention, thus stiffening the resistance of those holding counter ideologies. What had begun a half century earlier as concern with the miseries of "the poor" had evolved into a very complex issue.

The Rising Level of Living and the Elusive Poverty Line

The increasing concern over economic insecurity was expressed during a half century when the level of living of Americans at least doubled, on the average. By the sixties, according to the estimate noted in Chapter 1, the typical American's income would buy about three times as much as in 1910. Ogburn maintained that the increase in production was due mainly to technological growth, accompanied by better education and management.[4] Probably the extremely rapid rate of growth was facilitated by the capitalist system.[5] At any rate, *considerable concern over economic insecurity developed during a time of unprecedented improvement in the objective conditions of material existence.*

To avoid confusion, let us adopt the concept of *level of living* to refer to *the actual plane on which people are living*—the amount of *basic economic goods and services being consumed.* This can then be compared with the *standard of living, the desired level of consumption* of goods and services. Levels of consumption are usually discussed in terms of family units, and in terms of *real income, the goods and services the family can buy with its dollar income.* If a family gets a raise in dollar income of 10 per cent, and the items purchased

---

[4] William F. Ogburn, "Technology and the Standard of Living in the United States," *American Journal of Sociology,* 55 (January, 1955), 380–86.
[5] Oliver C. Cox, "Technology and the Standard of Living," *American Journal of Sociology,* 56 (July, 1955), 51–52.

by the family go up in cost by 10 per cent, the family has exactly the same real income it had before the raise. If costs increase faster than dollar income does, the real income drops; if costs decrease faster than dollar income does, the real income rises.

According to the Bureau of the Census, more than one-fifth of American families of two or more persons had incomes below $3000 in 1961, and nearly 31 per cent had incomes below $4000. About 22 per cent had incomes between $4000 and $6000, often called the "deprived" category in discussions of the sixties.[6] Most estimators were using the poverty line of $3000 for families (of two or more) and $1500 for persons living alone; others have used $4000 and $2000, or other levels. President Johnson must have been using the $3000–$1500 line in 1964, if he had reference to the Census estimate, when he classed one-fifth of the nation as poverty-stricken.[7]

Estimates by the Conference on Economic Progress of changes in the distribution of family incomes are summarized in Table 4.1. (Notice that the estimated percentage of families with incomes below $4000 is lower for 1960 than the Bureau of the Census estimate for 1961, while the amount between $4000 and $6000 is about the same.) The percentage figures in Table 4.1 have been adjusted for rises in prices; they reflect the real incomes in 1929 and 1947 in terms of the buying power of 1960 dollars, not the actual distributions of dollar income in those years. Table 4.1, then, shows that the percentage of families below the poverty line as conceived in the sixties was much higher in 1929 than in 1947, and a great deal higher than in 1960.

Because real income for many families in the Depression fell well below that of 1929, President Roosevelt's view of "one-third of a nation ill-housed, ill-clad, ill-nourished"[8] was very conservative from the standpoint of the definition of poverty in the sixties. The Depression notwithstanding, the nation has witnessed dramatic increases in family real income over a period of several decades. But the issue of poverty has revived strongly, reminding us that a social problem is more than an objective condition. *The minimum standard (desired level) of living has evidently raced ahead of our fast improving level of living.*

---

[6] U.S. Bureau of the Census, *Current Population Reports*, Series P-60, No. 39 (February 28, 1963).
[7] *Message on Poverty*, March 16, 1964. The President's Council of Economic Advisers had been using the $3000–$1500 level.
[8] Franklin D. Roosevelt, *Second Inaugural Address*, January 20, 1937.

TABLE 4.1

THE CHANGING DISTRIBUTION OF INCOME IN THE
UNITED STATES, 1929, 1947, AND 1960*

Family Incomes	Percentage with a Given Income		
	1929	1947	1960
Less than $4,000†	65.2	37.3	23.1
$4–6,000‡	17.2	29.3	22.7
$6–7,500	6.1	12.4	16.2
$7,5–15,000	9.1	17.2	30.7
$15,000 or more	2.4	3.8	7.3

* All income data have been expressed as constant (1960) dollars.
† Defined in original source as poverty.
‡ Defined in original source as deprivation.

SOURCE: An abridgement of a table in Murray Gendell and Hans L. Zetterberg, A Sociological Almanac for the United States (2nd ed.; New York: Charles Scribner's Sons, 1964), 70, based in turn on Conference on Economic Progress, Poverty and Deprivation in the U.S.: The Plight of Two-Fifths of a Nation (Washington, D.C., 1962), 26–27 and 37–38.

NOTE: The sources indicate that for unattached individuals the percentage changes are smaller but in the same direction.

The estimate for a given year will depend, of course, on where the poverty line is drawn. In 1965 the Department of Health, Education and Welfare took such variations as size of household, age of breadwinner, and place of residence into account in estimating dollar incomes needed for a minimum budget. They varied from $5000 for a family of seven down to $1000 for older persons living alone on a farm, with $3130 needed for a nonfarm family of four. Eighteen per cent of all Americans were below the minimum budget. Thirty million were in families, one-half of them children, and five million were living alone.[9] Most public references continued to be to the fixed

[9] Herman P. Miller, "Who Are the Poor?" The Nation (June 7, 1965), 609–10; reprinted in Judson R. Landis, Current Perspectives on Social Problems (Belmont, Calif.: Wadsworth Publishing Co., Inc., 1966), 239–41.

$3000–$1500 line, and *in the sixties it became fairly common to consider about one-fifth of the nation's people to be "poor" and about one-fifth "deprived."*

During the fifties, American sociologists usually drew the poverty line at or near $2000 and tended to estimate that fewer than 10 per cent of the population fell below it.[10] The prevailing emphasis on the affluence of Americans seemed consistent with clear evidence of the rising level of living and the decreasing percentage of unskilled workers in the labor force. Ogburn pointed out that the great increases in per capita income during the first half century had increased the level of living at an average rate of 0.4 per cent per year, that the proportion of urban families living below one widely used yardstick of the minimum standard of living declined from 40 per cent in 1901 to less than 10 per cent in 1950, and that poverty virtually would be eliminated if per capita income doubled again by the year 2000.[11] The level of living has continued to climb, but Ogburn's forecast now seems optimistic in light of (1) the serious rise in unemployment in 1958, lasting through 1963, (2) the changing public definition of the poverty line, and (3) the revelation that poverty has a hard core.

Conceiving of poverty as unacceptably low consumption of goods and services, Americans devoted considerable attention from 1910 to 1920 to defining the minimum standard of consumption.[12] In 1937 the Gallup Poll began asking representative national samples the question indicated in Table 4.2, which presents the results of a poll published in early January, 1965. The Table shows that those with annual incomes below $3000 believed that $3796 ($73 for each of 52 weeks) was needed to meet the barest living expenses of a family of four. The variations by region and dollar income level probably reflect different price levels, but also different styles of life, because they must influence the family's perception of what it "needs" to "get along in this community." This phrase implies minimum social acceptability, as well as health and work efficiency—what clothes a child must have to attend school, for instance, or what the minimum

---

[10] Wilensky and LeBeaux, *op. cit.*, 100; Bernard, *op. cit.*, 22–23; Kahl, *op. cit.*, 111; Jack L. Roach, "Sociological Analysis and Poverty," *American Journal of Sociology*, 71 (July, 1965), 68–69. Roach suggests, pp. 70–75, that the dominant type of sociological theory—that of Talcott Parsons—is oriented toward middle-class concerns and overlooks physical needs.
[11] William F. Ogburn, "Implications of the Rising Standard of Living in the United States," *American Journal of Sociology*, 55 (May, 1955), 542–46.
[12] *Ibid.*, 541.

TABLE 4.2

RESPONSES OF A REPRESENTATIVE SAMPLE OF AMERICANS AT THE MID-
POINT OF THE SIXTIES TO THE QUESTION, "WHAT IS THE SMALLEST
AMOUNT OF MONEY A FAMILY OF FOUR (HUSBAND, WIFE, AND TWO
CHILDREN) NEEDS EACH WEEK TO GET ALONG IN THIS COMMUNITY?"

Income Group	Median Average Response
Over $10,000	$ 99 per week
$7,000–$9,999	$ 99 per week
$5,000–$6,999	$ 80 per week
$3,000–$4,999	$ 78 per week
Under $3,000	$ 73 per week

Region	Median Average Response
Far West	$101 per week
East	$100 per week
Midwest	$ 82 per week
South	$ 62 per week

SOURCE: *George Gallup, American Institute of Public Opinion, Los Angeles Times, Friday, January 8, 1965, Part I, 30.*

NOTE: *In early 1966, after a year of continued rises in prices, the median average national response to the above question had increased from $81 to $99 per week. See, Gallup Political Index, Report No. 10 (March, 1966), 24.*

standard of housing is. Drawing this line of minimum needs—whether by the bread winner, the home economist, the social worker, or the voter—requires value judgments and an order of priority. And these have undergone marked changes in twentieth-century America.

Reaching for New Norms

CHANGING BELIEFS OF FACT. Increases in agricultural and industrial productivity have been raising the level of living of Americans during the twentieth century to such an extent that the belief has grown that poverty can be controlled and reduced, perhaps eliminated. Too, beliefs have developed that the insecurities attending industrial accidents, unemployment, aging, physical handicaps, and even death of the breadwinner are not inevitable, and that they can be minimized. As the technological revolution lighted factories, streets, and homes, produced more foods and other wondrous new consumer goods, and ushered in the marvels of modern travel, the vision of the possible underwent considerable metamorphosis.

"Pauperism," being poor and dependent to the point of destitution, had caused great public concern during the first half or so of the nineteenth century. It was attributed to a weakness of character, a condition thought to be encouraged by poor relief. Both in England and America, despite differences in details, the measures adopted followed the Puritan spirit of the Elizabethan Poor Law of 1602. Assistance was granted only upon proof of total lack of means, was limited to bare survival needs, and was administered so as to humiliate the recipient and set him apart from society.[13]

Later in the nineteenth century the dominant Anglo-American views of poverty were based on "Social Darwinism," which attributes poverty to biological inferiority.[14] Aid to the poor helps the unfittest to survive, was the view held by such writers as Spencer, Sumner, Huxley, and Mill.[15] In this light, attempts to alleviate the suffering of the poor only make the condition worse. A turn-of-the-century view that presented poverty as a positive good was based on different beliefs of fact—that being poor provides a valuable school-of-hard-knocks education and helps build character. In Andrew Carnegie's version, childhood poverty was considered necessary for high achievement in any field. Pity the disadvantaged, soft child of the wealthy![16]

---

[13] Karl Polanyi, *The Great Transformation* (New York: Rinehart, 1944), 100–02; Martin Rein, *The Strange Case of Public Dependency* (Selective Reading Series No. 5; Sacramento: California State Department of Public Welfare, 1965), 1–3. A condensation of this pamphlet appears in *Transaction*, 2 (March–April, 1965), 16–23.

[14] Robert E. Will and Harold G. Vatter (eds.), *Poverty in Affluence* (New York: Harcourt, Brace & World, 1965), 58–68.

[15] Herbert Spencer, *Social Statics* (New York: D. Appleton & Co., 1880; 1st pub., 1850), 353–56; A. G. Keller and M. R. Davie (eds.), *Essays of William Graham Sumner* (New Haven: Yale University Press, 1934), Vol. II, 56; Thomas H. Huxley, *Evolution and Ethics and Other Essays* (New York: D. Appleton & Co., 1902; 1st pub., 1894), 36–37; John Stuart Mill, *Principles of Political Economy* (London: Longmans, Green and Co., 1909; 1st pub., 1848), 365–66.

[16] Andrew Carnegie (ed., Edward C. Kirkland), *The Gospel of Wealth* (Cambridge: The Belknap Press of Harvard University Press, 1962), 53–64.

Various environmental explanations of crime and other behavior emerged to challenge biological determinism during the first quarter of the twentieth century, and poverty was one of the most emphasized conditions. Both the developing social sciences and the mass media demonstrated countless links between poverty and crime, ill health, unemployment, and other deplored social conditions. Often the explanation involved direct, single-factor causation, with poverty presented as the cause of the other conditions.

But what caused poverty, if not the genes? During the Great Depression the conviction became widespread that even a very able person could be unemployed and poor through circumstances beyond his control. Employment rose sharply with World War II and remained relatively high during most years until 1958. By the mid-sixties, after the public discovery of large "pockets of poverty," a national poll showed that a slight majority believed poverty to be caused more by "lack of effort" than by "circumstances." Republicans were more inclined to believe this way than Democrats, as were people with the most education and with incomes above $10,000. A sizeable majority of those with incomes below $3000 blamed circumstances.[17]

The view held on this question affects not only one's thinking about poverty, but also about the many conditions associated with it. Finding an almost equal division of opinion about whether "lack of effort" or "circumstances" are responsible helps explain why poverty and many associated phenomena pose continuing national dilemmas. Some of those who point to lack of effort attribute this to heredity while others link it with the processes of socialization. More knowledge of the sizes and characteristics of these subgroups, and their modes of thought, would be helpful.

What light can sociology and the other social sciences throw on beliefs of fact about poverty? From a quarter-century of community studies and some other sources, we have considerable factual information about social stratification, and the conviction that the subject is complex and elusive. Since the forties much of the effort to interpret the findings has taken the form of a defense or a criticism of the functionalist theory of social stratification, which stresses occupations.[18] According to the Davis-Moore statement of it, a role-occupant is rewarded with goods and services proportionate to the contribution

---

[17] George Gallup, *Gallup Poll Report*, Spring, 1964.
[18] *e.g.*, see the brief discussion in Thomas E. Lasswell, *Class and Stratum* (Boston: Houghton Mifflin Co., 1965), 61–62.

of the *role* to society.[19] One of several criticisms is that the rank accorded to a *person* cannot be taken as an objective measure of his *capacity* to contribute to society, because some groups and individuals begin with more opportunities than others.[20] Current sociological literature can enlighten the general public on these matters considerably, but clearly it does not provide final answers concerning which beliefs of fact about poverty are correct and which are false.

There is doubtless some interplay between beliefs of fact and those of value in the emergence of new norms in the economic arena. One's value preferences may well influence his beliefs of fact about the causes of poverty. Conversely, the way a person explains the unfolding drama of economic development may affect his value priorities. However, new norms may be supported on the basis of changes in beliefs of fact alone, or solely on the basis of changing values.

SHIFTING PRIORITIES OF VALUE. A basic value judgment began to emerge in economic discussions around the turn of the century, the *belief that no one should experience extreme economic insecurity, usually stated in terms of the "minimum standard of living."*[21] As this phrase entered the language, it was given an objective connotation by those who labored to define precisely the minimum acceptable level of consumption. Eventually this belief of value was accepted very widely in America and the Western world, and it spread rapidly throughout the globe after World War II. Its implications are far-reaching for economic and political institutions. It supports other humanitarian goals, such as health; but it has often come into conflict with traditional values, especially those of economic individualism.

It seems unlikely that this value would have received such strong support except for the growth of at least two beliefs of fact: (1) that

---

[19] Kingsley Davis and Wilbert E. Moore, "Some Principles of Stratification," *American Sociological Review*, 10 (April, 1945), 242–49.
[20] Melvin Tumin, "On Inequality," *American Sociological Review*, 28 (February, 1963), 19–26; see Moore's "Rejoinder," pp. 26–28. For other criticisms see Dennis Wrong, "The Functional Theory of Stratification: Some Neglected Considerations," *American Sociological Review*, 24 (December, 1959), 772–82; Robert A. Ellis and Thomas C. Keedy, Jr., "Three Dimensions of Status: A Study of Academic Prestige," *Pacific Sociological Review*, 3 (Spring, 1950), 23–28; Werner Cohn, "Social Status and the Ambivalence Hypothesis: Some Critical Notes and a Suggestion," *American Sociological Review*, 25 (August, 1960), 508–09.
[21] William Ebenstein, *Today's Isms* (3rd ed.; Englewood Cliffs, N.J.: Prentice-Hall, 1961), 180.

technology would develop to such an extent that poverty could be eliminated, and (2) that numerous other problems, including some emergent concerns such as ill health, could not be controlled unless poverty were alleviated. On the basis of the second belief, one would support maintenance of the minimum standard of living for all as an *instrumental value*, even if he might otherwise not consider economic insecurity undesirable. As to the role of the first belief, early in Chapter 2 we noted Waller's suggestion that the "humanitarian mores" are very old in human experience. Loss of the ability and willingness of primary groups to undergird the economic security of the individual resulted in widespread distress, and the search for new norms. As new visions of productive capacity soared, then, the old humanitarian values were applied to the wider community, to be implemented by secondary institutions.[22]

The development of new norms of responsibility at the societal level was to be no simple task. The views of the poor held by the Puritans, not greatly modified, lived on into the twentieth century to compete with humanitarian views. Early in the century, Georg Simmel, a German sociologist, defined the poor not as people without means, but as those who accept assistance. The givers thus created the social category of the poor; the takers accepted the classification and were then excluded from society.[23] By the thirties Waller thought that the humanitarian mores received little support when they conflicted with the pertinent "organizational mores"—the existing economic system and a cluster of values traditionally associated with it. Applying this view to unemployment compensation, as follows, he apparently considered the Puritan views still much in evidence:

> Confusing conflicts of mores appear in those situations, frequent enough in unemployment relief, in which human misery and misbehavior are intermingled. When people suffer privation, the humanitarian mores dictate relief. If these people are willing to work, if the old live in strict monogamy and the young do not contract marriage until they are off the relief rolls, if they obey the law, if they do not conceal any assets, if they spend absolutely nothing for luxuries, if they are grateful and not demanding, if the level of relief does not approach the income of the employed, relatively few objections are raised to the giving of relief. But let any of the above violations of the organizational mores defining the situation of the recipient of

[22] Willard Waller, "Social Problems and the Mores," *American Sociological Review*, 1 (December, 1936), 925.
[23] Georg Simmel, "The Poor," *Social Problems*, 13 (Fall, 1965), 118–40, trans. by Claire Jacobson from Simmel, "Der Arme," Chapter 7 in *Soziologie* (Leipzig: Duncker & Humblot, 1908).

charity arise, and the untrained investigator will quite possibly cut off relief in a storm of moral indignation. Herein he is in agreement with the moral sense of the greater part of the community.[24]

While such a restrictive approach to unemployment benefits no longer predominates, it is a fairly common public response in situations regarded as major moral lapses. An example is the MARS (man assuming the role of spouse) type of aid-to-dependent-children case, in which the man is not the father of any of the children of the woman he is living with. Even when perceived moral degeneracy is not involved, there is still some stigma attached to confessing dependency in a nation that values highly the initiative, independence, hard work, and success of the individual.[25] The modern poor are not complete outcasts, but their status is defined negatively, in terms of the characteristics they do not have. They are not expected to make a contribution to society.[26] The status dimension remains important for an adequate understanding of programs for economic security.

In spite of considerable opposition and much controversy, the belief that everyone should have a minimum standard of living received more support as the decades passed. Some idea of the nature and strength of the concern for this value can be obtained by studying Table 4.3, which summarizes responses of a representative national sample in 1965 to statements about economic insecurity and other conditions. It shows a great deal of concern in all income levels for hunger in the United States, and for other conditions associated with poverty. People with lower incomes exceeded those with higher ones in their concern about lack of medical care and neglect of the elderly; but the reverse was true for the treatment of minorities and for hunger abroad. The greatest amount of concern for the problems as a whole was indicated by the highest income group.

Far from being just pious words, such expressions of conscience about economic insecurity have been associated with a great deal of public discussion and action. At the end of the nineteenth century, most of the activity involved spontaneous charity; then came the emergence of such influential organizations as the charitable founda-

---

[24] Waller, *op. cit.*, 927; cf., C. LeRoy Anderson, "Development of an Objective Measure of Orientation Toward Public Dependence," *Social Forces*, 44 (September, 1965), 107–13.

[25] David Matza, "Poverty and Disrepute," Chapter 12 in Robert K. Merton and Robert A. Nisbet, *Contemporary Social Problems* (2nd ed.; New York: Harcourt, Brace & World, 1966), 620, 626.

[26] Lewis A. Coser, "The Sociology of Poverty," *Social Problems*, 13 (Fall, 1965), 141–42.

TABLE 4.3

PERCENTAGES OF A REPRESENTATIVE NATIONAL SAMPLE IN-
DICATING CONCERN OVER SELECTED SHORTCOMINGS IN THE
UNITED STATES

Statements about Shortcomings in the United States	Percentage in Different Income Groups Who Said They Feel Concern "Often" or "Sometimes"		
	Under $5000	$5000– 9000	Over $10,000
Some people in the United States still go hungry	82	83	86
Some people can't get proper medical care in the U.S. because of lack of money	84	79	69
Older people have been neglected	72	70	59
United States has food surpluses when people abroad are starving	49	66	76
Some people in big cities still live in slums	60	67	70
Way Negroes have been treated in the U.S.	54	64	74
Way American Indians have been treated	35	53	66
Way some Jews have been treated in the U.S.	40	45	50
Pollution of rivers and streams	36	43	50
Way some Catholics have been treated the United States	23	12	11
United States strictness in keeping immigrants out	12	10	11

SOURCE: Louis Harris, Washington Post Co., Los Angeles Times, Monday, August 9, 1965, Part III, 10.

tions, the Red Cross, and the Community Chest. Paid personnel increasingly replaced volunteers, and professional social work began to emerge to provide leadership. Governmental efforts increasingly supplemented the private ones, especially after the thirties, and most current issues involve public programs.

MAJOR ISSUES ABOUT ECONOMIC SECURITY

The Role of Government

According to the *laissez-faire ideology*, which crystallized in the nineteenth century, *the economic system works best when free of government controls of any kind, since intervention prevents the survival of the fittest.*[27] This position gave business owners and managers a free hand in the great industrial expansion of the time. A key value in this ideology is the *economic freedom of the individual.* This value is also central in the welfare ideologies, in the sense of freedom for all individuals from hunger, disease, unemployment, and so on.

The belief has gradually grown in the twentieth century that it is the proper role of government at all levels to take measures to ensure a minimum standard of living for all.[28] It has had sufficient acceptance to support many far-reaching governmental efforts, yet many people still accept this position with reservations and some reject it. The federal government has assumed much of the responsibility, but state and local governments have provided welfare measures of their own, as well as those designed to utilize federal grants-in-aid.

Of the three areas of governmental action discussed below, the first was motivated primarily by the desire to provide the minimum standard of living for all. It supplements the welfare efforts of private groups. The other two areas involve regulation of the economy, undertaken in the belief that they guard the capitalist economic system against threats to its survival and help it to operate at maximum capacity. These results, in turn, are believed to be instrumental in reducing economic insecurity for the individual, as well as in supporting such values as industrial and agricultural development, efficiency, private property, free enterprise, and national security. Opponents challenge the beliefs of fact involved in these wide departures from *laissez-faire* and maintain that they infringe on the economic freedom of the individual.

[27] Bernard, *op. cit.*, 159–61.
[28] Ebenstein, *op. cit.*, 236.

I. PROTECTING THE INDIVIDUAL AGAINST ECONOMIC HAZARDS. Among the early state and local programs were workmen's compensation, widows' pensions, care of the medically indigent, and general family relief. The early federal programs involved disability, unemployment, and retirement provisions for veterans, federal employees, and railway workers. The federal Social Security Act of 1935 has been the most comprehensive attempt to provide a minimum standard of living for the individual. Although passed during the Depression, it was conceived as the foundation of a growing program of supplements to other public and private efforts, to help ensure a floor of economic security for everyone. The Act of 1935 provided for:

A. Certain governmental services
   (1) Vocational Rehabilitation
   (2) Public Health services
   (3) Child Welfare services
   (4) Employment services
B. Financial aid for the dependent or incapacitated
   (1) Dependent children
   (2) Dependent mothers
   (3) The needy aged
   (4) The blind
C. Insurance against certain hazards
   (1) Unemployment Insurance
   (2) Old Age and Survivor's Insurance

The novelty of the last item resulted in so much publicity that many people still are unaware that it is but one provision of the Act. OASI is entirely a federal program. An employee's OASI payroll deduction is matched by his employer's contribution. (A self-employed person who is covered pays one and one-half times what an employed person would pay alone.)

Unemployment insurance is a federal-state program which is financed in nearly all states solely by a tax on the employer. The other provisions of the Act, administered in various ways, are supported by federal grants-in-aid to states. As the coverage of the insurance programs increases, along with the size of the benefits, the need for financial assistance programs declines.[29] This has important status implications.

---

[29] Martin H. Neumeyer, *Social Problems and the Changing Society* (New York: D. Van Nostrand Co., 1953), 296–301. For details of programs, see issues of the

At first the various provisions of the Act of 1935 covered 30 million people, but it continued to be amended under the administrations of Presidents Roosevelt and Truman. In the fifties, during President Eisenhower's first term in office, coverage was extended to 70 million. The system then involved billions of dollars of taxes and benefits every year, and had become a major force in the economy. There were further extensions during the fifties. Statements to Congress about social security legislation by President Eisenhower[30] were very similar to those of President Roosevelt[31] when he proposed the original Act. Both affirmed the view that it is the proper function of government at all levels to protect the individual against the hazards of economic insecurity.

During the fifties and sixties the U.S. Chamber of Commerce and the AFL-CIO, despite their differences, agreed on several extensions of social security coverage. Thus, *social security had clearly become national policy, in the fifties if not before, broadly supported by political and economic interest groups.* Strong conservatives (such as Senator Goldwater of Arizona) generally opposed the extensions, and many of the more extremist conservatives felt betrayed because they had fully expected the Republican administration to void the social security laws.[32] (See the discussion of political extremism in Chapter 3.)

It was frequently alleged that the welfare measures adopted by Congress during President Kennedy's administration, such as financing nursing home care through social security contributions and building medical and dental schools, were the same as those proposed earlier by President Eisenhower.[33] The expansion of social security provisions continued under President Johnson, including such changes in 1965 as hospital insurance and optional supplementary medical coverage for persons 65 years of age and over ("Medicare," put into

---

monthly *Social Security Bulletin* and the *Social Security Year Book,* published by the Social Security Administration. The annual *World Almanac and Book of Facts* and *Information Please Almanac* also carry summaries of social security provisions.

[30] Message to Congress, January 14, 1954.

[31] Message to Congress, January 17, 1935.

[32] Raymond E. Wolfinger, Barbara K. Wolfinger, Kenneth Prewitt, and Sheilah Rosenhack, "America's Radical Right: Politics and Ideology," in David E. Apter (ed.), *Ideology and Discontent* (New York: The Free Press, 1964), 288.

[33] *e.g.*, see statement by Robert A. Forsythe, Assistant Secretary of Health, Education and Welfare under President Eisenhower, reported in *St. Paul Pioneer Press,* Sunday, February 12, 1961, II, 3.

effect in 1966), larger retirement benefits, inclusion of self-employed physicians, larger earnings allowed for the retired, and liberalization of admission requirements for the disabled, the blind, and for the children and widows of deceased workers. These changes affected nearly every family in the United States in some way.

Supporters of social security legislation still frequently criticize the program, demanding coverage for groups not included, larger benefits, and better coordination of the various programs. Further extensions must be paid for, of course, so they are tied to the nation's productivity. The "system" is still growing, and its diverse programs seem to have proven capable of adapting to changing circumstances, from the Depression and World War II to the present.[34]

2. REFEREEING AMONG INTEREST GROUPS. In Chapter 3, we saw that Big Government has acted increasingly as a balance wheel to prevent any economic interest bloc from becoming all-powerful. Each grouping has received tangible support of its interests and its countervailing power, but each also has had checks put upon it. Although one economic group or another often objects to government regulation for itself, it usually is quick to accept special protections and to have opposing groups controlled. The shifting fortunes of the contest, and changing public priorities of value, make the determination of a reasonable balance both difficult and endless.[35] The increased support to agriculture and labor since the thirties has been justified to a considerable extent by the value judgment that the people in these groups are entitled to a decent standard of living.

The main basis for the public acceptance of the government's role of economic referee evidently has been a dislike of monopoly, even fear of it. At the least, monopoly goes against fair play and the rights of minorities. It has been thought capable of producing depressions, extreme unrest, and even revolution, thereby threatening such values as peace and order, prosperity, individual freedom, and even the capitalist economic system and democratic government.[36] The belief that such basic American values were jeopardized by economic monopolies has made possible consideration and support of some sharp departures from *laissez-faire* economics.

---

[34] Neumeyer, *op. cit.*, 299–300.
[35] Ebenstein, *op. cit.*, 182–83.
[36] Alfred W. Blumrosen, "Legal Process and Labor Law," in William M. Evan (ed.), *Law and Sociology* (New York: The Free Press, 1962), 208–20.

3. PROMOTING MAXIMUM PRODUCTION, EMPLOYMENT, AND PURCHAS-
ING POWER. Even when the unemployed receive compensation and
other aids, their floor of economic security is quite bare compared to
the level of living made possible by a steady job. And the real income
of everyone, employed or not, can be drastically reduced by extreme
inflation of commodity prices. In the *Full Employment Act of 1946*
the aim of economic security for the individual was strongly endorsed,
along with the idea that prevention is more effective than a cure.[37]
*The Congress emphatically affirmed that it is the federal govern-
ment's continuing responsibility to do everything in its power to promote the fullest employment, production, and purchasing power.* The
main result was the creation of a Council of Economic Advisers to the
President, especially to interpret trends in unemployment. The President is required by the Act to submit an Economic Report to each
session of Congress, and other reports as necessary.

Downward swings in the business cycle (recessions) had produced
cyclical unemployment many times before the thirties, but never on
so drastic a scale. Unemployment went as high as 25 per cent for the
nation, and vast numbers of the employed received very low wages.
The diagnosis by President Roosevelt's advisers was that too many
people had been cautiously accumulating savings rather than invest-
ing, with consequent decreases in production, thus in payrolls, and in
expressed demand for goods. Industry was producing at about half
capacity. To reinvigorate capitalism they prescribed measures designed to enable people to buy more goods, thus to stimulate production and encourage more investment. Among the measures were
emergency relief, subsidies, loans, crop controls, and the social
security program. Although the economic analysis[38] and these "pump-
priming" techniques provoked lively debate, the economy began to
respond.

While still recovering from the Depression, and almost totally
unprepared, the nation assumed the burdens of an all-out conflict.
World War II would have been lost without the vigorous response of
the economy. Following the war, Americans rejoiced when the tight
wartime economic controls were removed, but most seemed convinced

---

[37] Bernard, *op. cit.*, 485–86.
[38] This was an application of the theory of the English economist John May-
nard Keynes. See his, *The General Theory of Employment, Interest and Money*
(New York: Harcourt, Brace & Co., 1936); also, Alvin H. Hansen, *Economic
Policy and Full Employment* (New York: McGraw-Hill, 1947).

that the government could never allow another major depression or runaway inflation to occur. A substantial majority believed that the federal government must at all times help the economy perform at its best, a conviction that evidently has been reinforced by the Cold War, the conflicts in Korea and Viet Nam, and the space program. The philosophy of the *Full Employment Act not only strongly supports the economic welfare of the individual, but also continuing economic development, free enterprise, and the national security.*[39]

Thus great changes in policy and in beliefs of fact and value about the economy have taken place in a matter of decades. Traditional norms were increasingly considered inadequate for the situations faced by twentieth-century Americans, and new norms have been emerging during a series of crises and continued growth in productivity. There have been bitterly contested issues, with some people considering the changes unthinkable and many having great difficulty accepting what they feel must nevertheless be done.

The Republican Party has continued its traditional inclination toward *laissez-faire*, yet the interparty differences concerning the role of government in the economy often are greater in the words used to express them than in the actions taken. Frequently there is accord on the aims and on the necessity for government action, but disagreement about specific means to use. The administrations of both parties have watched the business cycle closely since World War II, and both have taken corrective and preventive measures to influence the flow of money and credit, wage and price levels, taxes, and other matters, in order to control recessions and to prevent undue inflation.

Most Americans who support the three "Welfare State" measures discussed above believe they strengthen our capitalistic economic system, and thus the nation.[40] There is very little acceptance of the ideology of *Socialism* (*government ownership and control of basic industries to achieve welfare objectives*), and almost none of *Communism* (*total ownership and command of the economy by a totalitarian government, a supposedly temporary "Dictatorship of the Proletariat"*).

The argument often called "Creeping Socialism" holds that any government regulation inevitably leads to more complete control, which inevitably leads to government ownership, which inevitably leads to Socialism, which inevitably leads to Communism. Taken

---

[39] William Haber, F. H. Harbison, L. R. Klein, and Vivian Palmer, *Manpower in the United States* (New York: Harper & Bros., 1954), p. x.
[40] Ebenstein, *op. cit.*, 180.

literally, this is powerfully suggestive name-calling, identifying any governmental action with the hated label of Communism. It can lend support to a stereotype in which all "planners," "liberals," even all Democrats and moderate Republicans, are seen as Communists, or at least as "fronters" or dupes. Then it becomes impossible to consider rationally such beliefs of fact as these: that judicious regulation may forestall public ownership, that the actions of government have enabled American capitalism to be more vigorous than ever,[41] and that Socialism and Communism are incompatible.[42]

Even the milder form of the "creeping" argument, that government officials have unintentionally started an irreversible chain of events, has evidently not been widely convincing. Government programs for economic security and full employment are strongly supported. The harsher contention, that the nation's leaders for decades have been advancing a *conspiracy* to take the country down the road to Socialism and Communism[43] evidently now appeals only to the most extreme economic and political conservatives (see Chapter 3).[44] Similarly, the argument of both the Old and New Extreme Left, that leaders in government are engaged in a reactionary conspiracy against the people, appeals only to the most extreme liberals. Evidently government is an instrumental value in greater or lesser degree to most Americans, and not the evil that economic-political extremists make it out to be.

Unemployment: Some Specific Issues

THE MEASUREMENT OF UNEMPLOYMENT. Cyclical unemployment has been discussed above, and we will consider the seasonal and technological varieties below. Also classed in terms of their causes, there are three other kinds: *intergenerational* (when young people are entering the labor force and older ones leaving it), *permanent shut-down* (when an industry leaves a community or goes out of business), and *transitional* (when people are moving to a new job). Considering the nature of some of these types, especially the last, we might expect

---

[41] *Ibid.*, 192–93.
[42] *Ibid.*, 205–11, 225.
[43] John T. Flynn, *The Road Ahead: America's Creeping Revolution* (New York: Devin-Adair Co., 1949), condensed in the *Reader's Digest* (February, 1950), 2–19.
[44] Richard Dudman, *Men of the Far Right* (New York: Pyramid Books, 1962), 9–10; Seymour Martin Lipset, "Three Decades of Radical Right: Coughlinites, McCarthyites and Birchers," in Daniel Bell (ed.), *The Radical Right* (Garden City, N.Y.: Doubleday & Co., 1963), 373–446.

that there will always be some unemployment.[45] Not until the rate
exceeds 5 per cent is unemployment considered to have reached the
danger level for the national economy.

The national rate has fluctuated a good deal since 1946, reaching
a high of 7.5 per cent during the peak months in 1958, when a rather
severe recession started.[46] The annual average rate was 7 per cent in
1958 and 1961, and 6 per cent in 1959, 1960, 1962 and 1963.[47] The
rate reached a low of 3.7 per cent in three of the months of 1966. Some
of the specific low points were 1.8 for married men, 2.4 for all adult
men, 3.6 for adult women, 11.7 for all teen-agers, and 7 per cent for
nonwhites (mostly Negroes). In reporting these lows, the administration indicated a labor shortage in several areas for the first time since
World War II and expressed concern for the inflationary effects.[48] This
high level of employment was reached at a time when over half the
national budget was being spent for defense, but this also was true
during the preceding decade,[49] including the year 1958. Toward the
end of 1968 the rate of unemployment fell as low as 3.5 per cent.

These figures on unemployment are compiled by the Bureau of
Labor Statistics of the U.S. Department of Labor and are widely
publicized by the news media as an index of the health of the economy. *The unemployed are defined as persons able and willing to work
but who cannot find a job.* A survey is made of 35,000 representative
households, and the unemployed are counted as all civilians 14 years
of age or older who answer "Yes" to the question, "Have you been
looking for work"? Thus everyone involved can be classed as employed, unemployed, or not in the labor force. The uncertain meaning
of "looking" casts doubt on the validity of many of the interviews. The
figures include all types of unemployment and are therefore difficult
to interpret without looking at the breakdowns by age, marital status,
degree to which loss of job is permanent, and so on. Many economists
consider the rate reported for married men to be the best available
indicator of national unemployment.[50]

---

[45] Neal W. Chamberlin, *Labor* (New York: McGraw-Hill, 1958); *op. cit.,* 483.
[46] Bureau of the Census, Labor Force, *Annual Report of the Labor Force, 1958,
Current Population Reports,* Series P–50, No. 89 (June, 1959) p. 10.
[47] Bureau of the Census, *Statistical Abstract of the United States: 1964,* 85th ed.
(Washington, D. C., 1964), 229–32.
[48] *Los Angeles Times,* May 7, 1966, I, 14.
[49] Galbraith, *op. cit.,* 312.
[50] Samuel Lubell, United Features Syndicate, Inc., *Los Angeles Times,* May 13,
1965, IV, 16.

UNEMPLOYMENT COMPENSATION, SUB, GAW, AND GAI. The states were quick to cooperate with the provisions for unemployment compensation in the Social Security Act of 1935, which stipulated that the federal government would pay for its administration if the states followed certain guidelines. Financing could be entirely by compulsory payments by employers, the path most states took. All states had passed such laws by the end of 1937. Since then, many amendments have increased the number of persons and the period of time covered. States have steadily raised the maximum dollar compensation, too, but the raises have barely kept pace with the increase in prices and dollar wages. Ever since 1935, all Presidents have encouraged the states to set compensation at least as high as 50 per cent of what the worker earned while employed, to ensure a minimum standard of living.

The average recipient of unemployment compensation in the United States in 1965 received $36.56 per week, for an average of 12.6 weeks.[51] A fairly typical beneficiary at that time would be one who had been earning $85 a week and was the sole breadwinner in a family of four. The poverty line usually drawn in the sixties, $3000 per year, is equivalent to approximately $58 a week. Also, as we saw in Table 4, representative low-income families at that time believed they needed $73 a week for barest living expenses, so $36.56 would be about half that requirement. Much of it must be spent for food, so prolonged unemployment very often means loss of any savings and life insurance policies, and of items being purchased on installment payments— automobile, household appliances, and furniture, for example—along with the accumulated payments. Also, a recipient often must supplement his benefit by accepting family relief. And after 18 weeks, more or less depending on the state concerned, unemployment compensation terminates (until the next fiscal year at least). All along the line, households with more than one wage earner have some additional built-in insurance, as long as at least one of them can remain employed.

It should now be apparent why labor leaders have contended that the minimum standard of living is not assured even when the state brings unemployment benefits up to half a worker's weekly earnings. The problem is especially acute in seasonal industries, notably agriculture, building, and garment and automobile manufacturing. The

---

[51] *The World Almanac and Book of Facts, 1966* (New York: New York World-Telegram, 1966), 175–176.

first Supplementary Unemployment Benefit (SUB) agreement was won in 1955 by the CIO United Auto Workers Union, in contracts with the Ford Motor Company and General Motors. The provision was that in the event of layoffs, workers were guaranteed 65 per cent of their normal take-home pay for 26 weeks. Thus, in a state paying a maximum benefit representing 50 per cent of usual pay for 24 weeks, the company would add 15 per cent for 24 weeks and pay the entire 65 per cent for two weeks. In another state, paying a benefit of 30 per cent of normal pay for 15 weeks, the company would add 35 per cent for 15 weeks and 65 per cent for the remaining 11. Obviously the company pays less SUB in states with the larger and longer benefits.

If SUB were increased from 65 per cent of normal pay to 100 per cent, it would be a company guarantee of regular income for half a year; if it were increased to 100 per cent for 52 weeks, it would be a Guaranteed Annual Wage (GAW). This is a goal of the large labor unions, particularly in the auto and building industries, but so far SUB does not show signs of spreading rapidly. It seems unlikely that the principle will be accepted at all by industries other than those seasonal ones with a strong interest in keeping a skilled labor force readily available during frequent, and sometimes extended, layoffs.

Since the rediscovery of poverty there have been endless proposals for more government action to guarantee the minimum standard of living. One logically possible extension which has received some mention is the long step of the government's guaranteeing every household an annual income (GAI). One argument for the plan is efficiency—eliminating the need for coordinating a profusion of separate programs. GAI would be comprehensive insurance against unemployment and substandard pay—against economic insecurity in general. It would presumably make most programs of financial assistance unnecessary, and make minimum income a matter of right.

Two national polls indicate strong public opposition to GAI. One in 1965 found 67 per cent against the principle, 19 per cent in favor, and 14 per cent with no opinion. No major segment of the population gave major support, but there was significantly more approval by those with the lowest income and educational levels, more by Negroes than by whites, and more by Democrats than by Republicans.[52] A 1966 poll found less than one voter in 12 who approved of having the govern-

---

[52] George Gallup, American Institute of Public Opinion, *Los Angeles Times*, October 8, 1965, I.

ment provide all families with a GAI of $3000.[53] In both surveys the main basis for opposition was the belief of value that one should work for what he gets, and the belief of fact that one must do so if he is to feel useful. Many interviewees said GAI would destroy individual initiative and self-reliance, and most of them favored job retraining for persons who cannot find work. *There is much support in America for the value of the minimum standard of living, but through a variety of private and public means rather than a single governmental guarantee, and through the individual's own efforts as far as possible.*

TECHNOLOGICAL CHANGE. Before turning to technological unemployment, let us consider briefly a wage issue resulting from ongoing technological change. Productivity (output per man-hour) has been increasing, and organized labor has argued that the fruits of technological innovating should be shared by continuing raises in workers' pay, to parallel the increases in managers' salaries and investors' profits. This principle was accepted by General Motors in its 1950 labor negotiations, the agreement calling for an "Annual Increment" —a 2 per cent automatic raise each year based on the (compromise) assumption that this was the average annual amount by which the productivity of the national economy had been increasing during the first half of the century.[54] The Ford Motor Company agreed to the same principle, calling it the "Annual Improvement Factor"—a five-cent-an-hour yearly raise, increased to six cents an hour in the 1955 contract. Even though there are technical issues concerning how large this annual increment should be, acceptance of the principle by industry considerably reduces disagreements over wages.

This annual pay increment is received by all workers covered by the contract, so it is in addition to merit raises. It must also be distinguished from the "Escalator Clause," a provision in a labor-management contract that adjusts paychecks upward or downward every three months with changes in the level of commodity prices. Such agreements are designed to keep a worker's real income constant over the contract period, so that he is protected against rises in prices and the company is protected against drops. And, of course, quite different

[53] Samuel Lubell, United Features Syndicate, Inc., *Los Angeles Times*, February 28, 1966, IV.
[54] The average annual gain had been at least 2 per cent, perhaps higher, until the end of War II. Then, according to U.S. Department of Labor reports, it averaged about 3 per cent for the next dozen years or so; then at least 4 per cent for the 1958–63 period.

considerations are involved in SUB. The same contract may contain all these wage provisions, and more.

The adoption of new machinery increases output per man-hour, but it also results in *technological unemployment*. New agricultural machinery has been having this effect for a long time, resulting in urban migration, as fewer farmers are needed to produce more food than before. New industrial machines make older skills obsolete, hence the hostility with which workers have often greeted innovations. Yet their long-run effect has been to create new jobs at a faster rate than older ones are outmoded,[55] to put countless new products and services on the market, and to raise the level of living in the process. However, persons thrown out of work often experience considerable insecurity before they are reemployed. A costly family move may be necessary. Retraining often is required, and if this period is very extensive, middle-aged and older workers are likely to find younger persons preferred.

Automation, the automatic control of a process by electrical or mechanical devices that replace human judgment, became a frequent form of technological innovating by mid-century. Capable of replacing large numbers of workers not previously threatened by technological unemployment, such as accountants, clerical workers, inspectors, testers, packagers, and materials handlers, automation created wide concern.[56] Continuous-processing systems, begun in oil and chemicals, spread to milling and other processing industries.[57] "Detroit automation," the integrating of separate processes by automatic materials-transferring devices that facilitate a continuous flow as a product is shaped, spread from the auto industry. Computers and other new automatic office machines began to revolutionize the handling of customer accounts, billing, payrolls, and statistical reports. Machines controlled by feedback mechanisms proved capable of turning out huge quantities of items meeting precise specifications, and numerical-control machines (receiving instructions from tapes or other devices) began performing chains of complex operations.

---

[55] A. J. Jaffee and Charles D. Steward, *Manpower Resources and Utilization* (New York: John Wiley & Sons, 1951), 164.
[56] U.S. Congress, House Committee on Education and Labor, *Impact of Automation on Employment Report* (Washington, D.C.: U.S. Government Printing Office, 1961).
[57] Robert Blauner, *Alienation and Freedom* (Chicago: University of Chicago Press, 1964), 124.

The forty-hour work week, upheld in 1940 by federal legislation, was based on the value judgment that workers needed more leisure time. Since World War II, labor's push for a still shorter work week has been connected with the unemployment factor, especially with the effects of automation. Concern became great during the recession of the late fifties and early sixties,[58] but when total unemployment declined markedly the question of the work week seemed irrelevant. A national poll in mid-1965 found half the adults believing that automation does more good than harm, 32 per cent that it does more harm, and 18 per cent that it makes no difference. Only 8 per cent said they felt personally threatened, but significantly more unskilled (16 per cent) and skilled (14 per cent) laborers felt threatened than was true of managerial, professional, white collar, and sales workers (all 4 per cent).[59] When unemployment dropped to very low levels in the spring of 1966, automation was seen generally as a great asset in combating the labor shortage.[60] *Perceptions about automation, and the length of the work week, evidently vary with the business cycle.*

Some industries and some jobs are more adaptable to automation than others. The new machines have replaced a great many people in semiskilled and clerical jobs, and some in skilled work, while personal service, craft, professional, managerial, and sales work so far have not been so amenable to automatic equipment. Among new jobs created by automation are engineering and management positions involved in designing, building, installing, and controlling new machines, machine repairing, computer programming, keypunch operating, systems analysis, advertising, and sales. Many monotonous, routine jobs have been outmoded, and a higher proportion of the newer ones are more satisfying, more challenging, and better-paying.[61] In fact, automation has accelerated the decrease in the proportion of unskilled and semiskilled workers in the labor force, and the increase in professional, technical, managerial, sales, and service workers. And

---

[58] Department of Labor reports showed that productivity was increasing faster than total production. After the recession the opposite was true.

[59] Louis Harris, Washington Post Co., *Los Angeles Times*, May 24, 1965, I, 22.

[60] *Los Angeles Times*, February 7, 1966, I, 14; and March 13, 1966, C, 2. The Presidential Commission on Automation, in its report of January 1, 1966, included the GAI among its proposals—but more to combat poverty than the effects of automation.

[61] There is probably a less sharp division of labor, thus less social isolation on the job. See, William A. Faunce, "Automation and Division of Labor," *Social Problems*, 13 (Fall, 1965), 149–60.

it has continued to increase productivity, and thus the general level of living.

Increased educational requirements accentuate and dramatize the problem of the least educated, unskilled workers. Neither for industry nor government is it easy to fashion effective retraining programs for them. In addition to retraining where it can be effective, industry has often practiced reduced hiring and nonreplacement policies in order to find jobs for as many displaced workers as possible. Unemployment compensation is likely to be inadequate for a person whose skill has been made obsolete, so SUB makes a significant contribution. Other proposals are severance pay, displacement insurance, GAW, and GAI (see above).

The Culture of Poverty

THE CONCEPT OF POVERTY AS A SUBCULTURE. This concept means that poverty is a distinctive way of life, with norms and supporting beliefs of fact and value that are transmitted from generation to generation.[62] Certainly the poverty-stricken share common experiences: unsteady work, crowded housing, educational handicaps, inadequate diet, frequent illness and inadequate medical and dental care, and uneconomic buying.[63] Certainly too there are barriers to escape; thus the term, "vicious circle of poverty." If we add to this the society's beliefs of value in economic security and in individual opportunity to climb the economic ladder, we get the concept of *cultural deprivation*.[64]

But how many of the poor share a unique outlook on the world, one almost certain to perpetuate poverty unless there is decisive intervention? *The concept of a subculture of poverty applies most clearly to the "hard-core" poor,* also described as "abject" and "disreputable."[65] This corresponds to the class group identified as "lower-lower," in contrast to the "upper-lower,"[66] or "lower" in contrast to the "working"

[62] Will and Vatter, *op. cit.*, 71–86; Harrington, *op. cit.*, 15–17, 161, 170.
[63] David Caplovitz, *The Poor Pay More* (New York: The Free Press, 1963).
[64] Frank Riessman, *The Culturally Deprived Child* (New York: Harper & Row, 1962).
[65] Matza, in Merton and Nisbet, *op. cit.*, 628–69.
[66] Robert J. Havighurst *et al.*, *Growing Up in River City* (New York: John Wiley & Sons, 1962), 12; A. B. Hollingshead, *Elmtown's Youth* (New York: John Wiley & Sons, 1949), 110–20; W. Lloyd Warner, Marcia Meeker, and Kenneth Eels, *Social Class in America* (Chicago: Science Research Associates, 1949).

class.[67] Their position at the bottom of the status structure results from four stigmas: (1) Persistent poverty, associated with erratic employment and often with personal failure, (2) Dependency— frequent acceptance of financial assistance, (3) Perceived immorality, often involving a casual approach to sex and family patterns, heavy drinking, drug addiction, gambling, prostitution, and close police surveillance, and (4) Rejection of the middle-class values of self-improvement and upward mobility.

Why are many of society's dominant values rejected? First, most of the hard-core poor share the fatalistic belief of fact that it is useless to struggle to better their lot. Poorly educated, many illiterate or semi-literate, they tend to be apathetic about formal learning.[68] The school is an agency of the other social classes, so it is expected that even the brightest children of the hard-core poor will receive humiliating treatment and poor grades.[69] The same feeling of hopelessness applies to work; a job is a way of surviving—a way to "get by," not to "get ahead." There is no reason to hurry.[70] Second, the hard-core poor resent the low esteem in which they are held and share a set of defensive attitudes and pride in their own values. People in the "higher" classes are considered insincere, snobbish, rude, inhibited, hypocritical, exploitative, and shallow.

LACK OF PROTECTION AGAINST HAZARDS. The poor as a whole, hard core included, have received much less protection from the many welfare programs than those who achieve some economic stability.[71] The "transfer" (insurance) type protections, including OASI and unemployment compensation, are designed for those regularly connected with the labor force and are related to amounts earned. Almost one-fourth of all paid employment was not covered by unemployment

---

[67] Richard Centers, *The Psychology of Social Classes* (Princeton, N.J.: Princeton University Press, 1949); S. M. Miller and Frank Riessman, "The Working Class Subculture: A New View," *Social Problems*, IX (Summer, 1961), 26.
[68] Kahl, *op. cit.*, 211; Lasswell, *op. cit.*, 270–75.
[69] See, Havighurst *et al.*, *op. cit.*, 37–46, and Hollingshead, *op. cit.*, 121–203, for evidence in support of this belief. Counselors often advise promising poor students against going to college; see Aaron Cicourel and John I. Kitsuse, *The Educational Decision-Makers* (Indianapolis: Bobbs-Merrill Co., 1963).
[70] Lasswell, *op. cit.*, 278; Horacio Ulibarri, "Social and Attitudinal Characteristics of Spanish-Speaking Migrant and Ex-Migrant Workers in the Southwest," *Sociology and Social Research*, 50 (April, 1966), 361–70.
[71] Harrington, *op. cit.*, 161, 170.

compensation in 1964, and one-fifth (mostly unskilled) was still excluded from workmen's compensation. Only about half of all the poor were receiving either of these, or OASI, or any other type of public transfer payments.[72] Few of the poor have the benefits of union-management contracts,[73] or of private pensions and disability insurance.

But what about public assistance—including the federally subsidized programs for dependent children, the aged, the blind, and the disabled—measures seemingly designed for the desperate? In 1959, it was estimated that less than a quarter of all poor families received any type of public assistance.[74] In most cases this apparently supplemented some type of transfer payment, since not much more than half of the poor were receiving either type. Assuming that over half of the poor are hard core, it seems plausible to suggest that as many as two-thirds of the hard-core poor received no official help in 1959, with the highest proportion being in the rural areas. Some with disabilities or other serious problems do not know they are eligible; others are discouraged from applying. Some are denied assistance because of minority group status, and some because of charges of immorality. Some reject all help, unless extremely desperate, because of the stigma of dependency and the pressure to prove that they are gaining in ability to "help themselves."[75]

THE BUREAUCRATIZATION OF WELFARE. Large formal organizations have been relied on increasingly to accomplish specific goals in society; but the poor mistrust these complex, powerful, impersonal structures, including the welfare administrations established to help them.[76] Like all bureaucracies, client-centered ones are expected to be efficient, so there is a temptation to select clients who are most likely to contribute to a record of accomplishment. Thus the charge that such organizations avoid the very clients they were ostensibly designed to serve—as when

---

[72] Council of Economic Advisers, *Economic Report of the President* (Washington, D.C.: U.S. Government Printing Office, 1964), 62–69. Coverage of the poor by private pensions, disability insurance, *etc.*, is small.

[73] In 1960, 23.3 per cent of the total labor force (32.1 per cent of nonagricultural workers) belonged to the large national and international unions. See *Statistical Abstract of the United States*, 1962, Table 319, 241.

[74] James Morgan, Martin David, Wilbur Cohen, and Harvey Brazer, *Income and Welfare in the United States* (New York: McGraw-Hill, 1962), 216.

[75] Rein, *op. cit.*, 14–15.

[76] Gideon Sjoberg, Richard A. Brymer, and Buford Farris, "Bureaucracy and the Lower Class," *Sociology and Social Research*, 50 (April, 1966), 325–37.

"nonreceptive" children are not accepted in child guidance clinics, or young men with criminal records are not taken in the Job Corps.[77] Criticisms of this type are unwelcome because they challenge the norms of the organization and its policy makers.

THE PROFESSIONALIZATION OF SOCIAL WORK. Welfare personnel represent the public in administering these programs, which are led by professional social workers. The process of professionalization has been accompanied by increasing concentration on the economic security of the stable working and middle classes, and on their emotional and family stability as well. There is more satisfaction in this than in the frustrating task of dealing with the poor, especially the resentful hard core. Professionals seek tangible results, pleasure, recognition, and income from their work.[78] Much financial aid is administered to the poor, of course, but public assistance departments find it difficult to recruit MSW's (those professionally trained, with the Master's Degree in Social Work). They tend to hold the administrative positions rather than to have direct contact with the poor.[79] The professionals seek control over their own standards, so they resist the bureaucracy and attempt to influence its policies as much as possible. Some escape entirely into private practice.[80]

COMPOSITION OF THE POOR. Let us take a closer look at the clients. About three-fourths of the nation's poor are white, but nonwhites (mostly Negroes) are represented twice as heavily as their numbers in the population. The majority are in other regions, but Appalachia and the entire South are considerably overrepresented. Poverty is heavy among the "industrial rejects," urban workers not covered by minimum wage laws.[81] Other groups in which poverty is disproportionately concentrated are the aged, farm workers (notably the mi-

---

[77] *Ibid.*, 327–330; Raymond G. Hunt, Orville Gurrslin, and Jack L. Roach, "Social Status and Psychiatric Service in a Child Guidance Clinic," *American Sociological Review*, 23 (February, 1958), 81–83.

[78] Rein, *op. cit.*, 14; Coser, *op. cit.*, 145–47; S. M. Miller, "Poverty and Inequality in America: Implications for the Social Services," *Child Welfare*, 42 (November, 1963), 444–45.

[79] Sjoberg, Brymer, and Farris, *op. cit.*, 327.

[80] Sidney Levenstein, *Private Practice in Social Casework: A Profession's Changing Pattern* (New York: Columbia University Press, 1964).

[81] Harrington, *op. cit.*, 21–22, 185–91; Miller, *op. cit.*, 240. Some 16 million domestic workers, hotel employees, bus boys, dishwashers, and some workers in retail stores were not covered in 1961. About half of all poor households have full-time workers, but their pay is insufficient.

grants), and families with a female head.[82] Most of the 20 million classed as "abject poor" in 1960 (over half of all the poor) fell into one or more of these groups: nonwhite, aged, rural-farm, headed by females. At least two thirds of them were chronic "multiproblem" families, outside the mainstream of the economy and the social structure in general.[83]

ANTI-POVERTY MEASURES. The rediscovery of poverty was followed by determined efforts to stamp it out. The foundation of the War on Poverty is the federal Economic Opportunity Act of 1964, which provided for:

I. Programs for Youth
   A. a Job Corps—for education, work, and vocational training of those aged 16–21, in training centers and conservation camps.
   B. a Work-Training Program—agreements with state and local governments and nonprofit organizations to subsidize employment of those aged 16–21.
II. Community Action Programs
   A. to subsidize local community anti-poverty programs.
   B. to help states with adult education and literacy training.
   C. to establish a clearing house for foster parents willing to provide financial support.
III. Programs to Combat Poverty in Rural Areas
   A. small loans—up to $2,500 for both farm and non-farm enterprises.
   B. migrant worker facilities—for housing, sanitation, education, and child day-care.
   C. indemnity to farmers for milk polluted by USDA-recommended pesticides.
IV. Employment and Investment Incentives for Small Business—loans and guarantees up to $25,000 on liberal terms.
V. Work-Experience Programs—pilot programs to encourage states to establish constructive work or training for unemployed fathers and others in need.

Much of the work was assigned to existing government agencies, but the Office of Economic Opportunity was established with separate staffs for the Job Corps, VISTA (Volunteers in Service to America), a Community Action Program, and migrant worker programs. It was

---

[82] Conference on Economic Progress, *Poverty and Deprivation in the United States: The Plight of Two-Fifths of a Nation* (Washington, D.C., April, 1962), 74.
[83] Oscar Ornati, *Poverty in America* (Washington, D.C.: National Policy Committee on Pockets of Poverty, 1964), 12–18.

declared that the Act should not influence the receipt of public assistance nor be influenced by it.[84]

A basic belief of fact of the Economic Opportunity Act appears to be that the means are at hand to reduce poverty to a small minimum, and to provide programs of support for the remainder that are satisfactory both to them and to the society. The attack is quite diversified. (1) Some measures seem designed to stimulate further economic growth and thus full employment, in the belief that poverty is thereby reduced, but not eliminated. (2) Some seem primarily to be financial assistance measures, of the work relief variety. (3) *The most novel aspect of the Act is the encouragement of education and training programs for the culturally deprived, in the belief that transmission of the subculture of poverty can be prevented.*

One of the early preventive programs to receive strong emphasis was Project Head Start. Begun in the summer of 1965 with over half a million four- and five-year-old children in low-income neighborhoods across the nation, it succeeded and grew. Based on the assumption that the preschool years are the most critical, emphasis has been given to health and physical abilities, self-confidence and social skills, verbal and conceptual abilities, parental interest, and family welfare. The largely favorable evaluation has been attributed mainly to the smallness of the groups and the individual attention given by the large number of volunteer teacher assistants and aides. Among the administrative problems have been those arising from the requirement of racial integration. Some parents have objected to the idea that their children are culturally deprived, while some more affluent ones want to utilize the program for their own children. A crucial question for all such efforts is how effectively the head start is followed up in the regular school program.[85]

Tutoring programs aimed at cultural deprivation have stressed the basic skills of reading, speech, and arithmetic in order to combat retardation and lower the drop-out rate. Programs like Operation Pebble (for an isolated section of Appalachia in Tennessee)[86] and Upward Bound have afforded low-income high school students summer learning experiences on college campuses. One aim is to in-

---

[84] From a summary by the President's Task Force on the War Against Poverty, August 20, 1964, reprinted in Will and Vatter, *op. cit.*, 217–20.
[85] Erwin Knoll, "Hasty 'Landmark,'" *Southern Education Report*, 1 (September–October, 1965), 2–9.
[86] John Egerton, "Pebbles," *Southern Education Report, ibid.*, 14–19.

fluence their beliefs of fact, so that they will consider college a realistic personal aspiration. Some programs, such as the Yale Summer High School,[87] are designed to interest those who score very high on intelligence tests in spite of their poverty.

The bulk of the expenditures under the Economic Opportunity Act have gone for the work program, the effect of which has probably been more supportive than preventive, and which have often been criticized as paternalistic.[88] Much of the anti-poverty controversy has involved the control, leadership, and methods of Community Action Programs (CAP). The Act states that CAP efforts shall be planned and administered with the "maximum feasible participation" of the people served, and the Office of Economic Opportunity has insisted that cities comply. This requires the creation of local boards to screen projects, request funds, and coordinate various efforts, board representatives being chosen from public agencies, private organizations, and the poor. City officials tend to be skeptical of leadership from the poor, and to want to keep control themselves. The poor, especially the hard-core, tend to mistrust the motives of both local and federal officials, and their modes of formal organization. Delays are seen as proof of lack of sincerity. Impasses have developed in some cities over organizational details, while in others the boards have been successfully established.

For the poor to have an opportunity to help determine community policy—especially for a national program involving considerable sums of money and their own destinies—is a marked departure from the traditional idea that those who receive aid can make no contribution to society.[89] Some of the poor accept the invitation to participate as genuine, but apparently more are inclined to consider the anti-poverty programs "just politics." In the low-income areas with heavy nonwhite concentrations, the issues of poverty and race have become intertwined, and representation of the poor on the boards has often been called "Uncle Tomism." It was in this climate, half a year after the rioting of August, 1965, in the Watts district, that less than 1 per cent

[87] James K. Batten, "Unorthodox Ivy Leaguers," *Southern Education Report, ibid.*, pp. 19–23. One boy at Yale in 1964 was a Negro from the upper South with nine brothers and sisters, all supported by their mother, a domestic worker. For discussions of class and I.Q. scores, see Lasswell, *op. cit.*, 399–402, and Havighurst *et al., op. cit.*, 12.
[88] Oscar Ornati, *Poverty Amid Affluence* (New York: The Twentieth Century Fund, 1966).
[89] Coser, *op. cit.*, 147–48.

of the eligible voters in poverty areas in Los Angeles County turned out to elect board representatives from their own ranks.[90]

A national poll in April, 1966, found 41 per cent favorable and 26 per cent unfavorable to the anti-poverty efforts, but one-third had no opinion. Twenty per cent had not heard or read of the War on Poverty, and 36 per cent of those who had did not know if there was a local program or not.[91] Considering the fact that widespread lack of knowledge about major issues is not unusual, and also considering the preoccupation with the war in Viet Nam, these results are not surprising. Also, recalling the 1964 poll showing that slightly more Americans believe poverty is due to lack of effort than to circumstances, we should expect considerable opposition to the program as well as apathy. The degree of normative consensus required to prosecute an all-out War on Poverty seems lacking, yet determined efforts continue.

Bringing more private enterprise into anti-poverty efforts would probably increase the support of the general public for them. This was assumed in the 1966 bill introduced into the U.S. Senate to create an Economic Opportunity Corporation to supervise job-training, help to small business, and other antipoverty programs.[92] A private business does not have to wait for appropriations before it invests money and gets a program started, and perhaps their organizational structures can be made more acceptable than governmental ones. The questions of control of policy by the city and by the poor remain, although they may be less difficult when the technical problems are delegated to private contractors. Perhaps the only organizations most of the hard-core poor can accept with enthusiasm are neither governmental nor private business arrangements, but structures they learn to develop themselves.

A proposal that might increase the confidence of those in need of anti-poverty programs is to employ many of them in such programs. Their personal experiences enable them to make unique contributions, it is assumed, and to be accepted. One suggestion is to develop sub-professional positions to assist social workers, teachers, recreation directors, and the health services. Such work might be made secure, it is thought, and could lead to meaningful careers.[93] The problems of

---

[90] *Los Angeles Times,* March 2, 1966, I, 1.
[91] *Gallup Political Index,* Report No. 11 (April, 1966), 7.
[92] *Los Angeles Times,* June 21, 1966, I, 10.
[93] Arthur Pearl and Frank Riessman, *New Careers for the Poor* (New York: The Free Press, 1965).

recruiting, training, placing, and articulating such new workers into existing bureaucratic and professional structures are no doubt immense, but trial programs might demonstrate their value to the anti-poverty campaign. It might accomplish breakthroughs in the areas of status and resistance to formal organizations, major factors in the persistence of the subculture of poverty.

PERSPECTIVE

The striking facts of twentieth-century economic life have been the continuing increases in productivity and the average level of living. Seeing new visions of the possible, people have reached for new norms. Primary group ideals of individual welfare were adapted to emerging industrial-urban conditions, at first through volunteer efforts. The instrumental value judgment that the society, through its government, should ensure the individual's minimum standard of living went directly against nineteenth-century beliefs embodied in the *laissez-faire* ideology. So did governmental refereeing among countervailing power groups, and all-out full employment measures.

The core value in the opposition to these actions is the economic freedom of the individual. Since most Americans believe in this value in one sense or another, and also in economic security, the issues involve questions of priority. Most oppose a single governmental guarantee of a minimum standard of living, preferring instead a variety of approaches and security based on the individual's own efforts as far as possible. Most evidently believe the continuing intervention of the federal government is essential to individual welfare and to the stability and strength of the capitalist economy, although issues remain concerning what to do and when. Democratic and Republican administrations alike now watch the economy closely, taking firm action to keep the swings of the business cycle under control. Rising productivity, the Great Depression, and the hot and cold wars have brought great changes in a few decades in beliefs of fact and value.

Increasingly during this century a long-standing belief of economic fact has been questioned—the assumption of scarcity. The English Poor Laws and Social Darwinism were oriented toward dividing up extreme scarcity; welfare programs of both the insurance and financial aid types seem to contemplate the avoidance of insecurity in a more productive but still relatively scarce situation; but the Full Employment Act of 1946 aims towards an economy of abundance.[94] This promise seemed almost fulfilled in the fifties, until the discovery of a durable subculture of poverty in the midst of affluence. Perhaps this disclosure was hastened by the recession of 1958–63.

The Economic Opportunity Act of 1964 affirmed the value of a minimum standard of living for all, but was it a retreat to the vision of scarcity? Some of its programs, it seems, are primarily supportive, though they require that recipients work. Some are extensions of full employment measures. But some of the programs suggest an alternative belief of fact to that of scarcity, that the hard-core poor are outside the economy and cannot contribute to and share in its abundance until they are brought into it. This requires intervention in the transmission of the culture of poverty through a variety of educational and other means, a task greatly complicated by considerations of status and bureaucracy.

The renewed concern about poverty and the determination to combat it occurred during a time when the proportion below a given poverty line was dropping ever lower, as productivity and average level of living climbed to new highs.[95] The definition of the minimum standard of living has risen too, as more and more goods and services are considered "essential." Today's modest living is tomorrow's deprivation. As poverty was being reduced closer to the hard-core, the society was confronted with this perplexing question: Must there always be that "bottom layer," transmitting from generation to generation its relative deprivation?

QUESTIONS FOR DISCUSSION AND STUDY

1. Why do you suppose that measures to support the individual's minimum standard of living have been called, "social security" rather than "economic security"?
2. Does an annual income of $2,000 now provide a minimum standard of living for the typical family? For any family? What about $4,000? $6,000? What about an hourly wage of $1.50 an hour?

[94] Bernard, *op. cit.*, 7, 485.
[95] Miller, *op. cit.*, 610.

3. Using present standards, how much poverty was there in America during the Depression of the 1930's?

4. What interpretations of Table 4.5 are in order, in addition to those made in the text?

5. What beliefs of fact are most likely to be associated with acceptance of the minimum standard of living value? Is there a causal relationship?

6. What beliefs of fact are most likely to be associated with the rejection of governmental programs to achieve a minimum standard of living for all?

7. Is *laissez-faire* policy completely dead in America? What about its supporting beliefs of fact and value?

8. Suppose you are a spokesman for a labor union. What specific wage provisions will you insist be included in the next labor-management contract you negotiate? Why?

9. Is automation a danger to the national economy? Explain.

10. What do you think has been the most effective effort so far in the War on Poverty? Why?

SELECTED READING

Brickman, William W., and Lehrer, Stanley (eds.), *Automation, Education and Human Values* (New York: School and Society Books, 1965).

Coser, Lewis A., "The Sociology of Poverty," *Social Problems*, 13 (Fall, 1965), 140–48.

Ferman, Louis A., Kornbluh, Joyce L., and Haber, Alan (eds.), *Poverty in America* (Ann Arbor: University of Michigan Press, 1965).

Harrington, Michael, *The Other America* (New York: The Macmillan Co., 1962).

MacIver, Robert M. (ed.), *The Assault on Poverty and Individual Responsibility* (New York: Harper & Row, 1965).

McDonagh, Edward C., and Simpson, Jon E. (eds.), *Social Problems: Persistent Challenges* (New York: Holt, Rinehart & Winston, 1965), Chapter 4, "Economics."

Meissner, Hannah H. (ed.), *Poverty in the Affluent Society* (New York: Harper & Row, 1966).

Miller, Herman P., *Rich Man, Poor Man: The Distribution of Income in America* (New York: Thomas Y. Crowell, 1964).

Ornati, Oscar, *Poverty Amid Affluence* (New York: The Twentieth Century Fund, 1966).

Pearl, Arthur, and Riessman, Frank, *New Careers for the Poor* (New York: The Free Press, 1965).

Pope, Hallowell, "Economic Deprivation and Social Participation in a Group of 'Middle Class' Factory Workers," *Social Problems*, 11 (Winter, 1964), 290–300.

Riessman, Frank, *The Culturally Deprived Child* (New York: Harper & Row, 1962).

Roach, Jack L., "Sociological Analysis and Poverty," *American Journal of Sociology*, 71 (July, 1965), 68–75.

Seligman, Ben D. (ed.), *Poverty as a Public Issue,* (New York: The Free Press, 1965).

Webster, Staten W. (ed.), *The Disadvantaged Learner* (San Francisco: Chandler Publishing Co., 1966). (Three paperbound volumes.)

Will, Robert E., and Vatter, Harold G., *Poverty in Affluence* (New York: Harcourt, Brace & World, 1965). (A paperbound book of readings.)

If health were entirely a matter of germs, or of tissue pathologies, it would be much easier to deal with. Actually it is part and parcel of the cultural pattern of a people.[1]

5. Ill Health

Wᴿɪᴛᴛᴇɴ ʀᴇᴄᴏʀᴅs ɪɴᴅɪᴄᴀᴛᴇ that epidemics have played a major role in human history,[2] and there is much evidence of disease among preliterates. The incidence of cancer, emotional stresses, and disorders of the heart, digestive system, and teeth appears to have increased under industrial-urban conditions;[3] but the statistical problems in charting long-run trends in disease are formidable and the evidence is debatable. At any rate, man's experience with disease and pain has been a long one.

But while the objective conditions have been at least relatively constant, there have been great cultural variations in health beliefs and practices.[4] Healing and religion have had a long and complex association.[5] Whenever man has attributed illness to evil spirits, the appropriate form of control has been magic. This approach predominated

---

[1] Jessie Bernard, *Social Problems at Midcentury* (New York: The Dryden Press, 1957), 179.
[2] Harry Elmer Barnes and Oreen M. Reudi, *The American Way of Life* (New York: Prentice-Hall, 1950), 237; Ralph H. Major, *Disease and Destiny* (New York: Appleton-Century, 1936).
[3] United Nations, *Preliminary Report on the World Health Situation* (United Nations, 1952), 29–31.
[4] Lyle Saunders, *Cultural Difference and Medical Care* (New York: Russell Sage Foundation, 1954); Leo W. Simmons and Harold G. Wolff, *Social Science in Medicine* (New York: Russell Sage Foundation, 1954).
[5] Bernard, *op. cit.*, 180.

in early Western Civilization, until the ancient Greeks developed naturalistic explanations of illness. These interpretations were improved upon and transmitted to medieval Europe by Arab and Persian medical scholars, whose works dominated the teaching and practice of medicine for hundreds of years.[6] There were many effective remedies in this tradition, and detailed knowledge of anatomy and bone-setting, but there also were large gaps and ancient errors.

American doctors before, during, and after the Civil War still practiced phlebotomy (bloodletting), based originally on the Hippocratic assumption that it would help restore the proper balance of the four humors. Ancient Greek explanations of infectious diseases, such as attributing malaria to breathing harmful gases from swamps, had not undergone improvement. Doctrines of contagion had been proposed from time to time in Europe and discouraged as heretical, disturbing, socially disorganizing ideas. Even after contagiousness was acknowledged, there was no way to demonstrate conclusively that a particular disease was communicable,[7] to explain why, or to take preventive action.

A REVOLUTION IN MEDICAL KNOWLEDGE

The Germ Theory and Other Developments

The key findings in support of Jacob Henle's germ theory (advanced about 1840) came in the latter third of the nineteenth century, from the work of Louis Pasteur in France and Robert Koch in Germany. A skeptical public was then shown that inoculation and sanitation measures could prevent contagion. Thus began the accumulation of knowledge that led to control of infectious diseases, including those that had long exacted a heavy toll of children. *Bringing the age-old epidemic diseases under control was dramatically sudden; and it rested directly on basic scientific discoveries, and on their acceptance.* The bacteriological innovators were either basic scientists or physicians with theoretical interests.[8] Their ideas eventually were

---

[6] Philip K. Hitti, *History of the Arabs* (London: The Macmillan Co., 1956), 363–69.
[7] In the 1840's, Oliver Wendell Holmes, Sr., could not convince his fellow physicians that puerperal fever was being carried from one woman to another by doctors and midwives; see Catherine Drinker Bowen, *Yankee From Olympus* (Boston: Little, Brown & Co., 1944), 87–89.
[8] Joseph Ben-David, "Roles and Innovations in Medicine," *American Journal of Sociology*, 65 (May, 1960), 557–68.

widely accepted, for they came at a time of increasing secularism, of debate over Darwin's evolutionary thesis and of enthusiastic encouragement of inventors. The issues were to arise over the social arrangements for putting the new techniques into practice.

The growth of basic knowledge of physiological systems—especially the circulatory, respiratory and digestive ones—has improved the treatment of many disorders. More knowledge about diet coincided with sustained increases in productivity and received mass dissemination as the concept of the minimum standard of living took hold. There has not yet been a major breakthrough in the control of the degenerative diseases, but they are now the focus of a vast amount of medical research. Perhaps developments in genetics, biochemistry, and the life sciences in general have already provided a scientific base for discoveries that will revolutionize our control of cancer, heart and circulatory diseases, and other deteriorative disorders.

Changing Beliefs of Fact

EFFECTS OF NEW HORIZONS. As word spread that technical means were being developed to combat one contagious disease after another, the belief grew that the dreaded epidemics might be eradicated. The belief also emerged that this aim could not be accomplished through traditional health facilities. Many people reached for new norms to guide the achievement of their new visions of the possible. Some inventions in social organization were necessary, it was argued, to make the most effective use of the new knowledge. Others countered with the belief that the new techniques could be exploited best by incorporating them into traditional medical arrangements.

The revolution in medical knowledge came while humanitarianism was on the rise, and probably contributed to it by encouraging the belief that human suffering could be greatly reduced. The high incidence of illness among the poor was not of great concern so long as paupers were considered morally unfit for society, and while fatalistic beliefs went unchallenged. The Social Darwinist view that attempts to combat disease among the poor would interfere with the survival of the fittest lent support to fatalism. But it had long been observed that epidemics struck rich and poor alike, and in this connection the germ theory suggested beliefs of fact such as that combating the conditions of poverty might help control epidemics that threaten the whole community, that perhaps poverty contributes to illness, and illness to poverty.

PERCEPTIONS OF THE PREVALENCE OF ILL HEALTH CONDITIONS. Once people began to define the social problem of ill health, evidence of the nature and extent of the condition was sought. Societies keep records of incidents that are considered important and believed to be subject to control. Although there are many hazards involved in gathering and interpreting health statistics, especially comparative figures, the alternative is to accept *a priori* beliefs of fact. Increasing reliance has been placed on data provided by governmental agencies, but voluntary groups also have played a large role. Mortality figures have been crucial, as the following statement indicates:

The marked decline in infant mortality since 1900, both in the United States and in other countries of the Western World, was stimulated considerably by vital statisticians. In the United States the American Association for the Prevention of Infant Mortality, organized in 1909, devoted its main effort during the first years to campaigning for the extension and improvement of birth and death registrations. As more accurate statistics on infant mortality became available, these denoted both the seriousness of the problem and the causes of death that most urgently required medical attention. Various authorities have pointed out the striking parallel between this attack on infant mortality a half-century ago and the present situation with respect to fetal mortality.[9]

Table 5.1 shows that in 1960 infant mortality in the United States was less than one-fifth what it was in 1900, and rates for children from one through four years of age had dropped even more sharply. Much of this drop had occurred by 1930.[10] These sharp reductions in deaths in infancy and early childhood were due mainly to applications of the germ theory, and they are primarily responsible for lowering the overall death rate from 17.2 per thousand in 1900 to 9.5 in 1960, and for raising the average expectation of life at birth from 49 years to 70 in the same period.[11]

The reduction in the incidence of the mass diseases, infectious and nutritional, enabled more children to grow to adulthood, shifting the frequency of various causes of death from the mass diseases to the degenerative ones.[12] During the sixties, the diseases of early infancy could vie for no higher than fifth place, in competition with the combined category of influenza and pneumonia. The leading cause of

[9] William Petersen, *Population* (New York: The Macmillan Co., 1961), 253–54.
[10] *Ibid.*, 251–52.
[11] U.S. Bureau of the Census, *Statistical Abstract of the United States, 1962* (Washington, D.C., 1962), 63–68.
[12] Bernard, *op. cit.*, 186–89; Petersen, *op. cit.*, 251–2, 573–74.

TABLE 5.1

DEATHS PER THOUSAND IN THE UNITED STATES
FOR 1900 AND 1960, BY AGE GROUPS

Age Group	Deaths per Thousand	
	1900	1960
Under 1 year	162.4	28.8
1–4	19.8	1.1
5–14	3.9	0.5
15–24	5.9	1.0
25–34	8.2	1.4
35–44	10.2	3.0
45–54	15.0	7.3
55–64	27.2	17.0
65–74	56.4	41.2
75–84	123.3	87.0
85 and over	260.9	209.6

SOURCE: *Statistical Abstract of the United States, 1962,* p. 63.

death became diseases of the heart, with cancer second, hemorrhages (strokes) affecting the central nervous system third, and accidents fourth.[13] So the run of attention in medical research has shifted to the deteriorative diseases, in the hopeful belief that they will yield to discoveries as far-reaching as the germ theory proved to be. As for accidental deaths, the rates for the nation declined in the fifties and through 1961, then started to increase.[14] Considerable research is now being conducted into the causes of accidents, reflecting the belief that much more prevention is possible.[15]

---

[13] See annual reports in the *Statistical Abstracts* and those of the National Center for Health Statistics, Public Health Service, U.S. Department of Health, Education and Welfare.

[14] See reports of the National Office of Vital Statistics and brief summaries in the annual *World Almanac.*

[15] William Haddon, Jr., Edward A. Suchman, and David Klein, *Accident Research Methods and Approaches* (New York: Harper & Row, 1964).

Changing Values

Health values did not receive extensive, active support until around the turn of the century. True, mass epidemics had periodically made crisis decisions necessary, and some sanitation reforms had been carried out;[16] but the relation of illness to sanitation, poverty, and personal contacts remained a mystery. Anesthesia had been introduced in the 1840's,[17] probably reinforcing the conviction that human beings should not have to suffer unnecessarily, a key value in the humanitarian movement. The many people who had considered illness deplorable, and a major threat to community life, had, however, believed little or nothing could be done about it. *The discovery of the means to control contagious diseases added the necessary ingredient for calls to action, combined with the belief by many that traditional and existing formal norms were not adequate for the task. So changing beliefs of value were activated by new beliefs of fact about illness.*

Health has risen in the pyramid of values.[18] It seems to be thought of as a positive good in itself, virtually synonymous with the enjoyment of life. But *health is also an instrumental value,* believed to help the individual achieve economic security and self-fulfillment, and to facilitate achievement of family, community, and national goals. In the following statement about programs for rehabilitating the disabled, notice the instrumental emphasis:

Vocational rehabilitation programs have variously been identified with the roles of federal government in conserving natural resources, assuring an equitable distribution of the nation's resources and the nation's burdens, providing for the "natural wards" of government, meeting the needs of persons who are "isolated" by various circumstances, and contributing to the betterment of all citizens. Programs have also been supported by an interesting combination of humanitarian and utilitarian motives. While the humanitarian theme has been prominently mentioned and supported by images of human misery, proposals for rehabilitation have consistently been tied to the utilitarian goal of employability. In recent years, the humanitarian theme has been enhanced by thoughtful considerations of the impact of disability on the family as well as the individual and by increas-

---

16 Bernard, *op. cit.,* 182–85, 190; Barnes and Reudi, *op. cit.,* 256.

17 Bowen, *op. cit.,* 92; Barnes and Reudi, *op. cit.,* 250.

18 Robert Straus, "Social Change and the Rehabilitation Concept," in Marvin B. Sussman (ed.), *Sociology and Rehabilitation* (Washington, D.C.: American Sociological Association and the Vocational Rehabilitation Administration of the U. S. Department of Health, Education and Welfare, 1966), 34.

ingly forceful efforts to eliminate employability as a criterion of eligibility for rehabilitation. At the same time, the utilitarian arguments have been strengthened by the argument that rehabilitation is a sound economic investment designed to remove the disabled and their families from the welfare rolls and to make them not just self-sufficient, but even tax-paying contributors to the federal treasury. Even the case for rehabilitation services for the homebound disabled has been justified primarily because they will release caretaking relatives to perform more socially useful roles.[19]

The view that the disabled can contribute to society's goals is a departure from the nineteenth-century picture of them as "deserving poor," which meant innocent but useless victims of circumstances,[20] and even more so from the Social Darwinist position that the unfit should not be helped to survive and propagate themselves.

Much the same can be said about concern for the health of the poor in general. Disease among paupers was part of the proof of their depravity; but humanitarian values condemned their suffering, and from the utilitarian standpoint the poor became potential community assets. The cost to society has been heavily emphasized as a basis for combating the illness of the poor, but the stress has been shifting to the positive contributions they can make when they are healthy. *Medical care has been included in the concept of the minimum standard of living, so concern for the health of the poor has been closely allied with the value of economic security for all* (see Chapter 4).

This concern has led to countless investigations of the relation of illness to economic status, and the record is clearly one of uneven incidence.[21] The lowest-income families suffer more frequent and longer periods of illness, lose more days from work, and have more preventable diseases; yet they have less health insurance and receive less medical care. The difference in dental care is especially great; the lower the family income, the greater the amount of tooth decay.[22] Low-income families also are most prone to delay seeing a doctor

---

[19] *Ibid.,* 33.

[20] *Ibid.,* 4–11.

[21] John M. Ellis, "Socio-Economic Differentials in Mortality from Chronic Diseases," *Social Problems,* 5 (July, 1957), 30–36.

[22] U. S. Department of Health, Education and Welfare, *Medical Care, Health Status and Family Income* (Washington, D.C., 1964). Only 1.3 per cent of Americans did not see a doctor from July, 1963 through June, 1964, but 16.6 did not visit a dentist. The main cause of work loss was respiratory ailments. See *Source Book of Health Insurance Data, 1965* (New York: Health Research Institute, 1965), 9.

because of the cost.[23] So poverty does contribute to illness, and there is evidence that illness is frequently the main or a contributing factor in requests for relief.[24]

The lower the economic status of a minority group, the lower its health status, as mortality rates clearly portray. Infant mortality rates for nonwhites in America are almost twice as high as for whites, and maternal mortality is about four times as high. In 1960 the life expectancy of white adult males was 6.3 years longer than for non-whites, and for women the difference was 7.8 years.[25] In recent years overall mortality rates have been falling more rapidly for nonwhites, thus narrowing the gap, as their communicable disease rates have been brought under greater control.[26] Health data provide an index of how well the value of equal opportunity for all groups is being achieved.

A study of a free Salk polio vaccine trial found a direct relationship between income and participation. The result may have been due to difference in information about the trial; but it may also reflect a greater tendency toward fatalism among low-income groups, and their lower evaluation of planning, time, medicine, and scientific research.[27] Many of the poor do not have access to free medical services, others lack information about them, and some are not accepted as eligible. But some will not accept free care unless they are extremely desperate, a rejection of formal organizations and middle-class values, including the low esteem accorded the recipient of any type of financial aid (see Chapter 4).

New health issues have continued to emerge and to command widespread attention during a time of marked improvement in the objective conditions of human health. People's level of health aspiration has moved ever higher as medical knowledge has advanced and as the level of living has risen. We saw in Chapter 4 (Table 4.5) that there was serious national concern in the mid-sixties over the inability of some people to afford proper medical care, nearly as much concern

---

23 H. Ashley Weeks, *Family Spending Patterns and Medical Care* (Cambridge, Mass.: Harvard University Press, 1961), 60.
24 Herbert Wolkin, *Health Research Opportunities in Welfare Records* (Research Series No. 8; New York: Health Information Foundation, 1959), 5.
25 U. S. Department of Health, Education and Welfare, *Vital Statistics of the United States,* 1960 (Vol. 2, Sec. 2; Washington, D.C.: 1960), 2–11.
26 Petersen, *op. cit.,* 227, 268–69.
27 Leila Calhoun Deasy, "Socio-Economic Status and Participation in the Poliomyelitis Vaccine Trial," *American Sociological Review,* 21 (April, 1956), 185–91.

as about hunger. There has been much poring over the statistics to establish the gap between what is believed possible and our actual achievements. A question posed over and over again is, How good is our health? The answer requires both data and value judgments. When we compare our mortality trends with those of other nations we find to our distress that the United States is not the lowest in any category, and that our obstetrical and child care have dropped comparatively to the point where they are now referred to as "underdeveloped."[28] We worry over the comparative percentages of military draft rejections for medical reasons, of failures by school children in physical fitness tests, of families with inadequate health care, and shortages of doctors, nurses, and hospital beds.

However, *there is not complete agreement on health values*. Religious and other subcultural differences affect our orientations to illness and disability,[29] and some Americans still hold fatalistic or Social Darwinist beliefs on the subject. *Health competes strongly with other values* and would apparently rank much lower if it were not widely believed to be instrumental in achieving some of our cherished goals.[30] Even among those who agree on health values there are conflicting beliefs of value and fact, particularly involving issues about economic security and means to employ. Some people rely more on faith healing, folk remedies, patent medicines or "quack" practitioners than on scientific prescription and the medical profession. More than a set of technical problems, ill health has emerged as a modern social problem.

THE PUBLIC HEALTH MOVEMENT

The Ideology of Public Health

The changing values and assumptions of fact discussed above in relation to the germ theory provided the foundation beliefs for the public health movement. The American Public Health Association was

---

[28] Roul Tunley, "America's Unhealthy Children: An Emerging Scandal," *Harper's*, 232 (May, 1966), 41–46; see the annual *Demographic Yearbook*, published by the United Nations. International comparisons are not very satisfactory, despite attempts to standardize the statistics.
[29] Norman Goodman, Sanford M. Dornbusch, Stephen A. Richardson, and Albert H. Hastorf, "Variant Reactions to Physical Disabilities," *American Sociological Review*, 28 (June, 1963), 429–35; Edward A. Suchman, "Sociomedical Variations among Ethnic Groups," *American Journal of Sociology*, 70 (November, 1964), 319–31.
[30] Straus, in Sussman (ed.), *op. cit.*, 3.

established in 1872. Its immediate goal was control of the spread of contagious diseases, which reflected the growing belief that existing health facilities could not accomplish the task. It was assumed that an all-out assault on the mass diseases required the authoritative coordination of diverse efforts, so *the norm that emerged was that community responsibility had to be assumed for mass health hazards, mainly through different levels of government.* "Just politics," was the general reaction of the medical profession, and of others who believed government had no business taking any responsibility for health. "Socialized medicine," said some, but all levels of government began in the field, and in 1912 the U.S. Public Health Service was established.

Public Health Measures

SANITATION SERVICES. Municipal governments have assumed the main responsibility for providing sanitation services, which include (1) disposal of wastes, and (2) provision of a pure water supply. Complex technical problems of sanitary engineering,[31] hydraulics, and chemistry are involved. While pure water, plumbing, and systematic disposal of refuse are largely taken for granted in America, their crucial role in the control of infectious diseases is highly appreciated by health workers in "underdeveloped" areas.

A supplemental municipal and state effort is mosquito control, directed especially against the carriers of malaria and yellow fever by using oil, chemical sprays, and by draining stagnant water.

SANITATION CONTROLS. Both state and local governments have attempted to control public behavior in the interest of sanitation. Measures include the provision and enforcement of standards for public drinking fountains, restrooms, hospitals and other public facilities, and misdemeanor penalties for littering and other unsanitary public conduct. Also, quarantine regulations were used extensively for a time to segregate the residences of persons with communicable diseases.

PURE FOOD AND DRUG ACTS. The federal and state laws in this area have had two aims: (1) to prevent the spread of infectious diseases, and (2) to prevent food and drug poisoning. The invention of countless new drugs and food preservatives has made this a very complex

---

[31] Barnes and Reudi, *op. cit.*, 255–56.

area to regulate. Foods and their handling are scrutinized all the way from the farm through processing plants to groceries, restaurants, and institutional food services.

HEALTH EDUCATION. Continuing health education has been assumed to have two desired results: (1) better public cooperation with sanitation and food and drug measures, and (2) voluntary preventive steps, such as brushing one's teeth, which go well beyond legal requirements. Health agencies educate directly through publications, conferences, talks, and consultations; but they encourage schools, voluntary organizations, and the mass media to share this responsibility. Sanitation has received heavy emphasis, but public health education covers a wide range of topics.

HEALTH RESEARCH. Epidemiology, the study of the extent, distribution, and control of diseases, is the mainstay of public health research. The amount of such research has grown considerably, especially that conducted or financed by the federal government. Preoccupied originally and for quite some time with the contagious diseases, epidemiologists began after World War II to devote increasing attention to degenerative disorders, especially those influenced by mass habit patterns and advertising. Smoking, overeating, and operating automobiles are examples. Sociology and other social sciences make two types of contribution to public health research: (1) data are gathered and analyzed by methods of social research, usually the sample survey, and (2) information is provided about the social factors involved in the complex chains of causation of illness and accidents.[32]

CLINICAL ACTIVITIES. Some medical consultation and nursing service is provided by public health agencies, which often result in medical and welfare referrals; but public health personnel are not oriented toward the individual case. Except for inoculation programs, clinical activities are designed to further sanitation, health education, and research to better control mass health hazards.

Recent Public Health Issues

The legitimacy of public health measures was generally accepted within a generation, with major administrative posts in the service

---

[32] Edward A. Suchman, *Sociology and the Field of Public Health* (New York: Russell Sage Foundation, 1964); Bernard, *op. cit.,* 190–91.

manned by members of the medical profession. Public health reports have for decades been considered objective and valuable. Their interpretations and recommendations, however, often arouse open opposition from interest groups concerned, creating issues over legislation and regulatory actions by agencies of government.

SMOKING. While smoking was at least a minor health issue before the sixties, it became a larger one after disclosure of its connection with lung cancer and other serious diseases. Growing pressure for the federal government to take a position on the accumulating evidence was brought by such private health organizations as the Sloan-Kettering Institute for Cancer Research and the American Cancer Society. A special advisory committee to the Surgeon General of the United States Public Health Service was appointed in 1962, consisting of ten scientists approved by representatives of both the health groups and the tobacco industry. The report, early in 1964, was unanimous in finding that cigarette smoking shortens life expectancy markedly, filter or no filter, and is closely associated with lung cancer, cancer of the larynx, emphysema, chronic bronchitis, and cardiovascular disorders.[33]

The response of the Federal Trade Commission to this report was to consider new regulations, including health warnings in cigarette advertising. This move evidently was thwarted by the tobacco industry when it influenced Congress to pass a bill in 1965 that appeared to be a strict regulation, requiring that cigarette packages carry the warning, "Caution: Cigarette Smoking May Be Hazardous to Your Health." But the bill prohibited warnings in advertising for at least four years and forbade states and localities to act on either advertising or package labeling.[34] The Southern bloc was solidly behind this ban, supported by other Congressmen strongly opposed to the extension of federal regulation over a large industry. The National Association of Broadcasters took a strong stand against warnings in advertising. The combined pressures of the Public Health Service and such private groups as the American Heart Association, National Tuberculosis

---

[33] *Smoking and Health: Report of the Advisory Committee to the Surgeon General of the Public Health Service* (Washington, D.C.: U. S. Government Printing Office, 1964).

[34] Elizabeth Brenner Drew, "The Quiet Victory of the Cigarette Lobby," *The Atlantic*, 216 (September, 1965), 76–77.

Association, and the American Cancer Society were no match for the tobacco and advertising interests.[35] More recently they have been.

In 1963, after some publicity about health hazards but before the Surgeon General's report had been issued, 637 college students at a state campus in Wisconsin completed a questionnaire on smoking. Evidently the national publicity had had deterrent effects. Some students had not taken up smoking because of health risks, and a number had successfully quit. About one-third of the cigarette smokers had cut down considerably, and some had switched to pipes or cigars; about three-fifths had tried to quit, most often for health reasons. The most frequent reasons given for having started smoking were group pressure and having friends who smoked.[36]

Cigarette sales reportedly dropped after the Surgeon General's report, but rose again after several months. The main public argument of the tobacco interests has been that the associations between cigarette smoking and respiratory and heart diseases are statistical, and not necessarily causal. They have fostered the impressions that medical opinion is split over the issue and that the only real problem is excessive smoking, and have argued that control of a large industry for health reasons is extremism.[37] The individual is caught between these arguments and advertising on the one side and the increasing efforts of health educators to persuade him on the other. The new knowledge about smoking and health has resulted in a complex personal and social dilemma, not just a set of technical-medical problems.

AIR POLLUTION. Public health officials in the sixties have publicized the connection between air pollutants and respiratory diseases, especially emphysema but also lung cancer, asthma, and chronic bronchitis. There are many difficult technical problems involved, such as effective smog control devices for motor vehicles and their counterparts for industry, but a few cities have shown that application of existing knowledge and technique can greatly reduce air pollution. Industry has attempted voluntary controls in some instances, and some individual consumers have also; but the individual tends to wait until controls are compulsory, and industries tend to resist them. Most city governments have found it extremely difficult to mobilize

---

[35] *Ibid.*, 78–80.
[36] Gus Turbeville, "Smoking Behavior and Attitudes on a College Campus," *Sociological Quarterly*, 6 (Spring, 1965), 147–56.
[37] Drew, *op. cit.*, 80.

sufficient political consensus on the need to reduce air pollution. It seems possible that the impasses will not be broken in many places until there are effective state controls, or until individual citizens bring successful lawsuits for health damage against manufacturers and other major sources of pollution.[38]

AUTO SAFETY. Almost half of all fatal accidents in the nation are caused by motor vehicles, and the cost of serious auto injuries—in lost wages, medical and insurance expenses—runs into billions of dollars annually. The several-year decline in motor vehicle accidental death *rates* through 1961 encouraged the belief that many casualties can be prevented. Researchers agree, although they insist that the etiology (pattern of causes) is complex and there is no simple answer.[39] After 1961 the rates began to increase. Following a series of hearings in 1965 and 1966, the U. S. Senate unanimously passed a bill to control safety standards in the manufacture of automobiles.[40] A national poll during the latter part of the hearings showed that many times more Americans believed that poor driving rather than unsafe cars is the main cause of accidents. When asked who should set higher standards for the manufacture of automobiles, 12 per cent said government, 29 per cent said the industry, and 55 per cent said both (4 per cent said, "don't know"); so the Senate was more rigorous than the general public would have been.[41] The control of the safety of used cars, and the driving standards, is left to the states. Prominent among the values competing against those of auto safety are freedom of the individual and freedom of business from government controls.

FLUORIDATION OF THE PUBLIC WATER SUPPLY. For a time, the combating of tooth decay by adding sodium fluoride to public water supplies was an issue frequently discussed in special scientific and medical publics, but since 1950 the few who oppose it have faced a virtually solid professional consensus. The U.S. Public Health Service endorsed fluoridation in 1950—followed by the American Dental Association, the American Medical Association, the World Health

[38] *Los Angeles Times*, July 30, 1966, I, 1. Water pollution is also claimed to be a serious health threat, but in public discussions it is linked more with beautification; see Donald E. Carr, "Death of the Sweet Waters," *The Atlantic*, 217 (May, 1966), 93–97, 100–106.
[39] Haddon, Suchman, and Klein, *op. cit.*
[40] *Newsweek*, July 4, 1966, 71.
[41] *Gallup Political Index*, Report No. 12, May, 1966, 14–15.

Organization, and other professional groups—and in 1951 began to campaign for it.[42] The usual claim is that one part fluoride to one million parts of water reduces tooth decay by approximately 60 per cent. Probably ten million Americans drink naturally fluoridated water containing from one to eight parts fluoride per million parts water, and perhaps twice that many get some fluoride but less than the recommended amount. Controlled fluoridation had been brought to about 60 million people in some 3,000 communities by 1966.[43]

From 1947 to 1951 fluoridation was widely adopted in Wisconsin, Michigan, Texas, and in scattered cities in 34 states. After Public Health endorsement it spread considerably in the Midwest, and after 1953 moved into other regions. It seemed possible that fluoridation might follow the rapid pattern of diffusion shown by some other technological innovations during this century, but the rate of adoption was slowed markedly by opposition beginning in 1953.[44] Municipal officials became less willing to make the decision, so it increasingly went on the referendum ballot and it became progressively harder to get approval by this route. The measure had been discussed in about three-fourths of eligible cities over 10,000 by 1960 but adopted in less than one-third.[45] Over four-fifths of the eligible cities had been fluoridated in Wisconsin but only six per cent in California.[46] The pattern of resistance continued in the sixties. Connecticut is the only state (by 1966) that requires fluoridation of municipal water supplies.

With polls showing around three-fourths of Americans in favor of fluoridation, and the U. S. Public Health Service ranking it as important as immunization, pure water, and pasteurization of milk,[47] why has the opposition been so effective? The answer does not lie in the cost, since only a dime a person can save at least one tooth per child, thus saving several hundred times the cost in dental bills. It does not lie in a self-interested pressure group that has opposed it politically; in fact the dental profession has been almost unanimous in its support. It lies only partly in the somewhat greater opposition of the

---

[42] Kurt Lang and Gladys Lang, *Collective Dynamics* (New York: Thomas Y. Crowell Co., 1961), 415.
[43] *Los Angeles Times*, February 7, 1966, I, 22.
[44] Robert L. Crain, "Fluoridation: The Diffusion of an Innovation Among Cities," *Social Forces*, 44 (June, 1966), 467–76.
[45] *Ibid.*, 69–70.
[46] *Ibid.*, 472; Lang and Lang, *op. cit.*, 414; see also Donald R. McNeil, *The Fight for Fluoridation* (New York: Oxford University Press, 1957), and reports of the U. S. Public Health Service.
[47] *Los Angeles Times*, February 13, 1966, G, 1–2.

aged, the less educated, the lower paid, and the childless than of their comparison groups.[48] *The answer lies in political extremism, combined with certain features of municipal government in action.*

Not only is there evidence that voting "no" on these referendums is a way of protesting against feelings of political powerlessness,[49] but the opposition has been spearheaded by conservative extremists such as Gerald Winrod, Gerald L. K. Smith, and William D. Herrstrom.[50] While Christian Scientists, food faddists, and other groups are opposed to fluoridation on other grounds, many ultraconservatives consider it a prime symbol of their cause and its defeat an index of their success. A common tactic of such coordinating organizations as the National Committee Against Fluoridation, when a city is considering the issue, is to sponsor speakers from out of town. These usually include a scientist or medical practitioner who typically challenges the professional consensus, rejects the assurance of the Public Health Service that all possible toxic side effects have been carefully investigated, and casts doubt on the integrity of professional associations, scientists in general and all public officials. Other opponents typically refer to basic American values, label the measure "socialized medicine," and charge that it violates a legal right.[51] Fluoridation ordinances have been upheld by the high courts of 14 states and the U. S. Supreme Court has refused to review these decisions.[52] To the right wing extremist this is not proof that fluoridation is constitutional, but only that the Supreme Court is part of the conspiracy.

Apparently most of those who vote against fluoridation do not accept the beliefs of fact of the extremists, yet they are influenced.

---

[48] Lang and Lang, *op. cit.*, 418; A. Stafford Metz, "An Analysis of Some Determinants of Attitude Toward Fluoridation," *Social Forces,* 44 (June, 1966), 477–84. Fluoridation seems to protect the aged against degenerative bone disorders and fractures, according to spokesmen for the American Dental Association.

[49] Maurice Pinard, "Structural Attachments and Political Support in Urban Politics: The Case of Fluoridation Referendums," *American Journal of Sociology,* 78 (March, 1963), 513–26; Arnold Simmel, "A Signpost for Research on Fluoridation Conflicts: The Concept of Relative Deprivation," *Journal of Social Issues,* 17 (December, 1961), 26–36; William A. Gamson, "The Fluoridation Dialogue: Is It an Ideological Conflict," *Public Opinion Quarterly* (Winter, 1961), 526–37.

[50] F. B. Exner and G. L. Waldblott, *The American Fluoridation Experiment* (New York: The Devin-Adair Co., 1957).

[51] Lang and Lang, *op. cit.*, 416–19; for an account of a typical public hearing on the issue, see *Los Angeles Times,* April 29, 1966, I, 3.

[52] Statement by Charles S. Rhyne, past President of the American Bar Association at a session of the National Dental Health Assembly, *Los Angeles Times,* February 9), 1966, I, 7.

One study showed that the majority of the "no" voters thought scientists should decide the question, so their political alienation was far from complete.[53] Perhaps some are simply stirred from apathy about local issues by the extremist charges and believe that there might be at least a little truth in them. By raising strong objections about the legitimacy of city officials to make the decision to adopt, opponents have often fostered a revolt against City Hall and gotten a Council decision rescinded.[54] This has worked so well that since 1956 fluoridation has increasingly been put to the ballot in the first place, providing a full political opportunity to influence the apathetic, the ill informed, the self-interested, and the moderately alienated. Thus the slow pace of a public health campaign with unusually strong professional backing and a high proportion of public support nationally, and the emergence of an unusual dilemma.

THE ORGANIZATION OF INDIVIDUAL HEALTH CARE

The Changing Context of Medical Service

Initially, the public health movement was opposed as an invasion of the doctor-patient relationship. The acceptance of the legitimacy of public health measures marked the adoption of collective responsibility for combating mass health hazards, but the belief that the ill individual should receive public care was rejected. The line between public health and individual care has not always been clear, but *the norm has remained that the individual shall arrange and pay for his own medical care when he is ill, if he possibly can.* All innovations have met resistance, yet the "if he possibly can" part of the norm has been expanded to cover large areas of public care.

We have seen that the germ theory, along with emergent humanitarian values, ushered in the public health innovations. It has often been argued that changes in medicine have created a corresponding need for new ways of organizing individual care and the reluctance to develop them has been portrayed as a cultural lag. It is very difficult to use the concept of lag objectively in this context. There actually has been considerable change in medical organization within the general framework of the traditional norm of individual

---

[53] Gamson, *op. cit.*, 536.
[54] James S. Coleman, *Community Conflict* (New York: The Free Press, 1957).

care. Let us note briefly some of the major conditions to which organizational adjustments have been made.

As medical knowledge has accumulated at a very rapid pace, it has become progressively more specialized. Longer and more expensive training is required, particularly for special practice, and research has become more central. The growing complexity of the specialization has increased the difficulties of professional communication, so that consultations, conferences, and professional journals are more essential. The nurse and the attendant have been joined by new supporting specialists such as physical therapists and medical laboratory technicians, so the physician has the problem of how to coordinate the efforts of all members of his growing "team."[55] Specialization has also been accompanied by expensive new equipment, raising the capital outlay for medical practice and increasing the number of short visits to hospitals and diagnostic clinics that have the most sophisticated machinery.

Another factor that has affected medical practice is increasing ability to control infectious conditions, which has reduced their danger and the amount of convalescent time required. More effective drugs have made it less necessary for the doctor to hasten to a patient's home whenever his fever rises, there to keep an anxious vigil. There is less risk in asking a patient to come to the office, and often the continuation of medication can be advised by telephone. These developments, combined with new equipment and increasing ability to afford preventive care, have taken most medical practice out of the family setting and placed it in the office and the hospital. There has been a considerable decrease in the *per capita* number of doctors in America during this century,[56] particularly in general practitioners, yet certainly the effectiveness of medical care has improved.

These changes have increased the cost of medical service. Table 5.2 shows that the dollar cost of medical care as a whole has more than doubled since World War II, increasing faster than any other category of family expenditure. It is evident from Table 5.3 that by far the steepest rise in medical costs in recent years has been in the area of hospital care. While the cost of prescriptions and drugs was slightly

---

[55] Leo W. Simmons, "Important Sociological Issues and Implications of Scientific Activities in Medicine," *Journal of the American Medical Association*, 173, (May, 1960), 120.
[56] David D. Dutstein, "Do You Really Want a Family Doctor?" *Harper's*, 221 (October, 1960), 144.

TABLE 5.2

CONSUMER PRICE INDEX, 1945–64*

Year	All Items	Food	Ap- parel	Hous- ing	Trans- porta- tion	Medi- cal Care	Per- sonal Care	Read- ing and Recrea- tion	Other Goods and Serv- ices
1945	62.7	58.4	71.2	67.5	55.4	57.5	63.6	75.0	67.3
1950	83.8	85.8	91.5	83.2	79.0	73.4	78.9	89.3	82.6
1955	93.3	94.0	95.9	94.1	89.7	88.6	90.0	92.1	94.3
1960	103.1	101.4	102.2	103.1	103.8	108.1	104.1	104.9	103.8
1964	108.1	106.4	105.7	107.2	109.3	119.4	109.2	114.1	108.8

* The base or comparison period is 1957–59, so for those years the index is 100.
SOURCE: Bureau of Labor Statistics, United States Department of Labor.

TABLE 5.3

CONSUMER PRICE INDEXES FOR MEDICAL CARE ITEMS, 1945–64*

Year	All Medical Care Items	Physi- cians' Fees	Den- tists' Fees	Optometric Examina- tion and Eyeglasses	Hospital Room Rates	Prescrip- tions and Drugs
1945	57.5	63.3	63.3	77.8	32.5	73.2
1950	73.4	76.0	81.5	89.5	57.8	86.6
1955	88.6	90.0	93.1	93.8	83.0	92.7
1960	108.1	106.0	104.7	103.7	112.7	102.3
1964	119.4	117.3	114.0	110.7	144.9	98.4

* The base or comparison period is 1957–59, so for those years the index is 100.
SOURCE: Bureau of Labor Statistics, United States Department of Labor.

less in 1964 than in the 1957–59 period, hospital room rates increased by 44.9 per cent. Important factors in the rising rates have been increases in the number of hospital employees per patient and in the pay of hospital personnel,[57] but equipment and other costs have risen also.

The rising level of living has made it possible for large numbers of Americans to afford these mounting medical costs, although some innovations have been necessary to prevent financial catastrophe when there are unusually large bills to pay. Low-income families and individuals have had great difficulty coping with the increased costs, yet their health aspirations have risen too. The special provisions made on their behalf have been part of the issue concerning the minimum standard of living for all.

The Fee-for-Service Tradition

The payment of fees to one's family doctor for services rendered has been the traditional medical arrangement. The most general norm of this tradition, within which the norm of direct payment by the patient or his family developed, was that the relationship between patient and doctor should be personal as well as confidential. Medical practice was likened to private business, with the addition of the professional fiduciary relationship. No doubt personal knowledge of the patient and his family often facilitated diagnosis and treatment, and under this system the prestige of the medical profession has been high.

Changes and Issues in Individual Care

COLLECTIVE MEDICAL CARE THROUGH PRIVATE ORGANIZING. The first communal responsibility taken for the treatment of the ill was private. It was based on the relationship between illness and poverty, emphasized children, and took the form of philanthropy. At first these efforts took the form of emotional, spasmodic campaigns for contributions, but these became institutionalized in the Red Cross, the Community Chest and its descendants, and in hospitals and special funds provided by churches and fraternal orders.[58] Both large private institutions of this type and those existing at different levels of government are formal organizations, parts of larger bureaucracies. "Private" in this

---

[57] *Source Book of Health Insurance Data*, 1965, *op. cit.*, 63.
[58] Robert L. Sutherland, Julian L. Woodward, and Milton A. Maxwell, *Introductory Sociology* (6th ed.; New York, 1961), 331–33.

context means collective, but nongovernmental, action to help the individual.

Since World War II much of the fund raising has been for medical research, and large amounts of foundation money have also been devoted to that end. The National Institutes of Health, operating under the U.S. Public Health Service, were established to make grants to private and public researchers in universities and other agencies. There are Institutes for research on cancer, heart diseases, allergies and infections, arthritis, metabolic diseases, dental disorders, mental health, neurology, and blindness. This operation has been characterized as a kind of middle road between governmental and private medical research, which is so in the sense that it is decentralized, autonomous within the terms of the grants, and conducted by diverse private groups and agencies at all levels of government.[59] Grants are, of course, made and monitored by the National Institutes.

TREATMENT IN GOVERNMENTAL FACILITIES. County and municipal hospitals provide both inpatient and outpatient care, largely for those without the means to pay. Both public health objectives and the minimum standard of living value are used to justify these institutions, along with emergency medical service for the general public. People are generally expected to pay if they are able to, so the large amount of health care dispensed is not considered a violation of the norm for payment for individual care.

State hospitals are provided in order to segregate tubercular patients, mental defectives and the mentally ill, and to absorb the cost on the basis of indigence as far as necessary. State medical schools and the hospitals connected with them are partly for medical education, partly for research, and incidentally to provide medical care free for the indigent, also at modest clinical rates and at private rates for those able to pay for the high-quality care available at these centers. At all levels of government, medical care is provided for institutional populations, limited in the case of students, but complete in the total institutions—prisons and other correctional facilities and the military services.

At the federal level, another huge program of medical treatment and research is conducted by the Veterans Administration. In 1965 approximately 750,000 patients were treated in 168 Veterans Hospitals

[59] *Ibid.*, 336.

and some were cared for under contract in other hospitals; outpatients were treated in 217 different facilities; and 7,000 research projects were under way in medicine and prosthetics.[60] Eligibility rules have varied, but the supporting values have continued to include fair compensation for national military service and the belief that all veterans should have at least minimum medical care.

GROUP PRACTICES. The trend toward partnership practice began decades ago with rising capital costs. Sharing the expense of office help and equipment is not usually thought of as group practice so long as each practitioner has his own patients. Three types of group practice may be distinguished: (1) that which involves sharing the cost of office facilities, referral to one another of patients on the basis of specialization, fees for service rendered, and division of income according to partnership agreement; (2) the same as (1) except for the prepayment of a fixed sum in exchange for whatever care (perhaps comprehensive) the agreement calls for; and (3) the group health cooperative plans, in which all staff members including doctors are on salary and are appointed by a board of directors representing the members.[61]

For a time all group practice was considered a betrayal of free choice of one's doctor; but the first type, above, came to be fairly acceptable, particularly for specialists. The number of American doctors in group practice has been growing;[62] but there is still considerable professional opposition to the second and third types.[63] In 1959, however, the American Medical Association dropped its formal opposition to prepaid practice, declaring that free choice includes selecting one's own medical system or plan.[64] The third type of group practice is anathema to many if not most members of the medical profession for the additional reason that it puts control of policy in the hands of the clients, who can then add more doctors to reduce waiting room

[60] *The World Almanac and Book of Facts,* 1966 (New York World-Telegram, 1966). 447.
[61] Examples: the Ross-Loos and Kaiser plans in California, and the Group Health Plan in the Twin Cities, Minnesota.
[62] U.S. Department of Health, Education and Welfare, *Medicine Groups in the United States, 1959* (Washington, D.C., 1963), 10.
[63] Dennis C. McElrath, "Perspective and Participation of Physicians in Prepaid Group Practice," *American Sociological Review,* 26 (August, 1961), 596–607.
[64] Policy statement, *Journal of the American Medical Association,* 170 (July 25, 1959), 155. Laws in many states still limit control of medical care plans to doctors, but their constitutionality has come under question.

time or get whatever service they want to pay for. A major claim advanced for both types of prepaid group practice is that they tend to emphasize preventive care, since it takes less staff effort to arrest a condition before it becomes severe. It is further claimed that costs are reduced by efficient use of staff and facilities, and drug prices are lowered.

VOLUNTARY HEALTH INSURANCE. Both types of prepaid group practice are forms of voluntary insurance covering doctor's care; but they involve innovations in the provision of service as well as in the manner of payment. The cooperative type especially may include coverage for hospitalization, thus providing comprehensive care unless there are exclusions. Only a small percentage of the population is covered by prepaid group practice plans, and except for them voluntary health insurance concerns the way a patient manages to finance his payment, not the way the service is provided. Billing by the hospital and the doctor is on a fee-for-service basis with the insurer either reimbursing the patient or paying the bill directly.

Highly controversial in the pre-World War II period, because the medical profession feared interference by the insuring companies and groups, voluntary health insurance has grown tremendously since. Only about one-tenth of the population was covered by some form of it in 1940, but the proportion had grown to about four-fifths by the mid-sixties. This is the way the vast majority have attempted to meet the mounting cost of medical care (see Table 5.2), especially of hospitalization (see Table 5.3), as the rising level of living has increased the ability to pay the premiums. As Table 5.4 indicates, coverage in 1940 was predominantly for hospital care; this has been greatly extended since then, but the growth has been even faster in other areas of expense.

Of those who had hospital insurance at the end of 1964, 93 per cent also had surgical protection (compared with 85 per cent a decade earlier), and 72 per cent had some degree of coverage of regular medical expenses (only 46 per cent ten years before).[65] Those with hospital coverage at the end of 1964 obtained it as follows: 57 per cent from insurance companies; 38 per cent from Blue Cross, Blue Shield, and Medical Society-approved plans; the remainder through independent plans. The figures were almost identical to those for

[65] *Source Book of Health Insurance Data*, 1965, *op. cit.*, 6.

TABLE 5.4

MILLIONS OF PERSONS WITH VOLUNTARY HEALTH INSURANCE
PROTECTION IN THE UNITED STATES BY TYPE OF COVERAGE,
1940–1964*

End of Year	Hospital Expense	Surgical Expense	Type of Coverage Regular Medical Expense	Major Medical Expense	Income Loss of
1940	12	5	3	—	NA
1945	32	13	5	—	NA
1950	77	54	22	—	38
1955	108	92	56	5	40
1960	132	121	88	27	42
1964	151	141	109	47	48

* *Figures represent number of people protected and are rounded to the nearest million; duplicate coverage has been eliminated. See text for explanations about type of coverage.*

SOURCE: *Source Book of Health Insurance Data, 1965, op. cit., p. 12; data originally from the Health Insurance Council.*

surgical insurers, but for regular medical expenses the percentages were, respectively, 48, 44 and 8. For loss of income, about three-fourths of the coverage was by insurance companies, nearly one-fourth by paid sick leave plans, and the small remainder by employee organizations. There is more insurance company coverage of all types in group policies than in individual and family ones.[66] Major medical coverage was started in 1951 by insurance companies as protection against unusually large bills.

The change in the stance of the medical profession from one of opposition to strong support of voluntary insurance is limited to hospital, surgical, and other major medical care, on the premise that more routine office calls and minor treatments are certainties rather than

---

[66] *Source Book of Health Insurance Data, 1965, op. cit., 15–20.*

insurable risks. Officials of Blue Cross and Blue Shield, controlled respectively by hospital administrators and doctors, oppose truly comprehensive insurance on this ground. There is also strong opposition to coverage for drugs and dental care. Remarkable as the growth of voluntary health insurance has been, then, there are still some issues unresolved. The policies provide partial protection only, with limitations involving time, number of visits, type of service, and dollar amounts. An estimate in 1961 was that three-fourths of the total medical expenses of those with one or more types of protection were not covered.[67] Yet voluntary insurance has taken the sting out of rising medical costs for a great many people, especially for hospital and surgical care. The one fifth or so with no coverage at all, and those with inadequate policies, are in a more precarious situation.

GOVERNMENT HEALTH INSURANCE: FROM TOTAL REJECTION TO MEDICARE. A bill was proposed in the U.S. Senate during the Truman administration to establish national insurance to cover the cost of hospital, medical, and dental care. It was to cover everyone under social security or similar federal systems, with the compulsory premium to be collected along with the social security tax. A partial precedent existed in the Workmen's Compensation Laws, which provided for various types of medical and hospital care occasioned by industrial accidents for those covered. Strong opposition to the bill was led by the American Medical Association, with frequent assertions that it would lead to a national health service such as England had adopted.[68] The proposal was not to provide government medical service, but mainly to help a patient finance his bills within a fee-for-service framework. It was more accurately described as "socialized insurance" than as "socialized medicine," but the fear persisted that it would lead to government influence over medical service. The bill was shelved decisively in 1949, and it seemed quite unlikely that a comprehensive government health insurance plan could be legislated in the foreseeable future.

Yet the question of the poor remained, and of others still not adequately protected despite the great rise in voluntary health insurance coverage. The majority of the poor (as defined in Chapter 4)

---

[67] Herman M. Somers and Anne R. Somers, *Doctors, Patients and Health Insurance* (Washington, D.C.: The Brookings Institution, 1961), 12.
[68] Barnes and Reudi, *op. cit.*, 266. It was referred to as the Wagner-Murray-Dingell Bill.

have no health coverage at all, and perhaps a third have minimally adequate protection.[69] Can the hospital and clinical care available free to the poor, along with welfare programs, take up where voluntary health insurance leaves off? One difficulty is that many in need reject free care, because of the stigma of admitting dependency or the dislike of bureaucratic procedures. Outpatient clinics are the medical version of mass production, complete with norms of efficiency, and it is hard for the financially dependent person to defend himself against their depersonalizing effects.[70]

The aged are disproportionately represented among the poor, and they suffer a heavy incidence of illness. Of the elderly poor, only about one-half had any form of voluntary health insurance in the early sixties, often insufficient; over half were getting social security or other small stipends.[71] Those on Old Age Assistance are entitled to some free medical care, and under the Kerr-Mills Act of 1960 there are federal grants available for hospital and nursing home care for the needy aged. The AMA supports both these programs because they are limited to those in greatest need. Both require that need for funds be demonstrated, which means accepting dependency status.

After years of discussion, the "Medicare" for the aged proposal came to a vote as part of the social security amendments of 1965, and passed.[72] This is a health insurance measure for all over 65 who qualify, and most people do; it is not limited to the very poor. Part A provides for compulsory hospital insurance through an increase in the social security tax. It also covers nursing-home care, post-hospital home visits, and outpatient diagnostic service, with certain limitations. Hospital coverage is limited to 90 days per illness, and the patient pays the first $40 of each hospital bill and $10 a day after the 60th day. Part B is optional, a bargain in voluntary insurance for medical care, the government paying half the cost by matching the patient's premium of $3 a month. The patient pays the first $50 of medical bills each year; thereafter, 80 per cent of all reasonable doctor bills are covered, exceptions including regular checkups, drugs, dental bills,

[69] Martin Rein, *The Strange Case of Public Dependency* (Selective Reading Series No. 5; Sacramento: California State Department of Public Welfare, 1965), 12.

[70] Herman Turk and Thelma Ingles, *Clinic Nursing: Explorations in Role Innovation* (Philadelphia: F. A. Davis Co., 1963).

[71] Michael Harrington, *The Other America* (New York: The Macmillan Co., 1964), 104–05.

[72] *Newsweek*, August 2, 1965, 27.

glasses, and hearing aids. Combined A and B coverage will pay for half or a little more of a typical older person's total medical expenses.

As a major extension of the social security program (also railroad retirement), Medicare was automatically available to the 17 million or so retired people receiving stipends when it went into effect, and well over a million others who had not claimed their benefits. For others there were these provisions: (1) increased grants to states to extend coverage of the Kerr-Mills Act; and (2) authorization for state welfare agencies to help persons over 65 who are on relief to enroll for supplementary medical insurance (Part B), and for the agency to pay the premiums. Thus a total approaching 19 million people were directly eligible when Medicare started in 1966, plus millions not under social security. But among eligible persons enrollment was far from complete at first, especially for Part B.

Strong pressure against the Medicare bill was led by the AMA and by insurance companies; leading lobbyists for it were the National Council of Senior Citizens and the AFL-CIO. After it passed, the AMA voted to comply with the law rather than boycott it. Months later, many insurance company spokesmen had concluded that the program would increase their business because of (1) increased awareness of health insurance, (2) the opportunity to drop the troublesome, high-risk comprehensive policies for the aged, (3) the use of insurance companies and private health plans as intermediaries in paying medical and hospital bills, and (4) the opportunity to write promising new policies for those with the means to supplement Medicare, because its coverage is far from complete.[73]

There have been difficulties, including the consequences of the requirement that nonsegregated facilities be used for beneficiaries; 250 Southern hospitals were declared ineligible during the first months of the program. The fear of serious hospital overcrowding did not materialize during the early months. Perhaps the greatest issue will prove to be over a provision (Title 19) passed along with Medicare but not limited to the aged, in which the federal government agrees to match state programs for the "medically indigent." The approximate effect of this provision would seem to be to extend Part B of Medicare to all age groups. Several states have passed legislation to take advantage of this offer, and New York's attempt created a storm of protest as soon as it was fully understood. It has guidelines making it possible

---

[73] Los Angeles Times, March 6, 1966, A, 2.

even for families with above-average incomes to obtain a good share of their medical expenses free. New York's generous interpretation of the definition of "medically indigent" included all those who cannot pay their medical bills but may be able to pay all others. The federal government accepted the plan. The AMA, and other groups opposed to extending government health insurance, have objected to it vigorously.[74]

NATIONAL HEALTH SERVICE. Finally, we shift our attention to governmental provision of medical *service,* as contrasted with government insurance to pay for hospital costs and the fees of private practitioners. We have seen that in addition to public health measures the United States provides some medical service at all levels of government, mainly for the indigent and for special categories of people. Thus, in addition to the partial "socializing" of health insurance through Medicare and other measures, America has partly socialized its medical service. Many nations have more comprehensively planned systems of care, which include supplementing government health insurance for all with hospital and other subsidies and certain free medical services such as maternity clinics and school health programs.[75] Private practice still plays a large role in such systems, including those of Sweden, France, and Canada. Great Britain's system comes much closer to being a fully socialized (nationalized) medical service. *A complete system of socialized medicine involves a tax-supported service in which private practice is prohibited; all hospitals, medical clinics, and equipment are state-owned; and the total medical staff is on the public payroll.* This is the case in the Soviet Union and presumably in all Communist countries.

Great Britain's national health service was chosen by elected representatives of the people, not imposed by totalitarian edict as in the Soviet Union. Most of the British medical profession originally had been opposed to the plan, and there were serious difficulties connected with overcrowding for a time; but the death rate dropped noticeably after the program started in 1948, and within two years popular support for the new system had become strong.[76] Public and profes-

---

[74] *Detroit Free Press,* May 20, 1966, A, 1–2; *Newsweek,* July 4, 1966, 10. Other early states to approve such plans, though less generous, were Hawaii, Ohio, California, Illinois, Minnesota, North Dakota, Oklahoma, and Pennsylvania. Puerto Rico has also approved a plan.
[75] Tunley, *op. cit.,* 42–44.
[76] Barnes and Reudi, *op. cit.,* 265.

sional support grew, though issues over administrative matters continued, and by the sixties 97 per cent of the population and 96 per cent of all British doctors were in the system.[77] A doctor may practice privately in his spare time, or all the time, and patients are free not to join the system. Conservative and Labour Party administrations alike have supported the service, and the cost has evidently not risen any faster than medical expenses have in the United States, if as fast.[78] Thus most Englishmen believe the system meets their needs, whether it would suit any other country or not. It would seem to have no chance of being adopted by the United States, where the opposition is strong to its predecessor—government health insurance.

Opponents of the system, including doctors, argued that Great Britain should stay with its compulsory health insurance plan rather than to nationalize medical service. Government insurance had been an admirable thing, in this view, as contrasted with "socialized medicine." At the same time in America the opponents of government health insurance were calling it "socialized medicine" and praising voluntary health insurance.[79] Not many years before that, voluntary insurance had been given the same bad name, as had the first forms of group practice and, still earlier, the provision of pure water and other public health measures. A belief of fact often used to justify lumping together such a variety of innovations is that any type of government health measure leads to more[80]—an apparently rather effective "creeping socialism" argument (see Chapter 4). Clearly, the term "socialized medicine" has meant so many different things that it must be defined with care for accurate communication and rational discussion of health care issues.

PERSPECTIVE

The discovery of the disease germ and effective ways to kill it wrought a medical revolution, challenging ancient beliefs of fact and

---

[77] William Ebenstein, *Today's Isms* (Englewood Cliffs, N.J.: Prentice-Hall, 1967), 224.

[78] Compare the discussion of costs earlier in the chapter with Almont Lindsey, *Socialized Medicine in England and Wales* (Chapel Hill: University of North Carolina Press, 1962).

[79] One AMA pamphlet in 1949 was entitled "The Voluntary Way Is the American Way."

[80] Lawrence Sullivan, *The Case Against Socialized Medicine* (Washington, D.C.: Statesman Press, 1949).

activating humanitarian values. Issues arose concerning the social arrangements best suited to put the new techniques into action, resulting in the emergence of a norm that supported public health measures. Mortality rates dropped so dramatically that health aspirations soared, and scientific research has been given strong private and public financial backing. Much slower progress in controlling degenerative diseases has resulted in redoubled research efforts.

But health, prized as it is and instrumental as it is in achieving other goals, competes with other values in complex ways when we grope for new norms for medical services. There are deeply divisive issues over how to attain our rising health goals, so ill health has become a social problem. The new medical knowledge not only increased the life chances of children and adults, but also changed public beliefs about what is possible, and thus changed active values, and demands. Eventually, medical schools brought social scientists in to help with research methods in epidemiology and to help explain the changing context of medical practice. Medical sociologists have contributed a great deal to knowledge of the organizational structure of the hospital and relationships between the medical and nursing professions, but have devoted relatively little effort to health service arrangements.[81]

There have been health care issues within the medical profession itself as well, but the AMA has long spoken firmly against any departures from the nineteenth-century ways of practicing and financing fee-for-service medicine. Everything from sanitation to Medicare has in its turn been labeled "socialized medicine," or a contributing agent of it. The first normative adjustment was to draw a line between public health measures, aimed at the whole environment, and the care of the ill individual. We need not assume that AMA leaders since then have callously used the "creeping socialism" argument for its economic propaganda value, or that they are conservative extremists who see Communists behind every innovation. Evidently they have long believed in what we might call "medical laissez-faire," the view that any change in either the financing of medical bills or in health care itself will lead to loss of professional control of medical services.

But we should not be blinded to the fact that the AMA has (grudgingly) accepted many changes, including extensive government

---

[81] Milton I. Roemer, "Social Science and Organized Health Service," *Human Organization,* 18 (Summer, 1959), 75–77.

hospital and medical service to indigents and other special groups. This acceptance has stretched considerably the traditional fee-for-service norm that ill persons shall pay for their own medical care, *if they can.* After much resistance the AMA accepted voluntary health insurance as a legitimate way for the patient to arrange to pay for his doctor bills, supporting it in opposition to compulsory insurance. It seems possible that Medicare will be extended, again after firm opposition, and that the AMA will grudgingly accept norms that legitimize government health insurance. Yet long-held beliefs of fact and individualistic values may prevent or at least delay these developments.

Health issues have aroused heated controversies, so the scientific base of health care is no guarantee of rational discussion. The reasoned and informative persuasion by which much public health education is conveyed contrasts sharply with the charges of extremists over water fluoridation, and with much of the discussion of issues like smoking and methods of financing health care. Economic interests threatened by health proposals often oppose them with every possible means. One study found that the greater the perceived danger of an illness, and the less the knowledge about it, the less rational are the responses to it.[82] Many groups and individuals reject science-based health care partly or entirely, despite its spectacular modern achievements, and countless others experience conflicts concerning proper diet or other medical advice. Health is, indeed, an integral part of our changing cultural pattern, one of its dilemmas.

QUESTIONS FOR DISCUSSION AND STUDY

1. With reference to health care, explain the significance of the statement that, "Scientific discoveries do not automatically change the lot of man."
2. Has the value of life itself remained constant in our society? Explain.
3. Explain the observation that, "Ill health and economic insecurity are distinguishable social problems, but at many crucial points they are intermingled."

[82] Lionel S. Lewis and Joseph Lopreato, "Arationality, Ignorance, and Perceived Danger in Medical Practices," *American Sociological Review,* 27 (August, 1962), 508–14.

4. Even though it is a prized value in itself, what would you say are the main values against which health competes?

5. Do you think health education produces behavioral results? Why or why not? If so, what types of education are effective?

6. What are the main themes of today's news stories about medical research? What diseases are being written about most, and what kinds of forecasts are made? Are any potentially new social issues indicated?

7. Referring to the health problem, explain the significance of the contention that, "It seems there is no end to the dilemmas man creates for himself; by solving one problem he creates two others."

8. Do you think smoking will continue to be a widely discussed public issue? Explain.

9. Do you know of other health issues that have followed a pattern similar to that of fluoridation of water? If so, why are there similarities? If not, why is fluoridation unique?

10. Select some health issue that has been in the news a good deal recently, and analyze the content of selected public statements for propaganda techniques and various types of persuasion.

11. Select some other country, and contrast what seems to be its dominant ideology of health care with that of the United States. Be specific about the beliefs of fact and value involved.

12. Summarize your personal ideology of health care and compare it with that of (1) the U.S. Public Health Service, and (2) the AMA.

SELECTED READING

Bloom, Samuel W., *The Doctor and His Patient* (New York: Russell Sage Foundation, 1963). A systematic summary of medical sociology.

Cates, Judith N., "Images of Health Professions," *Sociological Quarterly*, 6 (Autumn, 1965), 391–97.

Freeman, Howard E., Levine, Sol, and Reeder, Leo G., *Handbook of Medical Sociology* (Englewood Cliffs, N.J.: Prentice-Hall, 1963).

Haddon, William, Jr., Suchman, Edward, and Klein, David, *Accident Research Methods and Approaches* (New York: Harper & Row, 1964).

Journal of Social Issues, 17 (December, 1961). The entire issue is devoted to articles on water fluoridation.

Lerner, Monroe, and Anderson, Odin W., *Health Progress in the United States: 1900–1960* (Chicago: University of Chicago Press, 1963).

Mabry, John H., "Medicine and the Family," *Marriage and Family Living*, 26 (May, 1964), 160–65.

Mechanic, David, "Religion, Religiosity and Illness Behavior," *Human Organization*, 22 (Fall, 1963), 202–08.

Simmons, Ozzie G., "Implications of Social Class for Public Health," *Human Organization*, 16 (Fall, 1957), 7–10.

Smoking and Health: Report of the Advisory Committee to the Surgeon General of the Public Health Service (Washington, D.C.: U.S. Government Printing Office, 1964).

Suchman, Edward A., *Sociology and the Field of Public Health* (New York: Russell Sage Foundation, 1964).

Sussman, Marvin B. (ed.), *Sociology and Rehabilitation* (Washington, D.C.: American Sociological Association and the Vocational Rehabilitation Administration of the U.S. Department of Health, Education and Welfare, 1966).

U.S. Department of Health, Education and Welfare, *Medical Care, Health Status and Family Income* (Washington, D.C., 1964).

Vincent, Clark E., "The Family in Health and Illness: Some Neglected Areas," *The Annals*, 346 (March, 1963), 109–16.

Wright, George N., and Trotter, Ann Beck, *Rehabilitation Research* (Madison: The University of Wisconsin, 1968).

Whether or not one concludes that the middle-class family in contemporary America is going to the dogs seems to depend in part on which evidence one heeds and in part on which interpreter one reads.[1]

6. Family Issues

IN OUR HETEROGENEOUS SOCIETY there is considerable variation in family life, but public discussions of family issues are mainly in terms of the competing sets of norms that are predominant in the society, those of the middle class. *As an institution the family consists of a set of norms governing the basic function of replacing members of the society.* Except for interaction with nonmembers, these norms prescribe relationships among family members.[2] *As a set of norms legitimizing the union between husband and wife and specifying relationships between them, marriage is an institution within the family institution.*[3] The tasks of marriage, and of the family as a whole, have been performed in a great variety of ways throughout human history.[4] A number of basic modifications in our own traditional system were set in motion by broader changes in society, undermining older norms and creating family issues that have persisted.

---

[1] Robert F. Winch, *The Modern Family* (Rev. ed.; New York: Holt, Rinehart & Winston, 1963), 740.
[2] *Ibid.*, 12.
[3] *Ibid.*, 659–62, 685.
[4] Stuart A. Queen, Robert W. Habenstein, and John B. Adams, *The Family in Various Cultures* (2nd ed.; Philadelphia: J. B. Lippincott Co., 1961).

CHANGING INSTITUTIONAL PATTERNS

Changing Statuses and Roles

The most far-reaching change in the family pattern has been the considerable decline in patriarchal authority and prestige. Evidently there were issues concerning the status and role of women, child discipline, and mate selection in America even before the onset of urban industrialism.[5] Under Anglo-American common law a wife could not take any legal action except in her husband's name, so her status at law was about the same as that of a child. Well before the Civil War the states were legislating to allow married women to own separate property, and later to sell property, make contracts, and to sue and be sued. These trends toward family equalitarianism were probably encouraged by the growth of the public school system, the Jeffersonian ideal of equal treatment under the law and the abolition of slavery,[6] and were accentuated by industrialization and urbanization. After decades of militant action, women achieved the right to vote in America when the Nineteenth Amendment to the Constitution was passed in 1920. By now, married women have legal rights equal to those of their husbands, generally speaking, but some still carry on campaigns (non-militant) for more equal treatment in politics, education, and in jobs.[7]

But to what extent have these gains for the wife been accompanied by reductions in the husband's control of everyday family relationships? There evidently are many equalitarian families, especially among the most educated, urban, upper-middle and upper-class groups; there are also still many male-dominated ones, particularly among unassimilated ethnic minorities; and many female-dominated ones, notably among American Negroes.[8] But the general answer is that the United States is in transition from a patriarchal to an equalitarian system, so many ambiguities and issues about family authority exist. That *our system is still generally semipatriarchal* is indicated

[5] Frank Furstenberg, Jr., "Industrialization and the American Family: A Look Backward," *American Sociological Review*, 31 (June, 1966), 326–37.

[6] Henry H. Foster, Jr., Chapter 7, "Family Law in a Changing Society," in F. James Davis, Henry H. Foster, Jr., C. Ray Jeffery, and E. Eugene Davis, *Society and the Law* (New York: The Free Press, 1962), 247–49.

[7] *Ibid.*, 249; Helen M. Hacker, "Women as a Minority Group," *Social Forces*, 30 (October, 1951), 60–69.

[8] Winch, *op. cit.*, 81–84.

by the fact that a new wife is usually expected to cut her ties, whatever may be entailed, and establish residence in or near a community where her husband works. Also, the couple uses the husband's surname; men still are expected to take the initiative in dating and courtship; the wife is the one who gives up her job to stay home to care for the children; and despite greater sexual freedom there is still a sizable "double standard."[9] The system in general is becoming semi-equalitarian, however, with the husband tending to leave many decisions about family expenditures and other matters to his wife, and to be more of a companion and helper than a stern decision-maker and enforcer.

The law has also supported many improvements in the status of children,[10] and within the family the norm that the child should be "seen and not heard" has changed considerably. The father is less a stern, dignified taskmaster and disciplinarian and more a guide, helper, and companion to his son or daughter. Much of the disciplining of children is left to the mother, especially by the commuting father, although he often is the strong arm backing up his wife's actions. The decrease in both productive work and home maintenance chores by children, and the great increase in activities at school and under other outside auspices, has eliminated much of the work-supervisor role of both parents. As the level of living has risen, children have been allowed to spend more of the family's money, until now teenagers represent a huge mass market. Urban life and mass distribution of the automobile have given young people considerable freedom of action, rapidly diffusing the practice of unchaperoned dating and greatly changing courtship practices. Although there are still some uncertainties and issues about dating, the larger dilemma involves the conflict between greater freedom and the longer period of financial dependence that accompanies more education and later entry into the labor force.

Except for some of the later ethnic settlements, mainly the migrants from southern and eastern Europe, the United States has evidently had a *nuclear family* system—consisting of *parents and their children*—ever since the early settlers brought it over from England.[11] The extended patriarchal family includes grandparents

---

[9] E. E. LeMasters, *Modern Courtship and Marriage* (New York: The Macmillan Co., 1957), 29–33.
[10] Foster, in Davis *et al.*, *op. cit.*, 249–52.
[11] Sidney M. Greenfield, "Industrialization and the Family in Sociological Theory," *American Journal of Sociology*, 67 (November, 1969), 312–22.

and other close relatives on the father's side, with the senior male having authority over the entire household. It appears that the tradition that developed in America included only a weak survival of this system, in the expectation that the nuclear family would care for grandparents and other close relatives (especially father's) if necessary. This expectation diminished and became an issue while the proportion of the aged in the population was growing.

Changing Institutional Functions

The basic family function of replacement includes reproduction and sustenance, but it also includes socialization, which means guiding the development of the child so that the person becomes an acceptable member of society. Except for a child's earliest years, socialization has been taken over increasingly by the school and other agencies. Some other functions formerly performed by the family, such as religious education and worship, recreation, protection from physical harm and economic insecurity, and the conferring of status,[12] also have been largely taken over by other agencies.[13] The family as a unit has lost most of its function of economic production, according to the usual analysis, but retained its importance as a unit of consumption. One student of the matter, insisting that today's family has great economic importance, and that love and romance facilitate this function, has concluded the following:

. . . the function of romantic love in American society appears to be to motivate individuals—where there is no other means of motivating them— to occupy the positions husband-father and wife-mother and form nuclear families that are essential not only for reproduction and socialization but also to maintain the existing arrangements for distributing and consuming goods and services and, in general, to keep the social system in proper working order and thus maintaining it as a going concern.[14]

It is common for students of the family to consider it less important in the society today than it was when it performed more functions. Robert Winch holds this view toward the family as a whole,[15] and apparently also toward marriage, whose current func-

---

[12] One's place in the community once depended almost solely on membership in a family. Increasingly now it depends on occupation, and on such other factors as education and voluntary group memberships.

[13] Winch, *op. cit.*, 84–85, 748–49.

[14] Sidney M. Greenfield, "Love and Marriage in Modern America: A Functional Analysis," *Sociological Quarterly*, 6 (Autumn, 1965), 377.

[15] Winch, *op. cit.*, 86.

tions he lists as conferring position, sexual gratification, procreation, and emotional gratification.[16] Paul Landis represents the view that marriage has been freed of other functions and can now perform its unique tasks more effectively. He includes happiness, companionship, love, ego support, sexual loyalty, and a lasting relationship as current goals and as actual functions. He reasons that marriage must be very important today because "A greater proportion of the population in this country marry than ever before—marry younger and live together longer."[17] We will return to this last point in the discussion of divorce. Census figures show that the age of marriage for American males dropped from 26.1 in 1890 to 22.8 in 1961, and for females from 22.0 to 20.3.[18] If these figures are dependable, the declining age of marriage may be connected with (1) increased ability and willingness of couples to postpone having children, (2) increased entry of married women into the labor force, and (3) the rising level of living.

Changing Values

The traditional values emphasize the importance of the stability of the individual marriage and family, as well as of the whole institutional pattern. Obligations to the other members and to the family as a whole take precedence over the feelings and welfare of the individual, from this point of view, and over those outside the family who depend on it for economic, educational, religious, and other functions. The typical supporter of the institutional or stability-oriented position rejects divorce, considers the aim of marriage to be the bearing of children, and prefers that sex education be given at home rather than in school.

The competing norms that challenged this tradition were based on the happiness and welfare of the individual. As suggested by the Landis view, noted above, the emphasis in this value position is on personal development and fulfillment. The typical supporter of the individualist or person-oriented ideology considers the aim of marriage to be the personal happiness of the partners, divorce preferable to continuing an unhappy marriage, and sex education an appropriate task for both the school and home. The stability of the individual

---

[16] *Ibid.*, 685–86.
[17] Paul H. Landis, *Making the Most of Marriage* (3rd ed.; New York: Appleton-Century-Crofts, 1965), 3–32.
[18] U.S. Bureau of the Census, *Current Population Reports—Population Characteristics,* Series P–20, No. 114, January 31, 1962, 3.

marriage and family is valued, but escape hatches are considered necessary when personal happiness and welfare are jeopardized. While there are various shades and compromises between these polar positions, *issues persist because of the continuing conflict between proponents of the stability-oriented and the person-oriented positions, the ideological dimension of the gradual transition from the patriarchal to the equalitarian family.*

Changing Beliefs of Fact

The basic belief of fact in the traditional position is that family stability is necessary for orderly community life, and for the success and survival of its other major institutions. Thus a high divorce rate, a low birth rate, ineffective parental control of children, and other deviations from the traditional norms are seen not merely as indexes of family disorganization, but of social disorganization generally. Attempts have been made to demonstrate that civilizations fall mainly because the traditional family norms are not followed.[19] Many hold the belief that deviations from the norms of stability are biologically unnatural for man, and many believe that such departures are against the will of God. Another belief of fact is that people have marital difficulties or wilfully violate traditional expectations because they have not had the necessary moral training to build strong character; thus the way to deter deviation is to hold the individual responsible and to impose penalties for transgressions.

A basic belief of fact in the person-oriented ideology is that marriage, and family life as a whole, are capable of helping the individual to achieve maximum self-development, and thus personal happiness. It is believed that socialization of the person so that he knows what marriage is all about, and can accept and thrive on close interpersonal relationships, contributes to these ends. It is further believed that the person can change his behavior and thus influence interpersonal relations by rational effort, so that marriage education and counseling can make a difference both before and after marriage. It is assumed that the more knowledge one has about personality processes the more likely it is that he can contribute to mutually satisfying relationships.

Another belief of fact is that the individualistic family is more suited to the norms and structures of modern society than is the tra-

---

[19] Carle C. Zimmerman, *Family and Civilization* (New York: Harper & Row, 1947); see also Winch, *op. cit.,* 740–45.

ditional one. This belief implies that the family institution is not changing fast enough to prevent strains, and sometimes the concept of cultural lag is used explicitly in the argument. In one sociological treatment in which the person-oriented marriage is presented as the one now predominant, it is said to incorporate the deepest values of our economic, political, and religious systems, listed as follows:[20] free enterprise, equality, free competition, value of love, rights of the individual, the individual's worth, democracy. This position implies a factual judgment that individualistic marriage is instrumental in achieving these political, economic, and religious values, and *vice versa.*

A belief of fact fostered by most person-oriented marriage educators is that people who find satisfaction in their marriages and families will keep them together, and that this stability is instrumental in bringing about maximum personal fulfillment. In other words, we can have the best of both family worlds if more thoroughgoing modifications are made in the pattern and much more effort is devoted to making the individualistic marriage and family work. This view embodies the belief that the sources of much of the difficulty are the ambiguities and strains of our changing society, so that blaming and penalizing the individual for his problems does not achieve the desired results.

MAJOR FAMILY ISSUES

Divorce

Divorce, the legal recognition of the termination of a marriage, is unacceptable to family traditionalists except under the most strict limitations. Even the "poor man's divorce," desertion, is preferable because it is not legally condoned; in fact it is defined as a crime. An annulment is also preferred, because for some legal reason (fraud, coercion, *etc.*) the marriage is judged to have been improper. And separations are highly preferred because they may not be permanent. Traditionalists cannot accept the norm of *serial monogamy, one mate at a time,* in place of lifelong monogamy. *But most family individualists evidently are not enthusiastic about serial monogamy either; it is tolerated but not idealized. The ideal for most Americans seems still*

---

[20] LeMasters, *op. cit.,* 45.

to be lifelong marriage, and the majority achieve it.[21] *The issue, then, is over what should be allowed, not idealized. It is a question of priority of values.*

Many divorce statutes still strongly reflect the institutionalist view, especially in states in the East with large Roman Catholic populations and in the South. Even though lawyers, judges, and married couples resort widely to "patterned deviations" from these laws,[22] many people believe that the strict grounds are a barrier to an even higher divorce rate, as well as being a symbol of resistance. Divorce laws in general fix blame for wrongdoing in marriage and suggest an adversary proceeding, yet the most common result seems to be a rather ready allowance of divorce. The ground of cruelty once meant physical harm, but now very often is interpreted to mean incompatibility; proof of residence is often fabricated; the requirement of proof of adultery in New York is very often satisfied by false evidence, to everyone's knowledge, and annulment is often resorted to instead.[23] *Traditionalists oppose these patterned deviations; individualists try to bring the "lagging" statutes in line with dominant practices and to replace the legal combat approach with a clinical one.* Thus the law provides an index of the fundamental normative conflict over family patterns.

The legal norms, both written and in practice, make it more difficult to obtain a divorce if there are children. In our nuclear family system the child is heavily dependent on the marriage for emotional as well as physical support. So the law tries to prevent what it cannot fully remedy, and to guard the interests of the child when divorce is granted. Traditionalists oppose such a break under almost all conditions; individualists believe that the decision should depend on the circumstances. The welfare of children ranks high in the scale of values of both, and of society as a whole. There is some evidence that the effects on the child depend on the nature of the family relationships before the break; older children, and those who consider the home to have been happy, are more likely to suffer.[24]

The legal break is generally considered unfortunate if not tragic

---

[21] *Ibid.*, 25–26.
[22] Robin Williams, *American Society* (2nd ed.; New York: Alfred A. Knopf, 1961), 383–84.
[23] Foster, in Davis *et al.*, *op. cit.*, 235–36.
[24] William J. Goode, *After Divorce* (New York: The Free Press, 1956), Chapter 21; Judson T. Landis, "The Trauma of Children Where Parents Divorce," *Marriage and Family Living*, 22 (February, 1960), 7–13.

even if no children are involved. Regardless of what has occurred, a divorce symbolizes dashed hopes and failure in life's most intimate relationship. People often report that their friends avoid them when they need help with some difficult adjustments. Some turn to other divorced persons, sometimes in group support organizations such as Divorcees Anonymous. To the family traditionalist, the suffering of the divorced person is a deterrent to others; the individualist suggests that a further lessening of the stigma of divorce would reduce the suffering. Coming on the average after two years of a fitful and often agonizing process of alienation from the mate,[25] divorce is regretted by many of those involved whereas others welcome it with a great sense of relief. Some, especially women who move to a new area, make the status and role adjustments quite readily.[26] Nearly two-thirds of the national total remarry within five years,[27] uniting most frequently with other divorced persons, and running a risk of breakup about half again as great as for all first marriages.[28]

The recorded divorce rate has risen a great deal in the United States during this century until it is now the highest in the world.[29] But these considerations must be kept in mind in evaluating the trends in these rates: (1) it is impossible to tell how much of the increase is due to more efficient reporting of divorces by states, rather than in the number granted;[30] (2) the cultural definition and recording of divorce vary greatly from one nation to another; and (3) an unknown but probably considerable amount of the increase in America is due to the lessened stigma of divorce, resulting in more frequent formal recognition of permanent separations and other socially terminated marriages. A greater proportion of married people have resorted to divorce as the value of personal happiness has risen, but this does not necessarily mean that there has been a corresponding increase in marital conflict and failure.

Even if we accept the reported increase in the divorce rate as completely valid, it does not follow that there has been a similar rise

---

[25] Goode, *op. cit.*, 137.
[26] *Ibid.*, 241–42.
[27] Paul H. Jacobson, *American Marriage and Divorce* (New York: Holt, Rinehart & Winston, 1959), 69–70.
[28] Paul Landis, *op. cit.*, 717–18; Thomas P. Monahan, "The Duration of Marriage to Divorce: Second Marriages and Migratory Types," *Marriage and Family Living*, 21 (May, 1969), 134–38.
[29] Jacobson, *op. cit.*, 90–98. The peak was in 1946.
[30] Winch, *op. cit.*, 698.

in the instability of the family unit. One of the causes of dissolution, the death of a parent, has been greatly reduced during the same period. Note the following persuasive statement of the matter:

> The fact is . . . that modern marriage is more stable than marriage of any past age in that it lasts longer. This is a statistical fact which cannot be denied. Even as late as 1890, for example, 33 marriages in each thousand in the United States were terminated each year. . . . Of these marriages, 30 were terminated by death; their termination often left several orphaned children. Today, only 27 marriages per thousand are being broken each year. The proportion broken by death has been cut down to 17.5 per thousand. Divorce breaks not 3 per thousand, as then, but 9.3. In all, 6 more marriages per thousand survive today than survived in 1890.
>
> The average community today has less than half the funerals it had in 1890. Thus, even measured by this standard of stability, the human relationship of marriage is more lasting than ever before.[31]

To traditionalists this is not heartening news, but an indication of how much more stable marriage could be now if the divorce rate had not risen. *To the family traditionalists the problem is the high frequency of formal dissolution, and the remedy is to clamp down so that few divorces are granted. To the family individualists the problem is destructive family conflict*[32] *and personal unhappiness, and solutions lie in improving the quality of family life so that more married persons want their unions to be lasting.*

The Working Wife

The traditional status of the wife was limited to the roles of *housekeeping* and *supervising the children.* The spread of person-oriented ideals introduced the role of *companion,* thus increasing the importance of education for many women.[33] As women began working outside the home, the role of *partner* or *coprovider* became increasingly important.[34] This change was facilitated by three related developments: (1) technological change, involving both labor-saving machinery at home and the removal from the home of many tasks by new techniques for food-processing and for making and distributing clothing and many other commodities, (2) smaller families, and (3)

---

[31] Paul Landis, *op. cit.,* 31–32; see also Jacobson, *op. cit.,* 141.
[32] Evelyn M. Duvall and Reuben Hill, *Being Married* (Boston: D. C. Heath & Co., 1960), 284–89.
[33] Mirra Komarovsky, *Women in the Modern World* (Boston: Little, Brown & Co., 1953), 49.
[34] Clifford Kirkpatrick, *The Family as Process and as Institution* (New York: Ronald Press, 1955), 163–64.

the continuing transition from the patriarchal to the equalitarian family. Nearly 40 per cent of mothers with children from 6 to 17 and nearly one-fifth of those with preschool children were working outside the home in 1960.[35]

Being a coprovider is a major alternative for the wife and mother, because it takes more time than any other role and must be performed on schedule. It reduces the amount of attention that can be given to housekeeping and child supervising.[36] It gives modern woman new freedom of choice, and therefore confronts her with some difficult new decisions and responsibilities. Wives who prefer to stay at home often feel they must now do especially well at housekeeping, child care, or the companion role, or at participating in community affairs. According to the traditionalist orientation, a wife's place is in the home, so if she must work outside she should at least give the highest priority possible to child care and housekeeping. According to the individualistic view the wife should decide only after considering her personal fulfillment, along with other family interests.

The major ground for opposition to the role of coprovider is the alleged neglect of the children. Family role relationships are reciprocal, so changes in the wife's roles require adjustments in those of the husband and children. Studies seem to indicate either that there are no measurable effects on the child, or that when there are they may be beneficial as well as adverse. The outcome varies with the personality of the mother, her reasons for working, and with the family situation. Some seem to appreciate children more when not so restricted by them. According to one study, the mother who disliked her outside work tended to neglect her child, to provide little affection or discipline but to expect a great deal of help with household tasks, and have hostile, assertive children. A mother who enjoyed her outside job tended to be very affectionate, to be permissive and undemanding about household chores, and often to have passive children. Perhaps the mother's guilt feelings were involved in these different patterns, but the cause-and-effect relationships are by no means clear.[37] Developing effective norms for this situation is no simple matter.

[35] F. Ivan Nye and Lois Wladis Hoffman, *The Employed Mother in America* (Chicago: Rand McNally & Co., 1963), 16.
[36] *Ibid.*, 397–98. Part IV of this book summarizes studies of the mother's adjustment.
[37] *Ibid.*, 95–105. Ten studies of the effects on children are presented and discussed in Part II.

The major effects on the husband-wife relationship evidently are:
(1) an increase in household work done by the husband, (2) conflict
in many families over the reassignment of work roles, and (3) greater
influence by the wife over major economic decisions and less over
decisions about routine housework.[38] Statistical relationships between
a wife's working outside the home and dissatisfaction with her marriage have been reported. Perhaps this dissatisfaction contributes to
her decision to work outside, but perhaps the decision itself leads to
disagreement and thus to less marital satisfaction; or perhaps other
variables account for the association.[39] In a longitudinal study in
which this relationship appeared, it was found that the amount of the
wife's satisfaction with the marriage neither increased nor decreased
over a five-year period.[40] Other related findings are that dissatisfaction
with the fact of a wife's employment by either husband or wife is
associated with low marital adjustment scores; adverse effects on the
marriage seem greater in low-income families;[41] and the coprovider
role reduces tensions by lightening a husband's economic burden and
facilitating a higher family level of living.[42] *Is is no wonder that a
wife's working away from the home has been a key family issue, for
it is clearly a major development in the patriarchal-to-equalitarian
transition.*

Childrearing Methods

In the traditional view it is important to ensure the development of
character in a child so that he will assume his expected obligations
and conform to the moral norms of the community. The growth of
person-oriented ideals has been associated with widespread questioning of assumptions in this area and experimentation with different
approaches. Advice based on applications of the emerging sciences
of human behavior challenged various traditional beliefs of fact about
the original nature of the child, and effective ways to shape it in
desired directions. But different approaches to childbearing are

---

[38] Robert O. Blood, "The Husband-Wife Relationship," Chapter 20 in Nye and
Hoffman, *Ibid.*, 282–305. Part III summarizes this area. See also Robert O. Blood
and Donald M. Wolfe, *Husbands and Wives* (New York: The Free Press, 1960).
[39] Nye and Hoffman, *op. cit.*, 385.
[40] Bethel Logan Paris and Eleanore Braun Luckey, "A Longitudinal Study in
Marital Satisfaction," *Sociology and Social Research,* 50 (January, 1966),
212–22.
[41] Nye and Hoffman, *op. cit.*, 280.
[42] *Ibid.*, 398.

ideologies, since they also contain value judgments about the kind of person a child should become. Changing value priorities and a growing stream of research and new ideas on human development have kept a host of issues stirred up. In these discussions, child welfare emerges clearly as a very high-ranking value in this country, despite the transfer of a good deal of the function of socialization to the school and elsewhere, and despite the trend to a smaller family.

The issues have reflected a long-standing conflict between two polar positions, one centered on strict disciplining on a regular schedule and the other on meeting the expressed needs of the baby or older child. Published advice to parents reflected these opposing themes in the nineteenth century,[43] and continued to do so in the twentieth. The various editions of the U. S. Children's Bureau pamphlet on "Infant Care," beginning in 1914, have mirrored the conflicting views and the relative shifts in support of each stance. A baby's original nature has been presented variously as bad and strong-willed, good, and simply pliable; and the advice has ranged all the way from the most rigid scheduling and disciplining to indulgent fun and loving cuddling.[44] Issues have continued among the special publics of child care researchers and professionals. There has also been great variation in popular ideology and practice, particularly from one ethnic and social-class group to another. One generalizes at his peril about the advice given by Grandmas. Family traditionalists emphasize obedience and individualists stress personal needs, yet these positions cannot clearly be linked, respectively, with the regularity and self-demand schools.

With caution, major shifts since the 1890's in published middle-class advice on child rearing may be characterized broadly.[45] From loving indulgence of the child's needs around 1890, the counsel changed during the first quarter of the century to increasingly stern and regular discipline. Under the influence of the beliefs of fact of orthodox behaviorism (conditioned-response psychology) in the twenties the regimen of early and scheduled training of eating, sleeping, elimination, and other habits became fashionable. Many mothers seemed to thrive on the competitiveness engendered by this approach,

---

[43] Robert Sunley, "Early Nineteenth Century American Literature on Child-rearing," Chapter 9 in Margaret Mead and Martha Wolfenstein (eds.), *Childhood in Contemporary Cultures* (Chicago: University of Chicago Press, 1955), 150–67.
[44] Martha Wolfenstein, "Fun Morality: An Analysis of Recent American Child Training Literature," Chapter 10 in Mead and Wolfenstein, *ibid* 168–78.
[45] Winch, *op. cit.*, Chapter 14, "Rearing by the Book," 447–71.

and perhaps it was acceptable partly because of the strong drive for women's personal freedom during these years. The midthirties to the midforties saw a swing to the permissive or self-demand approach, with emphasis on the development of creativity and frequent citations of Freudian and Gestalt psychology, and of sociology and anthropology. Since World War II the most influential publication by far has been child psychiatrist Dr. Benjamin Spock's exposition of self-demand views, tempered with suggestions about a child's learning to sleep when it is reasonable to expect it and the importance of consistency in certain matters.[46]

There seems now to be a shift toward more limitations on the self-demand approach, linked with the value judgment that parents' desires and impulses are legitimate too, as long as the child is well cared for. One view is that this approach is just another fad or swing of fashion in childrearing, but another is that norms delegating more responsibility and stressing less catering to children are more in keeping with mother's entry into the labor force.[47] New parents often find that they disagree on many aspects of childrearing, and conflicting advice pours in from all sides, so mother's working away from home adds another face to an old dilemma.

Illegitimacy

Fornication (sexual relations with the other party's consent outside of marriage) violates a code of personal morality and is defined as a crime but rarely punished as such. If pregnancy occurs it is considered unfortunate but not extremely serious if the couple intends to marry; but failure to marry before the birth results in the strongly disapproved status of illegitimacy. The missing father is unable to confer legitimacy[48] and to complete the structure that society depends on to sustain and socialize the child. These facts cannot be changed by excluding mentions of illegitimacy from the birth records, although this may remove some of the handicaps faced by the child and help him to cope with his ambiguous status.

Complete chastity before and after marriage is a sure way to prevent illegitimacy, and some peoples have followed the practice of

---

[46] Benjamin Spock, *The Common Sense Book of Baby and Child Care* (New York: Duell, Sloan and Pearce, 1945), published in Pocket Book editions beginning in 1946.
[47] Nye and Hoffman, *op. cit.*, 6; *cf.* Winch, *op. cit.*, 462–63 for the faddist view.
[48] William J. Goode, "Illegitimacy in the Caribbean Social Structure," *American Sociological Review*, 25 (February, 1960), 27.

killing one or both of the offenders to deter others! Another approach that would doubtless strike most Americans as too drastic is to make contraceptive information and devices freely available and require either that they be used in premarital and extramarital relations or that an abortion be performed, perhaps at public expense, in case of pregnancy. This would eliminate the problem condition of children being born into the status of illegitimacy, often to people without contraceptive knowledge. Sufficient support for artificial birth control and for complete sexual freedom, however, is highly improbable in America. And the argument that abortions should be made easier than for the married couple who have the means to care for their unwanted child is not well received in a society whose religious and health values have so far kept induced abortion very restricted. Furthermore, to legitimize the separation of sexual relations from marriage might undermine the family system.[49] *Our conflicting values thus keep us from accepting effective means of preventing illegitimacy, and also from making the status a secure one.*

Adoption is the socially approved and legal way to eliminate the status of illegitimacy, but a mother often does not want to give up her child. She is most likely to be influenced to consent to adoption if her family is white and middle class, a segment of society in which illegitimacy is condemned and the expense of child care is high. Most illegitimate children are born in the large middle class, but the number in lower-income groups is proportionately higher. The rate for Negroes is declining as the traditional mother-centered family pattern becomes less common, but it still greatly exceeds that of whites. Nearly three-fourths of all illegitimate white children are offered for adoption, but less than 5 per cent of the Negroes.[50] In Chapter 4 we noted the resistance that exists to giving aid to illegitimate dependent children on the ground that such aid seems to reward immorality. We may now add that this resistance is to more than the act of fornication; the taxpayer is objecting to subsidizing the status of illegitimacy. This raises the question whether the values of the minimum standard of living and child welfare are to apply to all, or

---

[49] Kingsley Davis, "Illegitimacy and Social Structure," *American Journal of Sociology*, 45 (September, 1939), 221–33.
[50] Clark E. Vincent, *Unmarried Mothers* (New York: The Free Press, 1961). Estimates for 1958 were that 4.9 per cent of live births in America were illegitimate—2.1 per cent of white births and 18.3 per cent of all nonwhite ones; see, U.S. Bureau of the Census, *Statistical Abstract of the United States: 1961* (Washington, D.C.: Government Printing Office, 1961), 51–52.

to all but the illegitimate. Or, where the races are not measured by the same yardstick, to all but illegitimate Negroes. The impasse is not avoided by state laws that require a father to support his illegitimate child, because it is extremely difficult and expensive to enforce these laws.

Illegitimacy is often linked with youth and deviant behavior in public discussions. From 1947 to 1957 a little over one-fifth of America's illegitimate births were by girls of 17 or younger, and the rate for those 18 to 21 was comparatively high.[51] From the late thirties to the latter fifties, however, the rate for teenagers changed from one of the highest of the age groups to the lowest of any group under 35.[52] The high rate of failure of teenage marriages, especially when the male is quite young,[53] is probably due to the high percentage that are entered into to prevent illegitimacy. But the dilemma of illegitimate status is not limited to youth, to lower-class groups, or to people otherwise considered delinquent. It has become a general issue as the society has undertaken more responsibility for the welfare of the individual, an issue that exposes conflicting views on family change that seem irreconcilable.

Education for Marriage and the Family

Both family traditionalists and individualists support efforts to prepare people for marriage and family life and continuing education and counseling after the marriage. The former tend to emphasize traditional functions of the mother—reproduction, child care, housekeeping, and religious training—and opposition to divorce. They have opposed nursery schools as an abdication of parental responsibility. They stress the disciplinary role of the father and its reciprocal, obedience by the children, usually now in the spirit of gentle but firm love and understanding rather than of stern Puritanical dictation. They place considerable emphasis on marital happiness, without making it an absolute, sharing the individualists' belief of fact that it contributes to family stability. The individualists emphasize stability, without making it absolute, believing that it leads in turn to maximum personal happiness. So the traditionalists make use of much of the

---

[51] Department of Health, Education and Welfare, Bureau of Public Assistance, *Illegitimacy and Its Impact on the Aid to Dependent Children Program* (Washington, D.C., 1960), 9.
[52] Joseph Schachter and Mary McCarthy, *Illegitimate Births: United States, 1938–1957* (Washington, D.C.: National Office of Vital Statistics, 1960).
[53] Duvall and Hill, *op. cit.*, 109–11.

stock-in-trade of the individualists, the vast amount of material on the social psychology of the family. This is used in the belief of fact that people can cope with the problems of interaction better if they understand the concept of romantic love, similarities and differences in social background of their mates,[54] complementary personality needs,[55] initial adjustments in marriage,[56] parenthood, and adjustments to family conflicts and other stresses.[57] Acquaintance with and discussion of such material is directly associated with level of education.

A major point of divergence between family stability-oriented and person-oriented groups is sex education in the schools. The individualists believe that the home is a more ideal place for such instruction but that most families fail in this area and schools must fill the gap.[58] Some of the traditionalist opposition is based on the conviction that sex should not be publicly discussed, especially in a coeducational setting. The other major basis for opposition is that sex education usually includes discussions of mechanical and chemical contraception, methods not approved of by the Roman Catholic church. The Roman Catholic church wishes to present the subject of birth control to its members in relation to its theological doctrines concerning the family.

Courses or programs in sex education have been well accepted in a number of places, and it has been claimed that in Wisconsin and in the city of Pittsburgh the rates of illegitimacy and syphilis have been reduced considerably as a result.[59] But the opposition has kept most school administrators inactive in this area; actually, it seems that there is rather little sex educating done at home, in church, or in

---

[54] Paul Landis, *op. cit.*, Part III, "The Preface to Mate Choice," and Part IV, "Mate Choice;" Winch, *op. cit.*, Part Six, "Love, Mate Selection, and the Marital Relationship," and Duvall and Hill, *op. cit.*, Part One: "Anticipating Marriage."
[55] Winch, *op. cit.*, Chapter 18, "A Need-Based Theory of Love and a Theory of Mate-Selection Based on Complementary Needs"; Charles W. Hobart and Lauralee Lindholm, "The Theory of Complementary Needs: A Re-Examination," *Pacific Sociological Review*, 6 (Fall, 1963), 73–79.
[56] Beverly R. Cutler and William G. Dyer, "Initial Adjustment Processes in Young Married Couples," *Social Forces*, 44 (December, 1965), 195–201; Landis, *op. cit.*, Part V, "Marriage Adjustment."
[57] Duvall and Hill, *op. cit.*, Part Two, "Being Married"; Donald A. Hansen, "Personal and Positional Influences in Formal Groups: Propositions and Theory for Research on Family Vulnerability to Stress," *Social Forces*, 44 (December, 1965), 202–10.
[58] Paul Landis, *op. cit.*, 734–40.
[59] *Ibid.*, 737.

school.[60] And much of what there is comes toward the end of high school or in college, typically after years of misinformation and half truths picked up from friends and from personal experiences.

Aging Persons

We saw in Table 4.5 that the treatment older persons have received in our society ranks high among aspects of our national life that people are worried about, especially those with lower incomes. We have covered the economic (Chapter 4) and health (Chapter 5) aspects of aging, but need to relate these to the overall position of older people in the society. Evidently the aging have been the unfortunate victims of the dream-come-true made possible by the rising level of living—retirement. Earlier in the century this concept promised refreshing rest from a lifetime of toil, but it has since become something that must be planned for, and often dreaded. What has happened to the dream?

The coming of mass retirement brought a new status for those over age 65, a lower one rather than a secure and respected one, despite social security and all the references to our "senior citizens." Norms for behavior in different age groups were revised to include such innovations as retirement communities, planned travel for elderly groups, and babysitting by the grandparents. A study in the mid-sixties found a high degree of consensus among middle-class people in different regions about what behavior is appropriate at various ages. The aged people in the sample understood the expectations especially well, and exhibited strong emotions concerning age-norms.[61] They have become defensive about their new status, even rebellious at times.

Evidently those over 65 are now subjected to unfavorable treatment *as a group*. Being discriminated against as a member of a category instead of being evaluated as an individual is the plight of members of minority groups, and the aged have been classed as having "quasi-minority" status.[62] Employers fall back on stereotypes to justify compulsory retirement of older workers and their refusal to hire them. There is evidence that such stereotyped beliefs as the

[60] Duvall and Hill, *op. cit.*, 409–11; Winch, *op. cit.*, 125.
[61] Bernice L. Neugarten, Joan W. Moore, and John C. Lowe, "Age Norms, Age Constraints, and Adult Socialization," *American Journal of Sociology*, 70 (May, 1965), 710–17.
[62] Milton L. Barron, *The Aging American* (New York: Thomas Y. Crowell Co., 1961), Chapter 4, "The Aged As a Quasi-Minority Group."

following are false: that older workers produce less, are often absent, have more accidents, tend not to stay on the payroll long, lack job skills, and are inflexible and cantankerous at work. Companies with pension plans avoid hiring people in their fifties. Insurance companies advise that retaining employees after 65, or hiring women over 40 or men over 45, increases company premiums for workmen's compensation and disability and accident insurance.[63]

Just as other groups do under the appropriate conditions when they are subjected to stereotyped treatment, so the aging have become politically conscious and have made attempts to alter their status. One effort has been to push for legislation banning discrimination in hiring based on the age of the worker, a movement that met with success in several states before or during the fifties and in others later. In some instances, however, there is little enforcement power. Some of these bans are part of the Fair Employment Practices statute, such as the fairly successful one in Massachusetts. New York's statute, with considerable enforcement power lodged in the State Commission against Discrimination, has greatly reduced the practice of listing age restrictions in advertising and increased the placement of workers over 45.[64]

The original Social Security Act provided for a series of gradual increases in the tax and in Old Age and Survivor's Insurance benefits. OASI payments went up 7 per cent in 1965, the year the Social Security Amendments included Medicare, liberalized eligibility requirements, and an increase (to $1,500) in the annual amount a pensioner can earn. As the retired, the blind, and people in other categories began receiving higher benefits under these provisions, drops were registered in the proportion of the aged, blind, and the like, on public assistance rolls.[65] Further increases in social security benefits are expected to reduce public welfare costs further, which may improve the status of the retired worker considerably. Receiving a stipend one has contributed to and receives as a legal right is quite different from accepting dependency status, especially when the benefit becomes large enough to live on. Many now urge that coverage be extended to still more work groups, and that an escalator provision be established so that benefits vary with the cost of living.

What are the living arrangements of the aging? In the early sixties

---

[63] *Ibid.*, 60–61.
[64] *Ibid.*, 63–66.
[65] *Los Angeles Times*, Monday, May 2, 1966, I, 5.

most of them, four-fifths of the men and two-thirds of the women, lived in a household with a related person. For men this usually was the wife; for the women, who tend to be the survivors, it was often a son, daughter, or other relative. Only one in 25 lived in an institution, and one in four or five lived alone. About two-thirds were drawing social security benefits,[66] and total cash incomes were usually small, as we saw in Chapter 4. The nuclear family was taking some responsibility, but rarely was an elderly person living in a home with children under age 18.[67] The dominant value position apparently is that economic security for the aged is their own and society's responsibility, not that of the son or daughter, especially when it conflicts with child welfare.

Economic security not only provides the necessary base for other activities, but also is a symbol to the aged of their status. There are other aspects of their concern with their social position—relationships with the families of sons or daughters, role in the church, lodge, labor union, professional association, and the community as a whole. Much of the planning for the activities of retired people seems to assume that they no longer can or wish to be active in community affairs. Both the planning and the research on aging have been preoccupied with the interests of middle-class professionals—with such things as hobbies, discussion groups, the arts, visits to museums, and so on—which seem pointless to many people.[68] A study in the Twin Cities found that the lower-class aged had more problems, especially economic ones, but that those in the middle class were more likely to consider time a problem, and to say that they would live their lives over differently if they could.[69] The concerns may vary, but the aging in all segments of society indicate anxiety about their quasi-minority status, an outcome very different from the one anticipated for several decades.

PERSPECTIVE

Equalitarian ideals have combined with the effects of technological change—in industry, on the farm, and in the home—to move the

---

[66] Statement by the Senate Special Committee on Aging, *Congressional Record*, 108, No. 97 (June 14, 1962).
[67] Bureau of the Census, *Current Population Reports*, Series P-20, Numbers 114, 116.
[68] Barron, *op. cit.*, 72–74. Labor unions might play a very useful role here.
[69] Arnold Rose, "Class Differences Among the Elderly: A Research Report," *Sociology and Social Research*, 50 (April, 1966), 356–60.

American family well along the path from the patriarchal tradition to the equalitarian pattern. The American tradition in general was that of the nuclear family with kinship ties, not the extended household pattern, and father's authority was not absolute. It was challenged by both women and children in the nineteenth century, and women's legal and political rights became a major public issue. This major and open challenge to patriarchal authority became a successful social movement in the twentieth century and was replaced by less militant efforts for more equal treatment in employment, education, government, and in the home. Growing concern for child welfare has accompanied a sharp rise in the status of children. The growth of a new family ideology has strongly underscored the worth and happiness of the person, challenging the absoluteness of marital stability and lending support to the continuing transition away from patriarchalism.

Some of the issues that have been generated by this transformation have proven to be extremely knotty and persistent. Although the changes have been considerable, there is still strong support for the traditional ideology, the major interest group being the Roman Catholic Church. The views have been modified somewhat, at least partly through the influence of the new individualistic emphasis on personal happiness. Traditionalists and individualists share the belief that marital happiness contributes to family stability. For the traditionalists it is *the* major value; for the individualists, a prized instrumental value because of its presumed contribution to personal fulfillment. These idea systems thus share some common ground, but their differences involve matters of strong belief, so they clash over many issues—the role of the mother, divorce, modes of childrearing, and illegitimacy. There are many compromises we make and many patterned deviations and conflicting attitudes that arise within the person as we reach for and debate new norms, and apparently move from semipatriarchalism to semiequalitarianism.

The issues about marriage and the larger family are dilemmas of status—of the social place of the father, mother, child, and grandparents. Father's status has declined considerably in the pyramid of authority, and in prestige, both within the family and in the society. The social roles—the patterns of expected behavior of those who occupy the family statuses—have undergone a great deal of modification, and new questions about role-expectations continue to emerge. In public discussions the issues are usually formulated in terms of roles; people would know much more certainly who is to do what and when if fundamental matters of status were not at issue. We have seen dilemmas of status outlined sharply in the social problems of the working wife, divorce, and illegitimacy. And we have seen that retirement at 65 has lowered the status of those in the last stage of the family life cycle, who feel doubly deprived because the promise of a respected, carefree, and more secure position has in many cases been denied them.

QUESTIONS FOR DISCUSSION AND STUDY

1. What are three ways, or more, in which technological change has affected the American family in the twentieth century? Explain.

2. Are long-range developments in the structure and functions of the family consistent with (a) industrialization, (b) urbanization, and (c) bureaucratization? Explain.

3. Does evidence support the view that "Women are a quasi-minority group in American society"?

4. (a) Why may it be said that the person-oriented family ideology is individualistic, but not in the rugged or extreme sense?
   (b) Is the emphasis on stable marriages in the individualistic approach merely a compromise with the traditionalist approach? Explain.

5. Select five or more articles dealing with marriage from popular magazines; then, (a) Classify each article according to whether it is more traditionalist or person-oriented; (b) Identify any interest groups the author represents, and the ones he cites favorably, and (c) Classify each article according to whether its content is predominantly informative or suggestive.

6. Were trends in infant and child mortality during the first quarter of this century (see Chapter 5) consistent with the general shift in published advice on child care? What about the Great Depression, and the shift that began in the middle of it? Do you think these associations are causal or spurious?

7. What family issue discussed in this chapter is closest to being resolved? Why do you say so? Is the condition being eliminated, or are values changing to make the condition acceptable, or is something else happening?

8. What issue about family life most directly portrays the transformation from the patriarchal to the equalitarian pattern? Why? From the per-

spective of this particular issue, how far along does the transition seem to be?

9. Do you know of any instance in which one of the family issues has become the target of either extreme right-wing or left-wing tactics? If not, what issue do you think might be a "natural?" Why?

10. What are some ways in which the emergence of social problems in the economic, health, and family areas fit together into some master trends in society? Are any of the developments contradictory?

SELECTED READING

Burgess, Ernest W., Locke, Harvey J., and Thomas, Mary Margaret, *The Family: From Institution to Companionship* (3rd ed.; New York: American Book Co., 1963).

Cervantes, Lucius, "The Isolated Nuclear Family and the Dropout," *Sociological Quarterly*, 6 (Spring, 1965), 103–18.

Christenson, Harold T. (ed.), *Handbook of Marriage and the Family* (Chicago: Rand McNally & Co., 1964).

Deutscher, Irwin, "The Quality of Postparental Life: Definitions of the Situation," *Marriage and Family Living*, 26 (February, 1964), 52–59.

Hobart, Charles W., "Commitment, Value Conflict and the Future of the American Family," (with reply by William N. Kephart, and rejoinder), *Marriage and Family Living*, 25 (November, 1963), 405–14.

Kephart, William N., *The Family, Society and the Individual* (2nd ed.; Boston: Houghton Mifflin, 1966).

McKinney, John C., and deVyver, Frank T. (eds.), *Aging and Social Policy* (New York: Appleton-Century-Crofts, 1966).

Miller, Daniel R., and Swanson, Guy E., *The Changing American Parent* (New York: John Wiley & Sons, 1958).

Moberg, David, "The Christian Religion and Personal Adjustment in Old Age," *American Sociological Review*, 18 (February, 1963), 87–90.

Reiss, Ira L., "Social Class and Premarital Sexual Permissiveness: A Re-Examination," *American Sociological Review*, 30 (October, 1965), 747–56.

Rodgers, Roy, "Some Factors Associated with Homogeneous Role Patterns in Family Life Cycle Patterns," *Pacific Sociological Review*, 7 (Spring, 1964), 38–47.

Rose, Arnold, and Peterson, Warren A. (eds.), *Older People and Their Social World* (Philadelphia: F. A. Davis Co., 1965).

Stroup, Atlee L., *Marriage and Family: A Developmental Approach* (New York: Appleton-Century-Crofts, 1966).

Swinehart, James W., "Socio-Economic Level, Status Aspiration, and Maternal Role," *American Sociological Review*, 28 (June, 1963), 391–99.

Udry, J. Richard, *The Social Context of Marriage* (Philadelphia: J. B. Lippincott Co., 1966).

Williams, Richard H., Tibbetts, Clark, and Donahue, Wilma (eds.), *Processes of Aging: Social and Psychological Perspectives*, vols. I and II (New York: Atherton Press, 1963).

Winch, Robert F., McGinnis, Robert, and Barringer, Herbert (eds.), *Selected Studies in Marriage and the Family* (Rev. ed.; New York: Holt, Rinehart & Winston, 1962).

III

Problems Involving Deviant Behavior

In the United States, the insane were long treated in the same brutal manner as they were in Europe. . . . The number of hospitals for the insane grew slowly. As late as 1843, there were only 14 hospitals, both public and private, for patients suffering from mental disease. By and large, as late as the second third of the nineteenth century, the majority of the insane in this country were still confined in prisons, jails, and almshouses. They were brutally treated, chained fast or locked in miserable cells, poorly fed, and half clothed.[1]

7. Mental Illness

It MAY NOT BE EASY for today's student to comprehend such a state of affairs as this, although novels, movies, and television programs help the imagination. Also, there are many survivals in popular terms of reference, stereotyped jokes, and reactions to emotional disturbances. The underlying beliefs of fact and value, both for the past and the present, however, are not readily perceived.

MENTAL ILLNESS AS A SOCIAL PROBLEM

Until recent decades emotional aberration was not generally referred to in terms that associated it with ill health, and it is still set apart from physical illness by virtue of being deviant behavior. Physical illness is considered merely unfortunate; but emotional problems produce a sense of shame in the family and close friends, who often try to give plausible reasons for the behavior, thus denying that it is mental illness.[2] While members of the family may feel a sense of guilt for possibly having contributed to the emotional disturbance, the same may be true with respect to physical illnesses. The impor-

---

[1] Harry Elmer Barnes and Oreen M. Reudi, *The American Way of Life* (New York: Prentice-Hall, 1950), 801.
[2] John A. Clausen, "Social Science in the Mental Health Fields," *Items* (Social Science Research Council Bulletin), 9 (December, 1955).

tant difference is that the mentally ill person is behaving in a deviant manner, and to such a degree that it is considered a threat to community life.[3] *When violation of community norms beyond the tolerated limit becomes frequent enough to cause widespread concern, and when the resulting issues continue to resist resolution, the deviant conduct has become a social problem.*

The Role of Changing Values

When Dorothea Dix followed the lead of the European reformers and in 1841 began her campaign to get separate institutions built for the insane, the major goal was more humane treatment of the inmates. This new value judgment resulted in a major public issue over humane facilities and staff, not over the cure and prevention of insanity. Her campaign was highly successful in the sense that states began to build separate institutions,[4] but even where the treatment was more humane the judgment prevailed that insanity was a shameful condition. The location and management of the mental institutions betrayed a desire to deny the existence of mental illness as well as to isolate it, so that it was walled in, and kept out of sight. This mid-nineteenth century view still seems widespread today.[5] After World War II there was such a shortage of mental hospital facilities that charges of overcrowding and brutal treatment circulated widely, and for a time inhumane treatment again became a major public issue.[6]

An interview study of 300 married women provides us with some information about current attitudes toward the mentally ill. Rejection of emotionally disturbed people was found to be based more on the degree of deviance from community norms than on the seriousness of clinical symptoms. Men were rejected more firmly than women for the same deviations.[7] Also, the amount of rejection varied with the type of help sought by the disturbed person, from least rejection to most, as follows: no help, clergyman, physician, psychiatrist, and

---

[3] George A. Lundberg, Clarence C. Schrag, and Otto N. Larsen, *Sociology* (3rd ed.; Harper & Row, 1963), 645–51.
[4] Barnes and Reudi, *op. cit.*, 801–02.
[5] Elaine Cumming and John Cumming, *Closed Ranks: An Experiment in Mental Health Education* (Cambridge, Mass.: Harvard University Press, 1957), especially Chapter 7.
[6] Barnes and Reudi, *op. cit.*, 803–05; Albert Deutsch, *The Shame of the States* (New York: Harcourt, Brace & Co., 1948).
[7] Derek L. Phillips, "Rejection of the Mentally Ill: The Influence of Behavior and Sex," *American Journal of Sociology*, 29 (October, 1964), 679–87.

mental hospital.[8] Labeling a person as a dangerous deviant is most complete and ritualized when someone is committed to a state mental institution, with due process of law involving formal confrontation, judgment, and placement of the person. No ritual to remove the stigma occurs when the person is discharged, regardless of his condition.[9] It appears that a term like, "abnormal behavior" would be more suited to the public's deviance-oriented perception than is the medical term "mental illness."

Changing Beliefs of Fact

While some progress has been made in controlling and treating mental illness, there has been no discovery such as the germ theory that has brought about a treatment revolution. Freud's ideas produced a great deal of discussion and new thinking about emotional disorders, and there have been many important developments in abnormal and clinical psychology, and in psychiatry; but so far demonstrations of control have not been spectacular. The professional issues indicate little consensus on basic concepts and methods of diagnosis, and the honest answer to why controls and treatments sometimes work is that no one knows for sure.

After publication of his book about his experiences in a mental institution during the first three years of this century,[10] Clifford W. Beers began organizing state mental hygiene societies, and started the National Committee for Mental Hygiene in 1909. While there has been concern for humane treatment in the work forwarded by the mental hygiene movement, the main emphasis has been on influencing public beliefs of fact about mental illness, so that more people will believe it is a condition amenable to control. Public educational efforts have especially stressed the importance of "after care" to prevent relapses, and legislation to revise legal procedure. Mental hygiene was given some recognition as a field of public health as early as 1912. Major advances were made during both World Wars in treating the emotionally disturbed, and the National Committee secured passage

---

[8] ———, "Rejection: A Possible Consequence of Seeking Help For Mental Disorders," *American Journal of Sociology*, 28 (December, 1963), 963–72.

[9] Kai T. Erickson, "Notes on the Sociology of Deviance," *Social Problems*, 9 (Spring, 1962), 307–14; see also Jack P. Gibbs, "Rates of Mental Hospitalization: A Study of Societal Reaction to Deviant Behavior," *American Sociological Review*, 27 (December, 1962), 789–92.

[10] Clifford W. Beers, *A Mind That Found Itself: An Autobiography* (New York: Longmans, 1913, first publ. 1908).

of the Mental Hygiene Act of 1946, providing for the National Mental Health Institute at Bethesda, Maryland (one of the Institutes mentioned in Chapter 5). In addition to the work at the Institute there are grants for contract research and for psychiatric training centers. When the mental hygiene movement started, almost no Americans believed it was possible to control and treat mental illness;[11] now a great many do, thus creating issues about what type of facilities to develop. One basis for opposition to all proposals, however, is continued skepticism that anything effective can really be done.

The Nature and Amount of Mental Illness

DIFFICULTIES IN DEFINITION AND DIAGNOSIS. There are some variations in the way mental disorders are classified and in the terminology employed, reflecting the diversity of basic assumptions and emphasis on different schools of thought in psychiatry and pyschology. The same terms may be employed with somewhat different meanings in different schemes, but the measuring or operationalizing of the defined categories is a more serious difficulty. Two psychiatrists may use the same verbal definition of a disorder, but use different yardsticks in arriving at a diagnosis. Turnover in clinical personnel often results in large shifts in the percentages of patients diagnosed as falling in given categories. Practicing psychiatrists and psychologists often feel confident that they understand the dynamics of their cases, yet they have difficulty communicating accurately with others and in convincing them. Research into causes is hampered by lack of reliable and valid measures of particular mental illnesses, especially the functional ones (see below).[12] The problem of determining when and how much the functioning of a person is impaired is very complex.

The difficulty is enhanced by the fact that mental illness involves deviant behavior as well as impaired functioning. Clinicians often feel under pressure to relate their categories and explanations to traditional ideas about insanity, especially when they are called on for legal testimony. They feel compelled to note the danger to the community of particular symptoms, and to weigh this in making both diagnostic and treatment decisions. Yet deviance cannot be omitted from consideration from the pathological point of view, because impairment of functioning depends on what is normally expected of the person.

---

[11] Barnes and Reudi, *op. cit.*, 815–20.
[12] August B. Hollingshead, "The Epidemiology of Schizophrenia," *American Sociological Review*, 26 (February, 1961), 10.

There is wide variation in what is considered normal from one culture to another, and over time in a given culture that is changing. By considering the motivation for given conduct, and the situation within which it occurs, the diagnostician can make an informed judgment about what is abnormal for what and for whom,[13] but the application of this judgment is complicated when it comes to subcultural variations in our society. For example, is lack of career aspiration equally abnormal for all classes, races, regions and families? In mental health education the major themes are strongly oriented toward the goals and norms of the middle class, such as careful planning, striving to get ahead, and adjusting to dominant community norms.[14]

TYPES OF MENTAL ILLNESS. There is a fair agreement on the verbal definitions of the broad categories of mental illness.[15] Disorders are classed as *organic* if there is a recognizable physical basis, and *functional* if there is not. Organic mental illnesses are traceable to such conditions as a brain injury or tumor, disease germs, physiological impairments, and perhaps sometimes to heredity. One type, *paresis,* is the result of brain deterioration in the advanced stages of syphilis. Alcoholic psychoses occur in some cases of chronic alcoholism, and drug addiction is another habit which can damage the central nervous system through the blood stream. Aging is often accompanied by arteriosclerotic and other conditions that impair memory, concentration, and cause delusions. About one-third of all first admissions to state mental hospitals are people aged sixty years or over, and this is approximately the median age of all first admissions; but many are functional rather than organic cases.[16] (See the end of Chapter 6 for a discussion of the status anxieties of the aging.)

Another major distinction is based on how seriously the person's social participation is impaired. *Psychosis* is the most serious im-

13 Frederick C. Redlich, "The Concept of Health in Psychiatry," in Alexander Leighton, John A. Clausen, and Robert N. Wilson (eds.), *Explorations in Social Psychiatry* (New York: Basic Books, 1957), 145–46.
14 Orville R. Gursslin, Raymond G. Hunt, and Jack L. Roach, "Social Class and the Mental Health Movement," *Social Problems,* 7 (Winter, 1959–60), 210–18.
15 *Diagnostic and Statistical Manual: Mental Disorders* (Washington, D.C.: American Psychiatric Association, 1952); James C. Coleman, *Abnormal Psychology and Modern Life* (Chicago: Scott, Foresman & Co., 1956).
16 Milton L. Barron, *The Aging American* (New York: Thomas Y. Crowell Co., 1961), 50, 82–83. Probably many would receive more appropriate care in other types of facilities, 190.

pairment, involving marked loss of contact with reality, at least periodically. Presumably all organic disorders are forms of psychosis. *Neurosis* makes adjustment in some areas of life difficult, and often produces much stress and unhappiness for self and others, but the neurotic can get along reasonably well in occupational and other roles most of the time. Much mental hygiene effort is devoted to helping people cope with the still *milder personality problems* in order to prevent the disorders that require treatment—the neuroses and psychoses. Psychotics deviate more from community norms than neurotics do, although most are not physically dangerous.

Judging from hospitalizations, *schizophrenia* is by far the most common type of functional psychosis, occurring most often in adolescence and the early adult years. It involves a distorted perception of social reality and withdrawal from it. It takes many different forms, simple schizophrenia consisting of marked withdrawal from others into a private world, and progressive detachment from reality. The *hebephrenic* type involves inappropriate, silly forms of behavior and hallucinations. *Paranoid schizophrenia* involves delusions of persecution, or sometimes of grandeur. *Paranoia* is a separate psychosis involving permanent, rigid delusions of persecution or grandeur, but today most marked paranoids are classed as schizophrenic. The *catatonic* type involves extreme withdrawal, with long periods of sitting or lying in a motionless and speechless trance, usually alternating with states of excited activity.

Depression psychoses involve extreme feelings of despair, self-deprecation, and withdrawal. One form is the *manic-depressive* type, in which the person alternates between being highly excited, talkative and demonstrative, and markedly depressed. In the manic phase the person seems to be trying to break free of the feelings of depression. Mentally ill people in a depressed condition do not necessarily have a depression psychosis; they may be schizophrenic or neurotic.

The neuroses are characterized by marked feelings of anxiety, presumably resulting from contradictory treatment by parents,[17] or other childhood experiences. One explanation of the rigid nature of neurotic patterns is that the person is subconsciously attempting to adjust to strong feelings of conflict about relationships with other people.[18] Neurotic phobias presumably help the person hide from the

---

[17] Rollo May, *The Meaning of Anxiety* (New York: The Ronald Press Co., 1950).
[18] Karen Horney, *Our Inner Conflicts* (New York: W. W. Norton & Co., 1945), 40–95.

things he is really worried about. Obsessive-compulsive habits, such as counting things or excessive neatness, presumably give some re-assurance to those with strong guilt feelings. The various forms of hysteria, from seizures to loss of identity, help discharge tension or evade painful situations. Psychosomatic illnesses are ailments in which tensions have affected the stomach, intestines, heart or other bodily areas controlled by involuntary muscles.

AMOUNT OF MENTAL ILLNESS. The statistical measures of mental disorders are very unsatisfactory, so any statements about trends are suspect. The most cited figures are based on hospital admissions for mental illness, for which the recording and reporting procedure is not standardized. The National Institute of Mental Health estimate for December 31, 1963, was that a little over half a million patients were in state and county mental hospitals, about 13,000 in private mental hospitals, 9,000 in psychiatric wards of general hospitals, and about 176,500 on the rolls of outpatient psychiatric clinics.[19] If the number in Veterans' hospitals were added to the other inpatients, the total would doubtless be somewhat under 600,000 in hospital beds. The American Hospital Association estimate of the average daily hospital census in 1964 was approximately 1,421,000,[20] so evidently well below half of all hospital beds were occupied by mental patients. The usual figure for the fifties was that over half of all hospital beds were occupied by the mentally ill, with the estimate shifting downward a little to about one-half at the end of the decade.[21] Perhaps the increased use of tranquilizers, beginning in the midfifties, had by the beginning of 1964 decreased the length of hospital stays enough to reduce materially the proportion of mentally ill patients in hospital beds. From 1955 to 1960 the Census estimate of mental patients in hospitals dropped steadily, from about 631,500 in 1955 to 610,000 in 1960,[22] and an informal estimate by the National Institute of Mental Health in 1965 was 575,000.

Since many mentally ill people do not receive either hospital or

---

[19] *The World Almanac and Book of Facts* (New York: New York World-Telegram, 1966), 304. Perhaps mental patients in Veterans and other federal hospitals need to be added.

[20] *Ibid.,* 304.

[21] Joint Commission on Mental Illness and Health, *Action For Mental Health* (Science Edition; New York: Basic Books, 1961), 173.

[22] U.S. Bureau of the Census, *Statistical Abstract of the United States: 1963* (Washington, D.C., 1963), 84.

outpatient care, such figures underestimate the total incidence. Changes over time are more likely to reflect changes in the availability of facilities and in treatment practices rather than trends in the amount of mental disorder. Rejections for military service are often cited in an attempt to get a broader population base for an estimate, but the factors involved make this far from a representative sample of all men eligible for service. At any rate, about 12 per cent of all men called for service during World War II were rejected for personality reasons (over one and one-half million in all), and over half a million were discharged for neuropsychiatric reasons.[23]

Some community surveys have been made to estimate the amount of untreated mental illness, but the criteria used in the different studies have varied so greatly that the rates have ranged widely. One of the more intensive efforts, an interview study of 1,600 mid-town Manhattan residents, produced the estimate that 23.4 per cent had marked, severe, and incapacitating emotional symptoms.[24] By contrast, a study of Kalamazoo County, Michigan, produced an estimate of untreated mental illness of only 34 per 1,000 people, evidently a measure of only the extremely ill.[25] The Manhattan study found that only one in four of the seriously ill had ever seen a psychotherapist.[26] A national survey found that only 29 per cent of those who worried all the time, said they had received professional help.[27] It is clear that by any measure there is a great deal of mental illness, and that much of it goes untreated; but we cannot say exactly how much there is and whether it is increasing or not.

Social Variables

ECOLOGY OF MENTAL DISORDERS. The pioneering study of the distribution of mental illness in a metropolitan area was based on nearly 35,000 cases admitted to public and private hospitals in the Chicago

[23] Daniel Blaine and John H. Baird, "The Neuropsychiatric Program of the Veteran's Administration," *American Journal of Psychiatry*, 103 (January, 1947), 463–66.
[24] Leo Srole, Thomas S. Langner, Stanley T. Michael, Marvin K. Opler, and Thomas A. C. Rennie, *Mental Health in the Metropolis* (New York: McGraw-Hill, 1962).
[25] Jerome G. Manis, Milton J. Brawer, Chester L. Hunt, and Leonard C. Kercher, "Estimating the Prevalence of Mental Illness," *American Sociological Review*, 29 (February, 1964), 84–89.
[26] Srole *et al., op. cit.*, 151.
[27] Gerald Gurin, Joseph Veroff, and Sheila Feld, *Americans View Their Mental Health* (New York: Basic Books, 1960), 262.

area from 1922 to 1934.[28] For total admissions, there was a concentration of high rates near the city center and a progressive decline outward in all directions, except for outlying industrial zones. Rates for foreign born and Negroes as well as for native whites varied with the type of district in which they lived. The rates for poor people were not high unless they lived in high-rate districts. The rates in these districts were high for those who had grown up there, so the rates were not explained by transiency in the rooming-house districts or by "drifting" into the area to stay. Paresis rates were highest in rooming-house districts, where the patrons of houses of prostitution are concentrated. Alcoholic psychosis rates were highest in districts with the highest rates of chronic alcoholism, which were areas that tended to have poor housing, many lodgers and other renters, and many people on relief rolls. Other findings that suggest causal explanations will be noted below. In general, subsequent studies have supported the ecological findings of this study.[29]

SOCIAL CLASS AND MENTAL ILLNESS. Studies generally have agreed about the relationship of disorders to social class. A study in New Haven, Connecticut, was based on clinical outpatients as well as hospital admissions, and involved analysis of the social class groups from which the patients came.[30] Total illness, and particularly schizophrenia, was highest in the lowest class group. The higher the class position, the lower the proportion of schizophrenia. Neurosis was disproportionately high in the middle- and upper-class groups, and low in the lower. It is quite possible that the class differences in the incidence of different disorders are much smaller than was found, due to the fact that lower income groups tend not to seek treatment except for the most severe cases. Possibly there is much neurosis among the lower class, but not much treatment sought for it. Yet there are social forces in the different classes that seem to be associated with the illness rates, as we shall see in the following sections.

The New Haven study and most others to date have used the social class of the patient rather than his class of origin. Following

[28] Robert E. L. Faris and H. Warren Dunham, *Mental Disorders in Urban Areas* (Chicago: University of Chicago Press, 1939).
[29] H. Warren Dunham, "Current Status of Ecological Research in Mental Disorder," in Arnold Rose (ed.), *Mental Health and Mental Disorder* (New York: Norton, 1955).
[30] August B. Hollingshead and Frederick C. Redlich, *Social Class and Mental Illness* (New York: John Wiley & Sons, 1958).

the lead of some English researchers, a study has been made using the patient's father's class position, and the usual class differences were not found, particularly in the case of schizophrenia. In other words, schizophrenics came about equally from all five of the class groups, identified by occupation and education of the father. This was interpreted to mean that the patient's schizophrenia affects his occupational and other role performances, so that the illness affects the class position rather than the other way around.[31] Perhaps the common economic and educational statuses of parents are less important than other aspects of the style of life, suggesting the need to study the patient's particular interpersonal experiences in his family and other conditioning groups.

SOCIAL ISOLATION. Faris and Dunham found schizophrenia to be associated at least statistically with the processes that isolate the individual, experiences frequent for both children and adults in urban zones in transition. Faris suggested cautiously that actual experiences of isolation lead to schizophrenia,[32] and considerable evidence since then seems to bear him out.[33] A more recent study, however, provides findings which challenge this interpretation.[34] The schizophrenic person does withdraw from his social environment, but perhaps because his social contacts are too painful for him to cope with. There is indeed much isolation of the person in the anonymous transitional areas, yet in these areas there are families, gangs, schools, churches, fellow lodgers, and crowds. As we saw in Chapter 2, some persons in these anomic neighborhoods become alienated while others do not, and there are various forms of adjustment to alienation. Even if isolation is a causal factor in schizophrenia, we should note that the child can also be socially isolated in other urban areas and social classes. The person can evidently isolate himself emotionally in a variety of situations. Even lifelong, extreme social isolation appears less con-

[31] H. Warren Dunham, Patricia Phillips, and Barbara Srinivasan, "A Research Note on Diagnosed Mental Illness and Social Class," *American Sociological Review,* 31 (April, 1966), 223–27.
[32] Robert E. L. Faris, "Cultural Isolation and the Schizophrenic Personality," *American Journal of Sociology,* 40 (September, 1934), 155–64.
[33] E. Gartly Jaco, "The Social Isolation Hypothesis and Schizophrenia," *American Sociological Review,* 19 (October, 1954), 567–77.
[34] Melvin L. Kohn and John A. Clausen, "Social Isolation and Schizophrenia," *American Sociological Review,* 20 (June, 1955), 265–73.

ducive than marginal social adjustment to the development of various disorders that result in psychiatric hospitalization of the aged.[35]

CONTRADICTORY NORMS. The Chicago study and others have found schizophrenia rates high in areas with sharp cultural conflicts, particularly where different immigrant groups are present. The child experiences cultural conflict between the new culture and his parents' ways. Thus, far from being isolated, the person may be unable to cope with conflicting demands. Numerous researchers and clinicians have suggested that neuroses are associated with strong demands on the person, combined with inconsistent behavior on the part of parents or others making the demands. This creates dilemmas for the person that are somewhat similar to those sometimes resulting from the existence of contradictory role models, such as working wife vs. homemaker. The person is aware of alternatives, yet is unable to accept the consequences of any given choice. A study of the Hutterites found that they have low rates of schizophrenia and higher rates of manic-depressive psychosis, due apparently to the strong demands made on the person to do his part in a cooperative community. The person may become extremely anxious, but is not so likely to isolate himself from others. Rates of recovery were very high.[36]

Faris and Dunham found that the rates of neurosis and manic-depressive psychosis were distributed almost randomly over the Chicago area, and suggested that both were associated with childhood experiences of overprotection that produce what psychiatrists call "soft personalities," followed by sudden exposure to extreme hardships. For example, an extremely overprotected working-class son must support his family when his father dies, or the business tycoon's coddled son is told he must work his way through college. These are traumatic instances of the impact on the person of contradictory norms, involving discontinuity of experience.

Treatment Issues

HOSPITAL FACILITIES. The Veterans Administration produced a revolution in hospitalization of mental patients by pioneering in the use

---

[35] Marjorie Fiske Lowenthal, "Social Isolation and Mental Illness in Old Age," *American Sociological Review*, 29 (February, 1964), 54–70.

[36] Joseph Eaton and Robert J. Weil, *Culture and Mental Disorders* (New York: The Free Press, 1955).

of tranquilizers and anti-depressant drugs. When these were intro-duced generally in the treatment of inpatients in the midfifties, there was a serious shortage of hospital beds and the nation was still trying to correct the overcrowded, unsanitary conditions publicized so vividly a few years before. We have seen that within a decade the number of mental patients in hospital beds had been reduced considerably, yet in that same period the number of persons treated at least doubled. The use of the drugs resulted in shorter stays, since people could be returned to their homes sooner and their emotional reactions kept under control under outpatient supervision. So more people are enter-ing hospitals and more are being treated as outpatients,[37] and more people are entering hospitals voluntarily. Thus it would seem that an increasing proportion of people are getting professional help for their emotional problems. General hospitals have been more willing to take mental patients, since they can use the drugs to keep them under control, and Blue Cross and insurance companies have been adding coverage for hospital treatment for mental illness.

These changes have not only increased the amount of mental health care, they have also caused emotional disorders to be handled more like illness and less like deviant behavior. There has been some reaction against this trend, especially against the higher rates of dis-charge from state institutions. Sometimes this is because the family, which has usually made the commitment, does not want the person back in the home. This is not necessarily a matter of dislike or in-convenience, since the belief of fact is still held by many people that there is nothing that can be done to help a psychotic person. There seems to be some anxiety about the fact that a great many people are now abroad in the community who have been discharged from a mental institution or have been to an outpatient center. This conflicts with the century-old tradition of putting "insane" people behind walls and forgetting about them. Thus, in signing a 1965 bill to provide federal aid for payment of doctors, nurses, and other personnel in community mental health centers, President Johnson commented that even more mental patients can be taken out of hospital beds and cared for in their home communities. Perhaps we will yet give the most emotionally disturbed among us the sympathy and support they receive in many folk societies and among the Hutterites—quite

---

[37] Morris and Charlotte Schwartz, *Social Patterns of Mental Patient Care* (New York: Columbia University Press, 1964).

a shift from the bestial treatment of more than a century ago, and also from the out-of-sight orientation.

INVOLUNTARY TREATMENT. Much of the treatment for mental illness, especially of those committed to public institutions, is involuntary. Many patients, perhaps most, believe they do not belong in mental hospitals, and when they talk with researchers their reference groups are outside the institution.[38] One study found that the inmates of mental hospitals do not have pride in the institution as inmates of a correctional institution do, so the collective outbursts are much more individualistic and lacking in organized structure than those of a prison.[39] So long as identification with the outside community remains paramount, it seems unlikely that mental patients will develop strong inmate pride, especially in view of the preoccupation with self, combined with more rapid turnover.

Research in two different states indicates that the commitment hearings are very brief and that the complaint of insanity is almost always accepted.[40] This receives justification both on the ground of the person's welfare and that of his family and community, though involuntary detention and attempts to change behavior against the individual's will evidently often cause guilt feelings in the family and among the legal and medical personnel involved. The use of community power and bureaucratized psychiatry to control the conduct of the mentally ill person has been portrayed as a conflict between mass society and the individual. At least one psychiatrist has included community mental health centers and other places of community psychiatry (the open-door policy, integration of mental health facilities, and preventive efforts) in this perspective, objecting to the liberalization of psychiatric commitment proceedings as an unwarranted infringement of individual freedom.[41] The opposing view is

---

[38] H. Warren Dunham and S. Kirsen Weinberg, *The Culture of the State Mental Hospital* (Detroit: Wayne State University Press, 1960).

[39] Roland Wulbert, "Inmate Pride in Total Institutions," *American Journal of Sociology*, 71 (July, 1965), 1–9.

[40] Dorothy Miller and Michael Schwartz, "County Lunacy Commission Hearings: Some Observations of Commitments to a State Mental Hospital," *Social Problems*, 14 (Summer, 1966), 26–35; Thomas J. Scheff, "Decision Rules, Types of Error, and Their Consequences in Medical Diagnosis," *Behavioral Science*, 8 (April, 1963), 97–107.

[41] Ronald Leifer, "Community Psychiatry and Social Power," *Social Problems*, 14 (Summer, 1966), 16–22; *cf.* Leonard Schatzman and Anselm Strauss, "A Sociology of Psychiatry: A Perspective and Some Organizing Foci," *Social Problems*, 14 (Summer, 1966), 3–16.

that such procedures are designed to increase public acceptance, bring treatment to more people, and make treatment centers smaller and more personal and more subject to local control in spite of federal support.[42] At present this is an issue primarily among professionals, probably because the public at large perceives mental illness mainly as deviant behavior. Some politically ultraconservative groups have attempted to make this a general issue, claiming that involuntary treatment is a political weapon and a Communist plot (see Chapter 3).

PERSONNEL FOR MENTAL HEALTH. Federal and state attempts to increase the supply of mental health personnel meet with opposition for various reasons, including the resistance of many individuals and groups to any new public expenditures. As we noted in Chapter 5, health values compete with other values. Yet a number of attempts to increase the supply have been made, and some new types of professionals are being developed to supplement the work of the psychiatrist. The medical profession resisted the development of clinical psychology in the post-World War II years, but eventually the Ph.D.'s in that field outnumbered the psychiatrists, supplemented by many clinical psychologists trained at the Master's degree level. The psychiatrist has retained control of the mental hospitals and clinics, but has accepted clinical psychologists as valuable team members, along with psychiatric social workers. Psychiatric nurses are the most numerous professionals in the mental health field, and the number of public health nurses with mental health training is increasing.[43] Most numerous of all employees in mental health facilities are the attendants, usually ill-paid and not very well educated or trained. In view of the fact that they have the most contact with the patients, improvements in their pay and training could perhaps go far in making treatment more effective.

TREATMENT METHODS. Some professional and public issues have arisen over the use of the tranquilizing and antidepressant drugs. At first there were undue claims made for them, but now they have become accepted for their value in keeping patients calm and in a

---

[42] Gerald Caplan, "Some Comments on 'Community Psychiatry and Social Power'," *Social Problems*, 14 (Summer, 1966), 23–25. He calls attention especially to the provisions of the federal Community Mental Health Center Act of 1963.

[43] George W. Albee, *Mental Health Manpower Trends* (New York: Basic Books, 1959).

pleasant mood. There are occasional charges that the drugs are being over-used and that other attempts at therapy are being slighted, and sometimes that they have cruel effects analogous to those complained of in connection with electric shock therapy. These issues seem not to become major as long as there is a reasonable amount of information accompanying innovations.

Treatment issues today center on the emotional climate of treatment centers and of the home and community when the patient is discharged. Here the professionals find considerable resistance on the part of people who still identify mental illness closely with deviance. Families are upset when psychiatrists do not give them a label for the mental illness of one of their members, something now done deliberately by some professionals in order to avoid the stigma of such terms as "schizophrenia," "psychosis," or "paranoid."[44]

PREVENTION. The increased use of community mental health centers, along with more effective school counseling and other efforts, promises to prevent a good deal of mental illness from becoming serious. Getting support for this approach depends on acceptance of the belief of fact that mental illness is often developed rather than inherited, and perhaps also that good mental health is as contagious as poor emotional health is. A study of the use of a psychiatric outpatient clinic found that knowledge of psychological and psychiatric explanations of behavior is more important in decisions to use the service than is the location of the center.[45] Proposals for the expansion of preventive efforts bring mental health into competition with other values, especially when government expenditures are involved.

Mental Retardation

Both before and during the long period when the mentally ill were kept out of sight in institutions, the general public made little distinction between the mentally ill and the retarded, and often they were quartered together. Some mentally defective persons are emotionally disturbed, but the reason for their deviant behavior is usually that they do not understand community norms and the reasons behind them. As knowledge grew and attitudes changed about mental illness,

---

[44] Karl Menninger, "A New Approach to Mental Illness," *The Saturday Evening Post*, April 25, 1964, reprinted in *Reader's Digest*, March, 1965, 71–73.
[45] Edna E. Raphael, "Community Structure and Acceptance of Psychiatric Aid," *American Journal of Sociology*, 69 (January, 1964), 340–58.

the distinction between illness and retardation became somewhat better appreciated. However, for a long time the sole issue concerning the mentally retarded remained humane treatment, because it was generally believed that nothing could be done about their condition.

After the growth and dissemination of some new knowledge about mental retardation, the belief grew that something can be done, and demands for action received support. It has been shown that some forms of mental deficiency can be prevented, the incapacity reduced in some, and that a completely satisfactory social adjustment is possible in others. Idiots (I.Q. below 25) and imbeciles (I.Q. from 25 to 50) are assumed to result mainly from either heredity or brain damage, so prevention is the suggested emphasis. Morons (I.Q. from 50 to 75) are more likely to result at least in part from cultural deprivation, and therefore to be most susceptible to special training efforts. Children in middle and upper class families are most likely to be detected early if they deviate from official definitions of mental normality; ethnic minorities, and other groups with high levels of dependency and low levels of education are least likely to identify their children as retarded.[46]

Before 1954 the focus was on humane institutional care, but after that the state health departments began to offer special services for mentally retarded children. The federal government has encouraged such efforts, especially since President Kennedy's appeals that the problem be given more attention. The National Institute of Neurological Diseases and Blindness has been spending several millions of dollars each year for research, technical assistance, and grants to states and private groups, and considerable amounts are also being expended for mental retardation by the National Institute of Mental Health. The emphasis on research is heavy, in the belief that more knowledge will make possible some breakthroughs in prevention and treatment. School districts are being encouraged to offer special education for the mentally retarded, but a substantial majority of those who could probably benefit from such programs have no access to them. There is much educational effort designed to promote acceptance of mentally retarded people, but their deviant conduct is difficult for the community to tolerate and adjust to. Considering this fact, the amount of change in public attitudes and in programs of action

---

[46] Jane E. Mercer, "Social System Perspective and Clinical Perspective: Frames of Reference for Understanding Career Patterns of Persons Labelled As Mentally Retarded," *Social Problems*, 13 (Summer, 1965), 18–34.

in the past decade and a half has been considerable. Much publicity has highlighted the special talents of some of the mentally retarded, such as musical ability and memory powers, and of the spectacular improvements in literacy and social adjustment accomplished in some cases. Whether the hopes for prevention and cure exceed the possibilities of achievement remains to be seen, but beliefs of fact have been changing rapidly. These changes have in turn activated humanitarian values concerning the mentally retarded, but these conflict with other values when public expenditures are under consideration.

PERSPECTIVE

After a long history of treating the mentally ill and retarded as depraved and incurable, the application of humane values resulted in the construction of special institutions for them in the nineteenth century. They were then out of sight, and their afflictions still carried a heavy stigma. While no dramatic discovery such as the Germ Theory came along, increased knowledge of causes and the dissemination of Freudian and other ideas about treatment possibilities led to the slowly growing belief that mental illness could be controlled to some extent. Humane treatment has recurred as an issue from time to time, but in this century the emphasis has been increasingly on treatment and prevention of mental illness. As for mental retardation, the focus finally shifted to treatment and prevention in the fifties. Perspectives, and the officially recorded incidence of different disorders, vary a good deal from one social class to another.

Yet our knowledge of both causes and cures of emotional disorders and mental deficiency is still limited. Perhaps the wonder is that there is a willingness to commit so much money and effort to research in these areas, but the belief is evidently strong that new knowledge will be found which will make more effective control possible. There is also much opposition, however, to expenditures for research and for expansion of treatment facilities, some of it because of alleged infringement of individual freedom, some because of the belief that little or nothing effective can be done. But probably the main basis for opposition is still that the behavior of emotionally disturbed and mentally retarded people is deviant, and thus is perceived as a threat to the family and community. The open-door policy of the mental hospital, increased use of outpatient facilities, and other efforts to enlist the sympathy and aid of the total community in helping the mentally ill and retarded have been advanced in the face of the persistence of strong feelings about the conduct of these deviants. The freeing of many hospital beds by the use of new drugs for controlling patients and the resultant extension of care to a great many more of the mentally ill has aroused anxieties about how the community will cope with these deviants in its midst.

QUESTIONS FOR DISCUSSION AND STUDY

1. Can you think of some pattern of deviant behavior that is not a major public issue? Why isn't it?
2. Is mental illness a new social problem in the twentieth century? Explain carefully, keeping in mind the definition of a social problem used in this book.
3. In what ways has public discussion of mental illness been similar to that of physical illness, and in what ways different?
4. Why does a psychiatrist or clinical psychologist care about the general public's attitude toward mental illness?
5. Find and evaluate a statement in a newspaper or magazine about trends in mental illness.
6. Are there differences in mental illness among the different social classes, or only in the official treatment accorded to them? Explain fully.
7. Is there a causal relationship between schizophrenia and social isolation? If so, what is its nature and direction?
8. What was an unanticipated consequence of the experimentation by the Veterans Administration with tranquilizers and anti-depressant drugs? Does this represent a revolution in knowledge comparable to the Germ Theory? Explain.
9. In your own experience, what is the most discussed public issue concerning the treatment of the mentally ill?
10. What are the similarities and the differences in the way the public perceives mental illness and mental retardation?

SELECTED READING

Davis, James A., *Education for Positive Mental Health* (Chicago: Aldine Publ. Co., 1965).

Driver, Edwin D., *The Sociology and Anthropology of Mental Illness: A Reference Guide* (Amherst, Mass.: University of Massachusetts Press, 1965).

Dunham, H. Warren, *Community and Schizophrenia: An Epidemiological Analysis* (Detroit: Wayne State University Press, 1965).

Elinson, Jack, Padilla, Elena, and Perkins, Marvin E., *Public Image of Mental Health Services* (New York: Mental Health Materials Center, 1967).

Freeman, Howard E., and Simmons, Ozzie G., *The Mental Patient Comes Home* (New York: John Wiley & Sons, 1963).

Hollingshead, August B., and Rogler, Lloyd H., "Lower Socioeconomic Status and Mental Illness," *Sociology and Social Research,* 46 (July, 1962), 387–96.

Jackson, Elton F., "Status Consistency and Symptoms of Stress," *American Sociological Review,* 27 (August, 1962), 469–80.

Langner, Thomas, and Michael, Stanley T., *Life Stress and Mental Health* (New York: The Free Press, 1963).

Levinson, Daniel J., and Gallagher, Eugene B., *Patienthood in the Mental Hospital* (Boston: Houghton Mifflin Co., 1964).

Martin, Walter, "Socially Induced Stress: Some Converging Theories," *Pacific Sociological Review,* 8 (Fall, 1965), 63–69.

Riessman, Frank, Cohen, Jerome, and Pearl, Arthur (eds.), *Mental Health of the Poor* (New York: The Free Press, 1964).

Rushing, William A., *The Psychiatric Professions* (Chapel Hill: University of North Carolina Press, 1964).

Schwartz, Morris, and Schwartz, Charlotte, *Social Patterns of Mental Patient Care* (New York: Columbia University Press, 1964).

Srole, Leo, Langner, Thomas S., Michael, Stanley T., Opler, Marvin K., and Rennie, Thomas A. C., *Mental Health in the Metropolis* (New York: McGraw-Hill, 1962).

Strauss, Anselm, Schatzman, Leonard, Bucher, Rue, Ehrlich, Danata, and Sabshin, Melvin, *Psychiatric Ideologies and Institutions* (New York: The Free Press, 1964).

Turner, R. Jay, and Wagenfeld, Morton O., "Occupational Mobility and Schizophrenia: An Assessment of the Social Causation and Social Selection Hypotheses," *American Sociological Review,* 32 (February, 1967), 104–13.

Weinberg, S. Kirson (ed.), *The Sociology of Mental Disorders* (Chicago: Aldine Publ. Co., 1967).

As a topic of popular concern, the subject of crime, for a number of reasons, has been overlaid with an unusual amount of misinformation and misinterpretation. In the first place, the average person faces the problems of crime with certain basic biases and certain time-honored preconceptions steeped in the folklore of his culture. Secondly, it is evident that our knowledge of crime and criminals comes to us by highly selective routes—through gossip, the opinions of others, popular legend and fantasy, and through various forms of public reporting. Rarely do individuals come into direct contact with crime and criminals—not, at least, in a readily recognizable form. The result is an inevitable distortion brought about by fragmentary and indirect information, many steps removed from reality and based upon the most unusual and sensational cases.[1]

8. Criminal and Delinquent Behavior

DEFINITIONS OF CRIME AND DELINQUENCY

Crime Defined

Crime is behavior that deviates from the norms of a political community to a degree considered dangerously antisocial, so that it is defined and punishments are specified for it in the criminal law. Stated more technically from the standpoint of legal criteria, "Crime is an intentional act or omission in violation of criminal law, committed without defense or justification, and sanctioned by the law as a felony or misdemeanor."[2] Crime does not include all nonconformity, only that which is officially considered such a serious threat to the person, his property, or to community institutions that agencies of government intervene and use sanctions to control it. It does not include all law violation. Crime is only those acts prohibited by specific norms in the criminal law statutes and cases, not in other areas of public law (constitutional, administrative, *etc.*) or of private law (contracts, property, torts, *etc.*) Crime thus corresponds to vio-

---

[1] Herbert A. Bloch and Gilbert Geis, *Man, Crime and Society* (New York: Random House, 1962), 4.
[2] Paul W. Tappan, *Crime, Justice and Correction* (New York: McGraw-Hill, 1960), 10.

lations of the mores in simpler, stable societies, except that criminal law norms and their underlying values lack uniform support.[3]

Juvenile Delinquency Defined

Juvenile delinquency consists of acts committed by persons under 18 years of age (or 17 or 16 in some states) that would be crimes if committed by older persons, or conduct considered sufficiently deviant to warrant control by the juvenile court. Before the rapid diffusion of juvenile court statutes, the first of which was adopted in 1899 in Illinois, child offenders were punished under the criminal law and the concept of juvenile delinquency was unknown.[4] It was created to exempt child offenders from the procedures and punishments of the criminal court, and to emphasize protection and improvement of the child. Juvenile courts were also given jurisdiction over dependent and neglected children, and the same informal (court of equity) procedures were to be used for both this and the delinquency jurisdictions.[5]

CRIME AND DELINQUENCY AS A
SOCIAL PROBLEM

The occasional deviant in a highly stable society violates norms that are otherwise universally accepted and followed. A stable society based on kinship ties is relatively undifferentiated and the role of enforcer of the mores is assumed spontaneously by the wronged persons or, under appropriate circumstances, by other group members who see or learn of the deviant conduct. Deviators from the mores are few, and are either quickly brought into line or eliminated from the society by banishment or death. The swift response requires no reflection, being dictated by tradition, and it does not become a community issue. Violations of the mores thus do not constitute a social problem. When social change undermines the mores and political organization begins to replace kin organization, informal sanctions

---

[3] F. James Davis *et al.*, *Society and the Law* (New York: The Free Press, 1962), 56–58. Durkheim considered penal law to be based on "mechanical solidarity," that social unity made possible by social similarity. See Emile Durkheim, *On the Division of Labor in Society* (New York: The Macmillan Co., 1933), Chapters 1–3.
[4] Herbert H. Lou, *Juvenile Courts in the United States* (Chapel Hill: University of North Carolina Press, 1927), 12–19.
[5] *Ibid.* 2–7, 20–22.

against deviants from the mores are replaced by criminal law punishments, administered by occupants of official positions. The emergent criminal law norms presumably may become issues,[6] at least where some degree of public discussion is possible.

When courts and legislatures identify particular deviant acts as crimes, the values underlying the legal norms are by implication universally agreed upon in the society, or the officials believe they should be. If they were, law enforcement would involve technical problems of detection, detention, prosecution, punishment, rehabilitation, and prevention; but crime and delinquency would not be social problems, not unless the means of control posed major value dilemmas. Actually, there are strong conflicts about the desirability of enforcing criminal laws as well as over values related to the means of control. In addition to conflicting values there are disagreements over beliefs of fact about the causes of the deviance and about the effectiveness of various programs of social control. As new priorities of value and new beliefs of fact about behavior and new techniques of control are publicized, changes are brought about in programs of crime and delinquency control, when conditions are favorable. But new issues arise and old ones are more often continued or redefined than resolved, and the broader dilemma over frequent deviance from criminal law norms continues.

THE MEASUREMENT OF CRIME AND DELINQUENCY

Indexes of Crime

THE RELATIVITY OF CRIME. A major difficulty in the measurement of crime is that it is not a stable unit, but one that varies with official definitions of particular offenses and with law enforcement practices. A given crime, such as larceny, may be defined quite differently in different states at any one time. Crime varies from time to time within the same jurisdiction; new crimes may be added, some dropped or not enforced, and others given new definitions. There are also variations within a given jurisdiction because of differential law en-

---

[6] C. Ray Jeffery, "Criminal Justice and Social Change," Chapter 8 in Davis et al., op. cit., 264–77; Sir Henry Sumner Maine, Ancient Law (New ed.; New York: Holt, Rinehart & Winston, 1930, first publ. 1861); Sidney Post Simpson and Julius Stone, Cases and Readings on Law and Society, 3 vols. (St. Paul, Minn.: West Publishing Co., 1948), Book I.

forcement for different age, sex, and social class groups, and for different situations in which violations occur.[7] Thus crime is relative to place, time, social category, and circumstance; so it varies with the capriciousness of the general public as well as of legislators, policemen, judges, and other officials.

Statements about the amount of crime in the nation and about differences among states and cities must take into account the variations in definitions, and conclusions about trends are affected by changes in definitions over time. The Federal Bureau of Investigation has attempted to minimize this problem by providing all police departments with a set of standardized categories to use when forwarding data for the *Uniform Crime Reports*. This cannot correct for variations in law enforcement, but it has apparently helped somewhat on the relativity of definitions. In 1952, more than two decades after the introduction of standard categories, the Police Department of New York City reported that crime in 1951 had increased 254 per cent over 1950. The explanation was that a new method of recording crimes for the metropolitan area had been developed. Many other surprises have appeared in the data sent to the F.B.I., so the hope of stable statistical units is far from realized. Improved recording procedures were instituted in 1958 by the F.B.I., but this solves only a small part of the index problem.

Since the best official efforts have not eliminated the problems of relativity of the index, it has been argued that the legal definition of crime must be abandoned for scientific research. Sellin has proposed that crime be defined as violations of conduct norms;[8] others have suggested violations of the mores or other standards of societal welfare. One difficulty with this approach is in identifying the norms, presumably to be done by objective researchers rather than capricious legislators, judges, or other office-holders. Once the norms are clarified, the resulting subject matter would be different from the criminology based on the legal approach, but allegedly more dependable and capable of illuminating questions of law violation. Actually, complex societies do not have mores in the sense of norms of societal welfare uniformly supported by informal sanctions; so the researcher would have to decide what norms other than criminal laws he is

---

[7] Edwin H. Sutherland and Donald R. Cressey, *Principles of Criminology* (7th ed.: Philadelphia: J. B. Lippincott Co., 1966), 16–17.
[8] Thorsten Sellin, *Culture Conflict and Crime* (New York: Social Science Research Council, 1938), 17–32.

seeking, how they are to be classified, and how the existence of conflicting norms is to be handled. The problem of variations in criminal
laws and their enforcement is not really solved by this approach even
at best, since *other norms of conduct are also relative to place, time,
social category, and circumstance. Students of crime and delinquency
have therefore generally used the legal definitions, but have emphasized the limitations of the official indexes and have tried to relate
their efforts to broader knowledge of deviance and social control.*

THE IMPOSSIBILITY OF DETECTING ALL VIOLATIONS. No official index
measures all crime because a great deal of it goes undetected. In
addition to understating the total amount of crime at a given time,
statistics may provide a fuller estimate of some types of crime than
others, and may result in false conclusions about trends. Variations
in law enforcement, in willingness to notify legal authorities of
crimes, in keeping records—in all the factors that may influence the
index—may produce an unrepresentative picture of the amount of
different types of crime and of the total.

In the light of this problem, Sellin suggested that the least distorted index is the one closest to the crime, the crimes known to the
police.[9] This is the chief index relied on in the *Uniform Crime Reports*
for statements about the amount of crime, though they also report
arrests and other data. A great many crimes known to the police do
not result in arrest, especially for the different varieties of theft, the
most common type of felony. Crimes of violence are much more likely
to eventuate in arrests. Moving still further from the crime in terms
of law enforcement procedures, many of those arrested are not prose-
cuted, and many of these are not convicted. For every 100 felonies
known to the police in America in 1960, only 14 persons were convicted. Rates of prosecution and conviction vary widely from one type
of crime to another. The number of inmates in penal institutions
provides the smallest estimate of the amount of crime, and the most
unrepresentative, because selective processes occur at every stage of
law enforcement.

Yet the crimes known to the police index is an inadequate measure, since a large and unknown amount of crime is not reported, and
there is a greater chance that the police will learn of some types
rather than of others. *The "crimes known" index is the best one*

---

[9] Thorsten Sellin, *Research Memorandum on Crime in the Depression* (New
York: Social Science Research Council, 1937), Chapter 4.

available, but it is not very good.[10] *It is partial, unrepresentative of different types, and reflects unknown variations in law enforcement.* There is some evidence that almost all men and women have at some time committed crimes, often major felonies, suggesting a crime rate many times higher than officially recorded ones.[11] The use of the conduct norm type of definition would not solve this problem, since it would be even more difficult to develop an adequate index of such violations. Fortunately, research into the causes of criminal behavior does not depend on an adequate index, although knowledge of trends in the amount of crime does.

Indexes of Juvenile Delinquency

The two basic difficulties discussed above also hamper the measurement of juvenile delinquency, only more so. Statutory definitions of juvenile delinquency vary widely, and all of them include some kind of open-end phrase which can justify the inclusion of any conduct the court wishes to take under its jurisdiction. Even in the same state or city the procedures of detection, detention, court hearing, and subsequent official treatment of juvenile offenders are highly varied, so court statistics misrepresent the distribution of delinquency by sex, social class, racial, and ethnic groups. Further complicating the problem, delinquency figures sent to the U.S. Children's Bureau before 1955 were partial and highly unrepresentative of the nation. The statistics were mainly from urban areas, and the Northeast part of the country reported much more heavily than other regions.[12] From 1955 on the figures have been obtained by using 502 representative courts in 230 sample areas used by the U.S. Bureau of the Census in making population estimates. This resolution of the question of representativeness, however, has not eliminated the problem of relativity. The legal meaning of juvenile delinquency varies a great deal with respect to place, time, social category, and circumstance.

As for the other basic difficulty, official records enable us to make only the vaguest of guesses concerning the total amount of delinquent behavior. The best available index, the one reported to the U.S. Children's Bureau, is cases handled by the juvenile court. This cor-

---

[10] Bloch and Geis, *op. cit.*, 142–49; Sutherland and Cressey, *op. cit.*, 27–36.

[11] Sutherland and Cressey, *op. cit.*, 41–49.

[12] *Ibid.*, 37–38; James F. Short, Jr., and F. Ivan Nye, "Extent of Unrecorded Juvenile Delinquency: Tentative Conclusions," *Journal of Criminal Law, Criminology and Police Science*, 49 (November–December, 1958), 296–302.

responds roughly to the prosecution rate of adult crime, considerably more removed from the offense than the "crimes known" index. Making it an even poorer indicator, many if not most juvenile courts do not report half or more of their cases, the ones they classify as having been handled in some type of "unofficial" manner. Attempts have been made in some cities to get a fuller count by compiling in a central registry the names of children known by social work agencies to have committed delinquent acts. If these estimates are valid, less than half of all delinquent offenders are known to the courts, and so are not counted even as unofficial cases. Furthermore, the courts apparently undercount serious offenders as compared with minor ones and girls as compared with boys.[13] But the social work agencies index is also only a partial measure, judging by the studies of admitted delinquencies on the part of high school and college students. Evidently, most if not all students have engaged in minor delinquency at some time, and many have repeatedly committed serious offenses without being caught or at least without being officially recorded.[14] It would seem that a considerable amount of youthful deviation is tolerated and expected, but that immoderate amounts of offenses considered most dangerous are likely to call forth legal sanctions.[15]

Many referrals to the juvenile court are by parents, teachers, or acquaintances, but two-thirds or more nationally are by police officers. It is estimated that the police warn the child, take him home or to school, or take other independent action in about three-fourths of the cases that come to their attention, detaining only one-fourth for court handling.[16] The manner in which police officers use their discretion obviously has a great effect on delinquency statistics. One study found that police handling was influenced by prior records of delinquency, race, grooming, and demeanor. It appeared that the majority of cases of first offense were handled on the basis of the child's demeanor toward the police officer.[17] Both the fact and the nature of

[13] Ruth Shonle Cavan, *Juvenile Delinquency* (Philadelphia: J. B. Lippincott Co., 1962), 32–34; Sophia M. Robison, *Can Delinquency Be Measured?* (New York: Columbia University Press, 1936); Sophia M. Robison, *Juvenile Delinquency: Its Nature and Control* (New York: Holt, Rinehart & Winston, 1960), Chapters 2 and 4.

[14] Short and Nye, *op. cit.*, 297.

[15] Cavan, *op. cit.*, 32–38.

[16] *Ibid.*, 31.

[17] Irving Piliavin and Scott Briar, "Police Encounters with Juveniles," *American Journal of Sociology*, 70 (September, 1964), 206–14.

official treatment may influence more than the immediate statistics, because they affect the child's conception of self and the reactions of others toward him.

The Amount of Crime and Delinquency

The number of major crimes known to the police that were reported to the Federal Bureau of Investigation in 1964 was 2,604,400, a rise of 13 per cent over 1963, as recorded crime continued to increase faster than the rise in population. The figure for major crimes in 1963 was 10 per cent above 1962 and 16 per cent higher than the three-year average for 1960–62.[18] From 1940 to 1960 the number of reported major crimes nearly doubled while the population increased somewhat above one-third, and in recent years the F.B.I. has contended that crime is increasing four times faster than the population. It would be helpful if increases were reported as rates (the ratio of major crimes to the population base) rather than number of crimes, but it is clear that the *rate* of *reported* major felonies has been increasing during the last three decades.

In 1964 the property crimes of burglary, auto theft, and larceny of $50 and over made up 87 per cent of all major crimes. The violent crimes of murder, aggravated assault, forcible rape, and robbery accounted for only 13 per cent. Burglary (theft by breaking and entering) was the largest category, representing nearly one-half of all major felonies. Burglary, larceny, and auto theft comprised about 19 in 20 major thefts, so reports of robbery (theft by force or threat of force) are relatively infrequent. Forty per cent of all larcenies were thefts from autos and of auto accessories. From the news emphasis one could easily gain the impression that the proportion of violent crime is much larger than it is. All categories of major crime have been contributing to the continuing increase in recorded offenses, with the figures for given types sometimes fluctuating a good deal from year to year.

But do the reported figures measure increases in crime or something else? It is quite possible that people have been reporting more crime to the police, that police recording procedures have improved so that they keep more complete records, and that police departments have made greater efforts to make arrests and make full reports because of public pressure for them to "solve the crime problem."

---

[18] Federal Bureau of Investigation, *Uniform Crime Reports* (Washington, D.C.: Government Printing Office, 1963 and 1964).

Many new criminal statutes have been passed to cope with the dangers of the automobile and other changing conditions of life; rapid urbanization means more reliance on formal social controls, and police surveillance gets more intensive as a city grows. Urbanization, together with an increase in the proportion of youth in the population, may well have increased the prevalence of criminal behavior, but perhaps not nearly so much as the official indexes indicate.

For a generation in America there has been what anthropologists call a "run of attention" on crime and delinquency, and it has been especially heavy since about 1950. Delinquency and crime have repeatedly been referred to as the "number one social problem," and the belief of fact that offenses are increasing by leaps and bounds has been widely shared. Newspapers and the other mass media have headlined the F.B.I. reports and stories of violent crimes, thus reinforcing the belief. Evidently there is no relationship between fluctuations in the crime coverage from one newspaper to another or between the amount of crime news in a paper and trends in crime in the area of its readership.[19] It is very likely that the belief in a soaring crime rate has been a "self-fulfilling prophecy," with persistent actions on the basis of the belief increasing the number of officially recorded crimes. Any conclusions about crime trends are suspect, since even the best available index measures but a fraction of total crime, and crime may even be decreasing in this century.[20] There has long been a large (but unknown) amount of criminal behavior in America, and no dubious conclusions about trends are needed to support the contention that it is a serious social problem, whether increasing, decreasing, or remaining the same. However, the belief of fact about the trend has had much influence on the discussion of the problem and on efforts to cope with it.

The picture is much the same for trends in statistics on juvenile offending. The official rates of delinquency have risen sharply. Before World War II the estimate by the U.S. Children's Bureau was that roughly 1 per cent of American children aged 10 through 17 were officially delinquent each year, but by 1952 the estimate had grown to 2 per cent.[21] These estimates, based at that time on voluntary and

[19] F. James Davis, "Crime News in Colorado Newspapers," *American Journal of Sociology*, 57 (January, 1952), 325–30.
[20] Daniel Bell, "The Myth of Crime Waves," Chapter 8 in *The End of Ideology* (New York: The Free Press, 1960), 137–58.
[21] Herbert A. Bloch and Frank T. Flynn, *Delinquency* (New York: Random House, 1956), 26–33. For a discussion of indexes of delinquency, see Thorsten

unrepresentative reporting from the courts, were widely publicized, contributing to the concern that led to hearings on delinquency by the Judiciary Committee of the United States Senate. It seems likely that the official figures overrate the increase, but that there has been a real and possibly continuing rise. It is possible that during the immediate pre–World War II years there was an unusually low rate of offending, at least by official records, so that the reported increases produced alarmist reactions.[22] The anxieties caused by both cold and hot wars can promote fears of general disorder and demands for control of domestic difficulties, thus influencing official actions, and delinquency is an available, tangible problem. The growing belief of fact that it is possible to rehabilitate young offenders as well as to deter them may also have encouraged juvenile court officials to enlarge their efforts. *It is quite likely that the actual prevalence of both adult and juvenile offending has been increasing, though we cannot be sure, and that the recorded increase has been inflated unwittingly by official actions prompted chiefly by the belief that the "true" rates of offending are leaping upwards.*

TYPES OF OFFENDING

Types of Criminal Behavior

The assumption in delineating different behavior systems of crime is that the variables and causal sequences vary from one type to another. Thus Sutherland, to forward the development of a satisfactory general theory of crime, set an example by studying the behavior systems of white-collar criminality and professional theft.[23] Cavan has suggested that a general theory of crime must be social-psychological —one that relates the person to various group influences.[24] Her scheme of types of criminal behavior, with adaptations, is as follows:

Sellin and Marvin E. Wolfgang, *The Measurement of Delinquency* (New York: John Wiley & Sons, 1964).

[22] Negley K. Teeters and David Matza, "The Extent of Delinquency in the United States," *Journal of Negro Education*, 28 (Summer, 1959), 200–13; reprinted in Ruth Shonle Cavan, *Readings in Juvenile Delinquency* (Philadelphia: J. B. Lippincott Co., 1964), 2–15.

[23] Sutherland and Cressey, *op. cit.*, Chapter 13, "Behavior Systems in Crime"; Edwin H. Sutherland, *The Professional Thief* (Chicago: University of Chicago Press, 1937); Sutherland, *White Collar Crime* (New York: Dryden, 1949).

[24] Ruth S. Cavan, *Criminology* (3rd ed.; New York: Thomas Y. Crowell Co., 1962), 684–714; *cf.* Norman S. Hayner, "Characteristics of Five Offender Types," *American Sociological Review*, 26 (February, 1961), 96–102.

1. Essentially Law-Abiding Offenders:
   (a) Casual (minor, for convenience, such as speeding or parking violations)
   (b) Occasional (not necessarily minor; offender feels ashamed)
   (c) Episodic (once-in-a-lifetime situations).
2. White-Collar Offenders (regular violators of the criminal code who do not view themselves as criminals and are not treated as such).
3. Professional Offenders:
   (a) Informal Groups
   (b) Formally Organized Groups
       (1) Organized criminal gangs
       (2) Syndicates (organized prostitution, gambling, and other vices)
       (3) Rackets (organized extortion of money by threat of force)
       (4) Corrupt political groups.
4. Maladjusted Offenders:
   (a) Habitual (frequent but nonprofessional violators who view themselves as failures in life)
   (b) Emotionally Ill
       (1) Psychotic
       (2) Neurotic
   (c) Psychopathic (lacking in conscience, and also in clinical symptoms of emotional illness).
5. Conformers to a Subcultural Group (loyal to subcultural norms that conflict with criminal law norms, such as noncompliance with draft laws by pacifists).

Types of Juvenile Delinquency

If crime is not a unitary phenomenon perhaps juvenile delinquency is not either, yet many researchers continue to treat it as a single behavior system. The same problems of explanation and largely similar variables apply alike to adult and juvenile offenders, and attempts to account for adult behavior systems usually include childhood experiences. Most attempts so far to classify different patterns of juvenile offending have limited utility and bear little relationship to adult behavior systems being used. Cavan's attempt is as follows:[25]

1. Offenses Primarily Injurious to Others:
   (a) Theft (all types)
   (b) Vandalism
   (c) Homicides
   (d) Other Assaults
2. Offenses Primarily Injurious to the Delinquent:
   (a) Vices

---

[25] Cavan, *Juvenile Delinquency, op. cit.,* Part III, "Patterns of Delinquency."

 (b) Sex Offenses
 (c) Use of Alcohol
 (d) Use of Drugs
3. Group and Isolated Delinquency:
 (a) Gang Activities
 (b) Isolated Offending Patterns

In this scheme the emotionally ill do not appear as a separate category; they are stressed in connection with patterns of isolated offending, and also brought into the discussion of some of the subtypes under "1" and "2."

THE STUDY OF CAUSES

Up From Single Factorism

Until well into this century the study of the causes of crime was a quest for *the* cause, a search for the one factor that would be a complete explanation of the behavior. So the strategy was to keep testing one variable after another, as if each had to be the *sufficient cause* or else no cause at all.

BIOLOGICAL DETERMINISMS. Biological explanations of criminal behavior dominated nineteenth-century Europe and America, usually in the form of some type of hereditary determinism. It was held that criminal behavior itself is inherited, or that criminal instincts are, or that criminals are distinct physical types. A few physical anthropologists and psychiatrists in America are still working on a modification of this last approach, contending that behavioral scientists have minimized the role of biological factors. The single-factor quest flourished in the United States at the turn of the century in the form of the "psychopathic" explanation, with various investigators attempting to prove that crime is due entirely to feeblemindedness, or epilepsy, or a particular psychosis, or neurosis, or some composite configuration.[26]

Consensus was reached in the sciences of human behavior during the twenties that heredity provides the raw material for human development, and thus the potential for both law-abiding and criminal behavior, but does not determine personality and specific patterns of behavior. The concept of instinct was rejected as inapplicable to human behavior and replaced by other concepts. Hereditary defects and

---

[26] Sutherland and Cressey, *op. cit.*, Chapters 6 and 8.

other biological factors may contribute to antisocial behavior, in combination with certain social experiences, but they may also help make someone President. Much of this type of perspective has apparently filtered into the thinking of people generally, but public discussions of crime and delinquency still reflect a good deal of biological determinism.

ENVIRONMENTAL DETERMINISMS. Rejection of the biological determinisms did not lead at once to rejection of the single-factor quest. A series of factors in the social environment received considerable study, especially poverty, housing, and the broken home. Since only one of the many phenomena associated with crime in the urban slum could be *the* cause, by single-factor logic, the others could not be causes at all. Eventual conclusions, such as that the effect of the broken home depends on the cause of the break,[27] and that poverty and poor housing are more likely to be statistically associated with causes of crime and delinquency than to be causes in themselves, depended on some new methods of research.

THE CONTROL GROUP METHOD. Delinquency may show a high correlation with broken homes, the main type of evidence put forth to support the arguments for environmental determinisms. But what if a group of nonoffenders of the same age, sex, and residential area as a group of offenders have an average broken home rate just as high? Tests using a control group of nonoffenders found little or no difference for one environmental determinism after another. The control group method is an application of statistical tests for sampling error, and should not be confused with the experiment. It blocked off many blind alleys in the study of causes, and it remains an important method in studies of crime and delinquency.

CASE HISTORY STUDIES. In the late twenties and early thirties several researchers began using case histories, usually classifying the seeming causes as either major or minor. The studies often involved several hundred cases, but some cases were developed in great detail and published in order to convey the offender's own perspectives and to illuminate

---

[27] H. Ashley Weeks, "Male and Female Broken Home Rates by Types of Delinquency," *American Sociological Review*, 5 (August, 1940), 601–09; Richard S. Sterne, *Delinquent Conduct and Broken Homes* (New Haven, Conn.: College & University Press Services, Inc., 1964).

the processes linking up the variables that seemed to be causes.[28] There are difficult problems in using this method, but the repeated finding that there were three to five major factors in the average case and additional minor factors provided another blow to single-factor determinisms. No given factor was invariably present in all the cases, so the notion of a *necessary* cause was abandoned along with the sufficient cause. Apparently, variables combine in different ways in the experiences of different offenders.

THE NONDELINQUENT MAJORITY. Another type of evidence, usually a by-product of various studies, provided a basis for rejecting single-factor explanations. For a given variable, it was noted that the majority of people with this factor in their experience do not become offenders. So if most children from broken homes do not become delinquent, for instance, this cannot be a sufficient cause or even a necessary one. We must begin with a group of people from broken homes in order to answer the question: What proportion of people from broken homes become delinquent? We must note, however, that the conclusion that the majority of people influenced by any given factor are nondelinquent refers only to behavior officially treated as delinquency. We have mentioned the studies which show that most people commit some delinquent acts, so in that light there would be a delinquent majority for any given factor. The repeated observation of the (officially) nonoffending majority still today helps to prevent misinterpretation of findings.

THE NON-X MAJORITY. Still another type of evidence is pointed out to discourage interpretations of the single-factor type—the finding that most offenders did not have a particular factor in their experience. To continue the broken home example, most members of a given selection of adult or juvenile offenders did not come from broken homes. This is different from saying that the majority of people from broken homes do not become offenders. Conclusions about the nondelinquent majority require a different population for each variable, but evidence of the non-X majority type is available in any control group or case history study of a group of offenders.

---

[28] Clifford R. Shaw, *The Jack-Roller* (Chicago: University of Chicago Press, 1930); Clifford R. Shaw and M. E. Moore, *The Natural History of a Delinquent Career* (Chicago: University of Chicago Press, 1931); Clifford R. Shaw and Associates, *Brothers in Crime* (Chicago: University of Chicago Press, 1938).

THE MULTIPLE-FACTOR PERSPECTIVE. Any single-factor explanation is contrary to any one of the above types of evidence, and together such studies toppled the entire quest. It was replaced by the *multiple-factor perspective, the search for the ways in which various contributing factors combine to produce delinquency and crime.* Whenever an interpretation of a new finding strays back in the single-factor direction, critics block the way by pointing to the types of evidence we have just surveyed.

The multiple-factor perspective has been called a counting game by those seeking the common denominators in order to construct an adequate general theory of crime.[29] One reaction to this criticism has been to cast the many factors into an actuarial or risk-factor framework on the assumption that the combined weight of many factors might successfully predict delinquent and criminal behavior. Prediction would make control possible, and would provide at least some clues to causal sequences.[30] At any rate, a statistical association need not be perfect in order to indicate a possible causal relationship between a given variable and delinquent behavior; it need not be a necessary or sufficient condition, or be free of intervening variables.[31] The multiple-factor perspective is an approach to causal explanation, around which theories may be constructed that tie together many variables in meaningful ways and that may facilitate successful predictions.

The Ecology of Crime and Delinquency

Generally speaking, recorded crime and delinquency are much more frequent in urban areas, and the further one goes from a large city the lower the rates. Some exceptions to this have been reported in other countries, but differences in law enforcement and in recording procedures make international comparisons very risky.[32] The rural-urban differences in America are especially great for property crimes and much smaller for violent crimes. Rural homicide rates are a little higher.[33] Urbanization seems to create conditions that produce a

---

[29] Sutherland and Cressey, *op. cit.*, 61–65.
[30] Walter C. Reckless, *The Etiology of Delinquent and Criminal Behavior* (New York: Social Science Research Council, 1943).
[31] Travis Hirshi and Hanan C. Selvin, "False Criteria of Causality in Delinquency Research," *Social Problems*, 13 (Winter, 1966), 254–68.
[32] Sutherland and Cressey, *op. cit.*, 187–92.
[33] Federal Bureau of Investigation, *Uniform Crime Reports* (Washington, D.C., Government Printing Office, 1960), 33.

higher rate of offending, but the behavioral differences may not be so great as the records show.[34] Urban areas rely more on formal social controls, and the larger the community the more efficient the law enforcement and keeping of records are likely to be.

Within the city, the general pattern has been high rates of offending in the zone adjacent to the central business district, declining with the distance outward from the central area.[35] These areas of high delinquency and crime are *zones in transition* from land use for residential to business and industrial purposes, and thus they are blighted housing or slum areas. While holding land in anticipation of selling at greatly increased prices later on, owners let buildings deteriorate and crowd them with families in need of low-rent housing.[36] In these tenement and rooming house areas delinquent gangs flourish, along with professional crime, the vices, and high rates of all other types of offending. A great many "indexes of social disorganization" are concentrated here, so statistical associations are not hard to find; but what causes what?[37] In the search for adequate cause-and-effect explanations it is well to keep in mind that the vast majority of the residents in these areas of high rates of delinquency and crime remain law-abiding, at least according to official records. Thus, even for the census tracts with the highest rates of offending in our large cities, there is a nondelinquent majority of three-fourths or more.[38]

Age and Sex Differences

The youthful and young adult years are the ages at which arrests for felonies are most likely to occur. Over three-fourths of the persons arrested for burglary in 1960, for instance, were under 25, two-thirds were under 21, and about half were under 18, and for auto theft all

[34] Marshall B. Clinard, *Sociology of Deviant Behavior* (Rev. ed.; New York: Holt, Rinehart & Winston, 1963), 78–80, 83–85; Clinard, "A Cross-Cultural Replication of the Relation of Urbanism to Criminal Behavior," *American Sociological Review*, 25 (April, 1960), 253–56.

[35] Clifford R. Shaw *et al.*, *Delinquency Areas* (Chicago: University of Chicago Press, 1929); Clifford R. Shaw and Henry D. McKay, *Juvenile Delinquency in Urban Areas* (Chicago: University of Chicago Press, 1942); Terrence Morris, *The Criminal Area* (London: Kegan Paul, 1958).

[36] Clinard, *Sociology of Deviant Behavior, op. cit.*, 87–92.

[37] Calvin F. Schmid, "Urban Crime Areas: Part I," *American Sociological Review*, 25 (August, 1960), 527–42; "Urban Crime Areas: Part II," *American Sociological Review*, 25 (October, 1960), 655–78; Sarah L. Boggs, "Urban Crime Patterns," *American Sociological Review*, 30 (December, 1965), 899–908.

[38] Shaw, *op. cit.*, Sutherland and Cressey, *op. cit.*, 197–98; Solomon Kobrin, "The Conflict of Values in Delinquency Areas," *American Sociological Review*, 16 (October, 1951), 653–61.

three of these proportions were higher. Theft of all kinds is predominantly a "young man's game," or at least he is much more likely to be arrested. Violent crimes are not so concentrated in the younger years. About one-third of those arrested for homicides (all types) in 1960 were under 25, one-fifth under 21, and less than 8 per cent under 18.[39]

Men are arrested for felonies ten times more often than women in the United States, but the difference is decreasing and women are being arrested for a wider range of offenses than they used to be. Delinquency rates of girls are closer to those of boys than they used to be, but the ratio is still about four to one. There are large variations in the sex ratios from one region and country to another, and over time. Offending by boys tends to be concentrated in various forms of theft, while girls are more likely to be taken to juvenile court for ungovernability and sex offenses. It seems likely that female offenders are less likely to be subjected to official treatment than males, and that they often play roles that are harder to detect in stealing and in some other offenses; but it is also probable that males are more exposed to criminogenic influences because of their position in society.[40] Thus the proportion of male offending probably is much higher than that of females, but not so much as shown by the arrest and juvenile court statistics.

Family, Delinquency and Crime

Many different aspects of family life have been studied as possible contributors to delinquency and crime. The most careful control-group study made to date involved 500 official delinquents and 500 pair-matched nondelinquents. Several family variables were investigated, and among the larger differences found were those for: (1) discipline of boy by father, (2) supervision of boy by mother, (3) affection of parents for boy, and (4) family cohesiveness.[41] Following is Cavan's attempt to summarize available information about family experiences and delinquency:

In comparison with families of nondelinquent boys, delinquency-prone families as a group have a greater proportion of rejecting or harsh parents, parents who impress their sons as indifferent to their welfare,

---

[39] Federal Bureau of Investigation, *Uniform Crime Reports* (Washington, D.C., Government Printing Office, 1960), 93.
[40] Clinard, *Sociology of Deviant Behavior, op. cit.,* 206–07.
[41] Sheldon and Eleanor Glueck, *Unraveling Juvenile Delinquency* (Cambridge, Mass.: Harvard University Press, 1950), Chapters 8, 9, 10, 11.

parents who are erratic or lax in discipline, or who offer little for the sons to admire or emulate. Delinquency-prone families are more likely than other families to be broken (for some delinquents there is no family at all), with the female-based family a common type in some groups. The delinquency-prone family frequently is financially dependent on outside assistance or public relief; when the mother is employed it is usually at occasional jobs. There is evidence that an accumulation of unfavorable factors increases the likelihood that the boy will become delinquent and also that he will become a recidivist. However, some unfavorable factors can be balanced against favorable ones—for example, the effect of the harsh father may be neutralized by the loving mother. Thus families differ as to the number and combination of favorable and unfavorable factors.[42]

This contrasts with the single-factor thrusts frequently heard in everyday conversation, such as "the real reason is that parents neglect their children," or, "I think it's the lax discipline." Family experiences are apparently very often involved in the development of delinquent and criminal behavior, but there are many family variables, no single one of which evidently is a necessary cause. One suggestion is that the net effect of family interaction may be reinforced or offset by extra-familial experiences.

Emotional Disturbances

Estimates indicate that no more than one-fifth of all persons diagnosed as psychotic or neurotic have official records of crime or delinquency, so for the more serious mental illnesses there is evidently a large nonoffending majority. Studies of inmates of penal institutions, and of others convicted of felonies, show that from 15 to 25 per cent have symptoms of serious mental illness. Estimates of the proportion of juvenile court cases in which there is serious emotional disturbance range up to 10 per cent. Thus there is apparently a large non-mentally ill majority. The evidence is conflicting as to whether or not offenders and nonoffenders differ significantly in the incidence of mental illness.[43] The case studies show that major emotional problems are often involved as apparently major or minor causes, but that such disturbances are neither sufficient nor necessary to explain antisocial acts. Emotional disturbances may contribute to such behavior, and there is much yet to be learned about the conditions under which this happens.

---

[42] Cavan, *Juvenile Delinquency, op. cit.*, 125.
[43] Cavan, *Criminology, op. cit.*, Chapter 10.

The Mass Media

Movies, television, newspapers, and magazines contain a great deal of material about crime, and many claims are made about its effects on behavior. The available evidence indicates that there are great differences in response to particular media stimuli among different age, economic, educational, and other groups. The person's total organization of his experiences up to the time he perceives a given message—his *apperceptive background*—affects greatly his interpretation and other responses to the communication.[44] Thus the comics, movies, and the like, are neither sufficient nor necessary causes of crime and delinquency, and most students of the matter believe that they are rarely contributing factors. When they do play a role they are combined with other variables, so that they reinforce preexisting response tendencies.[45]

Professional Criminal Cultures

One learns to be a professional offender; he learns a specialized set of techniques to be used in a full-time career, and an appropriate ideology which provides justification for the way of life. The beliefs of value include materialism and strong loyalty to the subculture. Among the beliefs of fact are such convictions as: everybody in the society is dishonest when he gets a chance, that it is possible to make a safe and comfortable living without undue risk if one is sensible and knows his business, and that the more successful professional offenders are highly intelligent. The person who is getting initiated into this professional subculture must learn its special vocabulary in order to communicate about the specialized problems involved and the group's ideology.[46] Official indexes doubtless underestimate the extent of professional crime, since such offenders practice ways of escaping detection and "fixing" the case if they are caught. Prison sentences are a risk of the business, but professionals try to stay out of the limelight and to minimize all risks.

Much crime—notably certain kinds of larceny, burglary, and ways of obtaining money under false pretenses—is committed by small groups of professionals. Pickpocketing and confidence games, for instance, often involve highly developed skills in a division of labor. The

[44] Sutherland and Cressey, *op. cit.,* 257–65.
[45] Cavan, *Juvenile Delinquency, op. cit.,* 207–09.
[46] Sutherland and Cressey, *op. cit.,* 282–84.

necessary skills and accompanying attitudes are transmitted as part of the subculture, chiefly in areas of high delinquency and crime. Gangs are evidently crucial in this learning process, as suggested by the following characterization of the typical sequence of development:

1. The emergence of unsupervised play groups.
2. Predelinquent group conduct, reflecting needs for food, clothing, adventure, recreation, and sex.
3. Delinquent patterns, such as theft of auto accessories, with allegiance to the gang rapidly replacing the family, school, church, and other agencies.
4. Detention by police or other law-enforcement officials, usually resulting in a warning, unofficial court handling, or probation. (If families either ignore the matter or react so as to alienate the offender, the process of development is likely to continue.)
5. Contacts with older, professional offenders who begin to teach their skills to the gang members in exchange for cooperation in criminal activities.
6. Breaking contacts with family, school, and other law-abiding groups, and identifying with a career of professional crime.[47]

Presumably the above sequence holds for learning both the ways of small, informal professional groups and those of large criminal organizations. A small group of burglars or extorters differs from a large gang, syndicate, or racket in degree of organization, the latter involving many specialties, an accounting system, a hierarchy of leaders, and systematic ways of recruiting new members and eliminating disloyal ones. As large and successful organizations, they are a part of the social structure and their persistence is evidently facilitated by such aspects of society as the demand for illicit services, the wide sharing of attitudes of lawlessness, labor-management conflict (a seedbed for racketeering), the marketing system (providing opportunities for racketeering on middleman activities), the system of pricing whereby costs can be passed on to the consumer, and the high ranking of the values of individualism and sudden wealth. Sutherland has suggested that it is impossible to eliminate organized crime without basic changes in the social organization.[48]

Emotional stability and intelligence facilitate success in professional crime, and no single family, economic, educational, or other particular variable is necessary to the development of this pattern except the existence of the criminal subculture. Not even the delin-

[47] Cavan, *op. cit.*, 83–94.
[48] Sutherland and Cressey, *op. cit.*, 234–57, 276–86.

quent gang is necessary, though it usually seems to be involved. Explanations of professional criminality involve many contributing factors, then, and the necessary factor of the criminal subculture. The subcultural pattern is not a sufficient cause, since many variables combine in the processes by which it is learned.

Gang Delinquency

Most acts for which juveniles appear in court are committed in company with others. The friends of offenders are much more likely to be officially delinquent than are the friends of nonoffenders. These observations do not prove that most offenders belong to organized delinquent gangs, however, since the fellow offender may be a neighbor or brother who is neither a member of a delinquent gang nor even of an informal street group.[49] It is not necessary to belong to a delinquent gang in order to become an offender. Yet the gang is often a factor, especially in areas with high delinquency rates, and we have seen that it can become involved in systematic crime and the learning of professional patterns.

Street corner groups provide friendship and recreation, and meet other needs not met sufficiently by the family, school, and other agencies in high delinquency areas. Often these "social gangs" engage in borderline or casual offending, and some go on to develop the structure and subculture of delinquent gangs.[50] They do so, according to Cohen, because as lower class boys they cannot readily achieve the material things and the community status they have been taught to want as part of the American Dream. Frustrated, they see many criminal shortcuts in their neighborhoods, and thus reject and rebel against the middle class means of achievement through hard work, patient waiting for delayed rewards, and good manners.[51] In short, the norms of achievement are explicit but the youth concerned feel they are meaningless for them, so this is an application of Merton's formulation of the concept of anomie (see Chapter 2).[52] A related interpretation is that the frequent negativism, maliciousness, noninstrumental acts, hedonism, and the group unity among delinquents are

---

[49] *Ibid.*, 199–204.
[50] William R. Arnold, "The Concept of the Gang," *Sociological Quarterly*, 7 (Winter, 1966), 59–75.
[51] Albert K. Cohen, *Delinquent Boys: The Culture of the Gang* (New York: The Free Press, 1955).
[52] Albert K. Cohen, "The Sociology of the Deviant Act," *American Sociological Review*, 30 (February, 1965), 5–14.

reactions against the adolescent's powerless position in society.[53] In one study it was found that gang boys had weaker relationships with their parents than nongang boys did, but they did not appear to be alienated from adults and to be protesting against them.[54]

Earlier, from their ecological and case history studies, Shaw and his associates proposed an interpretation of delinquency in lower class neighborhoods in terms of the gap between learned aspirations and the opportunities available to achieve them.[55] Cloward and Ohlin revived this and put it in terms of Merton's concept of anomie, saying that illegitimate alternatives will be tried if desired goals are blocked through legitimate means. In pursuing their analysis of "opportunity structures," they classify delinquent gangs as (1) *criminal* (for status and illegal income), (2) *conflict* (for status and protection through gang fights and other violence, and vandalism, and (3) *retreatist* (through drugs and other sensual experiences, a rejection of both legitimate means as well as those of the criminal and conflict types.)[56] Gang boys have been found to verbalize middle-class goals quite readily, unless they are with fellow gang members.[57] Gang members have been found to perceive fewer legitimate opportunities and more illegitimate opportunities around them than do non-gang members in the same neighborhoods.[58] Leadership and fighting in conflict gangs has been interpreted both in terms of the management of status within the gang[59] and sociopathic personality traits of gang leaders,[60] explanations not necessarily incompatible. Perhaps differential opportunity structures is not a satisfactory explanation of middle-class de-

[53] Gerald Marwell, "Adolescent Powerlessness and Delinquent Behavior," *Social Problems,* 14 (Summer, 1966).

[54] James F. Short, Ramon Rivera, and Harvey Marshall, "Adult-Adolescent Relations and Gang Delinquency," *Pacific Sociological Review,* 7 (Fall, 1964) 59–65.

[55] Shaw and McKay, *op. cit.,* 435–41.

[56] Richard A. Cloward and Lloyd E. Ohlin, *Delinquency and Opportunity* (New York: The Free Press, 1960); Bernard Lander, *Towards an Understanding of Juvenile Delinquency* (New York: Columbia University Press, 1954); David J. Bordua, "Juvenile Delinquency and 'Anomie': An Attempt at Replication," *Social Problems,* 6 (Winter, 1958–59), 230–38.

[57] James F. Short and Fred L. Strodtbeck, *Group Process and Gang Delinquency* (Chicago: University of Chicago Press, 1965).

[58] James F. Short, Ramon Rivera, and Ray A. Tennyson, "Perceived Opportunities, Gang Membership, and Delinquency," *American Sociological Review,* 30 (February, 1965), 56–67.

[59] James F. Short and Fred L. Strodtbeck, "Why Gangs Fight," *Transaction,* 1 (September/October, 1964), 25–29.

[60] Lewis Yablonsky, *The Violent Gang* (New York: The Macmillan Co., 1960).

linquency,[61] and other questions have been raised in research oriented towards this concept;[62] but much of the evidence seems to support this explanation of gang behavior.

THEORIES OF CRIME AND DELINQUENCY

Anomie has emerged as an important theoretical perspective on delinquency with the publication of a spate of thought and research about gangs. Perhaps the explanation has limited appplication, but attempts are being made to develop it as a general theory of delinquency. The logical question would then be: To what extent can it explain adult crime? In Chapter 2 anomie was located within the general conceptual framework of social disorganization, and perhaps much that has been discovered and thought about crime and delinquency in terms of that general approach can be integrated into the focus on anomie. The focus is not new, but it has been vigorously rejuvenated.

Sutherland's theory of Differential Association has dominated much of the thinking about criminal and delinquent behavior, especially in sociology. According to this theory, the society provides the person with direct contacts with both law-abiding and law-breaking patterns of behavior and attitude, and his own behavior is determined by whichever persons and groups he has more association with. In addition to the frequency of contacts, this learning formula includes the variables of intensity of contacts, their duration, and priority in time.[63] Originally this theory was put forth as an explanation of professional and white-collar crime. Sutherland held that white-collar offenders learn from fellow business or professional associates, or from parents and friends in the same ways that the skills and attitudes of professional crime are transmitted. Later, he broadened this

---

[61] Harwin L. Voss, "Socio-Economic Status and Reported Delinquent Behavior," *Social Problems*, 13 (Winter, 1966), 314–24.

[62] Erdman A. Palmore and E. Phillip Hammond, "Interacting Factors in Juvenile Delinquency," *American Sociological Review*, 29 (December, 1964), 848–54; Delbert S. Elliott, "Delinquency, School Attendance and Dropout," *Social Problems*, 13 (Winter, 1966), 307–14; Judson R. Landis and Frank R. Scarpitti, "Perceptions Regarding Value Orientation and Legitimate Opportunity: Delinquents and Non-Delinquents," *Social Forces*, 44 (September, 1965), 83–91; Roland J. Chilton, "Continuity in Delinquency Area Research," *American Sociological Review*, 29 (February, 1964), 71–83.

[63] Sutherland and Cressey, *op. cit.*, 77, 83.

explanation and proposed it as a general theory of all criminal behavior,[64] a much criticized attempt.[65] One proposal was to restate the
position in terms of differential identification with competing models
of conduct.[66] Sutherland was trying to bring many factors together in
a systematic causal theory, first for two behavior systems and then for
all types, not to show the role of the single factor of contact with
antisocial patterns. His ideas have been widely disseminated and have
probably been instrumental in undermining biological determinism in
the general public.

The risk-factor idea is not in itself a theory, though it provides
part of the scaffold for constructing systematic explanations. There
have been other formulations of the multiple-factor perspective, apparently directed mainly toward the observation of the nondelinquent
majority for each of many variables. In their pre-World War II studies
the Gluecks suggested that no single factor is enough to produce delinquent behavior, but that the combined effect of a "number of handicaps" may do so.[67] Shaw proposed that each person can resist the
effect of one or two unfavorable factors, but that everyone has a "resistance limit." From psychology came the concept of, "frustration
tolerance,"[68] on the assumptions that (1) delinquency is aggressive
behavior, (2) that aggression is produced by frustration, and (3) that
everyone can tolerate frustration only up to a certain point. If there
is no measure of the breaking point other than the act of delinquency,
this is an exercise in circular reasoning. These conceptions are re-
minders of the multiple-factor perspective, but they have not helped
greatly in the difficult problem of explanation.

Reckless, not satisfied with his risk-factor suggestions, has more
recently conducted and stimulated research to test his "containment"
theory (see Chapter 2). The basic assumption is that both internal
(self) and external social controls must be effective if delinquency is
to be prevented, and Reckless believes this theory can explain a wider

---

[64] See the 1939 and 1947 editions of Sutherland's textbook, and his *White Collar Crime, op. cit.*
[65] Sutherland and Cressey, *op. cit.*, 84–98.
[66] Daniel Glaser, "Criminality Theories and Behavioral Images," *American Journal of Sociology*, 61 (March, 1956), 433–44.
[67] Sheldon and Eleanor Glueck, *One Thousand Juvenile Delinquents* (Cambridge, Mass.: Harvard University Press, 1934), 229.
[68] Maud A. Merrill, *Problems of Child Delinquency* (Boston: Houghton Mifflin Co., 1947), 14, 188.

range of criminal and delinquent behavior than any other so far developed.[69] One important insulator against delinquent conduct in high delinquency areas has been found to be a particular conception of self, that one is a "good boy" rather than the opposite.[70] In a sample taken from a Midwest training school, lower class boys were found to be more likely to conceive of themselves as "tough guys" and to have a record of violent offenses, conflict, the use of weapons and other harsh means, and low occupational aspirations. Boys in the sample from the lower middle class were more likely to conceive of themselves as a "loyal and daring comrade."[71] In an earlier study, recidivism (repeated offending) was found to be associated with both internal and external social controls, but more with the former.[72]

Few topics have received as much attention from sociological researchers and those in related disciplines as crime and delinquency, and the published findings are voluminous. Yet most students of these phenomena feel that we have but scratched the surface; we have not developed explanations that adequately predict and explain the behavior. There are hopeful developments, but the difficult task of testing plausible theories with adequate data stretches ahead. For the practitioner, there is the task of trying to keep abreast of the scientific progress, to continue to examine his own beliefs of fact and value, and to beware of the variety of beliefs of both kinds in the society he serves. Of these we shall see more in the next chapter.

---

[69] Walter C. Reckless, *The Crime Problem* (3rd ed.; New York: Appleton-Century-Crofts, 1961), Chapter 18.

[70] Walter C. Reckless, Simon Dinitz, and Barbara Kay, "The Self Component in Potential Delinquency and Non-Delinquency," *American Sociological Review*, 22 (October, 1957), 569; Frank R. Scarpitti, Ellen Murray, Simon Dinitz, and Walter C. Reckless, "The 'Good' Boy in a High Delinquency Area: Four Years Later," *American Sociological Review*, 25 (August, 1960), 555–58.

[71] Leon F. Fannin and Marshall B. Clinard, "Differences in Self Concept Among Delinquents," *Social Problems*, 13 (Fall, 1965), 205–14. cf. Scott Briar and Irving Piliavin, "Delinquency, Situational Inducements and Commitment to Conformity," *Social Problems*, 13 (Spring, 1965), 35–45.

[72] Albert J. Reiss, Jr., "Delinquency as the Failure of Personal and Social Controls," *American Sociological Review*, 16 (April, 1951), 196–207.

1. Why has crime not become a purely technical problem by now in our society?
2. What parts of the criminal code in your state do you suppose have changed most during the twentieth century? The least? Why?
3. If you were asked to study trends and causes of adult and juvenile offending in Thailand, how would you define crime and delinquency? Why?
4. Before 1931 the main source of figures on crime was the populations of prisons and reformatories. Has crime increased since 1776?
5. False advertising would seem to be a violation of the crime of obtaining money under false pretenses, but it is usually handled by administrative rather than criminal law procedures. Is it crime? Explain.
6. Do you think there are different "behavior systems" of juvenile delinquency? Explain.
7. Using some economic factor as an example, explain the difference between a finding of the nondelinquent majority and the non-X majority.
8. Would the control group method, without other types of evidence, necessarily have produced the rejection of the single-factor approach? Explain.
9. Why is the multiple-factor perspective not a theory?
10. Criticize this comment about a study that showed that nondelinquent children received more affection from their parents than their delinquent brothers and sisters did. "This discovery of a deeper essential cause of delinquency means that slum housing, type of family, and other social background factors are unimportant."
11. Is the gang a sufficient, necessary, or contributing cause of delinquent behavior? Explain.
12. Might anomie explain more about some behavior systems of delinquency and crime than others? How about containment theory?

SELECTED READING

Cameron, Mary Owen, *The Booster and the Snitch: Department Store Shoplifting* (New York: The Free Press, 1964).

Cavan, Ruth Shonle, *Readings in Juvenile Delinquency* (Philadelphia: J. B. Lippincott Co., 1964).

Clinard, Marshall B., and Quinney, Richard, *Criminal Behavior Systems: A Typology* (Holt, Rinehart and Winston, Inc., 1967).

Cloward, Richard A., and Ohlin, Lloyd E., *Delinquency and Opportunity: A Theory of Delinquent Gangs* (New York: The Free Press, 1960).

Cohen, Albert K., *Delinquent Boys: The Culture of the Gang* (New York: The Free Press, 1955).

Cressey, Donald R., *Other People's Money* (Glencoe, Ill.: The Free Press, 1953).

Glueck, Sheldon, and Glueck, Eleanor, *Unraveling Juvenile Delinquency* (Cambridge, Mass.: Harvard University Press, 1950).

Glueck, Sheldon (ed.), *The Problem of Delinquency* (Boston: Houghton Mifflin Co., 1959).

Hirshi, Travis, and Selvin, Hanan C., "False Criteria of Causality in Delinquency Research," *Social Problems*, 13 (Winter, 1966), 254–68.

Matza, David, and Sykes, Gresham M., "Juvenile Delinquency and Subterranean Values," *American Sociological Review*, 26 (October, 1961), 712–19.

Nye, F. Ivan, *Family Relationships and Delinquent Behavior* (New York: John Wiley & Sons, Inc., 1958).

Quinney, Richard, "A Conception of Man and Society for Criminology," *Social Problems*, 6 (Spring, 1965), 119–27.

Shaw, Clifford, *The Jack-Roller* (Chicago: University of Chicago Press, 1930).

Shaw, Clifford, and McKay, Henry D., *Juvenile Delinquency and Urban Areas* (Chicago: University of Chicago Press, 1942).

Short, James F., and Strodtbeck, Fred L., *Group Process and Gang Delinquency* (Chicago: University of Chicago Press, 1965).

Sutherland, Edwin H., *The Professional Thief* (Chicago: University of Chicago Press, 1937).

Sutherland, Edwin H., *White Collar Crime* (New York: Dryden, 1949).

Spergel, Irving, *Racketville, Slumtown, Haulberg: An Exploratory Study of Delinquent Subcultures* (Chicago: University of Chicago Press, 1964).

Wolfgang, Marvin E., Savitz, Leonard, and Johnston, Norman (eds.), *The Sociology of Crime and Delinquency* (New York: John Wiley & Sons, 1962).

Yablonsky, Lewis, *The Violent Gang* (New York: The Macmillan Co., 1960).

. . . neither the punitive reaction to law-breaking nor any specific method of implementing that reaction is rooted in the human organism or in universal traits of human nature. On the contrary, reactions to crime are seen to change with variations in the culture. Some kind of reaction to criminal behavior is universal, but the reaction may be either punitive or nonpunitive. Even when the societal reaction is punitive there are great variations in the specific methods used to implement the reaction.[1]

9. Crime and Delinquency Control

SOCIETY'S PROGRAMS of crime and delinquency control are based on value judgments in two different areas: (1) those the criminal law norms are designed to protect, such as the security of person and property; and (2) those related to the means of control, such as health, and freedom from physical pain and mental suffering. The programs are also based on two areas of judgments of fact: (1) the causes and extent of the behavior, and (2) the probable effectiveness of alternative means of control. Assessment of alternative means requires the consideration of competing explanations of the causes, but it also raises many new questions about what is in fact possible. The more systematic thinkers about the control of crime and delinquency make explicit a number of judgments of value and fact and integrate them into ideologies for the support of particular programs.

THE "MODERN" PRISON SYSTEM

What Came Before?

It is easy to misunderstand the statement that the "modern prison system" began about 1800. There was no prison system before then,

---

[1] Edwin H. Sutherland and Donald R. Cressey, *Principles of Criminology* (7th ed.; Philadelphia: J. B. Lippincott Co., 1966), 332–33.

not in the sense of places in which the punishment for crimes is confinement itself. Before this practice began, prisons were either (1) places of *detention,* for use before trial or before the carrying out of sentence, or (2) places of *torture,* whether by mechanical means or by starvation and extreme neglect. The supporting ideologies were those of *retribution,* of balancing the score with the offender by making him suffer.[2] The penalty for a large number of offenses was death, even for petty theft by children. But the blanket use of capital punishment had come to be considered too severe in England, America and elsewhere, and patterned deviations to avoid the penalty were widely practiced.

During the eighteenth century such influential men as Voltaire and Beccaria had questioned the practices and ideologies of retribution.[3] They and others were often accused of heresy, since the beliefs of value and fact undergirding retributive practices were largely theological. A belief of fact that had provided much support for physical torture was that offenders are possessed by demons or by the devil, and that bodily torture drives the evil spirits out. Courts also had often referred to the Roman idea of retribution, that an "eye for an eye" evens up the universal "scales of justice." It had been widely accepted that criminal offenders lacked human desires and feelings, and that they were incapable of ever participating in community life again. The questioning of such beliefs of fact led to the application of emergent humanitarian values to offenders against the criminal law.

The Role of Humanitarian Values

As the view of the nature of the convicted offender changed, factual conditions in the jails and prisons became relevant to public policy-making. The most influential of the early modern criminal law reformers in England was John Howard, a Quaker who publicly deplored the wide use of the death penalty and presented detailed evidence about mixing all types of offenders regardless of sex or age, confining offenders with debtors and the insane, the bad food, the unsanitary conditions, the neglect and cruelty, and the resulting high

---

[2] Ruth Shonle Cavan, *Criminology* (3rd ed.; New York: Thomas Y. Crowell Co., 1962), 271–73.
[3] Marcello T. Maestro, *Voltaire and Beccaria as Reformers of the Criminal Law* (New York: Columbia University Press, 1942).

rates of death.[4] Following the belief of fact that criminal offenders are capable of human feelings and responses, he pleaded for acceptance of the view that they deserve humane treatment. The rise of the modern prison system was built on two pillars of belief, this humanitarian one, and the judgments of fact incorporated in the new legal theories about the criminal law.

Legal Theories of Punishment by Imprisonment

Retributive thinking has not yet vanished from the minds of criminal law officials or the public at large, as suggested by a phrase such as, "I hope he get what's coming to him." But in the Anglo-American system of law, retribution has had no official standing since the rise of the modern prison system. In order to justify the new method of punishment by imprisonment, three new major criminal law theories were developed. Goals are specified in these "utilitarian theories" and reasons given to demonstrate how punishment by confinement can attain them. Capital punishment was not to be abolished, but greatly reduced in order to make the maximum contribution to the success of the new system.

PROTECTION OF SOCIETY. One legal theory holds that imprisonment protects the society from the offender by removing him from it. This rationale has been expressed most with reference to major offenses, especially the violent ones. The emphasis is on protection of the person or his property from further attack, not on restitution for loss already incurred. The use of this idea system is consistent with the provision of maximum precautions against escape, and it is most relevant to the life sentence. Key questions about how this works out in practice are: (1) how many offenders of various types return to the community, (2) after how long, and (3) what are they like when they return?

DETERRENCE. The dominant and most thoroughly developed of the legal theories of imprisonment has been deterrence. Jeremy Bentham worked out a graded series of punishments on the hedonistic assumption that the offender gets a certain amount of pleasure from a given offense; thus the punishment must be made severe enough so that the anticipated pain outweighs the pleasure. The length of imprisonment

---

[4] John Howard, *The State of Prisons in England and Wales* (2nd ed.; London: Cadell and Conant, 1780).

was his chief deterrent for felonies, the size of the fine or length of a jail sentence for misdemeanors. Bentham assumed that the punishment must be swift and sure, and administered in a uniform manner in order to deter others effectively.[5] The person was assumed to have a free will and to act solely on the rational basis of the pleasure-pain calculation, so this ideology rests on an oversimplified view of the causes of criminal behavior. These ideas, bolstered by humanitarian arguments, provided the main justification for building prisons, and they became the backbone of all phases of law enforcement. This theory of deterrence is also known as the Classical School of Criminology.[6]

The main argument used to justify the death penalty since Bentham has been that it deters potential murderers and other violent offenders. The most careful comparisons in twentieth century America, however, indicate that murder rates in a given jurisdiction are unaffected by the presence or absence of the death penalty.[7] Opponents of capital punishment have usually made their stand chiefly on the supremacy of the value of human life, though sometimes they also attack the belief (of fact) in deterrence. The use of the death penalty has been declining for well over a century,[8] and support for it in the United States has declined in recent years. In 1953, 68 per cent of a representative national sample said they favored the death penalty for persons convicted of murder, but only 42 per cent favored it in 1966.[9] The balance of support seems to have shifted, but sentiment is almost equally divided and three-fourths of the states are reluctant to abolish the death penalty completely. The usual argument in favor of the penalty is deterrence, and opponents are accused of "coddling" offenders and encouraging crime. Many proponents seem sincere in holding the evidently mistaken belief of fact that it is a deterrent; others often clearly indicate that they are more interested in retribution, in given expression to strong feelings of revenge.

Belief in deterrence has placed much pressure on the police to

---

[5] Jeremy Bentham, *An Introduction to the Principles of Morals and Legislation* (London: Pickering, 1823).
[6] Sutherland and Cressey, *op. cit.*, 54–55.
[7] *Ibid.*, 347–53.
[8] *Ibid.*, 314–17.
[9] *Gallup Political Index*, Report No. 13, June, 1966, 16. Two of the larger differences in 1966 were found for sex and political affiliation. The percentage of men in favor of the death penalty was 47, of women, 38; 51 per cent of the Republicans were in favor and 39 per cent of the Democrats.

detect and arrest offenders and push for prosecutions. Judges and prosecutors feel this pressure too, and it has very often been so strong that the traditional presumption that an accused person is innocent until proven guilty beyond a reasonable doubt has been more violated than observed. "Third-degree" methods of obtaining confessions had become so commonplace in our state systems of prosecution that it came as a surprise when the U.S. Supreme Court began holding that constitutional rights of accused persons were being violated. A series of decisions over several years[10] led up to the 1966 decision in the case of *Miranda vs. Arizona* that the police and prosecutors cannot question a suspect until he has been advised of his right to remain silent and of his right to legal cousel, which must be provided for him if he has no lawyer. Otherwise, the Court reasons, the accused person's right not to incriminate himself is insecure. Those who criticize this line of decision, place their faith in the theory of deterrence, and they state or imply the value judgment that it is desirable to convict all who are guilty even if some innocent ones are wronged in the process. Those who support the decisions believe it is preferable to avoid infringing on the individual rights of the innocent (and the amateur offender) even if some guilty ones escape. The supporters also assume that after the police and courts reorganize their procedures in keeping with the new guidelines that the rate of convictions will be about as high as before.

REFORMATION. The legal theory of reformation began as one of the justifications of punishment by imprisonment. It took shape gradually, while deterrence was being publicized in its developed form. The idea of reformation was implicit in Bentham's provision of less-than-lifetime sentences for most crimes, and in the idea of John Howard and others that prison is a place where offenders might become repentant. The first prisons were constructed to keep each inmate in solitary confinement, to give him a maximum chance to commune with his God, thus the term "penitentiary." This plan of continuous solitary imprisonment was introduced into Pennsylvania and into many European countries, but the American pattern came to consist of working and eating together during the day and confinement in cells at night. This plan was introduced in 1824 in the prison at Auburn, New York,

---

[10] Two key cases are: *Gideon v. Wainwright,* 372 U.S. 342 (1963); and *Escobedo v. Illinois,* 378 U.S. 478.

and became known as the *Auburn system*. At first the rule of strict silence at all times was followed, and confinement was in individual cells. This was the beginning of the familiar cell block plan, which evidently prevailed over the Pennsylvania system for economic reasons: the productivity of congregate prison labor, lower cost of construction of the cell areas, and healthier inmates.[11]

The idea of reformation became more explicit in the law and in public debate with the importation of the *reformatory system* from Ireland. The first American reformatory opened in 1876 at Elmira, New York, with an age limit of 16 to 30, and several other states followed. The key idea was that reformation could occur if the inmate could earn his way to freedom by his own efforts, originally by accumulating "marks" for daily work, schooling, sanitation, military drill, and moral training. A legal feature essential to this system, the indeterminate sentence, is a clear departure from Bentham's idea of deterrence by a fixed term for each crime. *Parole was introduced along with the indeterminate sentence, making it possible to stipulate conditions of liberation and to provide for supervision for a time. The offender who completes a fixed sentence is freed unconditionally and without supervision.*

The reformatory movement failed in the sense that it did not accomplish widespread reformation of inmates, and not all states built such institutions. Perhaps Elmira and other early reformatories could have accomplished more if they had not had the same maximum precautions against escape and disorder as other prisons of the Auburn type. There were from the beginning of the use of reformatory procedures some basic conflicts between the legal theories of deterrence and protection of society on the one hand and reformation on the other. Yet reformation was begun as a theory to justify imprisonment, one assumption being that the punishment impressed on the offender the necessity for developing law-abiding habits. In practice, prisons and reformatories became more similar than different.

But the reformatory movement succeeded in another sense; its procedures were eventually adopted in prisons and in correctional institutions as a whole,[12] thus modifying the Auburn system in several ways: (1) Parole came to be used for the penal system as a whole,

---

[11] Elmer Hubert Johnson, *Crime, Correction, and Society* (Homewood, Ill.: The Dorsey Press, 1964), 335–41.

[12] *Ibid.*, 333–35, 342–44; Sutherland and Cressey, *op. cit.*, 509–10; Cavan, *op. cit.*, 392–405.

along with different varieties of the indeterminate sentence. (2) Prison labor, originally conceived of as punishment, came to be considered useful in teaching inmates new habits and preparing them for a job after release. (3) Classification of inmates with a view to individualizing the "treatment procedures" became generally accepted at least in name. (4) The idea of progressing from one stage to another on the way to release resulted in the provision of institutions with different degrees of security measures, varying from maximum through medium to minimum. The federal system became the model in this regard to be followed eventually by a number of states. (5) Even fixed sentences came to be reduced for good behavior, by formulas providing for time off for "good time" (a period, usually a month, served with no black marks for bad conduct) and "honor time" (additional reduced time for serving as a "trusty").

REHABILITATION VERSUS PUNISHMENT

From the above it can be seen that the penal system has incorporated as regular features a number of contradictory beliefs and practices. Correctional personnel have faced the continuing dilemma of how to manage both security and reformation, and have tended to give increasing attention to the latter. They have also preferred the term "rehabilitation" to the more punishment-oriented concept of reformation. Police and the legal profession have continued to give high priority to beliefs about deterrence and protection of society, while usually recognizing the legitimacy of attempts to change attitudes and behavior. Debate on these issues goes on and on, both in various special groups and the general public, accompanied by ideological attempts to minimize the inconsistencies.

The Juvenile Court Philosophy

While some special institutions for children had been built, and some states had tried special hearings and probation for them, it was not until 1899 that legal action was taken to exempt juvenile offenders (in most situations) from the system of criminal law punishment. Following the lead of that first juvenile court statute in Illinois, other legislatures provided that the child offender is not a criminal in the eyes of the law, but a child needing care and protection. The supporting ideology, developed mainly by child welfare workers, criminologists, and a small group of judges and lawyers, was so widely publicized that some legislatures did not even bother to define the aims. Little was said about the procedures to be used in the court hearing, except that they were to be informal, like those of a court of equity. By this the promulgators of the juvenile court philosophy meant: (1) no jury, (2) no rules of evidence, (3) no defense attorney, (4) an informal, closed hearing rather than a public trial, (5) no publicity in the news media, and (6) full use of the report of a pre-hearing investigation to facilitate the best disposition of the case. The machinery of the criminal court, designed to protect the constitutional rights of a person being tried for a particular offense, were considered irrelevant and harmful to the interest of the child.[13] The courts upheld these acts, but it became quite common to have the family's lawyer present at the hearing. A wide variety of juvenile court practices developed, usually involving some degree of mixture of the juvenile and criminal court models.

Probation

The juvenile courts greatly extended the use of probation, which had first been legislated in Massachusetts in 1878, but little used.[14] *Probation is a substitute for punishment because it is conditional supervised release before any time is spent in a correctional institution.* This became the most common disposition of cases going to juvenile court hearings, with no more than 5 per cent being committed to juvenile institutions in most courts. The use of informal disposition procedures and of probation thus replaced criminal law punishment for nearly all juvenile offenders. Since probation later came to be used increasingly for older youth and adults as well, the suggestion that *the juvenile court movement has had revolutionary effects on our criminal law system* can be appreciated. It has greatly increased the use of substitutes for criminal law punishment, and the emphasis on rehabilitation.

The Youth Correction Authority Acts

After its start in New York City, the Youth Correction Authority movement received impetus with the publication in 1940 of the American Law Institute's model statute. The purpose was to extend

---

[13] Sutherland and Cressey, *op. cit.*, 455–67.
[14] *Ibid.*, 480–83.

the juvenile court philosophy up to the age of 21, since youth from 17 or 18 to 21 cannot vote or be treated as adults in the civil courts. The key belief of fact is that probation and other juvenile court procedures are more effective in controlling offending by this age group than imprisonment or other punishment. Where there is a requirement that the person be "adjudicated" to the status of "youthful offender" or "wayward minor,"[15] compromise procedure is used which centers on a specific charge in a manner more like a criminal trial than an informal hearing. Generally speaking, in the states with YCA laws and in the federal system, the accused youth stands criminal court trial and may then be committed to the Youth Correction Authority if found guilty. Juvenile courts send some of their more serious offenders to the Authority, especially those 17 years of age. Only where the Authority can also (or instead of the court) grant probation, and where it has some special institutions, is it likely to function very differently from the adult correctional system.

If the Youth Authority should spread more rapidly, and especially if probation became used for the 17-to-21 year-olds almost as much as it is by the juvenile court, it would effect a revolutionary change in the criminal law. In Chapter 8 it was noted that two-thirds of all persons arrested for burglary are under 21, and the figure is higher still for auto theft. The ages of 19 and 20 are peak years of felonious offending, especially in major forms of theft. So the extension of the juvenile court philosophy to age 21 can greatly extend the use of substitutes for punishment for society's major offenders. Up to now, however, except for publicizing the idea that youthful offenders can be rehabilitated, the Youth Authority programs have not produced major changes in correctional systems.[16]

Juvenile Court Issues

How much rehabilitation has been accomplished by juvenile and youth programs? Alongside the claims made for many a local court or special program, we must note that a number of careful attempts to study the extent of recidivism have produced dismal evidence. Most studies show that from one-third to two-thirds of those handled by the juvenile court are repeaters within five years,[17] and the Gluecks re-

[15] Paul W. Tappan, *Delinquent Girls in Court: A Study of the Wayward Minor Court of New York* (New York: Columbia University Press, 1947), 234.
[16] Sutherland and Cressey, *op. cit.*, 473–76.
[17] *Ibid.*, 467–73.

ported a figure of 88.2 per cent.[18] Yet we lack an adequate measure
of the outcomes, especially in comparison to those of a straight punishment approach for the same age groups. One may approve or not
of the substitutes for punishment on the basis of value considerations,
but there have been no satisfactory tests of the beliefs of fact. Proponents of probation and other substitutes for punishment often make
the point that such programs have been too poorly supported, financially and otherwise, to indicate what they can do. Believers in the
ideology of deterrence have often maintained that it has not been
adequately tested either, since punishment is far from being uniformly
swift and sure.

It costs several times as much to run a juvenile court with a staff
of paid probation officers and other professionals, yet two Detroit
studies are interpreted as evidence that the results are no better than
they were before such staff members were hired. The researchers argue
that rehabilitative programs should therefore be divorced from the
court, so that both these and the control functions of the court can be
accomplished more effectively.[19] It has been very hard to identify the
basis for a specific disposition.[20] It is possible that the juvenile courts
have been accomplishing more than they used to, but that this is offset by other variables. It must also be kept in mind that few courts
have had the number and caliber of professionals considered essential
for adequate investigation and supervision.

It was long doubted that judges could implement the juvenile
court philosophy and related ideologies, since they run counter to
training and experience in deterrence-oriented criminal law. However,
it is evidently true that most judges understand the philosophy and
try to follow it, even those who spend little of their time in the juvenile court and who lack the facilities to accomplish its goals.[21] The
trouble is, according to the view advanced by Tappan and others
beginning in the late 1940's, that the juvenile courts have very often

[18] Sheldon and Eleanor Glueck, *Juvenile Delinquents Grow Up* (New York: The
Commonwealth Fund, 1940), 16–26, 43, 59.
[19] Mildred R. Chaitin and H. Warren Dunham, "The Juvenile Court in Its Relationship to Adult Criminality: A Replicated Study," *Social Forces,* 45 (September, 1966), 114–19; Mary E. Knauer, "The Juvenile Court in Its Relationship to
Adult Criminality," *Social Forces,* 32 (March, 1954), 290–96.
[20] David Matza, *Delinquency and Drift* (New York: John Wiley & Sons, 1964),
114–15.
[21] F. James Davis, "The Iowa Juvenile Court Judge," *Journal of Criminal Law,
Criminology and Police Science,* 42 (September–October, 1951), 338–50; Sutherland and Cressey, *op. cit.,* 464–66.

violated the constitutional rights of children. Under the guise of helping them, the argument runs, the courts often act in the spirit of either retribution or deterrence and use broad powers to punish the young more surely and more severely than they would be punished in the criminal courts. The solution usually proposed has been a more formal adjudication procedure, requiring witnesses and competent evidence (but no jury), thus limiting the intake and leaving prevention and rehabilitation to agencies able to perform these tasks well.[22]

For decades the dominant position among probation officers and other correctional personnel was to press for more and better staff and facilities—for the court clinic ideology—and the constitutional issue seemed settled. Tappan's argument that rehabilitative efforts should be removed from the court revived the constitutional and correctional issues and began to convince many lawyers, judges, and law enforcement officials. Some legislatures enacted statutes in the 1950's and early 1960's requiring or allowing a lawyer to represent the juvenile, to permit newspapers to print his name in the hope of deterring others, or to make other modifications in procedure. After several years of increasing concern over the constitutional rights of the accused adult and the child, the U.S. Supreme Court in 1966 decided in the case of a 16-year-old boy that strict standards of due process should apply to the juvenile court hearing.[23] Acting on the Court's *dictum*[24] that this view will be extended to other juvenile court situations, state judges and legislators have begun to make the juvenile court hearing more formal.

A pattern that seems likely to become general requires a three-step proceeding: (1) a detention hearing within 48 hours, to determine if there is sufficient evidence to hold the juvenile further; (2) a formal hearing limited to charges of a particular delinquent act, to determine if the court shall take jurisdiction; and (3) a disposition hearing, to be held within three weeks of the original detention. Only in the third step is the probation officer present, and the report of his investigation of the child's social environment is not read by the judge until this

---

[22] Tappan, *op. cit.*, 89–110, 196.
[23] *Kent v. United States*, decided in March, 1966. The case involved multiple felony charges: the District of Columbia Juvenile Court waived the hearing completely, sending it directly to the U.S. District Court for criminal trial. In jurisdictions where juveniles may or must go to criminal trial for certain felonies, evidently, they must first have a fair juvenile court hearing.
[24] *Dicta* are statements in an appellate court's written opinion that go beyond the facts of the case decision, to explain the reasoning.

stage. This is comparable to the criminal court, where the judge may not see the report until after guilt is determined, so that it can affect only the determination of sentence. The more formal hearing is still defined as a civil proceeding, with adjudication by the preponderance of the evidence rather than beyond a reasonable doubt.

Whether this development will ultimately facilitate prevention and rehabilitation remains to be seen. It will probably reduce the court intake and the length of detention considerably, so recidivism will presumably be reduced to the extent that official labeling of delinquents is itself a factor.

OFFENDER TYPES AND TREATMENT

Custodial Classification

Most correctional institutions have a classification committee, consisting of several key members of the staff. Each new inmate is classified with respect to housing (type of cell area, or dormitory), job, school, and other programs, and reclassification is considered from time to time. Parole recommendations are usually initiated in this group, as well as those concerning transfer to another type of institution. This continuing task of classification involves the two interests of custody and rehabilitation, and they often conflict.[25] From the custodial point of view there are the two security risks—escape and internal disorder. A maximum security institution puts its emphasis on custodial considerations, and treatment programs are also often secondary in medium security facilities. The former are surrounded by castle walls and house many armed guards; the latter are ringed by fences, usually, and employ fewer armed guards. Minimum security institutions allow considerable freedom of movement, utilize dormitory housing for the most part, and take minimum precautions against escapes.

The different types of security risk that classification committees apparently have in mind in making individualized predictions have not been highly systematized. One suggestion is to use the categories referred to in the argot of the prisoners. Four groups are identified in one such effort: (1) Antisocial inmates, or "right guys," who follow the norms of the prisoner society; (2) Prosocial inmates, "square Johns," who support law-abiding norms; (3) Pseudosocial inmates,

[25] Cavan, *op. cit.*, 448–51.

"politicians," who shift their allegiance back and forth; and (4) Asocial inmates, "outlaws," who reject both prisoner and law-abiding norms.[26] Some apparent subtypes appear in another classification scheme involving eleven groups identified by inmates.[27] These different inmate roles have value for custodial classification and actions, but they also have implications for treatment, especially when related to preprison behavior systems.

Treatment Types

Classification for purposes of rehabilitation focuses consideration on matters bearing little relation to custody. One possibility is to use the types of behavior system discussed in Chapter 8, yet treatment involves other considerations in addition to the patterns of causes. Also, we saw that the schemes for classifying delinquent behavior systems have been less satisfactory than those for adult offending. Gibbons has suggested the following treatment types for juvenile delinquency:[28]

1. Predatory gang delinquent
2. Conflict gang delinquent
3. Casual gang delinquent
4. Casual delinquent, nongang member
5. Automobile thief—"joyrider"
6. Drug user—heroin
7. Overly aggressive delinquent
8. Female delinquent
9. "Behavior problem" delinquent

He has developed a scheme of criminal behavior with 15 types,[29] all differentiated in terms of their treatment requirements. He proposes the following classification of modes of treatment, to be used both for crime and delinquency:[30]

---

[26] Clarence C. Schrag, "A Preliminary Criminal Typology," *Pacific Sociological Review,* 49 (Spring, 1961), 11–16; Schrag, "Some Foundations for a Theory of Correction," in Donald R. Cressey (ed.), *The Prison* (New York: Holt, Rinehart and Winston, 1961), 309–57.

[27] Gresham M. Sykes, *The Society of Captives* (Princeton, N.J.: Princeton University Press, 1958), 84–108.

[28] Don C. Gibbons, *Changing the Lawbreaker* (Englewood Cliffs, N.J.: Prentice-Hall, 1965), 74–97.

[29] *Ibid.,* 97–128; see also Don C. Gibbons and Donald L. Garrity, "Definition and Analysis of Certain Criminal Types," *Journal of Criminal Law, Criminology and Police Science,* 53 (March, 1962), 27–35.

[30] Gibbons, *op. cit.,* 129–88.

A. Psychotherapy
  1. Individual "Depth" Psychotherapy
  2. Group Psychotherapy
  3. Client-Centered Therapy
B. Environmental Therapy
  4. Group Therapy
  5. Milieu Management
  6. Environmental Change

Gibbons then proceeds to discuss specific modes of treatment for the different types of crime and delinquency. In the following excerpts from his discussion of treatment suggestions for different forms of gang delinquency, there are references both to patterns of causation and to other social control considerations:

> The basic proposal for dealing with predatory gang delinquents centers around tactics involving group intervention. In brief, the task of treatment is to convert predatory offenders into members of an "antidelinquent society" by using group members as the agents of behavioral change.[31]

> The recommendations for the treatment of conflict gang members are much the same as those for predatory offenders because the two types of delinquents are relatively similar. Both types of juveniles define themselves as without "problems" and both are supported in their antisocial values by a relatively well-organized peer system.[32]

> There seems little question that the general tack being taken with conflict gang members is appropriate for such persons. Streetworker programs and similar ventures which are directed at utilizing gangs as the vehicle for rehabilitation seem to make good sense. The same could be said of the more complex approaches which try to alter the environment. It is highly doubtful that efforts to redirect the behavior of gang members by breaking up gangs or other strategies of that kind would be effective. The consequence of disrupting the peer associations of the offender would be to leave him without any supportive social system. In turn, he might then be driven to even more serious deviant activity such as drug use. Along the same line, conflict gang members are not likely candidates for psychotherapy.[33]

> The major problem presented by casual gang offenders is to prevent their contamination by more serious delinquents. Thus group treatment should be used with these juveniles to isolate them from older, more so-

---

[31] *Ibid.*, 231.
[32] *Ibid.*, 238.
[33] *Ibid.*, 239; *cf.* Frank R. Scarpitti and Richard M. Stephenson, "The Use of the Small Group in the Rehabilitation of Delinquents," *Federal Probation*, 30 (September, 1966), 45–50.

phisticated delinquents. This group activity, in turn, should be designed to reinforce their nondelinquent self-images and attitudes.[34]

In an institution for girls in California attempts have been made to develop effective classification for purposes of rehabilitation, using four levels of interpersonal maturity and three types based on an attitude inventory. The interpersonal maturity types have proven more useful than the psychiatric categories used before. The program of treatment had been entirely psychiatric in its orientation, and it was concluded that most of the girls could not profit from it.[35] Such efforts appear capable of increasing the effectiveness of rehabilitation programs, especially where blanket assumptions and procedures are in vogue. Effective placement and work with the individual depend on the use of a set of categories that facilitate the understanding and prediction of his behavior.

DANGEROUS MYTHS?

Are the Legal Theories Wrong?

Questions have been raised that challenge all the legal theories, including rehabilitation. Let us push this questioning further. The average male adult inmate of a penal institution in the United States serves less than two years time. We cannot place much credence in the legal theory of protection of society, then. Most persons who commit major felonies are not behind bars for life; they are back in the community in a matter of months. Many are released on parole, but others have completed fixed sentences and go free without any supervision. The average length of time served under indeterminate sentences is longer than under fixed ones.[36] To keep most offenders imprisoned for several decades would require the building of hundreds of new prisons in the United States, or perhaps vast concentration camps.

What of deterrence? Whether increasing or not, crime and delinquency are very widespread, so our control measures are not deterring it very well, perhaps very little. Would there be more deterrence if punishment were more swift, sure, and perhaps more severe? How likely is our society to give up its deterrence measures? Its rehabilita-

[34] Gibbons, *op. cit.*, 241.
[35] Edgar W. Butler and Stuart N. Adams, "Typologies of Delinquent Girls: Some Alternative Approaches," *Social Forces*, 44 (March, 1966), 401–07.
[36] Sutherland and Cressey, *op. cit.*, 633–35.

tive ones? Can uniformity and individualization of justice be achieved in the same system of crime and delinquency control? Can one approach perhaps succeed for some deviant behavior systems and the other for others?

And what of the legal theory of reformation? One view is that this is a dangerous myth about our custodially oriented prisons.[37] If the common estimate is sound that less than 5 per cent of all prisoners require maximum security measures, how much more reformation could be accomplished if tax money for thick stone walls and machine guns were used for correctional programs? Is society likely to support a marked increase in probation and minimum security facilities for adults? Many people appear to have a sacred outlook toward a particular ideology of crime and delinquency control; a secular outlook on the various programs requires a willingness to examine fully the competing ideologies.

Research, we might agree, is the most systematic way to raise questions and to provide at least partial, tentative answers to them. And lest we draw unqualified conclusions about the dangerous mythology of our legal theories, we should note that there is research evidence that the effects of prison experience vary with the type of inmate and with the type of institution.[38] Perhaps careful use of treatment types can enhance correctional success. Concerning nonpunitive efforts at rehabilitation, there is evidence that group counseling with juvenile probationers markedly increases the success of probation, and that detached workers can achieve considerable success with violent gangs.[39] Such research cannot resolve value controversies, but it can give tentative answers to questions about the beliefs of fact in the conflicting ideologies of crime and delinquency control.

Is Reintegration Possible?

Some employers are willing to hire exprisoners or probationers, but many are not. Credit and insurance agencies usually are skeptical,

---

[37] John Bartlow Martin, *Break Down the Walls* (New York: Ballantine Books, 1954).

[38] Donald L. Garrity, "The Prison as a Rehabilitative Agency," in Donald R. Cressey (ed.), *The Prison, op. cit.*, 358–80; Oscar Grusky, "Organizational Goals and the Behavior of Informal Leaders," *American Journal of Sociology*, 65 (July, 1959), 59–67; Bernard B. Berk, "Organizational Goals and Inmate Organization," *American Journal of Sociology*, 71 (March, 1966), 522–34.

[39] Stuart Adams, "The Value of Research in Probation," *Federal Probation*, 29 (September, 1965), 35–40.

and the press and law-enforcement groups often are openly hostile toward those with criminal records. Embarrassments are frequent, so the released offender who wants to be law-abiding and who expects to be accepted by the community is likely to become frustrated.[40] Parolees have at least part of their civil rights restored at some point in many states, but others require the same thing as for fixed term releasees, a governor's pardon. To the extent that he is permanently labeled and rejected as an exconvict, he is physically in the community but psychologically and socially not a part of it.[41] This is in sharp contrast to the practice of forgiving the offender, after punishment or the threat of it, and helping him to become a contributing member of the community.[42] Since the rise of parole and probation staffs there has been little support for prisoner aid societies,[43] and one expedient is to form "restoration clubs" where parolees can discuss common problems and lend mutual support. Apparently there is increasing sympathy for the "half-way house," the ones designed for prerelease as well as those for help after release. These centers in the community provide a base from which to obtain employment and housing, and to establish other contacts.[44]

PREVENTION OF CRIME AND DELINQUENCY

Efforts at all-out mobilization of the machinery of deterrence are sometimes referred to as crime prevention. The assumption is that many potential offenders will be deterred if they know they are very likely to be caught almost instantly. With this exception, the preventive emphasis is centered on adolescents, chiefly boys. Efforts to strengthen and supplement the community institutions that support law-abiding behavior—by supervised recreation, family life education, moral training—are often designed to influence children in a particular area in the desired direction. (In fact, an argument likely to be thrown

---

[40] Walter C. Reckless, *The Crime Problem* (3rd ed.; New York: Appleton-Century-Crofts, 1961), 553–54.
[41] Richard R. Korn and Lloyd W. McCorkle, *Criminology and Penology* (New York: Holt, Rinehart & Winston, 1959), 76–83.
[42] Karl N. Llewellyn and E. Adamson Hoebel, *The Cheyenne Way* (Norman: University of Oklahoma Press, 1941), Chapters 4–7.
[43] Ruth P. Baker, "What Happened to 'Prisoners Aid'?" *Federal Probation*, 29 (March, 1965), 54–55.
[44] Sutherland and Cressey, *op. cit.*, 426, 633; Robert G. Meiners, "A Halfway House for Parolees," *Federal Probation*, 29 (June, 1965), 47–52.

in for almost any proposal for community betterment is that it will "combat delinquency.") Such "scattershot" efforts are aimed at children in general, so it is extremely difficult to determine how much delinquency they prevent. The "pinpoint" programs are for individuals identified as potential offenders, so evaluating them is more manageable, though not easy.

Some Types of Delinquency Prevention

THE AREA PROJECT PLAN. This plan grew out of the studies of delinquency areas by Shaw and others, and came to be considered an application of Sutherland's Theory of Differential Association. There are several variations, but the basic idea is to find people who are liked and respected by the children in the neighborhood to turn the interests and activities of the local boys in law-abiding directions. There may be outside consulting and financing, but the assumption is that the rapport the "natural leaders" have with the boys enables them to accomplish more than a better trained outsider could.[45] It is difficult to tell whether the lowering rates of delinquency reported in several of the areas is a result of the program or of the tendency to use unofficial methods of handling delinquency. Many strong claims have been made by the supporters of this method, and at least it has the advantage of being based on a well known theory of delinquent behavior. It has both "pinpoint" and "scattershot" utility. Also, its supporters point out that it is a democratic method, since local leaders make the decisions and carry them out.[46]

COMMUNITY GROUP WORK. Some group work sponsored by community agencies is of the pinpoint variety, and some is directed toward the children at large. Recreation programs tend to be scattershot, whether run by park and recreation departments, service organizations, police departments, schools, churches, settlement houses, or other community centers. In some community programs, especially those run by police departments, probation departments, and community centers staffed by trained social workers, predelinquents are identified for group counseling or other special handling. Many delinquent boys make considerable use of recreational facilities, so

---

[45] Clifford R. Shaw and Henry D. McKay, *Juvenile Delinquency in Urban Areas* (Chicago: University of Chicago Press, 1942), 442–46; Solomon Kobrin, "The Chicago Area Project—A 25-Year Assessment," *The Annals*, 322 (March, 1959), 19–29.
[46] Sutherland and Cressey, *op. cit.*, 685–87.

the group program is not a panacea; but when pursued with realism it can evidently help discourage delinquent behavior.[47]

COMMUNITY CASE WORK. A variety of public and private agencies engage in case work in the interest of delinquency prevention, often as a part of family service. This is a major aim of visiting teacher (school social work) programs.[48] Despite many claims it is hard to measure the success of such preventive efforts. Child guidance clinics operating in high delinquency areas apparently are not very successful,[49] and a ten-year study found little difference in offending between the boys who received counseling and special help and an experimentally matched group that did not.[50] Before concluding that this proves that intensive work with near-delinquents is impotent,[51] the possibility of varying the approach for different treatment types needs to be considered. Despite the drive in case work to tailor the treatment to the individual, it is quite possible for such programs to be dominated by a particular procedure and even to proceed from overly simplified assumptions about causation.

SOCIAL CODE AGREEMENTS. In the more affluent new suburbs and other situations where the activities of young people from "good" families have become highly dangerous and destructive, a frequent diagnosis has been that the expected behavior is unclear. Some attempts were made in the early fifties to eliminate this presumably normless situation by working out explicit norms, so that both parents and children would know what was expected. At first these social codes were on a neighborhood basis and were negotiated by representatives of high school students and their parents, under the urging and

[47] Roscoe C. Brown, Jr., and Dan W. Dodson, "The Effectiveness of a Boys' Club in Reducing Delinquency," *The Annals*, 322 (March, 1959), 47–52.

[48] Sutherland and Cressey, *op. cit.*, 691–92.

[49] Helen L. Witmer and Edith Tufts, *The Effectiveness of Delinquency Prevention Programs* (Washington, D.C.: U.S. Children's Bureau, 1954), 40.

[50] Edwin Powers and Helen L. Witmer, *An Experiment in Prevention of Delinquency—The Cambridge-Somerville Youth Study* (New York: Columbia University Press, 1951); H. Ashley Weeks, *Youthful Offenders at Highfields* (Ann Arbor: University of Michigan Press, 1958); William McCord and Joan McCord, *Origins of Crime: A New Evaluation of the Cambridge-Somerville Youth Study* (New York: Columbia University Press, 1959).

[51] Jackson Toby, "Early Identification and Intensive Treatment of Predelinquents: A Negative View," *Social Work*, 6 (July, 1961), 3–13; Jackson Toby, "An Evaluation of Early Identification and Intensive Treatment Programs for Predelinquents," *Social Problems*, 13 (Fall, 1965), 160–75.

guidance of school administrators. The codes included norms for such matters as dating behavior, time to be home, home entertaining and other parties, driving, drinking, and family cooperation.[52] Evidently such codes are most likely to be effective when they are (1) local, and (2) developed by joint representatives of students and parents. When attempts were made to develop such codes for entire cities and even states, the movement seemed to lose its appeal. Apparently this type of normative agreement is more meaningful at the level where young people and their parents can relate their expectations to those of their neighborhood peers. Some of the claims of local successes have been strong, but knowledge of the extent and the conditions of delinquency prevention by such programs requires careful research.

COORDINATING COUNCILS AND COMMISSIONS. Much of the effort at delinquency prevention is undertaken without consideration of other programs in the same areas. Community coordinating councils for the prevention of delinquency are in a position not only to reduce the overlapping, but also to facilitate the sharing of ideas and experiences and even of common planning by various public and private agencies. At the state level, commissions for prevention can perform educational functions, and encourage municipal efforts by providing consultation and by channeling state and federal funds into local projects.[53] Coordinating bodies are in a strategic position to stimulate and to conduct research, and to encourage innovations in prevention.

Predicting Delinquent Behavior

Programs in which individuals are pinpointed for preventive effort require some method of identifying potential delinquents. The only way to estimate the chances with confidence is with some measures that have been found to predict successfully for groups similar to the one under consideration. In other words, information with which there has been experience can be put into probability tables, as insurance companies do. The chances that a person will have an accident are determined on the basis of past experience with other individuals of the same age, sex, occupation, marital status, health status, etc. If the

[52] Hartzell Spence, "Connecticut Tames Its Teen-Agers," *Saturday Evening Post* (October 4, 1952), 24–25, 108–09; Robert C. Taber, "A Code for Teen-Agers," *Parents Magazine* (December, 1955), 47–49, 105–08.
[53] Robert P. Capes, "New York State's Blueprint for Delinquency Prevention," *Federal Probation*, 18 (June, 1954), 45–50.

probability is that 12 persons in 100 with a certain combination of traits will have an auto accident in a year's time, then the probability that one person *with that same combination* will have an accident is 12 in 100. Scientific predictions are statements of the chances (and the conditions) of an occurrence, not absolute forecasts.

Experience tables have been used considerably in attempts to predict parole success or failure,[54] but not a great deal for predicting delinquency for a population in the community, such as a school. The Gluecks developed a Social Prediction Table based on the five family factors for which they found large differences between offenders and pair-matched nonoffenders[55] and three other efforts at prediction based on psychiatric and psychological classifications. Such variables, although derived from control group rather than from longitudinal research, can be assigned weights and used in experience tables to see if they will successfully predict delinquency. Considerable success with the Glueck Social Prediction Table has been reported,[56] yet obtaining careful ratings presents a problem. Psychiatric classifying for gathering predictive data for programs of prevention is even more expensive and slow. Much quicker is the use of standardized personality tests,[57] or attitude questionnaires filled out by the children.[58] The KD Delinquency Proneness Scale and Check List has both an attitude questionnaire and a set of items to be checked by someone who knows the child, usually a teacher.[59] The measurement of the self-concept by Reckless and others may be useful in predicting delinquent behavior.[60] In addition to decisions about the costs and accuracy of different

---

[54] Sutherland and Cressey, *op. cit.,* 655–60.

[55] Sheldon and Eleanor Glueck, *Unraveling Juvenile Delinquency* (New York: The Commonwealth Fund, 1950), Chapter 20; Sheldon and Eleanor Glueck, *Predicting Delinquency and Crime* (Cambridge, Mass.: Harvard University Press, 1959).

[56] Eleanor Glueck, "Efforts to Identify Delinquents," *Federal Probation,* 24 (June, 1960), 49–56; Maude M. Craig and Selma J. Glick, "Ten Years' Experience with the Glueck Social Prediction Table," *Crime and Delinquency,* 9 (July, 1963), 249–61.

[57] Starke R. Hathaway and Elio Monachesi, *Analyzing and Predicting Juvenile Delinquency with the MMPI* (Minneapolis: University of Minnesota Press, 1953).

[58] Jay Lowe, "Prediction of Delinquency With An Attitudinal Configuration Model," *Social Forces,* 45 (September, 1966), 106–13.

[59] William C. Kvaraceus, *The Community and the Delinquent* (New York: Yonkers-on-Hudson, 1954), 139–54.

[60] Michael Schwartz and Sandra S. Tangri, "A Note on Self-Concept As An Insulator Against Delinquency," *American Sociological Review,* 30 (December, 1965), 922–26.

methods of prediction, it is necessary to establish cutting points or standards for the inclusion of potential offenders in programs of prevention.

PUBLIC OPINION AND CORRECTIONAL CHANGE

Programs of law enforcement and correction depend on public support, so the issues of the special publics quickly become general issues. Correctional and law enforcement groups are continually concerned with educating the society to their views, though frequently divided among themselves, and they often take partisan positions on particular proposals. Spokesmen for the mass media, economic interests, political groups,[61] education, the churches, and other groups join the controversies over particular programs and comment on the ongoing ideological dilemmas.

At the state level, one way of mobilizing support for correctional change is to appoint a commission of respected leaders from various walks of life, usually including a well known university criminologist and at least one consultant from the federal system or a highly regarded state system. Public acceptance is enhanced by publicity of firm support by the governor and the state's leading correctional officials. While the commission is investigating the system and deliberating, news releases can prepare the way for significant changes, a mood to which legislators are responsive. It is possible to make major changes in this manner, even to transform a state system considered a national scandal into a national model, within a few years.[62] But conditions are rarely favorable to major changes, and there is no easy road for those seeking correctional reform.

The theme of saving tax dollars apparently can be effective, when accompanied by certain assurances. The argument that a minimum security facility will be relatively inexpensive to build and operate will appeal to some because of its emphasis on rehabilitation, but those opposed to or skeptical of this emphasis may not want to save the money unless they believe security risks can be eliminated by careful selection of the inmates. The argument that even an excellent probation system costs many times less than imprisonment becomes impressive when translated into an estimated saving such as that an

---

61 Johnson, *op. cit.,* 387.
62 Reed Cozart, "What Has Happened to America's Worst Prison?" *Federal Probation,* (December, 1955), 32–38.

increase by 150 in the number granted probation would save a given state one million dollars a year. But before supporting this saving, many people must be persuaded that it is possible to select probationers who do not endanger the community, or that an all-out faith in Bentham's formula of deterrence is not warranted.

If a proposed program of rehabilitation will not cost less money than maximum-security confinement, it seems very unlikely to be acceptable to the public as a whole. For example, prison labor has for decades been limited almost entirely to the state-use system, due to pressures to limit both tax expenditures and competition with private industry.[63] Some alternative systems of prison labor are considered to have more rehabilitative potential, but the greater costs have eliminated them from serious consideration. Programs of work release during the day for those serving jail sentences have evidently been accepted because they reduce the cost to the taxpayer, both for confinement and for the support of the inmate's family.[64] Observers and officials who believe this system is suited to reintegration into the community[65] can argue in addition that it saves money. Yet, as with probation, this dollar argument is not sufficient for many people, so pertinent beliefs of fact and value concerning crime and delinquency control must be discussed.

Security considerations apparently loom large in public thinking. The rash of prison riots in 1952–53 and other outbursts since then have prompted major additions to the correctional systems of many states: medium and minimum security facilities, classification centers, diagnostic clinics, expansion of probation, and other changes. A major argument has been that such changes relieve overcrowding, making better security possible for those requiring maximum custody. The money-saving argument has also been prominent. Prison officials and researchers incline to the view that the riots have been due more to loss of control and special privileges by inmate elites than to such publicized conditions as overcrowding, bad food, and harsh discipline.[66] Riots nevertheless provide officials with a dramatic opportunity to press for relief from overcrowding, and for more diversified facilities, for probation, and other reforms. Public assent probably is

[63] Sutherland and Cressey, *op. cit.*, 588–603.
[64] David R. McMillan, "Work Furlough for the Jailed Prisoner," *Federal Probation*, 29 (March, 1965), 33–34.
[65] Stanley E. Grupp, "Work Release and the Misdemeanant," *Federal Probation*, 29 (June, 1965), 6–12.
[66] Sutherland and Cressey, *op. cit.*, 578–81.

based less on faith in rehabilitation than on the beliefs that costs will be lowered and prison custody made more secure.

The "modern" prison system remains the dominant symbol of the control of crime and delinquency, and expressions of belief in deterrence, protection of society, and retribution are much in evidence. Yet the ideology of rehabilitation has many supporters, and there have been some determined preventive efforts. There have been many modifications of the criminal law, often supported for divergent reasons, in this century. It is difficult if not impossible to formulate an ideology capable of integrating the collection of practices that make up the present "system" of crime and delinquency control. It is also impossible to measure adequately the full potential of any one of the approaches, since none receives the uniform support assumed necessary for its success. Particular issues keep emerging, and the larger dilemmas of law enforcement and correction continue.

QUESTIONS FOR DISCUSSION AND STUDY

1. Apply the following statement to long-range changes in societal attempts to control crime and delinquency: "The liberalism and heresy of one age often become the conservatism and orthodoxy of another."

2. From the standpoint of your knowledge of psychology, what do you think of the legal theory of deterrence?

3. Suppose a police officer is a biological determinist in his thinking about the causes of crime and delinquency. Will this influence the way he does his work? Explain.

4. Spokesmen for the Federal Bureau of Investigation have often defended the legal theories of deterrence and protection of society, and have been critical of those of reformation and rehabilitation. Why do you suppose this is so?

5. Suppose a judge is about to pass a criminal sentence or to make a disposition of a juvenile case. Explain how his beliefs of fact about the causes and control of the deviant behavior may influence his actions at this point.

6. Why is there some justification for saying that none of the following has ever been really tested: (a) deterrence? (b) the juvenile court philosophy? (c) parole and probation?

7. What are the implications for law enforcement and correction of the age distribution of those who commit felonies?

8. Has juvenile court procedure moved in the direction of more formal hearings because of value considerations, or beliefs of fact, or both? Explain.

9. In which program(s) of delinquency prevention can Containment Theory best be utilized? Differential Association Theory? Theories of Anomie? Explain.

10. Do you think societies are capable of making rational decisions about programs of crime and delinquency control? Explain.

SELECTED READING

Alexander, Myrl E., "Current Concepts in Corrections," *Federal Probation*, 30 (September, 1966), 3–8.

Clemmer, Donald, *The Prison Community* (New York: Rinehart, 1958).

Cressey, Donald R. (ed.), *The Prison: Studies in Institutional Organization and Change* (New York: Holt, Rinehart & Winston, 1961).

Dressler, David, *Practice and Theory of Probation and Parole* (New York: Columbia University Press, 1959).

Fisher, Sethard, "Informal Organization in a Correctional Setting," *Social Problems*, 13 (Fall, 1965), 214–22.

Giallombardo, Rose, *Society of Women: A Study of a Women's Prison* (New York: John Wiley & Sons, 1966).

Glaser, Daniel, *The Effectiveness of a Prison and Parole System* (New York: The Bobbs-Merrill Co., 1964). Report of a study of the federal system.

Kay, Barbara, and Vedder, Clyde B., *Probation and Parole* (Springfield, Ill.: Charles C. Thomas, 1963).

Johnston, Norman, Savitz, Leonard, and Wolfgang, Marvin E. (eds.), *The Sociology of Punishment and Correction* (New York: John Wiley & Sons, 1962).

Miles, Arthur P., "The Reality of the Probation Officer's Dilemma," *Federal Probation*, 29 (March, 1965), 18–23.

Savitz, Leonard, *Dilemmas in Criminology* (McGraw-Hill Book Co., 1967).

Seeman, Melvin, "Alienation and Social Learning in a Reformatory," *American Journal of Sociology*, 69 (November, 1963), 270–85.

Simpson, Jon E., "Institutionalization as Perceived by the Juvenile Offender," *Sociology and Social Research*, 48 (October, 1963), 13–23.

Street, David, "The Inmate Group in Custodial and Treatment Settings," *American Sociological Review*, 20 (February, 1965), 40–55.

Street, David, Vinter, Robert D., and Perrow, Charles, *Organization for Treatment: A Comparative Study of Institutions for Delinquents* (New York: The Free Press, 1966).

Sykes, Gresham, *The Society of Captives* (Princeton, N.J.: Princeton University Press, 1958).

Ward, David A., *Women's Prison: Sex and Social Structure* (Chicago: Aldine Publishing Co., 1965).

*The public attitude toward drug addiction is very much like the atti-
tude toward alcoholism before the 1930's. There is shame and disgrace associated with it.*[1]

10. Drug Addiction and Alcoholism

DRUG ADDICTION

Societal Definition of the Problem

BEFORE THIS CENTURY the drug addict in America was
apparently considered pathetic but not dangerous.[2] His problem was
personal; he could go to a doctor for help, and he could buy drugs at
modest prices. During a time of growth of organized crime, of increasing trade between East and West, dramatic international migrations,
and considerable fear in the West of being overrun by the "yellow
peril," the opium den became a symbol of the underworld. Self-ad-
ministered drugs came to be considered instrumental in undermining
the values of thrift, industry, health, personal safety, the home,
public order, and even national security. A three-year series of international meetings culminated in 1912 in the agreement at the Hague
Opium Convention to restrict the drug trade. The result in the United
States was the Federal Narcotics (Harrison) Act of 1914.

The effect of the Harrison Act was to make the sale *and possession*
of drugs criminal acts, unless done for "legitimate medical purposes."

---

[1] Jessie Bernard, *Social Problems at Midcentury* (New York: The Dryden Press,
1957), 261.
[2] Alfred R. Lindesmith, *Opiate Addiction* (Evanston, Illinois: Principia Press,
1947), 183.

Technically, arrest under the Act and its subsequent amendments is for avoiding an excise tax, which is the reason enforcement is lodged in the Bureau of Narcotics (at first the Narcotics Division) of the Treasury Department. This special police unit brought actions in 1919 against doctors for prescribing opiate drugs to addicts, and the convictions were upheld by the U.S. Supreme Court. Prosecution was then zealously pursued until the Court reversed its interpretation in 1925;[3] but the medical profession stayed away from treatment efforts, leaving a breach to be filled by the illegal "pusher."[4]

The Harrison Act was not limited to addictive (narcotic) drugs as now understood in science, since it mentions cocaine and other coca products. *Opium and its derivatives*—morphine, heroin, and codeine—*are addictive because the body becomes physiologically dependent on them.* They produce sleep and combat pain, and the body develops tolerance, so that progressively larger amounts are required to produce these effects and to prevent the onset of painful withdrawal symptoms. There are also synthetic narcotics, such as demerol and methadone. Cocaine is a stimulant (sometimes combined with a narcotic) which does not induce physiological dependence.[5] Marihuana, also a nonnarcotic, produces relaxation from tensions and inhibitions, and a sense of slowing down of time. It was brought under the purview of the Bureau of Narcotics by the Marihuana Tax of 1937. Other stimulants (like peyote, benzedrine, and amphetamine) and sedatives (including the barbiturates) have also been brought under the control of the Bureau. Alcohol has not been, although (like barbiturates) the body can become physiologically dependent on it if used in extreme amounts, in which case it is a narcotic. There are probably 25 times as many alcoholic addicts in America as there are users of opiates and other narcotics.

Dominant public opinion in America has supported the legal actions under the Federal Narcotics Act. Both drug users and illegal sellers have generally been conceived of as criminal offenders. A questionnaire study of middle-class people in various parts of San Francisco

---

[3] *Linder v. United States*, 268 U.S. 5 (1925).
[4] Rufus King, "Narcotic Drug Laws and Enforcement Policies," *Law and Contemporary Problems*, 22 (Winter, 1957), 122–23; John A. Clausen, "Drug Addiction," Chapter 4 in Robert K. Merton and Robert A. Nisbet, *Contemporary Social Problems* (2nd ed; New York: Harcourt, Brace & World, 1966), 201–04.
[5] David W. Maurer and Victor H. Vogel, *Narcotics and Narcotic Addiction* (Springfield, Ill.: Charles C. Thomas, 1954), 47–77.

showed considerably less public tolerance of drug addiction than of homosexuality and abortion.[6] Evidence was also found of lack of knowledge about drugs, especially among the less educated, and the more the misinformation the greater was the support for existing policies of legal control.[7] The distribution of new knowledge about drugs has raised new issues, but changing beliefs of fact about the physiological effects of various drugs apparently are not sufficient to produce a quick mass conversion to new policies.

Extent and Distribution of Drug Use

In 1955, according to one estimate, there were 60,000 drug addicts in the United States. The incidence was reportedly about one-tenth as great in 1963 as it was in 1914.[8] Even with some increases, including a reported 15.1 per cent rise during 1964 and one of 2.3 per cent during 1965, arrests for narcotics violations were still less than 1 per cent of all arrests listed by the F.B.I.[9] The frequency of drug addiction is quite small in comparison to other forms of deviance, although experimentation with drugs by youth has evidently increased since World War II.[10] Table 10.1 shows a marked increase from 1940 to 1960 in the proportion of those under age 25 admitted at the hospital for drug addicts operated by the United States Public Health Service at Lexington, Kentucky, and a lowering mean age. Commitment to such hospitals is not an adequate measure of addiction, especially of its early stages, but the marked age shift probably reflects a genuine increase in youthful addiction.

Drug addiction is highly concentrated in our largest cities and in a small number of census tracts in those cities, those areas of greatest deprivation and minority group concentrations. In New York City in the early fifties, 87 per cent of the young male addicts from age 16 to 20 were living in 13 census tracts. As many as 10 per cent of the

---

[6] Elizabeth A. Rooney and Don C. Gibbons, "Social Reactions to 'Crimes Without Victims'," *Social Problems*, 13 (Spring, 1966), 400–10. There was more tolerance of abortion than of homosexuality.

[7] *Ibid.*, 405–06.

[8] Alfred R. Lindesmith, "The British System of Narcotics Control," *Law and Contemporary Problems*, 22 (Winter, 1957), 141–42; *New York Times*, March 22, 1965, C, 28.

[9] *The World Almanac and Book of Facts, 1966* (New York: New York World-Telegram and The Sun, 1966), 118, 307; *The World Almanac and Book of Facts, 1967*, 693–94.

[10] Maurer and Vogel, *op. cit.*, 3–9. The Bureau of Narcotics reported that 17.5 per cent of the nation's new addicts in 1965 were under 21 years of age; see *The World Almanac and Book of Facts, 1967, ibid.*, 694.

TABLE 10.1

AGES OF PERSONS ADMITTED DURING SELECTED YEARS TO
THE LEXINGTON HOSPITAL*

AGE	1940		1950		1960	
	No.	%	No.	%	No.	%
19–Under	4	0.4	252	8.7	73	2.9
20–24	45	4.8	671	23.1	608	24.4
25–29	80	8.5	367	12.7	673	27.0
30–39	282	30.1	512	17.7	714	28.7
40–49	329	35.1	549	18.9	211	8.5
50–Over	185	19.7	520	17.9	213	8.5
Unknown	13	1.4	28	1.0		
Total	938	100.0	2,899	100.0	2,492	100.0
Mean Age	41.4		35.5		31.9	

* United States Public Health Service Hospital, Lexington, Kentucky.

SOURCE: William M. Bates, "Narcotics, Negroes and the South," Social Forces, 45 (September, 1966), Table 6, p. 66.

young males in some of the tracts were users.[11] On January 1, 1965, slightly over half of the nation's 55,899 reported addicts were in New York City! The State of New York had about 52 per cent, Illinois (mostly Chicago) had 13.2 per cent, and California was third with about 11.6 per cent. Over four-fifths were male, and more than nine-tenths of the total used heroin. More than 53 per cent of the national total were Negro, over 12 per cent Puerto Rican, and nearly 6 per cent of Mexican background.[12] Judging by admissions to the U. S. Public Health hospitals at Lexington, Kentucky, and Fort Worth, Texas, Negro addicts are highly concentrated in a few large cities.[13]

---

[11] Isidor Chein and Eva Rosenfeld, "Juvenile Narcotics Use," Law and Contemporary Problems, 22 (Winter, 1957), 52–68.

[12] The World Almanac and Book of Facts, 1966, op. cit., 118.

[13] William M. Bates, "Narcotics, Negroes and the South," Social Forces, 45 (September, 1966), 61–67. Southern white patients are mainly from rural areas,

Addiction and Crime

Drug addiction is highly correlated with other crime and delinquency in the same area, but what is the causal connection? One view is that both are caused by other variables, so that those who commit crimes to obtain narcotics would probably be committing felonies even if they were not addicted.[14] Another possibility is that other criminal behavior precedes, and leads to, addiction. One reason suggested is that access to drugs in most cases requires illicit contacts. Drug use is apparently especially prevalent among prostitutes and other lower ranking members of the underworld. Studies of addicts have produced estimates ranging from less than one-fifth to a majority with criminal records prior to addiction, and this proportion has probably been increasing.[15] Perhaps prior criminal conduct increases the probability of drug addiction, but this is not clearly established.

The third causal possibility is that addiction results in the commission of other crimes, and there is evidence that it often does. Arrests after addiction exceed the number expected of persons of a given age and other characteristics. The increase is in money-making crimes, not violent ones, and in drug offenses. Furthermore, the increase is greatest for those using the most expensive drugs, so it is evidently a result of the need to maintain the habit. Yet, while drug use resulted in considerably more crime in one study, addiction was not followed by arrest in about one-third of the cases.[16] Some just had not been caught, we must assume, yet perhaps not all addicts proceed to commit crimes. Their need to do so in most cases is great because of the expense of illicit drugs. Heroin costs up to fifty times as much here as in Italy, for example, and most addicts do not have the $20 to $150 per week required for their personal needs. Men addicts needing money usually resort to various forms of theft, women and girls to prostitution. Boys usually perform petty thefts and run errands for professional criminals.

Criminal syndicates are organized to make profits on those vices

---

and they average almost ten years older than Southern Negro patients (who are mostly urban). Northern Negro and white patients are the same age.

[14] Harold Finestone, "Narcotics and Criminality," *Law and Contemporary Problems,* 22 (Winter, 1957), 69–85.

[15] John A. O'Donnell, "Narcotic Addiction and Crime," *Social Problems,* 13 (Spring, 1966), 374–76, 385.

[16] *Ibid.,* 377–85.

that violate public morality to the extent of being prohibited by criminal law, chiefly prostitution, gambling, liquor law violations, and drug addiction. The Harrison Act drove the drug traffic underground, thus greatly increasing the cost. Illicit drugs are largely if not entirely imported by smuggling. Thus the Act spawned enormous profits for the syndicated middlemen who buy, transport, smuggle, and distribute drugs. Syndicates made large profits from illegal sales of liquor until the Prohibition era was ended, after which they redoubled their efforts in the other vices. Criminal syndicates have a vested interest in the pattern of drug use and its prosecution under the Harrison Act, the Marihuana Tax Act, and supporting laws. Individual pushers are expendable, so long as they can be replaced and the organization is not threatened.[17] The addict has a vested interest in the syndicate activity, and the Bureau of Narcotics has a vested interest in the system of control.

Causal Variables

From clinical observation of addicts it has been reported that they have such personality problems as excessive dependence on others, inability to make lasting friendships, difficulty (for males) in taking the male role, low frustration tolerance, and strong feelings of anxiety, failure, futility, and depression. A major research problem involves determining when such personal traits develop—before or after drug use. And even when they existed before, we must note the non-addicted majority among people with such personality problems. Also, since it seems quite possible for people without such problems to experiment with drugs and become physiologically dependent on them, the majority of addicts may well come from people not seriously disturbed. Physiological variables obviously are involved. The high ecological concentration of addiction indicates the importance of association with drug users, yet the vast majority of people in these areas remain free of it. Those in occupations with legal access to drugs—physicians, dentists, nurses, and pharmacists—have disproportionately high rates of addiction, yet most people in these groups are nonusers. Some people become addicted through the medical use of narcotics during illness.

It should be clear that a multiple-factor explanation of drug ad-

---

[17] Ruth Cavan, *Criminology* (3rd ed., New York: Thomas Y. Crowell Co., 1962), 181.

diction is in order.[18] Some type of contact with drugs is obviously necessary, and subcultural processes seem essential to the explanation of the extreme concentration of addiction. Yet the location of addict subcultures in areas of marked disorganization must be explained, along with the nonaddiction of most people in these districts, and the addiction of some people who live in quite different areas. One suggestion is that addiction fits in well with the "cool cat" subcultural pattern of accommodation of minority groups in urban slums, particularly of Negroes.[19]

Evidently the pusher usually is not directly involved in the first use of drugs. Adults typically are invited to try them by friends, often at a party. Invitations to teen-agers are usually extended by persons of the same age, in group situations. When pressures are applied for members of delinquent gangs to try drugs, they are difficult to resist.[20] Much of the youthful adventuring involves marihuana, which sometimes serves as an introduction to the use of narcotics, especially in some delinquent gangs.[21] Experimentation with marihuana by middle-class youth has increased in recent years, and many have tried LSD (lysergic acid diethylamide).

LSD is a powerful drug that produces vivid hallucinations, sensory distortions, often a sense of being outside one's body, and sometimes a feeling of being at one with the universe. Middle-class prospecters seem more interested in stimulants for new and vivid experiences than in a retreat from society through narcotics, and some insist that drug experiences are psychologically beneficial and even religious. There may be 25,000 or more frequent users of LSD in the nation, and apparently a great many more (perhaps mostly students) who have tried it. A research group which made an interview study of 92 adult users found them typically to be successful professional people, law-abiding, white and Protestant, who were introduced to the drug by high prestige professionals. The dominant ideology was not that of a deviant group, but rather of people with loving concern for others.[22] Since the varied and powerful effects sometimes produce

---

[18] Chein and Rosenfeld, *op. cit.*, 60.
[19] Harold Finestone, "Cats, Kicks and Color," *Social Problems*, 5 (July, 1957), 3–13.
[20] Chein and Rosenfeld, *op. cit.*, 55–56.
[21] Harry Manuel Schulman, *Juvenile Delinquency in American Society* (New York: Harper & Bros., 1961), 496.
[22] Richard Blum and Associates, *Utopiates: The Use and Users of LSD-25* (New York: Atherton Press, 1964).

panic,[23] a concerned group might help prevent utter terror from spreading in such cases. The cultural definition of drugs influences their use and their effects on the person and also societal attempts at control.[24]

While new patterns have emerged, at least one older one has virtually disappeared from the American scene. For decades there was a comparatively high frequency of addiction among Chinese-Americans,[25] but this decreased sharply in the fifties and sixties.[26] During the long period of the marked segregation of Chinatowns, and before the take-over of China by the Communists (1949), the sojourner way of life was quite common among Chinese-Americans. The sojourner is a migrant who intends to accumulate wealth and return to his native land to become a businessman or landowner.[27] From a study of Chinese patients discharged from the federal hospital at Lexington, Kentucky, from 1957 to 1962, it was concluded that the Chinese addict was usually an unsuccessful sojourner. Typically 53 years of age, and a restaurant or laundry worker, he lived an alienated, rooming-house existence. The increasing assimilation of American culture by Chinese-Americans has been eliminating the sojourner pattern, and apparently with it the addict subculture.[28]

Control of Drug Use

PENAL CONTROLS. The reduction of known addiction in America to one-tenth of the 1914 level suggests that its official handling as crime has been quite effective. However, the criminal label may have caused many users to take precautions against detection, so perhaps the drop has not been so great as reported. The crimes-known-to-the police index is a partial and selective measure, as we saw in Chapter 8, so all we know for sure is that the addiction known to the Bureau of Narcotics has decreased greatly. Assuming that there has been a large drop in addictive behavior, it is possible that the criminal label

---

[23] *Los Angeles Times,* July 11, 1966, II, 1–3; July 12, 1966, II, 1–2.
[24] Clausen, in Merton and Nisbet, *op cit.,* 198–99.
[25] *e.g.,* see Bingham Dai, *Opium Addiction in Chicago* (Shanghai, China: The Commercial Press, 1937), 46.
[26] John C. Ball and M. P. Lau, "The Chinese Narcotic Addict in the United States," *Social Forces,* 45 (September, 1966), 72.
[27] Rose Hum Lee, *The Chinese in the United States of America* (Hong Kong: Cathay Press, 1960), Chapter 5.
[28] Ball and Lau, *op. cit.,* 68–72.

and the zealous enforcement have deterred many from trying drugs. But in view of the extreme spatial concentration of addiction since the twenties, a more likely explanation would be that the supplies have been curtailed and are difficult to obtain except where there are direct contacts with the underworld. An undesired consequence has been the rise of a thriving black market. Another factor that may have prevented some drug use is public education about addiction, led by the United States Public Health Service.

Critics of the penal approach point out that the arrest and prosecution of drug users neither helps the addict nor slows down the traffic. Detection of individual users, pushers, and even peddlers (who supply the pushers) does not threaten the criminal syndicate. No such illicit profits are possible in Western European countries, which take a medical rather than a criminal law approach. They have programs of prevention and rehabilitation, and they have much lower rates of addiction than our current one.[29] Repression creates both the syndicated black market and addict subcultures that integrate the various roles, facilitate contacts with the suppliers, and provide ideological justification and warning systems.[30]

The spread of new knowledge about drugs has increased public awareness, especially among the better educated, that many drugs are non-addictive. The penal treatment of users of marihuana and some other non-narcotics has become a public issue. Defenders of LSD insist that the chances are small of becoming psychotic or committing a violent crime under the influence of the drug or of shifting to heroin, and they object to being classed as criminals. Some point out that after marihuana came under the control of the Bureau of Narcotics it became tied in with the traffic in heroin, and they join federal officials in the fear that the same thing is happening to LSD. The 1966 federal law is designed to stop the manufacture and distribution for sale of LSD, says nothing about use, and provides for enforcement by a unit for the control of drug abuse in the Food and Drug Administration. A California law (1966) makes unlawful possession or use a misdemeanor, illicit manufacture and distribution a felony, and lodges control in the Board of Pharmacy.[31]

---

[29] Alfred R. Lindesmith, *The Addict and the Law* (Bloomington: Indiana University Press, 1965).
[30] Edwin M. Schur, *Crimes Without Victims* (Englewood Cliffs, N.J.: Prentice-Hall, 1965), 141–45.
[31] *Los Angeles Times,* July 10, 1966, C, 9.

PROGRAMS OF REHABILITATION. Treatment efforts within the framework of repression of drug addiction in the United States have been very unsuccessful; rates of relapse have been high. Yet certain things have been learned and some modest successes reported. Experience in hospital treatment centers has indicated that controlled withdrawal is not enough, that it must be followed by attempts to change attitudes and role habits.[32] Imprisonment and hospitalization of convicted offenders strengthen the in-group feelings of addicts, and those in hospital wards tend to develop an antitreatment consensus. This is difficult to overcome, but there has been some success with programs designed to shift prestige to the rehabilitated person.[33] A study was made of the results of various lengths of hospitalization at the federal center at Lexington, Kentucky, and the presence or absence of parole supervision. The highest rate of abstinence for one year in the community, 67 per cent, was found for the combination of the long (9 to 12 months) stay and parole supervision on release.[34] While later relapses may have occurred, this is an extremely high rate of post-release success in comparison with most of those reported in this study and others.

Since 1959 California has given exceptionally close supervision to addicts on parole, under the Narcotic Treatment Control Program. Readjustment from prison to community life is facilitated for as many as possible by the East Los Angeles Halfway House. All parolees are given a Nalline (an anti-narcotic drug) test each week and one or two surprise tests a month to see if they are under the influence of an opiate drug. Quick detection of a relapse makes it possible to remove the parolee from the community for up to 90 days before he reverts to crimes to sustain the habit. The parolee may return more than once to the Control Unit at Chino or San Quentin, where he receives counseling and group therapy. Most relapses occur during the first six months on parole, about half of them during the first month. Early detection is considered essential both for deterrence and to salvage the possibility of rehabilitation. California's programs for treating addiction are based on the beliefs of fact that (1) legislative and public support requires the inclusion of methods to protect the

---

[32] Schulman, op. cit., 497.
[33] James J. Thorpe and Barnard Smith, "Phases in Group Development in the Treatment of Drug Addicts," International Journal of Group Psychotherapy, 3 (January, 1953), 66–78.
[34] George E. Vaillant and Robert W. Rasor, "The Role of Compulsory Supervision in the Treatment of Addiction," Federal Probation, 30 (June, 1966), 53–59.

community from crimes by addicts, and (2) addiction can be cured, not just controlled.[35]

California has also provided for *civil commitment* to the California Rehabilitation Center. Convicted addicts may elect this procedure if they are not guilty of a violent felony and are otherwise considered good risks. Also, completely voluntary commitments may be made by the addict or his family. The program includes vocational, academic, and physical training, but emphasizes group counseling. A period of time at the Center is followed, where possible, by halfway house experience, and then by intensive parole supervision and Nalline testing. Relapses entail compulsory return to the Center, which is operated by the Department of Corrections. The civil commitment program in the State of New York is under the control of the Department of Mental Hygiene[36] and is conceived of as hospital care, followed by supervision and outpatient care.[37] Civil commitment is a major step away from handling drug addiction as crime, especially in New York, and toward replacing it with a clinical approach. A further step, the establishment of public narcotics clinics, has been proposed from time to time.

A residence for former addicts (of both sexes) was established in 1958 in Santa Monica, California, and called *Synanon* when an early resident mispronounced the word "seminar." Other Synanon houses have since been set up in other cities, all run by the residents. Started by a member of Alcoholics Anonymous,[38] Synanon bears such similarities to that organization as: (1) voluntary membership, limited to narcotics users who admit the futility of addiction; (2) acceptance of complete dependence on Synanon in order to remain drug-free; (3) unquestioning and lifelong loyalty to the norms of Synanon; (4) continuing, relentless group evaluation of the person in relation to these norms; and (5) the conferring of prestige for conformity to the norms and for long residence.[39] The program is

[35] Gilbert Geis, "Narcotic Treatment Programs in California," paper presented at the Conference on Perspectives on Narcotic Addiction, sponsored by the Massachusetts Health Research Institute and the United States Public Health Service at Chatham, Mass., September 9–11, 1963, 1–15.

[36] *Ibid*, 18–22.

[37] Richard H. Kuh, "Civil Commitment for Narcotic Addicts," *Federal Probation*, 27 (June, 1963), 21–23.

[38] Charles E. Dederich. Other houses are operating at Westport, Conn., Reno, Nevada, San Francisco, and San Diego.

[39] Geis, *op. cit.*, 15–18; Lewis Yablonsky, *The Tunnel Back: Synanon* (New York: The Macmillan Co., 1965).

based on a single-cause explanation of addiction, "emotional infancy." Research evidence is scanty, but at one point it was reported that 86 per cent of those who had remained at the original house for seven months or more were not using narcotics.[40]

The control of addiction in Great Britain under the Dangerous Drugs Act of 1920 has been designed to accomplish rehabilitation. Under this law the addict has been treated as a medical problem, his physician being free to prescribe essential doses of narcotics. The doctor is subject to penal controls if he violates the laws of drug distribution, but the user of legally prescribed narcotics is not classed as a criminal. The aim has been to cure as many as possible, but also to facilitate a fairly normal life for those believed to be incurable. The cost of the drugs is modest.[41] The lack of the criminal label has made a relatively normal community life possible, facilitated cooperation with treatment efforts, and made it unnecessary to commit crimes to sustain the habit.[42] For forty years the system was heralded for its low rate of addiction; in 1955 it was estimated that there were 335 addicts in Britain as compared with at least 60,000 in the United States.[43]

In the sixties the reported rate of addiction in Great Britain began rising, together with increased experimentation by young people with nonnarcotic drugs. Even though the *rate* of addiction had risen to only about 4 per cent of the rate reported in the United States by the mid-sixties, there was fear of a continued increase. Some doctors had allegedly given unduly large prescriptions to their patients, who had shared them with their friends; but the pusher was also reported to have appeared. The proposal to limit the handling of narcotics to physicians in special treatment centers began to be seriously considered.[44] This would tighten up control of the supply but would still be a medical rather than a criminal law approach to the addict.

PREVENTION. Rehabilitative efforts have so far not been very successful, so it is argued that prevention deserves greater emphasis. Strict

---

[40] Rita Volkman and Donald R. Cressey, "Differential Association and Rehabilitation of Drug Addicts," *American Journal of Sociology*, 69 (September, 1963), 129–42.

[41] Clausen, in Merton and Nisbet, *op. cit.*, 233–34.

[42] Edwin M. Schur, *Narcotic Addiction in Britain and America* (Bloomington: Indiana University Press, 1962), 154–55, 206.

[43] Alfred R. Lindesmith, "The British System of Narcotics Control," *op. cit.*, 141–42; *cf.* Schur, *op. cit.*, 118.

[44]*Los Angeles Times*, May 23, 1965, A, 22, and June 17, 1966, II, 5.

control of the supply of drugs prevents most people from gaining ready access to them. Judging by the comparative experiences of Great Britain and the United States, this policy is far more effective when combined with a medical approach to the addict because of the large black market created by criminal prosecution. It seems unlikely that other variables could account for so large a difference between the rates of addiction in the two countries. The medical approach also prevents the crimes that are committed by buyers of illicit drugs.

The other main preventive effort is public health education, a combination of information about the effects of dangerous drugs and persuasion against their use. Much of this persuasion in the United States has been designed to emphasize the criminal status of users of prohibited drugs. Little is known about the amount and conditions of success of this and other appeals. Preventive educational effort apparently has been complicated by the rise of issues concerning the criminal status of users of a number of nonnarcotic drugs.

ALCOHOLISM

The Redefinition of an Issue

While some individuals and groups consider any drinking of alcoholic beverages to be a social problem, the predominant view in America today is that the problem is alcoholism—excessive drinking. The temperance movement was correctly named when it began in the eighteenth century, since its supporters called for moderation rather than abstinence. The widespread use of wine and beer during the seventeenth century had been controlled by norms of moderation, enforced by families. The greater ease of transporting distilled liquors led to a marked increase in their use, and the lack of traditional family restraints on the frontier became associated with the heavy drinking of hard liquor. Americans became polarized into heavy drinkers and abstainers, and by 1840 the adherents of the "temperance" movement were calling for abstinence from the use of all alcoholic beverages. This became associated with another movement, for women's rights. More than one-third of the states passed prohibition laws in the 1850's, only to repeal or restrict them within a few years. Similar laws passed by eight states in the 1880's met the same fate. During the World War I period, a drive spearheaded by the Anti-Saloon League resulted in such laws in 25 states, and in the Eighteenth

(Prohibition) Amendment to the federal Constitution in 1919.[45]

After several years of widespread violation, the Prohibition Amendment was repealed in 1933 by referendum, with only 30 per cent voting to retain it. National polls from 1936 to 1956 showed a variation from 33 to 38 per cent (excluding the undecided) in favor of returning to prohibition, and then the percentage dropped to 26 in 1960 and to 22 in 1966.[46] The South has been the stronghold of prohibition sentiment, and half the people of the region still favored it in 1960. Table 10.2 shows that support for prohibition in the South had dropped to 37 per cent in 1966, but that the percentage in other regions was much lower. The table also indicates considerably more support by farmers, persons with limited education, those over age 50, Protestants, rural dwellers, and persons with low incomes. Smaller differences were found for sex and political affiliation.

The decline in support for prohibition has occurred during a time of proportionate decrease in the use of distilled liquors, and a corresponding increase in the percentage of beer and wine drinkers. Nearly nine-tenths of the alcohol consumed in 1850 in America was in hard liquor, and only about seven per cent in beer. In 1960 only 38 per cent of the alcohol used was in distilled liquor, while 51 per cent was in beer.[47] The increase in the drinking of beer and wine in the late nineteenth and twentieth centuries apparently resulted from the large migrations of people from Germany and the countries of Southern and Eastern Europe, but the use of these beverages has now been diffused widely among other Americans. Perhaps norms of moderation similar to those of early Colonial times are again developing, but at any rate a substantial majority of Americans view alcoholism as the social problem rather than all forms and amounts of drinking.

Extent of Drinking and Alcoholism

Alcoholism consists of drinking so excessively that (a) it is viewed by the community as extremely deviant, and (b) it markedly impairs

---

[45] Robert Strauss, "Alcohol," Chapter 5 in Merton and Nisbet, *op. cit.*, 244–49; Raymond G. McCarthy and Edgar M. Douglass, *Alcohol and Social Responsibility* (New York: Thomas Y. Crowell Co., 1949), 25–41; Robert Strauss and Seldon D. Bacon, *Drinking in College* (New Haven, Conn.: Yale University Press, 1953), 20–35.

[46] *Gallup Political Index*, Report No. 9 (February, 1966), 20.

[47] Mark Keller and Vera Efron, *Selected Statistical Tables on Alcoholic Beverages, 1850–1960, and on Alcoholism, 1930–1960* (New Brunswick, N. J.: Quarterly Journal of Studies on Alcohol, Inc., 1961), 3.

TABLE 10.2

REPLIES OF A REPRESENTATIVE SAMPLE OF ADULT AMERICANS IN FEBRU-
ARY, 1966, TO THE QUESTION, "WOULD YOU FAVOR OR OPPOSE A LAW FOR-
BIDDING THE SALE OF ALL BEER, WINE AND LIQUOR THROUGHOUT THE
NATION?"

	Favor %	*Oppose* %	*No Opinion* %
National	21	76	3
Sex			
Men	18	79	3
Women	24	72	4
Education			
College	14	83	3
High School	19	77	4
Grade School	28	69	3
Occupation			
Professional & Business	16	83	1
White Collar	14	84	2
Farmers	39	56	5
Manual	21	74	5
Age			
21–29 years	16	80	4
30–49 years	16	80	4
50 & over	26	71	3
Religion			
Protestant	27	69	4
Catholic	8	90	2
Politics			
Republican	19	79	2
Democrat	23	74	3
Independent	17	79	4
Region			
East	7	91	2

TABLE 10.2 (*Continued*)

	Favor %	*Oppose* %	*No Opinion* %
Midwest	21	75	4
South	37	57	6
West	18	80	2
Income			
$7,000 & over	13	85	2
$5,000–$6,999	19	78	3
$3,000–$4,999	28	66	6
Under $3,000	34	62	4
Community Size			
500,000 & over	11	86	3
50,000–499,999	19	78	3
2,500–49,999	22	76	2
Under 2,500, Rural	33	62	5

SOURCE: Gallup Political Index, *Report No. 9* (*February, 1966*), 20.

the health of the person and his ability to meet his role obligations.[48] The available measures—deaths attributed to (alcoholic) cirrhosis of the liver, numerous arrests for drunkenness, and the records of mental hospitals, clinics, and social work agencies[49]—probably underestimate the amount of alcoholism. One estimate for the United States in 1960 was approximately four and one-half million alcoholics.[50] Five million is probably a conservative figure for the midsixties, about one in 18 adult users of alcoholic beverages, with men

[48] Mark Keller and John R. Seeley, *The Alcohol Language* (Toronto: University of Toronto Press, 1958), 19; Mark Keller, "Definition of Alcoholism," *Quarterly Journal of Studies on Alcohol*, 21 (March, 1960), 125–34.
[49] William and Joan McCord, *Origins of Alcoholism* (Stanford, Calif.: Stanford University Press, 1960), 10–11.
[50] Keller and Efron, *op. cit.*

outnumbering women alcoholics by more than five times.[51] *Judging by available statistics, there are nearly one hundred times more alcoholics in the United States than there are drug addicts.*

The most readily recognized alcoholics are the chronic ones, constituting an estimated *one-fourth of the total. The chronic alcoholic is an addict, since he is physiologically dependent on alcohol and must drink almost continually or suffer withdrawal symptoms;* he has completely lost control over his drinking and his ability to fulfill his role responsibilities.[52] Others presumably drink to excess because of emotional rather than physiological dependency on alcohol, and are able to meet their role duties part of the time. This contrasts sharply with the take-it-or-leave-it approach of the "social drinker," especially the "occasional" type who has only a few drinks a year. The "regular social drinker" may drink three or more times a week, but still in a controlled manner. The "heavy drinker"—who takes three or more drinks at a time more than once a week—often becomes intoxicated and has some difficulty controlling his drinking. Heavy drinkers are able to reduce the amount or stop entirely, but some continue the heavy pattern for a lifetime and some become alcoholics. Alcoholism usually involves progressively more drinking over a period of 10 to 20 years.[53]

One-third of a representative national sample of adults in 1945 said they were total abstainers from the use of alcoholic beverages. In annual polls, thereafter, the figure increased to a high of 45 per cent in 1958, then decreased to 35 per cent in 1966. Twelve per cent of the 1966 sample said liquor had been a cause of trouble in their families.[54] Table 10.3 indicates the distribution of the 1966 responses by several variables; it should be noted that it includes occasional as well as heavier drinkers. There is a close correspondence between Tables 10.2 and 10.3. The groups with the most abstainers tend to favor prohibition, although the totals indicate that many of their numbers are opposed to it. Evidently the percentage of women who drink is approaching that of men, but women are still much less likely to become heavy drinkers and alcoholics.

---

[51] Strauss, *op. cit.*, 267.
[52] *Ibid.*, 260–62.
[53] Marshall B. Clinard, *Sociology of Deviant Behavior* (Rev. ed.; New York: Holt, Rinehart & Winston, 1963).
[54] *Gallup Political Index, op. cit.*, 18–19.

TABLE 10.3

REPLIES OF A REPRESENTATIVE SAMPLE OF ADULT AMERICANS IN FEBRUARY, 1966, TO THE QUESTION, "DO YOU HAVE OCCASION TO USE ALCOHOLIC BEVERAGES SUCH AS LIQUOR, WINE OR BEER—OR ARE YOU A TOTAL ABSTAINER?"

	Yes, Use Alcoholic Beverages %	No, Total Abstainers %
National	65	35
Sex		
Men	70	30
Women	61	39
Education		
College	75	25
High School	70	30
Grade School	51	49
Occupation		
Professional & Business	78	22
White Collar	72	28
Farmers	33	67
Manual	65	35
Age		
21–29 years	76	24
30–49 years	70	30
50 & over	57	43
Religion		
Protestant	56	44
Catholic	85	15
Politics		
Republican	69	31
Democrat	63	37
Independent	69	31
Region		
East	83	17

Midwest	65	35
South	38	62
West	77	23
Income		
$7,000 & over	81	19
$5,000–$6,999	70	30
$3,000–$4,999	46	54
Under $3,000	41	59
Community Size		
500,000 & over	84	16
50,000–499,999	67	33
2,500–49,999	62	38
Under 2,500, Rural	44	56

SOURCE: Gallup Political Index, *Report No. 9 (February, 1966), 18.*

Social Effects of Alcoholism

Alcoholism damages the individual's health and impairs his performance as a member of the family, on the job, and in other roles. Alcoholics have a life expectancy from 10 to 20 years lower than that of other Americans. Tensions in the family or other groups may promote excessive drinking, but this in turn aggravates family problems, often resulting in severe conflicts and divorce. Large amounts of family income go for alcoholic beverages, drastically reducing the amounts available for food, clothing, shelter, health, and education. Excessive drinking threatens family security and may undermine it completely, especially when it becomes impossible to keep a job.

This frequent impoverishment of families increases community welfare costs. Employed alcoholics miss an average of nearly a month of work each year; the annual cost to the economy in absenteeism and inefficiency is probably at least as high as two billion dollars.[55] Excessive drinking is probably responsible for at least 2,000 industrial deaths a year, and for many times that number of accidental deaths at home, on the highway, and elsewhere. The primary factor in driver-

---

[55] *Los Angeles Times*, October 21, 1966, I, 22.

caused automobile accidents is alcohol; but, of course, drinkers who are not alcoholics contribute heavily to this result. It has been difficult to enforce strict laws against driving after drinking, due apparently to the high valuation of both the right to drink and the right to drive.[56]

About half of all arrests in the nation in 1965 were for drunkenness, driving while under the influence of alcohol, liquor law violations, or disorderly conduct.[57] There is no way to estimate the proportion of these arrests attributable to alcoholism, but it is no doubt considerable. Drinking, both by alcoholics and others, is a factor in many arrests for other offenses also. However, the causal relationship between drinking and crime is not at all clear when the arrest is not for intoxication as such. The fact that a person has been drinking, although alcohol does lower inhibitions, does not prove that it is a contributing cause of a subsequent burglary, assault, or other crime.[58]

It is evident that the total monetary cost to society of excessive drinking is great, although exact estimates are not possible. Another way to reckon the cost is to estimate the number of people directly affected, recognizing that some suffer more than others. Besides the alcoholics, these would include the members of their families, and persons suffering injuries, crimes, economic privation, or marked emotional stress through the excessive drinking of others. If there are five million alcoholics in the nation, and an average of six persons directly affected by each, the total (including the alcoholics) is 35 million people.

The Elusive Causes of Excessive Drinking

Among the theories of alcoholism are explanations stated in terms of emotional stresses that are very similar to those suggested for drug addiction. Alcoholics have been described clinically as being extremely dependent on others, and as having marked feelings of inadequacy, guilt, masochism, and anxiety. But why do most people with these personality problems adjust in other ways: by other forms of deviance, including drug addiction, or by socially accepted forms of adjustment such as overworking? Also, does the presence of these

---

[56] Strauss, in Merton and Nisbet, *op. cit.,* 256–59.
[57] *The World Almanac and Book of Facts, 1967, op. cit.,* 693.
[58] Howard T. Blane, "Drinking and Crime," *Federal Probation,* 29 (June, 1965), 25–29.

emotional symptoms prove that they existed before excessive drinking began? Perhaps they are more result than cause of a dozen or more years of alcoholic behavior. Despite these difficulties it seems reasonable to suggest that emotional problems contribute to excessive drinking, at least in many cases, and treatment efforts in which the person's current feelings are ignored would probably be futile.

Various physiological conditions have been investigated as possible causes of excessive drinking, including nutritional deficiencies, and malfunctioning of the liver, endocrine glands, and central nervous system. Even if most alcoholics have a given physical condition, there is the problem of determining when it developed, and why. Was it cause or effect of excessive drinking? And, if it in fact preceded alcoholism, do not most people probably cope with such a condition without excessive drinking? If so, such bodily conditions can be neither sufficient nor necessary causes of alcoholism, though they might contribute to it.

Explanations in terms of socially induced stress have been advanced. Occupations with low prestige and income have a high incidence of alcoholic psychosis,[59] but the anxieties and practices of the middle and lower-upper classes apparently often cause excessive drinking.[60] Social isolation has been found to be associated with alcoholic behavior, notably in the case of the homeless man on Skid Row.[61] Another stressful situation associated with alcoholism is living in an all-male community, such as the work camp, the military, or on shipboard.[62] Yet most people experiencing such conditions, even in groups with a high rate of heavy drinking, do not become alcoholics; and perhaps a good many are in such situations as a result of excessive drinking. So the contribution of social stresses to alcoholism is complex and not yet clear.

---

[59] Robert E. Clark, "The Relationship of Alcoholic Psychoses Commitment Rates to Occupational Income and Occupational Prestige," *American Sociological Review,* 14 (August, 1949), 539–43.

[60] McCord and McCord, *op. cit.,* 41; Clinard, *op. cit.,* 352–55.

[61] Robert Strauss and Raymond G. McCarthy, "Nonaddictive Pathological Drinking Patterns of Homeless Men," *Quarterly Journal of Studies on Alcohol,* 12 (December, 1951), 601–11; Nels Anderson, *The Hobo: The Sociology of the Homeless Man* (Chicago: The University of Chicago Press, 1923; reissued by Phoenix, 1961), 134–35; W. Jack Peterson and Milton A. Maxwell, "The Skid Road 'Wino'," *Social Problems,* 5 (Spring 1958), 308–16.

[62] David J. Pittman and C. Wayne Gordon, *Revolving Door* (New York: The Free Press, 1958), 67.

Evidently a major factor is the presence or absence of norms of control of drinking. Italians of both sexes have customarily used wine with family meals, and Jews traditionally drink wine during family religious observances. As the child is socialized into these groups he comes to associate the moderate drinking of wine, and the abhorrence of heavy drinking and drunkenness, with family unity and religious values. Cultural definitions of drinking vary greatly, and these two groups stand in sharp contrast to the Irish. In Ireland, at least for well over a century, heavy drinking and drunkenness have been accepted ways for the adult male to gain release from economic privation, late marriage, and other tensions. Thus in America, persons with an Irish background are far more likely than those of Jewish or Italian parentage to become excessive drinkers, although a smaller percentage of Irish adults drink anything and far fewer of them drank any alcoholic beverage as a child.[63] A related finding is that persons who grow up in religious groups that teach abstinence have far greater difficulty controlling drinking than those from groups that teach moderation.[64] Perhaps the reason American women as a whole are so much less likely to become alcoholics than men is no longer that a small percentage of them drink, or that they experience few tensions, but that they are more likely than men to be taught norms of moderation.

Research to date suggests that there are many variables that contribute to excessive drinking, and no single discipline seems capable of providing a complete explanation. More adequate general theories of causation would seem to depend on more effective cooperation among physiologists, psychologists, psychiatrists, sociologists, and anthropologists. When alcoholism was becoming defined as an illness in the thirties and forties, public support was developed for biological and medical research. As public beliefs of fact about deviant behavior have shifted away from biological determinism and toward the inclusion of personality, social, and cultural variables, research efforts have been broadened. Evidently norms of control of drinking play a large role in preventing alcoholic behavior, but little is known yet about the interaction of cultural definitions of drinking with other variables.

---

[63] Robert Freed Bales, "Cultural Differences in Rates of Alcoholism," *Quarterly Journal of Studies on Alcohol*, 6 (March, 1946), 400–99; Charles R. Snyder, *Alcohol and the Jews* (New York: The Free Press, 1958), 9–10, 182, 202.
[64] Jerome H. Skolnick, "Religious Affiliation and Drinking Behavior," *Quarterly Journal of Studies on Alcohol*, 19 (September, 1958), 452–70.

Control of Alcoholism

LEGAL CONTROLS. There are no criminal laws against alcoholism as such, but alcoholics are often among those arrested for drunkenness, disorderly conduct, drunken driving, or liquor law violations. There are legal controls over liquor sales and the age and place of public drinking, but otherwise the criminal law approach to drinking contrasts sharply with that taken toward the possession and use of drugs. Those alcoholics who are drug addicts from a medical standpoint, being physiologically dependent on alcohol, are not subjected to narcotics laws. From the standpoint of formal laws, alcoholism is not a crime, but an illness. However, most legal agencies, especially those of local government, take little or no responsibility for its treatment. Alcoholics convicted of major felonies are more likely to receive some kind of treatment for their condition than are those arrested and jailed briefly for drunken and disorderly conduct. Despite distinctions in the legal norms, the effect of repeated jailing for drunken behavior is that alcoholism is handled primarily as a crime rather than an illness.

PROGRAMS OF REHABILITATION. Founded in 1935, and greatly expanded after favorable publicity in the forties, Alcoholics Anonymous has become the most important program for arresting uncontrolled drinking and for sustaining sobriety. In keeping with the Oxford Group religious movement, A.A. asks its members to confess their helplessness to control their drinking, and to acknowledge their complete dependence on A.A. and on God for the maintenance of their sobriety. Two key beliefs of fact are (1) that only an alcoholic can help another alcoholic, and (2) that an alcoholic must help his fellow victims in order to stay sober himself. The group therapy of frank discussion meetings is supplemented by many acts that lend group support to the person trying to stay sober.

On the basis of the claim of a success rate of at least two-thirds, the A.A. program has often been credited with being the most successful program yet devised to control alcoholism, and with being a major influence in convincing the general public that excessive drinking is an illness. But it has also received criticism. It has allegedly tended to become a ritualistic cult with a dogmatic ideology, and a vested interest with great influence as a pressure group. It has been criticized for contending that those who cannot stay sober with the help of

A.A. are psychotics rather than true alcoholics, that those who learn to drink moderately could never have been alcoholics, that scientific evidence contrary to A.A. ideology is false, and that other programs of control are worthless. Critics usually acknowledge that A.A. offers the most hope for the majority of alcoholics, but insist that many cannot profit from it and often become desperate when told there is no other way.[65]

Community clinics for alcoholism under both public and private auspices have been operating in many cities since the forties. A major task for them has been the provision of hospital facilities for the addictive alcoholic. The medical profession has assumed only limited responsibility for treating excessive drinking, even in public institutions, so the provision of hospital facilities for acute cases is usually a part of a clinical program. Such clinics rely heavily on family ties for the effectiveness of their outpatient programs, so they do not reach most homeless men alcoholics. Most of these men evidently avoid the demands of the clinical bureaucracy unless they become extremely desperate.[66]

Numerous programs for alcoholics have been provided within penal systems. Chapters of Alcoholic Anonymous have become widely accepted in correctional institutions. The half-way houses for alcoholics operated in some systems have been credited with a success rate of about one-third.[67] Parole officers often cooperate with A.A. and community clinics. Some probation officers have included special discussion groups for excessive drinkers in their case-loads.[68]

PREVENTING EXCESSIVE DRINKING. Since alcoholism has come to be classed as an illness it has been considered a public health problem, and is now usually listed as the third or fourth most serious one. Public health agencies, schools, churches, and other agencies have devoted considerable attention to education about drinking. The Yale Center of Alcohol Studies has provided leadership in research. In 1966

[65] Arthur H. Cain, "Alcoholics Anonymous: Cult or Cure?" in Judson R. Landis, *Current Perspectives on Social Problems* (Belmont, Calif.: Wadsworth Publishing Co., 1966), 46–54.
[66] Robert Strauss, "Alcoholism," in Arnold Rose (ed.), *Mental Health and Mental Disorder* (New York: Norton, 1955), 441–47.
[67] Edward Blacker and David Kantor, "Half-Way Houses for Problem Drinkers," *Federal Probation*, 24 (June, 1960), 18–23.
[68] Edward W. Soden, "Constructive Coercion and Group Counseling in the Rehabilitation of Alcoholics," *Federal Probation*, 30 (September, 1966), 56–60.

a national center for controlling and preventing alcoholism was established within the National Institutes of Health, to coordinate research, treatment, and preventive efforts.

It has been claimed that Alcoholics Anonymous controls most of the public information about research, treatment, and community activities in this area. A.A.'s allegedly hold key positions in most governmental and private agencies dealing with the problem. One consequence claimed is the neglect of psychological and sociological knowledge, since the A.A. view is that alcoholism is a physical problem only.[69] Since a multidisciplinary approach seems in keeping with knowledge thus far, a particularistic line would appear to pose obstacles to treatment and prevention. Widespread knowledge about the role of variables such as norms of moderate drinking might prevent much alcoholism, although such knowledge is not automatically translatable into effective action.

The agencies of the criminal law treat many alcoholics and prevent a great deal of alcoholism, and could do much more. They treat alcoholism as a problem that often contributes to criminal offending, and thus combat excessive drinking in order to prevent more crimes. They are in a position to know about excessive drinking at all stages in the criminal law process, and to take authoritative action. We have already pointed out that felonious offenders are more likely to receive this type of attention, so the greatest room for more criminal law responsibility in preventing alcoholism is in the municipal courts and their jails.

PERSPECTIVE

Beliefs of both fact and value concerning drug addiction and alcoholism have undergone changes in American society. Defining the possession and use of narcotics as crimes limited the supplies to underworld channels, thus reducing the known rate of addiction by nine-tenths and restricting it largely to a few urban areas. The criminal image of the addict has been reinforced, and the cost of narcotics has been made so high that to maintain the habit most people must resort to lucrative crimes. Dangerous non-narcotic drugs also have been subjected to criminal law controls, and this has recently become a public issue as new knowledge of the properties of drugs has spread.

---

[69] Cain, in Landis, *op. cit.*, 49–51.

Since the repeal of the Prohibition Amendment, moderate drinking has been increasingly accepted, and alcoholism has come to be seen more as an illness than as a crime. Yet frequent arrests for drunken behavior perpetuate the criminal treatment. Evidently there are at least 100 times more alcoholics than there are drug addicts, so far more people have direct contact with excessive drinking. One-fourth or so of the alcoholics are physically addicted, yet they are seen in law and in public opinion as ill and unfortunate people, in contrast to the definition of the drug user as a criminal. In England and other countries of West Europe, drug addiction is treated as a medical problem and the incidence is but a fraction of that in the United States. It is noteworthy that the supplies are restricted, along with the medical approach, and that moderate costs prevent a large black market traffic in drugs from developing. For excessive drinking the medical approach alone seems insufficient, and the American public is unwilling to limit the supply of alcoholic beverages. Research findings suggest that one promising alternative would be to promote norms of moderation, and perhaps this idea also has some merit in connection with (at least some of) the nonnarcotic drugs.

Are alcoholism and drug addiction "crimes without victims?" Technically, alcoholism is not a crime, although the effect of arrests for drunken conduct is that much of it is treated as such. We have seen that the number of people directly harmed by excessive drinking is very large, so it is not only the alcoholic who suffers. The drug addict is also not the only victim of his practices, and the black market gives rise to crime and supports syndicates. In criminal law it is not necessary to prove that a person intends the particular harm he causes, and any conduct that violates the stability and security of society or its individual members may be included in the criminal code. But when criminal laws are ineffective, they accomplish little except to express condemnation of certain behavior. And if they have undesired consequences, such as creating a black market in drugs, they do not resolve the general problem. Whether they should then be revised or abandoned is a very complex issue.

The Oxford Group has spawned an innovation—the group support organization—that has spread from Alcoholics Anonymous to other compulsive habits, and to other areas involving difficult common problems of personal adjustment. The Synanon organization for drug addicts consciously borrowed and adapted its basic beliefs from A.A., and Gamblers Anonymous (formed in 1957) did also. Fairly similar organizations for divorced persons and for other areas of shared suffering have also been formed. Their spread must be due to more than the urban, and American, propensity to form voluntary organizations around special interests. One suggestion is that seeking help from one's fellow victims is an extension of the individualistic value of helping oneself rather than asking taxpayers to support a program. Also, the person wrestles with his conscience, admits the complete error of his ways, and acknowledges his dependence on others (and on God) for his salvation. At any rate, the claims are that Synanon and A.A. have been much more successful than other programs for controlling drug addiction and alcoholism. Much more research on these and other group support organizations is needed before we can say how effective they are, and why, and the same may be said of other programs of treatment and prevention.

QUESTIONS FOR DISCUSSION AND STUDY

1. Was drug addiction a new social problem in the twentieth century? Was alcoholism? Explain.

2. Apparently there has been a marked increase in the use of both narcotics and nonaddictive drugs by young people. Why? How do the patterns differ from one social class to another?

3. Why do you think Negroes and Puerto Ricans are disproportionately represented among drug addicts?

4. What beliefs of fact about the causes of drug addiction underlie the American approach to its control? The British approach? Explain.

5. Can you think of more than one way to take the syndicate's profit out of the drug traffic? Explain.

6. Is there a variable that seems to you to be either a sufficient or a necessary cause of alcoholism? Of drug addiction? Explain.

7. Why do you think outlawing the possession and use of narcotics is acceptable to the American people while the same approach to alcoholic beverages has been rejected by a substantial majority?

8. In the future, do you think American legal controls on marihuana, LSD, and other nonnarcotic drugs will likely be more similar to the present controls on narcotics or to those on alcoholic beverages? Why?

9. Do you think group support organizations can support norms of mod-

eration as effectively as A.A. and Synanon seem to be able to support abstinence? Explain.

10. As a nation, do you think America is likely to move further toward or away from norms of moderation in drinking? In the use of nonnarcotic drugs? In each instance, what evidence do you have in mind?

11. Outline what you believe might be an effective program for preventing drug addiction. For alcoholism. Indicate your supporting beliefs of fact.

SELECTED READING

Alexander, C. Norman, "Consensus and Mutual Attraction in Natural Cliques: A Study of Adolescent Drinkers," *American Journal of Sociology*, 69 (January, 1964), 395–403.

Bacon, Selden (ed.), "Understanding Alcoholism," Special Issue of *The Annals*, 315 (January, 1958), 1–200.

Ball, John C., and Bates, William M., "Migrations and Residential Mobility of Narcotic Drug Addicts," *Social Problems*, 14 (Summer, 1966), 56–69.

Baur, E. Jackson, and McCluggage, Marston M., "Drinking Patterns of Kansas High School Students," *Social Problems*, 5 (Spring, 1958), 317–26.

Blum, Richard, and Associates, *Utopiates: The Use and Users of LSD-25* (New York: Atherton Press, 1964).

Cavan, Sherri, *Liquor License: An Ethnography of Bar Behavior* (Chicago: Aldine Publishing Co., 1966).

Cramer, Mary Jane, and Blacker, Edward, " 'Early' and 'Late' Problem Drinkers Among Female Prisoners," *Journal of Health and Human Behavior*, 4 (Winter, 1963), 282–90.

Gusfield, Joseph R., *Symbolic Crusade: Status Politics and the American Temperance Movement* (Urbana: University of Illinois Press, 1964).

Klonsky, George, "Extended Supervision for Discharged Addict-Parolees," *Federal Probation*, 29 (March, 1965), 39–44.

Lindesmith, Alfred R., *The Addict and the Law* (Bloomington: Indiana University Press, 1965).

Lorch, Barbara Day, "The Perception of Deviancy by Self and Others," *Sociology and Social Research*, 50 (January, 1966), 223–29. The process is illustrated with material on alcoholism.

Maddox, George L., and McCall, Bevode C., *Drinking Among Teenagers* (New Brunswick, N.J.: Rutgers Center of Alcohol Studies, 1964).

McCarthy, Raymond G., *Alcohol Education for Classroom and Community* (New York: McGraw-Hill, 1966).

Mulford, Harold A., and Miller, Donald E., "Measuring Public Acceptance of the Alcoholic As a Sick Person," *Quarterly Journal of Studies on Alcohol*, 25 (June, 1964), 314–24.

O'Donnell, John A., and Ball, John C. (eds.), *Narcotics Addiction* (New York: Harper & Row, 1966).

Pittman, David J., and Snyder, Charles R. (eds.), *Alcohol, Culture and Drinking Patterns* (New York: John Wiley & Sons, 1962).

Roebuck, Julian, "The Negro Drug Addict As an Offender Type," *Journal of Criminal Law, Criminology and Police Science*, 53 (March, 1962), 36–43.

Rubington, Earl, "Grady 'Breaks Out': A Case Study of An Alcoholic's Relapse," *Social Problems*, 11 (Spring, 1964), 372–79.

Schur, Edwin M., *Narcotic Addiction in Britain and America* (Bloomington: Indiana University Press, 1962).

"Symposium on Alcoholism," Special Issue of *Social Problems*, 5 (Spring, 1958), 292–338.

Trice, Harrison, *Alcoholism in America* (New York: McGraw-Hill, 1966). Includes a comparison with drug addiction.

Yablonsky, Lewis, *The Tunnel Back: Synanon* (New York: The Macmillan Co., 1965).

IV
Continuing National Dilemmas

A quick and easy way to assess historical growth is to note how long it took to reach each billion of population. The world's people first totaled a billion about 1820 and thereafter arose to two billion around 1930 and three billion about 1960. Thus after requiring hundreds of thousands of years to achieve the first billion, the people of the world added another billion in only about three decades. The four- five- and six-billion marks are expected to be reached by about 1975, 1985, and 1995 respectively.[1]

11. Population Problems

BY ABOUT 1650 there were an estimated one-half billion people on earth, the result of a very long period of slow and uneven growth. Then the rate of population growth greatly accelerated, with consequences felt around the globe. Why did this human population explosion begin in the mid-seventeenth century, and why in the West, more particularly in Northwest Europe? What have comparative patterns of growth around the world been like since then? What accounts for the variations, and how are population issues related to them?

THE DEMOGRAPHIC TRANSITION

If migration into a given territory equals the migration out of it, the population can grow only by natural increase—*i.e.*, by an excess of births over deaths. Throughout most of man's existence this natural increase has been uncontrolled, with neither births nor deaths subject to effective limitation. The uncontrolled birth rate was high, yet growth was slow because the uncontrolled death rate was almost as high, and sometimes higher because of famines, epidemics, and major

---

[1] Ralph Thomlinson, *Demographic Problems* (Belmont, Calif.: Dickenson Publishing Co., 1967), 14.

wars. This ancient balance of human population began to disappear in Europe about 1650, when the first population explosion signaled the beginning of the transition to a new kind of balance, one involving the control of births and deaths.[2]

The Effect of "Death Control"

Hypothetically, holding migration constant, a rapid increase in the rate of population growth of an area could be due to a marked increase in the birth rate or a sharp decrease in the death rate, or a combination of the two. Demographers (systematic students of human populations) usually have attributed population explosions mainly or entirely to a declining death rate. As the birth rate remains high, and the death rate drops well below it, the rate of natural increase booms because more of those being born are staying alive. Any simultaneous increase that may occur in the birth rate, such as apparently took place during England's industrial revolution because of increased illegitimacy and other factors, accentuates the population explosion.[3]

This discussion is in terms of the "crude birth rate" (number of live births in a given year per 1,000 of total population) and the "crude death rate" (number of deaths in a year per 1,000 of total population). An uncontrolled birth rate of 50.0 per 1,000 and an uncontrolled death rate of 47.0 yields a rate of natural increase of 3 per 1,000, or .3 per cent per year. If the birth rate remains at 50.0 while the death rate drops to 30.0, the increase jumps to 20 per 1,000, or 2 per cent per year. If the birth rate then drops to 35.0 and the death rate to 10.0, the growth is 2.5 per cent per year. A new population balance, in which the rate of natural increase is slow again, depends on a fall in the birth rate almost to the new low level of the death rate. For example, Table 11.1 shows that Sweden's rate of growth in 1960 had fallen to .37 per cent, in contrast to a country such as Mexico with a rate of 3.36 per cent. A rate of increase of 3 per cent a year doubles the population every 23 years; one of 2 per cent doubles it every 35 years.

TECHNOLOGY AND THE LEVEL OF LIVING. In Chapters 1 and 4 we noted the effect of the agricultural and industrial revolutions on the level of living. In the developing countries of the West, long before the com-

---

[2] *Ibid.,* 14–15.
[3] William Petersen, *Population* (New York: The Macmillan Co., 1961), 11–14, 393–402.

TABLE II.I

CRUDE BIRTH AND DEATH RATES,* AND RATE OF NATURAL
INCREASE, FOR SELECTED COUNTRIES, 1960†

	Birth Rates	Death Rates	Rates of Natural Increase‡
United States	23.6§	9.5§	14.1§
Sweden	13.7	10.0	3.7
Japan	17.2§	7.6§	9.6§
Soviet Union	24.9	7.1	17.8
Puerto Rico	31.7§	6.7§	25.0§
Taiwan	39.5	6.9	32.6
Tunisia	43.7	10.8	32.9
Mexico	45.0	11.4	33.6

§ *Provisional*
* *Crude rates indicate the number of births or deaths for every 1,000 persons of all ages.*
† *The selection of countries has been limited by the fact that many countries do not yet have reliable vital statistics.*
‡ *The rate of natural increase is merely the difference between the birth rate and the death rate.*

SOURCE: *Murray Gendell and Hans L. Zetterberg (eds.),* A Sociological Almanac for the United States *(2nd ed.; New York: Charles Scribner's Sons, 1964, Table 1.21, p. 41 (based on United Nations,* Demographic Yearbook 1961, *pp. 162ff. and 264ff.).*

ing of the medical revolution (see Chapter 5), food production was increasing, along with more and better housing, clothing, and other goods and services, and a (probably slowly) rising level of consumption by the poor. There were significant reductions in scurvy, rickets, and other food-deficiency diseases, and they ceased to be major threats to life. The death rate declined, due probably in the main to the improving food supply.[4] The result, apparently accentuated in some areas by a somewhat higher birth rate for a time, was an unprecedented burst of population growth.

---

[4] *Ibid.,* 385–93.

It is apparent in Table 11.2 that the coming of the technological revolution altered the continental distribution of the world's population. The population of Europe constituted less than one-fifth of the world's total in 1700, but nearly one-fourth of it during the first half of the twentieth century. Moreover, European migrants and their descendants accounted for most of the great increase in the Americas and other areas of colonial settlement. Most of Asia and Africa had not experienced the technological revolution by 1950, and their proportions of the world's population had declined from the 1700 percent-

TABLE 11.2

POPULATION OF THE WORLD BY CONTINENTS, 1700–1950
(POPULATION ESTIMATED IN MILLIONS)

Continent	1700	1800	1900	1950
North America	1	6	81	166
South and Central America	12	19	63	162
Europe	110	187	401	559
Asia	400	602	937	1302
Africa	98	90	120	198
Oceania	2	2	6	13
Total	623	906	1608	2400

Percentage Distribution

	1700	1800	1900	1950
North America	0.2	0.7	5.1	6.9
South and Central America	2.0	2.1	3.9	6.7
Europe	17.7	20.7	24.9	23.3
Asia	64.2	66.4	58.3	54.3
Africa	15.7	9.9	7.4	8.3
Oceania	0.3	0.2	0.4	0.5
Total	100.0+	100.0	100.0	100.0

SOURCE: *Harold A. Phelps and David Henderson,* Population in Its Human Aspects *(New York: Appleton-Century-Crofts, 1958), 6, Table 1–2. Based on W. S. and E. S. Woytinsky,* World Population and Production *(New York: Twentieth Century Fund, 1953), 34, 260.*

ages. Now the rate of growth in the Western world has slowed down considerably, and the spread of the technological revolution has brought population explosions to the undeveloped countries. It is estimated that by the year 2,000 only about 15 per cent of the world's people will be in Europe and the U.S.S.R., about 5 per cent in America north of Mexico, above 9 per cent in Latin America, while Asia's percentage will have increased again to nearly 62 per cent.[5]

THE MEDICAL REVOLUTION. Not until the latter part of the nineteenth century, as we saw in Chapter 5, was the necessary knowledge available to bring the contagious diseases under control. To the inadvertent death control brought about by the higher level of living in developing countries was now added the public health campaigns to wipe out the ancient killers of babies and small children. This medical revolution has greatly reduced infant and child mortality, further cutting the death rates in these countries, and thus intensifying their population explosions. A dramatic example of this is the fact that the rate of population growth in the United States was five times greater than that of India from 1871 to 1941, despite an American birth rate only about half as high as India's.[6]

The medical revolution came to most of the undeveloped countries after World War II, primarily through the auspices of the World Health Organization of the United Nations. The all-out battles against malaria, typhus, yaws, trachoma, endemic syphilis, and other ancient communicable diseases have produced remarkable results. Ceylon's death rate was cut in half in ten years by DDT spraying, and it later fell to below 10 per thousand; yet its birth rate remains near 40 per thousand. Since little has been done to promote economic development, these "extra" children who have been kept alive by the medical revolution must be subsidized by the United Nations. Countries that are not technologically advanced cannot absorb the rapid population growth resulting from disease control, yet medicine is usually what these countries want first. The demographic transition is taking place at a much faster pace than it did in Europe and North America, in decades rather than centuries.

---

[5] *Ibid.*, 500–01; Thomlinson, *op. cit.*, 24; United Nations, Department of Economic and Social Affairs, *The Future Growth of World Population* (Population Studies, No. 28; New York, 1958), 23–24.
[6] Kingsley Davis, *The Population of India and Pakistan* (Princeton, N. J.: Princeton University Press, 1951), 27.

The Effect of Birth Control

The "short-run" effect of technological revolution—both of economic development and disease control—is to cut the death rate, and thus to promote explosive population growth. Major technological change eventually results in the "long-run effect" of control of the birth rate, which in turn slows down the rate of natural increase. When the controlled birth rate drops to about the same level as the controlled death rate, the period of explosive growth is over. The transition to this condition lasted a long time in the Western countries that began developing well before the Germ Theory came along, with the results over time on world growth patterns noted in Table 11.2.

The population of the United States more than doubled every 25 years for nearly a century after the first national census of 1790, as Table 11.3 shows. The birth rate was high and uncontrolled. Immigration was smaller during much of this period of great growth than it was after mid-century, reaching its peak in the years before World War I;[7] so the figures on "Intercensal Increase" in the table understate the first several drops in the rate of *natural* increase. Keeping in mind that these drops continued after public health measures began to push the death rate lower, we can see that the crude birth rate was falling rapidly.

Except for a reversal for several years after World War II, the general trend in the American birth rate for a century has been down. It was reported to be 30.1 in 1910, 18.3 at the bottom of the Great Depression in 1933, and 26.6 in 1947 at the height of the post-war "baby boom." By 1965 the birth rate had fallen to 19.4, and a death rate of 9.4 per thousand that year[8] meant a rate of natural increase of 1 per cent. In 1967 the birth rate dropped further, to about 17.9.

Effects on Population Distribution and Composition

Technological revolution displaces agricultural workers, especially the youth, and opens new jobs in industrial areas, thus creating both push and pull factors for migration to cities. Under certain conditions displaced ruralites have sought new opportunities abroad, but most of these "surplus" people have moved to cities in their homelands. In Chapter 1 we noted how both agricultural and industrial change ac-

---

[7] Peterson, *op. cit.*, 9–10.
[8] Provisional figures cited in *The World Almanac and Book of Facts, 1967* (New York: Newspaper Enterprise Association, Inc., 1967), 683.

TABLE 11.3

POPULATION OF THE UNITED STATES, 1790 TO 1960,
COMPARED WITH A "MALTHUSIAN PROJECTION"

	Census Population	Percentage of Intercensal Increase	Population Doubling Each 25 Years
1790	3,929,214	—	3,929,214 (1790)
1800	5,308,483	35.1	
1810	7,239,881	36.4	
			7,858,428 (1815)
1820	9,628,453	33.1	
1830	12,866,020	33.5	
1840	17,069,453	32.7	15,716,856 (1840)
1850	23,191,876	35.9	
1860	31,443,321	35.6	
			31,433,712 (1865)
1870	39,818,449	26.6	
1880	50,155,783	26.0	
1890	62,947,714	25.5	62,867,424 (1890)
1900	75,994,575	20.7	
1910	91,972,266	21.0	
			125,734,848 (1915)
1920	105,710,620	14.9	
1930	122,775,046	16.1	
1940	131,669,275	7.2	251,469,696 (1940)
1950	150,697,361	14.5	
1960	179,323,175*	18.5*	
			502,939,392 (1965)

* *Does not include armed forces, their dependents, and other persons living abroad.*

SOURCE: *William Peterson,* Population *(New York: The Macmillan Co., 1961), Table 1–1, p. 10.*

celerated rapid urbanization of the United States in the twentieth century.

When agricultural production enables a population to develop a relatively high density by slow growth over a long period of time, at a level of living not much above survival, food shortages cause mass starvation. But when the level of technology is sufficiently high and the rate of its development quite rapid, great increases in population density are associated with rising affluence rather than hardship. England, for example, has one of the densest populations on earth (much higher than that of India), yet one of the highest levels of living, and a labor shortage. "Population pressure" can be very severe in a sparsely populated area if resources and technology are in short supply.

Migration often produces changes in the racial and ethnic composition of a population, frequently resulting in intergroup tensions and conflicts. The outcomes vary from virtually complete segregation to racial amalgamation and cultural assimilation. International migrants are predominantly young, single males, which affects the age and sex ratios of both the sending and receiving countries. Rural-urban migrants within a given country are preponderantly young females. For the total population, a burst of growth at first increases the proportion of children, later the proportion of those in the reproductive and working years, and of the aged.[9]

We saw in Chapters 1 and 4 that the technological revolution in the West pushed the level of living upward for a rapidly growing population. The effect on the level of living has been especially marked during the present century, after birth control began to slow down the rate of population growth. One result of this is a great increase in the proportion of middle-class people, whether measured by income groups, occupational categories, or status perceptions. Other factors affect the social class structure, but undeveloped countries generally have a small ruling elite, a small middle class, and masses of poor villagers. Rapid technological development requires a fast-growing middle class, which means upward social mobility for many people. It also means shifting priorities of value, anxieties, and changing institutional patterns.

---

[9] Peterson, *op. cit.*, 627–28. For a discussion of various aspects of internal migration, see Ralph Thomlinson, *Population Dynamics* (New York: Random House, 1965), Chapter 11.

Changing Beliefs of Fact

A persistent belief for two centuries or more has been that rapid population growth will outrun the supply of food. In 1798 Thomas Malthus synthesized a number of ideas about the economics of rapidly growing populations and subsequently revised his work several times.[10] He contended that population tends to grow at a geometric rate (doubling every generation) while the food supply can at best grow at an arithmetic rate (an increase by one unit each generation or so). Thus the food supply sets limits, and the "positive checks" on population growth are periodic wars, famines, and natural catastrophes such as floods and earthquakes. He held that man's only hope is to limit births, and the only method he considered both effective and moral is "moral restraint"—late marriage, with no premarital or extramarital sexual relations.

Malthus was unable to see that agricultural and industrial technology can, under certain conditions, increase the supply of food and other goods faster than the population increases. He also did not foresee the effectiveness and widespread acceptability of various other means of birth control than the one he proposed. His treatise was widely read and discussed, however, and it apparently helped spread the belief that the birth rate and thus population growth are subject to deliberate limitation. This contrasts with the traditional belief of fact that man's numbers are beyond the control of human will. Malthus classed attempts at contraception as "vice," but proponents of artificial methods of birth control would have gained no support without the secular idea that man can limit his numbers.

Another belief of fact encouraged by Malthusian thought is that mankind may run out of living space if population explosions continue. Demographers have made projections of present growth rates of the world's population, with startling results, such as that people will be stacked several feet deep over the entire surface of the earth! The medical revolution came after Malthus' time. Its recent spread to undeveloped countries has revived his basic reasoning among demographers, many of whom have functioned as a special public, attempting to alert the world that living space and the world supply of food are threatened unless nations adopt birth control programs,

---

[10] Thomas Robert Malthus, *An Essay on the Principle of Population* (7th ed.; London: Reeves and Turner, 1872). The 6th ed., in 1826, was the major one; he died in 1834. Malthus was an English political economist.

and soon. Modified Malthusian ideas are thus very influential in current demographic scholarship,[11] and in the public discussion of population issues.

In Chapter 5 we noted the rise of the belief that man can reduce disease and pain, and deaths, in response to the public demonstration of the soundness of the Germ Theory. Without this belief, and the public health measures built upon it, populations could not have grown so explosively during the present century. And without more children staying alive per family, fewer parents would have been motivated to test the belief that man can control his numbers.

Changing Beliefs of Value

We saw in Chapter 5 how the spread of the belief of fact that diseases could be controlled led to the judgment that they *should* be, thus supporting the values of health, freedom from pain and disability, and of life itself. We noted that health became a part of the value of the minimum standard of living, and so did the values embodied in the concept of child welfare. The spread of the belief that these values are threatened by rapid world population growth has evidently caused increasing numbers of people to conclude that something can and must be done about the condition. Sixty-nine per cent of a national sample of Americans in April, 1966, said they thought this is a "serious problem."[12] Population explosion has become a dilemma within the nation as well as internationally because of continuing disagreement over the means for coping with it.

Support for birth control as a positive, instrumental value for planning the size and spacing of the family has been increasing for over a century, very slowly at first and against strong opposition. The motivation for family planning is not yet clearly understood. The majority of adults in a representative sample of Americans in 1966 said the ideal family should have 3 or 4 children, and the differences in response between Catholics and Protestants were small.[13] This is not

[11] Warren S. Thompson and David T. Lewis, *Population Problems* (5th ed.; New York: McGraw-Hill, 1965), Chapter 2; Peterson, *op. cit.*, Chapter 17; Thomlinson, *Population Problems, op. cit.*, 5–7.

[12] *Gallup Political Index*, Report No. 11, April, 1966, 16.

[13] *Ibid.*, 17. The percentage results were: 3, 27 per cent; 4, 27 per cent; 2, 18 per cent; "as many as you want," 11 per cent; 5, 4 per cent; 6, 3 per cent; 1, 1 per cent; 7–10, 1 per cent; no opinion, 8 per cent. There is little support for the one-child family, or for five or more children. Childlessness is also rejected; see, Ronald Freedman, Pascal K. Whelpton, and Arthur A. Campbell, *Family Planning, Sterility, and Population Growth* (New York: McGraw-Hill, 1954), 401–02.

only far from the 25 or so children most women could have (fecundity) during the child-bearing years,[14] but also well below the 10 or so the average woman actually has (fertility) when there is little or no attempt to prevent conception.[15] Most children now survive in medically advanced areas, and each additional child in an industrial-urban setting potentially hampers the realization of highly prized family values, including the care and education of children already in the family.[16] Living space, health, learning opportunities, recreation, privacy, travel, and the amount and quality of consumer goods are among the values jeopardized by too many children. But many who are thus motivated to practice birth control face difficult value choices concerning the means to be used, especially if their major reference groups take firm stands on the matter.

At the level of national policy, the traditional view has been to encourage births, in the belief that a large, growing population protects the nation from foreign powers. A large family is thus seen as an instrumental value in the quest for national security. Pronatalist policies have been prominent in modern military dictatorships, in some rapidly developing countries with plenty of land space (such as Canada and the U.S.S.R.), and in countries such as France and Sweden where the aim is to stabilize the population rather than to allow it to decline.[17] But otherwise the most developed countries now seem to be more fearful of an exploding population than of one that is not growing. In the United States there is much support for the policy of influencing the newly developing countries to limit births, partly on behalf of their health and welfare and partly out of fear for our own national security. Such policies have aroused persistent conflicts of value within both the more advanced and the less developed countries.

MAJOR ISSUES OF POPULATION CONTROL

The Means of Birth Control

CONTRACEPTION. Much of the discussion of the voluntary prevention of conception has revolved around the use of specific methods that

---

[14] Thomlinson, *Population Dynamics, op. cit.,* 146–58.
[15] Thompson and Lewis, *op. cit.,* 385–86. Among the cultural practices that limit the number of births are: abortion, marriage well after puberty, female infanticide, and segregation of mothers for periods of time after childbirth.
[16] Thompson and Lewis, *op. cit.,* 325–33.
[17] Thomlinson, *Population Dynamics, op. cit.,* 396–400, 404–24.

have become available. Each method has its technical advantages and disadvantages, and its use is affected by beliefs of fact and value. Some available methods are highly effective and others much less so. The main reason why any given method in practice gives less protection than it is capable of is incorrect and inconsistent use by the individual, which in turn is due to lack of knowledge, acceptance, or motivation.[18]

Formal religious opposition to contraception has gradually diminished during the twentieth century, especially on the part of the Protestant churches. The Roman Catholic Church has continued its opposition to *artificial* means, but since the early 1930's has accepted the rhythm method—abstention during periods of female fertility—as natural. A major difficulty at present is the lack of effective and simple means for determining the safe period. The rhythm method works best for the best educated, and for wives who are carefully instructed and strongly motivated.[19] A national study published in 1959 indicated that at least 30 per cent of all Catholic wives, and at least half of those married ten years or more, use means of contraception considered artificial.[20] Catholic families as a whole do have somewhat higher birth rates than Protestant ones, with Jewish rates lowest of the three, but the differences apparently are becoming smaller.[21]

In the 1960's the pressures on the Catholic church to change its position became stronger with the development of ovulation-suppressing pills. They proved to be at least 98 per cent effective, and their use increased rapidly in spite of the need to take them daily and some undesirable side effects (usually minor) in some women. A national poll on the pill in January, 1967, found small-to-moderate differences between the views of Catholics and Protestants.[22] For example, 63 per cent of the Protestants and 56 per cent of the Catholics thought the pills should, "be made available free to all women on relief of childbearing age."[23] The Roman Catholic hierachy has not actively opposed the view that this type of pill is a natural means of contra-

[18] Christopher Tietze, "The Use-Effectiveness of Contraceptive Methods," in Clyde V. Kiser (ed.), *Research in Family Planning* (Princeton, N.J.: Princeton University Press, 1962), 357–69.

[19] Peterson, *op. cit.*, 555–56.

[20] Ronald Freedman, Pascal K. Whelpton, and Arthur A. Campbell, *Family Planning, Sterility, and Population Growth* (New York: McGraw-Hill, 1959), 182–83.

[21] Peterson, *op. cit.*, 222–25.

[22] *Gallup Political Index*, February, 1967, 10–14.

[23] *Ibid.*, 10.

ception.[24] Catholic theologians are sharply split on the issue of contraception, but the Church has paid increased attention to appeals for controlling population growth.[25]

In general the relationship between social class position and family size has been inverse in this century if not before—at least in Europe and countries of European settlement. The usual sociological explanation has been that those with higher status and more education have had (1) more motivation for birth control (appropriate beliefs of value), and (2) better knowledge about how to achieve it (more effective beliefs of fact). The knowledge, at least, has evidently spread from people of higher to those of lower status and education.[26] The 1967 national poll mentioned above suggests that knowledge and favorability toward the pill are following this pattern. This is yet another female-controlled and clinically supervised method, about which those lower status groups with a tradition of male dominance cannot be expected to be enthusiastic.[27]

What motivates people to use birth control methods is not well understood, but limiting the family size has evidently facilitated upward mobility for many; and it is noteworthy that Catholics have constituted a disproportionately large percentage of Americans who have climbed the class ladder during the past decades.[28] While the differential class birth rate is complex, it seems likely that it will continue to grow smaller, perhaps disappear, or become reversed. In the meantime there is in general a direct (but now modest) association of norms of low fertility and rational family planning with class position,[29] and upward mobile families tend to adopt these norms.

[24] Thompson and Lewis, *op. cit.*, 567–68.

[25] Thomlinson, *Demographic Problems, op. cit.*, 60–63; Peterson, *op. cit.*, 556–59.

[26] Thompson and Lewis, *op. cit.*, 289–307.

[27] J. Mayonne Stycos, "Obstacles to Programs of Population Control," *Journal of Marriage and the Family*, 25 (February, 1963), 5–13. Except for male sterilization, no major male-controlled device has been introduced since the condom, which in practice is a relatively inefficient contraceptive.

[28] Peterson, *op. cit.*, 221–22, 225–26; Ronald Freedman and Lolagene Coombs, "Childspacing and Family Economic Position," *American Sociological Review*, 21 (October, 1966), 631–48. *Cf.* Alan E. Bayer, "Differential Fertility of Nativity-Parentage Groups in the United States: The Assimilation of European Female Foreign Stock," *Sociological Inquiry*, 37 (Winter, 1967), 99–107.

[29] Charles F. Westoff, Robert G. Potter, Jr., Philip Sagi, and Elliott G. Mishler, *Family Growth in Metropolitan America* (Princeton, N.J.: Princeton University Press, 1961), Chapters XIII and XIV; Dennis H. Wrong, "Trends in Class Fertility in Western Nations," *Canadian Journal of Economic and Political Science*, 24 (May, 1958), 216–29; Mary G. Powers, "Socioeconomic Status and the Fertility of Married Women," *Sociology and Social Research*, 50 (July, 1966), 472–82.

The manufacture, sale, and dissemination of information about contraceptives is restricted by state and federal statutes. Most of these were enacted during the nineteenth and twentieth centuries by Protestant legislatures, but have been maintained primarily through Roman Catholic pressure. Some such statutes have been nullified or repealed, but in 1966 twenty-two states still prohibited the sale of contraceptive equipment and supplies and thirty prohibited advertising them. Federal controls include criminal law *punishments* for sending contraceptive information and materials through the mails.[30] Court decisions have modified the effects of many of these statutes. There has been a great deal of patterned evasion of these legal norms, accompanied by the continuing movement to legalize open information about, and sale of, contraceptive materials.

A turning point in governmental action on birth control came in the mid-1960's, despite continuing opposition. For over a decade such groups as the Population Reference Bureau (a private organization) had been trying to persuade governments to take steps to control explosive population growth. The rising concern about poverty in the sixties, and the linking (by such groups as the Planned Parenthood Federation of America) of poverty with uncontrolled births provided additional impetus for action. In 1965 several states repealed their restrictive statutes, others authorized "family planning" services, and the U.S. Supreme Court nullified a long-standing symbol of resistance —Connecticut's 1879 law providing for criminal punishment for the *use* (or abetting the use) of contraceptives. Also in 1965 President Johnson became the first chief executive to announce support for birth control programs, and ex-President Eisenhower publicly reversed his previous stand and called on governments to accept the moral obligation to help families limit their numbers.[31] These declarations were followed by action, of a pilot nature at first, both in the United States and by agencies of the United Nations.

In a climate of great public concern over poverty, *the new governmental programs of family planning in the mid-sixties came to be justified mainly in terms of child welfare.* Publicity about the pill and other new devices lent backing to the belief of fact that something *could* be done to control births; appeals primarily in terms of the highly esteemed values of child welfare supported the judgment that something *should* be done. The American Medical Association agreed. Fam-

---

[30] Thomlinson, *Demographic Problems, op. cit.,* 59–60.
[31] *Los Angeles Times,* June 23, 1965, I, 1, 7, and July 6, 1965, I, 1, 8.

ily planning became part of the work of the Children's Bureau, later of other federal health and welfare agencies, and of the antipoverty program. The number of public birth control clinics in America had increased by early 1966 to 700. The United States Department of Health, Education and Welfare in 1966 adopted the policy of providing birth control information and services upon request to people, married or not, receiving its health services.[32] In 1968 a federal law was passed requiring states to provide birth control services to mothers receiving public assistance for dependent children.

Closely on the heels of the American developments, two United Nations agencies—the World Health Organization (WHO) and the Children's Fund (UNICEF)—shifted to a policy of active support of birth control efforts by host countries. Child welfare was cited immediately as the chief ideological justification.[33] The newly developed intrauterine device (IUD) became the mainstay of birth control efforts in India and some other countries. It now is used a good deal in American clinics, being nearly as effective as the anti-ovulation pill and much less expensive. The IUD is actually abortive (and so is the contragestive pill), but the growth of the ovum is stopped soon after fertilization and the device seems to be publicly regarded here and abroad as contraceptive.[34] Because of variations in beliefs of value and fact, no one method is equally acceptable in all societies and subcultural groups. Thus *which* method to use is often at issue in the continuing discussion of whether or not to use any.

ABORTION. Spontaneous abortions (miscarriages) are involuntary, but those induced by surgery or other means are conscious birth control. In France in the fifties it is possible that there were more abortions, including both types, than there were live births.[35] Recent estimates of the average annual total in the United States range from 700,000 to 2,000,000, which is from about 16 per cent to roughly one-half the number of live births in the typical year in the sixties.[36] Probably about

---

[32] *Ibid.*, March, 1966, C, 1–2, and April 2, 1966, II, A, 1.

[33] *Ibid.*, May 10, 1966, I, 10.

[34] Thomlinson, *Demographic Problems, op. cit.*, 53–55. The IUD must be distinguished from the well established vaginal diaphram, a device not well suited to women with little education or motivation. The IUD can be left in place indefinitely, although one-fourth of all women cannot use the device at all.

[35] United Nations Population Branch, *Survey of Legislation on Marriage, Divorce, and Related Topics Relevant to Population* (New York, 1956), 10.

[36] Thomlinson, *Population Dynamics, op. cit.*, 198–200.

one-third of all American abortions are induced. There is considerable evidence to suggest that an increase in the widespread use of effective contraceptives reduces the rate of abortion.[37]

Along with France and England, the United States has strict anti-abortion statutes, at least in comparison with the approach of the Scandinavian countries. In general the states have prevented abortion except when necessary to save the life of the mother. Since the majority of induced abortions in the United States probably are for other reasons, evasion of the laws is widespread. Whether or not these statutes should be liberalized is a continuing issue. The Roman Catholic position is that the existing laws are too liberal, that abortion is generally not justified to save the life of the mother.

The movement to legalize voluntary *therapeutic abortions*—those designed to protect mother or child from serious hazards to physical or mental health—is supported by a number of small but highly articulate groups, usually with medical or social work leadership. Some favor extending the laws to permit the avoidance of gross deformity or abnormality, severe poverty and dependency, extreme difficulty in placing the child at adoption, or extreme hardship in caring for the child. It is charged that the laws place the poor at the greatest disadvantage. Such proposals are based on the values of physical and mental health of both the mother and potential baby, the mother's life, and child welfare.

The major value cited against therapeutic abortion is the life of the unborn baby, combined with various beliefs about when life begins. Proponents reply that abortions occur anyway outside the law, and that 5,000 or so American mothers die each year due to improperly performed operations. The risk to the mother's life of an abortion induced by a physician in a hospital is small. So far these arguments have not won in the legislatures. The changes in abortion laws that began in 1967 in Colorado, North Carolina, and California were limited to situations where such criminal acts as rape, incest, and the impregnation of a young adolescent threaten the institutions of marriage and the family. These circumstances are not involved in the typical abortion, most of which are sought by married women who already have children.[38] If the politically effective rank order of values

---

[37] Thompson and Lewis, *op. cit.*, 311–12. Similarly, an increase in either abortion or contraception reduces infanticide, a practice which has the effect of birth control.
[38] Thomlinson, *Demographic Problems, op. cit.*, 54–55.

does not shift in favor of therapeutic abortions, it would seem that only a preventive program can curtail illegal abortions and the deaths that often result. We have seen that abortions evidently decline when motivated people have access to effective means of contraception, but this alternative is unacceptable to those opposed to all mechanical or chemical methods of birth control. Thus much patterned evasion of the abortion laws continues, and the dilemma remains.

Comparison of our experience with that of Japan helps provide perspective. The Japanese Eugenic Protection Law of 1948 was passed both to prevent the reproduction of defective stock and to protect the life of the mother. In 1949, after the law was extended to allow abortions for economic reasons, a great many families began using the facilities in public and private clinics to abort unwanted children. Induced abortion supplemented contraception so effectively that the Japanese birth rate was halved, from 34.3 to 17.2 per thousand, from 1947 to 1957. The preference seems to be to rely more on contraception, but abortion had for centuries been an accepted means (supplementing infanticide) of keeping the family small. The well-being of the heir was the major traditional value rather than having many sons, and industrial-urban development has reinforced this value. Neither Buddhism nor Shintoism is opposed to birth control.[39]

STERILIZATION. When contraception and abortion are not acceptable or effective enough, sterilization provides more certain and more permanent birth control. The inexpensive operation may be performed on either sex, but it is simpler on the male and may be reversed in about half the cases. Despite the persistence of contrary beliefs, the modern methods are not harmful to health, sexual activity, or hormonal balance. Sterilization has become the most popular method of birth control in Puerto Rico, despite Roman Catholic opposition, and is used a good deal in India and other countries.[40]

In America, three states require medical justification for all sterilizations, explicitly disallowing them for socio-economic reasons.[41] Except for this, and for ambiguities in some states, American families are legally free to use sterilization to limit their size. Yet it apparently seems an unnecessary alternative to most people, and its use as an

---

[39] Peterson, *op. cit.*, 486–90; Thomlinson, *Demographic Problems, op cit.*, 109.
[40] Peterson, *op. cit.*, 480–84, 548.
[41] Thomlinson, *Demographic Problems, op. cit.*, 52–53. The states are Connecticut, Kansas, and Utah.

ordinary birth control method is not widespread. Nevertheless, a substantial majority of Americans evidently opposes restrictions on the voluntary use of sterilization. Over three-fourths of a national sample said in April, 1966, that they approved of sterilization in cases where the mother's health is endangered, and where persons with physical or mental defects request it. Nearly two-thirds of the Catholics and over four-fifths of the Protestants agreed on these points. On the question concerning, "women who have more children than they can provide for properly and ask to be sterilized," almost two-thirds of the total approved—49 per cent of the Catholics and 71 per cent of the Protestants.[42] The further questions of whether and when involuntary sterilization should be used are prominent in eugenics discussions.

Population Quality

NEGATIVE EUGENICS. As knowledge about the processes of natural selection was disseminated, concern arose over the quality of human populations. Supporters of negative eugenics sought to eliminate biologically inferior strains by sterilizing or segregating those presumed to be unfit to keep them from procreating. Legislation permitting involuntary sterilization of hereditary defectives has been passed by about half our states, and supported by the United States Supreme Court. Most of the statutes were passed during the second and third decades of this century and were designed mainly to combat such presumed hereditary defects as epilepsy, deaf-mutism, blindness, marked body malformations, criminality, "feeblemindedness," and "hereditary insanity."[43] During the vogue of Social Darwinism, both physical handicaps and deviant behavior were widely attributed to biological factors, very often to heredity alone.

Scientific views of the causes of the conditions that concerned those in the eugenics movement two and three generations ago have undergone much change. Some defects present at birth evidently are due to prenatal infections, injuries, or malnutrition rather than to heredity, and others—including mental deficiency, malformations, deafness and blindness—in many cases may be. Experiences in the postnatal environment also influence many defective conditions, so the role of heredity is difficult to isolate. Nearly everyone carries some defective genes, evidently, yet they may remain latent for generations unless

---

[42] *Gallup Political Index*, Report No. 11, April, 1966, 14–15.
[43] Paul H. Landis and Paul K. Hatt, *Population Problems* (2nd ed.; New York: American Book Co., 1954), 502–04.

they combine with some of the mate's unfavorable genes. It is now considered quite unlikely that epilepsy is genetically transmitted; the fact that such a defect often runs in families does not prove it is hereditary.[44] As for criminality, drug addiction, alcoholism, dependency, much of mental illness, and other deviancy, we have seen that heredity provides the raw material for all human conduct, but does not determine specific forms of behavior.

Involuntary sterilization has been used with growing caution, probably due in considerable measure to publicity about changing beliefs of fact in genetics. A further deterrent is the high (but not absolute) value attached to the right to keep one's reproductive powers. Some carriers of defects or their parents have been persuaded to accept voluntary sterilization, but efforts to combat mental deficiency, mental illness, crime, and physical defects that pose severe social handicaps have turned increasingly in other directions. Some physical defects have been shown to be clearly hereditary, but states are not legislating to permit their carriers to be sterilized against their will. And, although there is opposition and anxiety about it, there is now less segregation of the mentally ill and deficient. Finally, with the dramatization of the world population explosion, public concern has largely shifted from the quality of human population to its quantity. Assuming that population growth can be brought under control, and that dramatic genetic discoveries are forthcoming, public concern may well shift back to population quality.

POSITIVE EUGENICS. While negative eugenics stresses elimination of the unfit, positive eugenics encourages those that are presumably most fit to have more children. The latter stemmed from observation of the differential class birth rate early in the century, when biological determinism was widely accepted. The key belief (a combination of fact and value) in positive eugenics is that narrowing or reversing the differential birth rate improves the biological quality of a population. This rests on the basic belief (of fact, colored by values) that economic success and higher status are measures of genetic superiority. This is highly dubious, since the different social classes have unequal opportunities to compete for educational and occupational success and community status.[45] Also, differential rates of disease and death

---

[44] Harold A. Phelps and David Henderson, *Population in Its Human Aspects* (New York: Appleton-Century-Crofts, Inc., 1958), 378–79.
[45] Landis and Hatt, *op. cit.*, 289–94.

are inadequate indexes of genetic strength because those families with more means obtain better food, health education, and medical care.[46]

There is little reason to question the socially selective effects of the differential class birth rate, as opposed to the genetic effects. Thus, reducing the gap presumably enhances the quality of life in the society by increasing the proportion of people who receive adequate care and favorable opportunities.[47] The accelerated reduction of this gap has evidently resulted from the increased use of contraception by lower income groups, a development hastened more by public concern over population quantity than over quality. It appears unlikely that appeals have persuaded families with more means to have more children, in order to contribute either to the overall quality of child care or to population quality.[48] However, such appeals may well have helped build support for programs that make contraception available to families of lesser means.

Immigration Control

Immigration policies have been much more controversial in America than those concerning emigration and internal migration. Emigration has been subject to some restrictions, for reasons of security and internal relations, but these have not become major issues. Within the country, countless rural-urban moves have accompanied industrial development, and freedom of horizontal mobility has facilitated the highly esteemed value of freedom of opportunity to climb the class ladder.[49] Immigration became a major issue when the value of keeping America open as a land of opportunity for the poor and oppressed of other lands came into conflict with other beliefs.

Until about 1830 immigration continued to be unregulated, as it had been during the long Colonial period, with most of the immigrants still coming from England, Scotland, and North Ireland. By 1830 the belief was widespread that increased immigration was aggravating the nation's problems. State legislatures began passing laws designed to keep out undesirable individuals, especially Europe's unwanted criminals and paupers. Immigration continued to increase, along with agitation for federal control, which began in 1882. As the state laws had been, a succession of federal laws were justified on the basis of

---

[46] Peterson, *op. cit.*, 582.
[47] Landis and Hatt, *op. cit.*, 296–99.
[48] Phelps and Henderson, *op. cit.*, 473.
[49] Landis and Hatt, *op. cit.*, 389–90.

individual selection, with mention of such classes of undesirables as the mentally ill, beggars, anarchists, prostitutes, and criminals.

During the first decade of the twentieth century there was an average of over a million immigrants a year into the United States, more than in any ten-year period before or since.[50] There was growing fear of cheap labor, Roman Catholicism, national clannishness, cultural dilution, and even of lowered population quality.[51] Public demand grew for *group selection* as the only way to stem the flow of people from Southern and Eastern Europe, but this approach met determined opposition because it meant a reversal of the historic policy of the open door to all desirable individuals from abroad. Finally in 1917 the literacy test was passed. Its language was that of individual selection, but the aim was group restriction. This method failed because ways were found for illiterate immigrants to learn enough to pass the test, but there was now considerable public support for more explicit and effective group selection. The result was legislation to limit the total amount and to control the source of immigration by the establishment of national quotas.

The temporary Immigration Act of 1921 permitted entry annually to 3 per cent of the natives of other nations living in the United States in 1910. This closed the "golden door" most of the way, and allotted almost half of the immigration to Southern and Eastern Europe, since they had sent many migrants in the years before 1910. The Immigration Act of 1924 superseded the 1921 statute, first with its own temporary provision, quotas of 2 per cent of the natives of other nations living in America in 1890. This reduced the total further, but it also greatly decreased the quotas for Southern and Eastern European countries, and increased those for Germany and other nations of Northern Europe that had contributed large numbers of migrants in the years prior to 1890. This shift is apparent in Table 11.4, which also shows that immigration from Asia and Africa was completely stopped. Immigration from Mexico and all other countries in the Western Hemisphere was not restricted by these, or later, national quota systems.

The final provision of the Immigration Act of 1924 established quotas on the basis of the national origins of the American population

---

[50] *Statistical Abstract of the United States,* United States Department of Commerce, Bureau of the Census, 1961, p. 92.
[51] Charles F. Marden and Gladys Meyer, *Minorities in American Society* (2nd ed.; New York: American Book Co., 1962), Chapters 4, 5.

TABLE 11.4

IMMIGRATION QUOTAS UNDER SUCCESSIVE LAWS, UNITED STATES,
1921–1952

	1921	1924	1929	1952
Northwest Europe*	197,630	140,999	127,266	126,131
Southern and Eastern Europe	159,322	20,423	23,225	23,536
Asia	492	1,424	1,423	2,990
Africa and Oceania	359	1,821	1,800	2,000
Total	357,803	164,667	153,714	154,657
Per Cent				
Northwest Europe*	55.2	85.6	82.8	81.6
Southern and Eastern Europe	44.5	12.4	15.1	15.2
Asia	0.1	0.9	0.9	1.9
Africa and Oceania	0.1	1.1	1.2	1.3
Total	99.9	100.0	100.0	100.0

* British Isles, Scandinavia, Germany, Low Countries, France, Switzerland.

SOURCE: William Peterson, Population (New York: The Macmillan Co., 1961), 105, Table 5–2. Based on President's Commission on Immigration and Naturalization, Whom We Shall Welcome (Washington: U.S. Government Printing Office, 1953), 76–77.

as of 1920. The Bureau of the Census had a most difficult time working out these ancestral fractions, and the "permanent" quotas did not go into effect until 1929. Great Britain (including North Ireland) received 40 per cent of the total allowed, since it was concluded that the ancestry of Americans in 1920 was 40 per cent British. Similarly, Germany received a quota of 16 per cent of the total, the Irish Free State 11 per cent, and all other countries less than 5 per cent. How could this be, in view of the fact that more immigrants have come from Germany than from any other country? The rank order of the next several countries in 1960 was: Italy, Ireland, Great Britain, Austria-Hungary, Russia, Canada, Sweden, and Mexico. Great Britain's total would be larger if data were available for the years before 1820,[52] but the main reason our national ancestry is so heavily British is that migrants from Great Britain came so much earlier than others and thus have had so many more descendants.

The quota laws passed in the 1920's reflected a sense of emergency on the part of organized labor, and many other groups. Perhaps the fears that attended the growing volume of immigration from Southern and Eastern Europe would have been calmed somewhat if our present knowledge of world population growth had been available to the general public. Why did our earliest immigrants come from Great Britain, large numbers during the latter part of the nineteenth century from the countries of North and West Europe, and still later from Italy and other nations of Southern and Eastern Europe?[53] After due allowance is made for the Irish potato famines, the introduction of the railroad and the steamship at a given time, political entanglements, and other factors, the major explanation seems to be that the technological revolution came first to Great Britain, then to other countries of North and West Europe, and finally to the rest of Europe. Many displaced agricultural workers and others seeking opportunity sought it in the beckoning lands abroad, although most tried the growing cities in their own homelands. Thus it was not a plot in Rome or anywhere else that produced such a heavy migration from Southern and Eastern Europe early in this century, and no mystery that Great Britain and Germany and other North European countries did not fill their immigration quotas. At a certain stage of development, many nations have felt they needed to export part of their exploding populations. But with the later coming of mass birth control and a new population balance, several nations have pleaded for immigrants, to take up the labor shortage! Of course, before Italy, Poland, and their neighbors would have reached this point they would have sent us a great many more immigrants before they were braked by the Depression and World War II.

The McCarran-Walter Act of 1952 continued the basic quota system, based on the national origins as of 1920, and continued to justify this policy on the basis of maintaining the cultural traditions of America. (See Table 11.4.) It permitted very little immigration from the countries of Asia and Africa, and it included several much criticized

---

[52] Thomlinson, *Population Dynamics, op. cit.,* 245.
[53] Landis and Hatt, *op. cit.,* 446–54.

provisions against subversive activity.[54] Amicable relations with other countries was a major argument advanced by three successive American presidents and their foreign policy advisers for the abolition of the quota system. The national quotas finally were abolished in 1965.

The total amount of immigration is limited by the Act of 1965, but by mid-1968 the discriminatory quotas were to be ended. The limit is 170,000 per year for nations outside of the Western Hemisphere, with no country to get more than 20,000. A controversial new provision in the Act of 1965, reflecting concern over the explosive rates of population growth in Latin America, is a limit of 120,000 immigrants per year from nations in the Western Hemisphere. The Act gives priority to the reuniting of families and the admission of people with special occupational skills, and continues safeguards against admitting criminals, those in poor health, subversives, and other undesirable persons. The golden door remains open only part of the way, but on the basis of individual rather than group merit. However, the application of the stipulated criteria, particularly the preference for those with special occupational skills, will probably result in a tendency to select individuals from the more advanced nations. Thus the Act of 1965 is at least partly an attempt to balance the values of America as a haven for seekers of new opportunities and a land of individual initiative against the minimizing of job competition and unemployment. It seems designed to support the maximum operation of the economy, family unity, and cultural and racial diversity.

PERSPECTIVE

Populations have grown explosively wherever modern agricultural and industrial revolutions have taken place, mainly by cutting the death rate, and have grown still faster with the control of contagious diseases. The spread of the population explosion around the globe has accompanied the introduction of medical controls to undeveloped areas and created difficult problems of support in the absence of economic development. Projections of present rates of growth have greatly increased American and international concern over questions of food supply and living space. Motivation to limit family size developed slowly with industrial-urban growth in the Western world, and

---

[54] Thomlinson, *Population Dynamics, op. cit.,* 255–56; Peterson, *op. cit.,* 104–09.

the conviction has grown since World War II that it must spread much faster in the new areas where population is exploding.

A major deterrent to international encouragement of programs of birth control has been the continued resistance to contraception, abortion, and sterilization in the United States. There is still much restrictive legislation, especially against abortion and contraception, despite the large amount of deviation from the legal norms. The resistance of the Roman Catholic Church and of the legislators in a number of states has lessened somewhat in recent years, under the heavy pressure of demands to do something about explosive population growth. In the mid-sixties the federal government shifted to a policy of encouraging contraceptive clinics at home and abroad, basing the action mainly on child welfare values. The pertinent United Nations agencies at once began fostering birth control more actively, pointing to child welfare. Yet such programs run counter to firmly held beliefs of value and fact of a highly varied nature. Where birth control is not strongly opposed there are still issues over the means; no one method seems equally acceptable everywhere.

The concern over numbers has replaced an earlier emphasis on the quality of population. Many of the beliefs underlying programs of eugenics have been discarded or seriously questioned by biologists. Concern about quality may again produce some major issues, assuming that the rates of population growth subside and that major genetic discoveries are made and publicized. The control of immigration in the United States has reflected shifting priorities of value throughout this century, and changing beliefs of fact as well, including growing understanding of the relation of international migration to population growth. The policy of allowing limited immigration on a non-quota basis is criticized rather little at this time. In view of the great anxiety about world population growth, one way to spark a major controversy would be to suggest removal of the annual limit on immigration!

QUESTIONS FOR DISCUSSION AND STUDY

1. How are population explosions since World War II different from those that began much earlier? How are they similar?

2. What are some of the major relationships between technological development and population growth?

3. Why do you think there was such a change in federal policy on programs of contraception in the mid-sixties?

4. Why is it maintained that laws of contraception and abortion work the greatest hardships on the poor?

5. Which do you think is more likely in the next decade or so, changes in statutes regulating contraception or abortion? Why?

6. Why do you suppose there are many legal restrictions on contraception and abortion in the United States, but not on sterilization? How are beliefs of value involved? Beliefs of fact?

7. Public attention has shifted away from programs of eugenics since the early decades of this century. To what extent has this been due to changing beliefs of fact? To changing beliefs of value? Explain.

8. What public policies seem capable of influencing the quantity or quality of population growth, and what ones do not? Explain, in each instance.

9. As a factor in international migrations, why would it be wise to use the concept of "population pressure" with much caution?

10. From various sources, what information can you find about the pressure groups that have been prominent in the public discussion of immigration control? What are the beliefs of each group?

SELECTED READING

Bogue, Donald J. (ed.), *Applications of Demography: The Population Situation in the United States in 1975* (Oxford, Ohio: Scripps Foundation for Research in Population Problems, 1957).

Calderone, Mary S. (ed.), *Abortion in the United States* (New York: Harper & Bros., 1958).

Davis, Kingsley (ed.), "A Crowding Hemisphere: Population Change in the Americas," an issue of *The Annals*, 316 (March, 1958).

Day, Lincoln H., and Day, Alice T., *Too Many Americans* (Boston: Houghton Mifflin Co., 1964).

Freedman, Ronald (ed.), Population: *The Vital Revolution* (Garden City, N.Y.: Doubleday Anchor Books, 1964).

Guttmacher, Alan F., *Babies by Choice or by Chance* (New York: Avon Books, 1961).

Hauser, Philip M. (ed.), *The Population Dilemma* (Englewood Cliffs, N.J.: Spectrum Books, Prentice-Hall, 1963).

Hill, Reuben, Stycos, J. Mayonne, and Back, Kurt W., *The Family and Population Control: A Puerto Rican Experiment* (Chapel Hill: University of North Carolina Press, 1959).

Hutchinson, Edward P. (ed.), "The New Immigration," an issue of *The Annals* (September, 1966).

Osborn, Fairfield (ed.), *Our Crowded Planet: Essays on the Pressures of Population* (Garden City, N.Y.: Doubleday & Co., 1962).

Rainwater, Lee, *Family Design: Marital Sexuality, Family Size, and Contraception* (Chicago, Ill.: Aldine Publishing Co., 1965).

Sauvy, Alfred, *Fertility and Survival: Population Problems from Malthus to Mao Tse-Tung* (New York: Criterion Books, 1961).

Sheps, Mindel C., and Ridley, Jeanne C., *Public Health and Population Change: Current Research Issues* (Pittsburgh: The University of Pittsburgh Press, 1965).

Thomlinson, Ralph, *Demographic Problems* (Belmont, Calif.: Dickenson Publishing Co., 1967).

Thompson, Warren S., and Lewis, David T., *Population Problems* (5th ed.; New York: McGraw-Hill, 1965).

Westoff, Charles F., Potter, Robert G., Jr., and Sagi, Philip C., *The Third Child: A Study in the Prediction of Fertility* (Princeton, N.J.: Princeton University Press, 1963).

Whelpton, Pascal K., Campbell, Arthur A., and Patterson, John E., *Fertility and Family Planning in the United States* (Princeton, N.J.: Princeton University Press, 1965).

Wrong, Dennis H., *Population and Society* (Rev. ed.; New York: Random House, 1967).

The Court's decisions of the mid-fifties, and its many supportive decisions since, are no more cause than result, part of a vast series of events that constitute the nation's major domestic development of the century. The vast migrations of the Negro from South to North and West, from farm to industry and country to city; the emergence of the new African nations and America's political role in international affairs; the military experiences of American Negroes and the broadening travels this service permitted; the research of scholars in the biological and social sciences on the nature of race and the consequences of discrimination; the response of the political system to the emergence of a major Negro voting bloc—these are a few major of many changes to which the social analyst must give proper due in explaining the contemporary nature of race relations in the United States.[1]

12. Racial and Cultural Minorities

INTERGROUP RELATIONS

When Peoples Meet[2]

GROUPS OF HUMAN BEINGS that are culturally or racially different, or both, have been coming into contact throughout history. Often this has resulted from migrations, both voluntary and involuntary. The shifting of political boundaries repeatedly has compelled formerly isolated groups to confront one another. The rise of new religious groups again and again has created new frontiers of cultural contact.

Some cultural and subcultural differences—such as language, modes of dress and decoration, and ways of walking and gesturing—immediately strike the senses and are easily confused with racial differences. Races are overlapping biological categories, sub-species groupings. On the basis of anatomical traits, one widely used scheme identifies three races—caucasoid, negroid and mongoloid—some sub-

---

[1] Ernest Q. Campbell (ed.), in the Introduction to "Analysis of Race Relations in Current Perspective," an issue of *Sociological Inquiry*, 35 (Winter, 1965), 3.
[2] This arresting phrase was taken from Alain Locke and Bernhard J. Stern (eds.) *When Peoples Meet* (New York: Hinds, Harden and Eldridge, 1946).

races, and some hybrids.[3] The meanings attached to racial and cultural differences have varied widely, but treatment of the other group as equal has been the exception.

Acculturation occurs as one group learns the way of life of the other, and *assimilation* as one loses its separate identity and becomes part of the other. *Amalgamation*, the biological mixing of once separate stocks, has been very frequent in human history. Groups that retain their identities are able to remain in contact by virtue of some type of *accommodation*, a structure of working arrangements that defines group statuses and roles. Accommodation may be equalitarian or stratified, and may vary from markedly segregated to highly integrated. Segregation may be voluntary (the separatist pattern) or imposed. Accommodation also varies from arrangements that are thoroughgoing and unquestioned to uneasy truces that readily give way to intergroup *conflict*. Changes in a long-standing pattern of intergroup accommodation require extensive changes throughout the society. Three extreme outcomes of intergroup contact are *extermination* of one group by another, *expulsion* from a given territory, and *voluntary emigration*.[4]

Minority-Dominant Relations

DEFINITIONS. A minority group in the sociological sense is a subordinate group, so its reciprocal is the dominant group (or majority). More precisely, *a minority group is a sub-group in a society that (1) is distinguishable by racial and/or cultural traits, (2) is regarded as inferior and as not belonging to the dominant group, and (3) is discriminated against and thus excluded from full participation in the life of the society.*[5] Minorities are not necessarily small; in fact they may make up most of a society's population, as in the typical colonial

[3] A. L. Kroeber, *Anthropology* (New York: Harcourt, Brace & Co., 1948), 140. Research indicates that somewhat better classification is possible on the basis of gene frequencies (of blood types and other traits), but it is the surface anatomy that strikes the eye—the head shape, hair, nose, lips, and skin color (which is very unreliable.)

[4] Charles F. Marden and Gladys Meyer, *Minorities in American Society* (2nd ed.; New York: American Book Co., 1962), 30–37; George E. Simpson and J. Milton Yinger, *Racial and Cultural Minorities* (Rev. ed.: New York: Harper and Bros., 1958), 205–32; Brewton Berry, *Race and Ethnic Relations* (2nd ed.; Boston: Houghton Mifflin, 1958), Part II, "The Consequences of Contact and Conflict."

[5] *Cf.* Marden and Meyer, *ibid.*, 24–26, 31. This concept of minority group was established by Donald Young in *American Minority Peoples* (New York: Harper and Bros., 1932).

situation. In the Union of South Africa the whites, only about one-fifth of the population, dominate the blacks and the "coloureds." Many groups are assigned minority status on the basis of more than one characteristic, but the dominant group tends to select one as primary. In one instance this may be race, in another a cultural identification—nationality, religion, or language, and politics in some countries.

AMERICAN MINORITIES. A great variety of cultural and racial groups have entered America's "melting pot." Discussions of immigration control (see Chapter 11) have reflected the minority status held by one national group after another. Many white immigrants have been thoroughly assimilated in the third generation, North European Protestants often in the second. With the curtailment of immigration in the twenties, there was a reduction of anxiety about alien groups on the part of "Anglos" (people predominantly of British origin) and groups already assimilated into the "Wasp" (White Anglo-Saxon Protestant) culture. Second-generation immigrants are not usually classed as having minority status now, and some students of minorities also omit the foreign born. A clear exception are the Puerto Ricans, who migrated in considerable numbers and concentrated in New York City in the years following World War II.[6]

If Roman Catholics are included they are America's largest minority group (over 38 million in 1960), Negroes are second (nearly 19 million in 1960), and Jews third (between 3 and 4 million).[7] Some students include foreign-born whites but exclude Catholics,[8] holding that discrimination against the latter group is disappearing. Some no longer include either the foreign born or Catholics.[9] At any rate, religious minorities include the Jews, a profusion of Protestant sects, and followers of many faiths from around the globe.

Negroes are by far the largest racial minority in America, con-

---

[6] Clarence Senior, *Strangers—Then Neighbors: From Pilgrims to Puerto Ricans* (New York: Freedom Books, 1961), 22, 60–61; Clarence Senior, "The Puerto Rican in the United States, Ch. VII, in Joseph B. Gittler (ed.), *Understanding Minority Groups* (New York: John Wiley & Sons, 1956), 109–25; Nathan Glazer and Daniel Patrick Moynihan, *Beyond the Melting Pot* (Cambridge, Mass.: The M.I.T. Press, 1963), 86–136.

[7] Arnold M. Rose, "Race and Ethnic Relations," Ch. 9, in Robert K. Merton and Robert A. Nisbet, *Contemporary Social Problems* (2nd ed.; New York: Harcourt, Brace & World, Inc., 1966), 412–17.

[8] Berry, *op. cit.*, 51; Simpson and Yinger, *op. cit.*, 811.

[9] Marden and Meyer, *op. cit.*, 14, 116–18, 384–90.

stituting about one-tenth of the population. This is based on the census practice of enumerating as Negroes all who are so considered in their communities. This means that a person of predominantly white ancestry is classed as Negro, since the Southern definition—a person with any known Negro ancestry—has long been the nation's definition. If we followed the practices of Latin American nations we would count far fewer of our citizens as Negroes, but census takers count those things that are considered significant in the nation concerned.[10]

Actually, the people officially classed as American Negroes are a mixture, mainly of the negroid and caucasoid races, with some American Indian (a mongoloid subrace) admixture. Most of this amalgamation took place during slave days, as a result of access to slave women by white men; but since Emancipation there has also been considerable white exploitation of Negro women. Little of the miscegenation (racial amalgamation) has had the benefit of interracial marriage, then; and it is much too late to keep the race pure! Probably less than one-fifth and perhaps as few as 5 per cent of American Negroes are of pure negroid ancestry. Despite the society's definition of the situation, the process of genetic mixing continues when a mulatto and a pure negroid person (or two racially mixed individuals) have children.[11]

Many Mexican-Americans are racially visible, and often experience discrimination on that basis. Most of the three million or so Spanish-speaking Americans in the Southwest (some now in the Midwest) came from Mexico during the past half century or more, or their forbears did.[12] However, many if not most Anglos apparently think of Mexican-Americans primarily as a cultural minority, one resistant to assimilation. The Hispanos are whites, located mainly in the poor, rural areas of New Mexico. They are descendants of the Spanish who were in the area over two centuries before 1848, when after the Mexican War it became part of the United States. All remaining nonwhite groups are relatively small, totaling less than 1 per cent of the population. In order of size, this remainder includes American Indians, Japanese-Americans, Chinese-Americans, and Filipinos.

---

[10] Ralph Thomlinson, *Population Dynamics* (New York: Random House, 1965), 440–44.

[11] Arnold Rose, *The Negro in America* (Boston: The Beacon Press, 1956), 44–51; E. Franklin Frazier, *The Negro in the United States* (Rev. ed.; New York: The Macmillan Co., 1957), 67–68, 185–87, 310–11.

[12] Marden and Meyer, *op. cit.*, 120–41. The population of Mexico in this century has been about 10 per cent white, 30 per cent Indian, and 60 per cent mestizo (mixed white and Indian).

Prejudice and Discrimination

Prejudice may be negative or positive. *Negative group prejudice is an unfavorable attitude toward the members of a group.* It is learned and can be unlearned, and much is now known about the variables involved.[13] Prejudiced attitudes against racial and cultural groups tend to be *ethnocentric; i.e.,* the other group's ways and/or physical features are seen not only as different, but as odd and inferior. This apparently has been the typical response throughout history when peoples have met. Ethnocentric feelings and responses accentuate consciousness of the differences, foster unity and pride in the in-group, and when extreme enough promote hostility toward the out-group.

Group prejudice also tends to involve *stereotypes* (see Chapter 3), which usually reflect ethnocentrism and find expression in derogatory names and other symbols of the out-group. These false images of racial and cultural groups tend to become strongly reified, but under the right conditions they are subject to change. They may become key beliefs of fact in ideological justifications of particular patterns of intergroup relations. When acted upon as if they were true, results are often brought about that support the stereotype. For instance, if the image of a given group as slow learners results in a very gradual and undemanding program of school instruction, children of the group will perform poorly on competitive tests. Merton calls this kind of vicious circle a "self-fulfilling prophecy."[14]

Group discrimination is action against members of a group which prevents their full participation in the life of the community. Examples are: promoting a restrictive housing covenant, excluding certain groups from a hotel, or enforcing group quotas for admission to professional schools. Prejudice and discrimination often reinforce

---

[13] *E.g.*, see Robin M. Williams, Jr., John P. Dean, and Edward A. Suchman, *Strangers Next Door* (Englewood Cliffs, N.J.: Prentice-Hall, Inc., 1964); Ernest Works, "The Prejudice-Interaction Hypothesis from the Point of View of the Negro Minority," *American Journal of Sociology*, 67 (July, 1961), 47–52; Donald L. Noel and Alphonso Pinckney, "Correlates of Prejudice: Some Racial Differences and Similarities," *American Journal of Sociology*, 69 (May, 1964), 609–22; Armand L. Mauss, "Mormonism and Secular Attitudes Toward Negroes," *Pacific Sociological Review*, 9 (Fall, 1966), 91–99; Donald J. Treiman, "Status Discrepancy and Prejudice," *American Journal of Sociology*, 71 (May, 1966), 651–64.

[14] Robert K. Merton, *Social Theory and Social Structure* (Rev. ed.; Glencoe, Ill.: The Free Press, 1957), 421–36; *cf.* William R. Catton, Jr., and Sung Chick Hong, "The Relation of Apparent Minority Ethnocentrism to Majority Antipathy," *American Sociological Review*, 28 (April, 1962), 178–91.

each other, but they may also occur independently.[15] An example of the *unprejudiced discriminator* is the person who agrees to keep Jews out of the club solely for fear of losing favor with his fellow members. An unprejudiced person who discriminates because of expediency is likely to feel guilty, and thus to feel relieved if the situational constraints shift into line with his attitudes. The *prejudiced nondiscriminator* is illustrated by the employer who goes against his own feelings and hires a minority person to avoid investigation by the Fair Employment Practices Commission. He is frustrated, and would be relieved if the legal restraints were removed so he could discriminate. The *prejudiced discriminator* is most difficult to control, since he considers his actions logical and right. The *unprejudiced nondiscriminator* is convinced that equal treatment of all racial and cultural groups is logical and right.[16]

CHANGES IN GROUP STATUS. Minority groups vary at any given time in the amount of discrimination experienced, and there may be variation over time in the status of a particular group. American minorities have experienced many ups and downs in status, some gradual and some sudden.[17] As European immigrants struggled up the educational and occupational ladders, and as newer immigrants arrived to take over the old jobs and residences, the statuses of entire national groups were raised.[18] Discrimination against Jews increased greatly during the years of Hitler's influence, and later decreased considerably. The status of Japanese-Americans declined during the thirties and hit bottom with their relocation after the attack on Pearl Harbor, to rise again remarkably after World War II. Clearly, minority group statuses are dynamic under certain conditions, and changes in international relations and in the economy are among the major variables involved.

CHANGING BELIEFS ABOUT RACE AND CULTURE. In the Social Darwinist thought of the nineteenth and early twentieth centuries, racial and

[15] Raymond W. Mack, *Race, Class and Power* (New York: American Book Co., 1963), 118–21.

[16] Robert K. Merton, "Discrimination and the American Creed," in R. M. MacIver (ed.), *Discrimination and National Welfare* (New York: Harper and Bros., 1949), 99–126.

[17] Rose, in Merton and Nisbet, *op. cit.*, 409–12, 474–78.

[18] Oscar Handlin, *The Newcomers* (Cambridge, Mass.: Harvard University Press, 1959); W. Lloyd Warner and Leo Srole, *The Social Systems of American Ethnic Groups* (New Haven, Conn.: Yale University Press, 1945); Fernando Peñalosa and Edward C. McDonagh, "A Socioeconomic Class Typology of Mexican Americans," *Sociological Inquiry*, 36 (Winter, 1966), 19–30.

cultural differences were interpreted in racist terms. Among the more systematic racist ideologies have been those justifying segregation in the South, Nazi Germany's expansionism and extreme actions against the Jews, and some of the writings in support of group restriction of immigration. Racism has been prevalent in other world civilizations also; witness Japanese expansionism earlier in the century and China today. Racist beliefs still have much support in Western Civilization, but many inroads have been made on them in the twentieth century.[19]

One basic belief in racism is the doctrine of physical superiority and inferiority of the races. One kind of evidence cited in its support is the higher rates of disease and mortality of the supposedly inferior races, but the environmental conditions of the groups compared must be held constant. The life chances of the members of a group are affected by the quality of its housing, sanitation, nutrition, medical care, and educational opportunities. Evidence cited for the related doctrine of mental superiority and inferiority of the races also must be related to environmental influences. After decades of intelligence testing, it was clear that racial differences in performance vary with differences in school experience, social class background, language, rapport with the tester, and group values concerning competition and speed. When different races have equal opportunities to learn what the I.Q. tests test, and are equally motivated, the average racial differences disappear.[20] The evidence fails to support the belief that racial crossing results in an inferior stock, physically and mentally.[21] Hybrids experience social handicaps, but this is due to the treatment accorded them.

In racist thought the tendency is to consider all distinctive groups, including the cultural ones, to be races. It has generally been assumed that national groups are highly in-bred, and thus that each one is a race group. This assumption of biological homogeneity is false for most nations, notably those of Europe. A pervasive belief in racism is that the reason the members of each (supposed) race share a way of life is that they inherit it genetically.[22] Cultures, of course, are

[19] Marden and Meyer, op. cit., 62–66; Rose, The Negro in America, op. cit., 31–44.
[20] Otto Klineberg, Social Psychology (Rev. ed.; New York: Henry Holt and Co., 1954), 305–11; Rose, The Negro in America, op. cit., 51–54.
[21] M. F. Ashley Montagu, Man's Most Dangerous Myth: The Fallacy of Race (4th ed.; New York: Meridian Books, The World Publishing Co., 1964), Chapter 10, "The Creative Power of 'Race' Mixture."
[22] Marden and Meyer, op. cit., 59–60, 63–64.

socially rather than biologically transmitted. Related here are the beliefs that race determines the characteristic temperament of a group and its morality. Such interpretations ignore wide variations in conduct by people with similar physical traits, especially from one cultural group to another, as well as the impact of group conditioning experiences—thus contributing to the confusion of race and culture.

The decline in racism must be attributed in considerable measure to the heavy academic attention and general publicity given to new findings and perspectives on race and culture, in biological and social science. Much publicity has been given to the failure to demonstrate the doctrines of racial superiority and inferiority, especially to the findings of the mental testers, and to data pertaining to the confusion of race and culture.[23] Many of the findings concerning the causes and consequences of prejudice and systematic discrimination have received extensive treatment in the mass media.

Many social forces have helped to break down stereotypes of racial and cultural groups during the past half-century or so and also to undermine many earlier beliefs about the nature of intergroup relations. The rapid assimilation of many nationalities brought them into intimate contact with millions of Americans, on an increasingly equalitarian basis, so stereotypes of national groups were widely challenged. The increased mobility of Negroes and other minorities during and after the two world wars also greatly increased the number and types of intergroup contacts, undermining both stereotypes and the belief that conflicts are inevitable whenever peoples meet.

Changes in the economic, educational, legal, and political statuses of minority groups have further undermined racist beliefs of fact, as well as the belief that law can have no effects on intergroup relations. Encouraged by gains, Negroes and other minorities have acquired new visions of the possible again and again; concurrently, the majority has come to believe less and less that minority groups are content with their lot. The general belief of fact has grown that things can be done to change intergroup relations in desired directions, and this has lent support to the value judgment that such things must be done.

[23] See Ruth Benedict, *Race: Science and Politics* (Rev. ed.; New York: The Viking Press, 1945); M. F. Ashley Montagu, *Statement on Race* (New York: Henry Schuman, Inc., 1951); Oscar Handlin, *Race and Nationality in American Life* (Boston: Little, Brown and Co., 1950); reprinted, New York: Doubleday Anchor Books, 1957).

VALUE PRIORITIES AND DILEMMAS OF INTERGROUP RELATIONS. Relations between groups, no matter how discriminatory, do not in themselves constitute a social problem. These relationships become a
public issue when members of the dominant community believe important values are threatened, and if the issue persists it becomes a
social problem. Since the minority has less power to control the relationships, it is primarily the dominant group's dilemma.[24]

The value of good international relations has assumed added
importance since the founding of the United Nations and the onset of
the Cold War, and the United States has been highly sensitive to
criticism from abroad of our treatment of racial minorities. Official
representatives from newly independent countries have sometimes
experienced discrimination personally in America. Foreign students
have come in large numbers since World War II and have often indicated concern about the racial situation. In studies of students from
the Middle East a substantial majority believed that Americans treat
their cultural minorities fairly but their racial ones unfairly; the
majority expressed surprise at finding so much racial discrimination,
and those here the longest were most likely to consider the treatment
unfair.[25]

A stable, growing economy has ranked high among national values
in recent decades, as we saw in Chapter 4. Excluding a minority
from whole occupational areas prevents efficient use of the abilities of
large numbers of people, thus wasting manpower. During World War
II, when national survival required maximum use of the labor force,
critical shortages developed in various skilled and semiskilled work
areas previously closed to Negroes and other minorities. A Presidential
order in 1941 established a Fair Employment Practices Committee for
the duration, and prohibited discrimination against racial or cultural
groups in government training programs and in all plants with defense contracts. The benefits to the economic status of Negroes and
other groups were great, and many of the doors remained open after

---

[24] Gunnar Myrdal, with the assistance of Richard Sterner and Arnold M. Rose,
An American Dilemma (New York: Harper and Bros., 1944), Chapters 1 and
2; Arnold Rose and Caroline Rose, *America Divided* (New York: Alfred A.
Knopf, 1948), 3–19.

[25] F. James Davis, "American Minorities as Seen by Turkish Students in the
United States," *Sociology and Social Research*, 46 (October, 1961), 48–54;
F. James Davis, "Cultural Perspectives of Middle Eastern Students in America,"
The Middle East Journal, (Summer, 1960), 256–64. Most Middle Easterners are
caucasoid (some of these the "dark white" Hindu type), some negroid, and a
few mongoloid; minorities have traditionally been religious groups.

the war, including those to many labor union halls.[26] Some of the concern about equal educational opportunity has been based on the desire to make maximum use of the work talents of the total population.

The value of maintaining peace and order enters often into minority issues, since community order is instrumental in guarding many cherished values that are threatened by intergroup tension and conflict, such as physical and mental health, property, and human life. The dominant community has shown much concern over the high rates of poverty, ill health, and deviant conduct in urban minority communities, indexes that show the inroads made on health, welfare, and family values. Thus the discussion of minority issues in this century has reflected the rising concern over minimum standards of living and related humanitarian values, including the dignity and worth of the human individual, and the growing inclination to apply them universally—to all human groups.

Central in the discussions of minority problems in America have been the constitutional guarantees of individual freedom and equal opportunity and the traditional value of fair play. Facts have frequently been marshalled to show that these basic values are being denied to minority groups, thus to large numbers of Americans. Since national unity is built around basic values, and would seem to imply reasonably consistent support of them, our minorities problem has been characterized as an "American Dilemma."[27] For a great many people it has also been a personal dilemma.

Acts of discrimination against racial and cultural groups support values prized within the dominant community, including economic advantage and security for one's family and friends. Discrimination can effectively eliminate whole groups from competition for desirable positions, even from entire businesses and industries. It helps dominant families to maintain their class status, homogeneous neighborhoods, and many have believed it helps maintain their property values.[28] It bolsters ethnocentric pride in race or cultural group and

---

[26] Marden and Meyer, *op. cit.*, 15–16, 281–83.

[27] Myrdal *et al.*, *op. cit.*; Rose, *The Negro in America, op. cit.*, 1–13; Ernest Q. Campbell, "Moral Discomfort and Racial Segregation—An Examination of the Myrdal Hypothesis," *Social Forces*, 39 (March, 1961), 228–34; Frank R. Westie, "The American Dilemma: An Empirical Test," *American Sociological Review*, 30 (August, 1965), 527–38.

[28] For evidence that property values do not fall in mixed areas unless there is the self-fulfilling prophecy of panic selling, see Luigi Laurenti, *Property Values*

helps those with a need for it to maintain a sense of superiority. Individual liberty is a value frequently appealed to in support of actions that circumscribe the individual liberties of members of entire groups.

A pattern of minority-dominant accommodation can become such an integral part of a social structure that any hint of change in it seems a threat to the noblest values and to the unity of the total way of life. This requires thorough acceptance of an ideology that answers all questions and explains away all contradictions, not with perfect logic but with certainty, and then the dominant group has no minority problem. This is not the picture in America today; conflicting values are involved in many complex ways as the dominant community struggles for agreement on intergroup goals, and on ways to achieve them. This is so particularly for the Negro problem, so let us examine it more closely.

THE DRIVE FOR EQUALITY FOR THE AMERICAN NEGRO

The System of Segregation

The Thirteenth, Fourteenth, and Fifteenth Amendments to the Constitution were intended to guarantee the newly freed Negro slaves equal treatment as American citizens. During the Reconstruction period many Negroes served in the legislatures and held other public offices, and the Civil Rights Bill of 1875 was passed by the Congress to ensure equal access to public facilities. In 1883 this bill was declared unconstitutional with respect to personal acts of "social discrimination," and the way was paved for a flood of Jim Crow legislation by Southern states and cities. The effect was to force the Negro back into an inferior position. The resulting system of discrimination was legalized in the South, with the support of federal courts, but was also backed by force and threats outside of the law. It was most rigid in the states of the Deep South, but the system prevailed throughout the South, with some variations. Considerable discrimination developed against the comparatively few Negroes in the North at this

---

and Race (Berkeley and Los Angeles: University of California Press, 1960), 47–48; Eleanor P. Wolf, "The Invasion-Succession Sequence as a Self-Fulfilling Prophecy," Journal of Social Issues, 13 (November, 1957), 7–20; Eunice and George Grier, "Market Characteristics in Interracial Housing," Journal of Social Issues, 13 (November, 1957), 50–59; Nathan Glazer and Davis McEntire, Studies in Housing and Minority Groups (Berkeley and Los Angeles: University of California Press, 1960).

time, but it was less severe and rigid than in the South, and in general not sanctioned by law.[29] The caste-like system in the South was crystallized by 1910, and was not threatened much until World War II.

The norms of this Southern system call for marked segregation, and for following a strict pattern of interracial etiquette when contacts are unavoidable. The white must make it clear in all interaction that he is in charge; the Negro must always show proper deference, indicating that he "knows his place." The white man must be addressed as "Mr.," and he must call the Negro man by his first name, or "boy," or "uncle," or something similar. The form, content, and contexts of interracial conversations are so restricted that group stereotypes are constantly reinforced. A "good nigger" is one who carefully follows the etiquette at all times; to do otherwise is to run serious risks. This extreme form of "social discrimination" is crucial in maintaining the whole segregated system, and it circumscribes the freedom of action of whites as well as Negroes.[30] This etiquette is facilitated by the racial visibility of most members of the Negro community.

The Rank Order of Discriminations

Myrdal and his associates found white attitudes favoring discrimination stronger in some areas of life than others. They proposed the following rank order, based on the hypothesis that the more intimate the contact the stronger the attitude of whites that discrimination must be maintained:[31]

1. Intermarriage and sexual contacts with white women.
2. Personal relations (greeting, talking, eating, dancing, swimming, and other matters governed by the interracial etiquette)
3. Public facilities (segregated schools, churches, trains, parks, *etc.*)
4. Political participation (voting and holding public office)
5. Legal treatment (in the courts, and by the police)
6. Economic activities (jobs, credit, housing, getting land, public assistance, *etc.*)

[29] Rose, *The Negro in America, op. cit.*, 189–203.
[30] *Ibid.*, 204–23; for treatments of the way "social discrimination" facilitates economic discrimination against Jews, see Carey McWilliams, *A Mask for Privilege* (Boston: Little, Brown & Co., 1948), and Alfred McLung Lee, *Fraternities Without Brotherhood: A Study of Prejudice on the American Campus* (Boston: The Beacon Press, 1955).
[31] Rose, *The Negro in America, op. cit.*, 24–26.

Research has shown some support for the existence of such a rank order, with some variation in the ranks, in the North as well as in the South.[32] A relatively recent study of the attitudes of students at the Universities of North Carolina, Texas, and Washington resulted in the following rank order: Intermarriage, personal relations, economic life, public facilities, political participation, and legal treatment.[33] It seems plausible that attitudes toward the economic area would vary with the degree of direct competition, and that the rank order would vary in different situations. It is difficult to arrange these areas as to degree of intimacy after the first two ranks, but the inclusion of housing in the economic category must be taken into account, since residential location influences personal contacts.

There is some support for further hypothesis that the Negroes have a rank order of attitudes of resistance to discriminations that is the inverse of the rank order of whites.[34] Assuming that behavior corresponds to these sets of verbally expressed attitudes, an optimistic suggestion is that orderly changes are possible since the Negroes want most those things that whites are least worried about losing. This has not been a successful prophecy, and evidently not because of some possible shifting in the rank orders. Changes have been strongly resisted in all areas of life, especially in the Deep South.

Why is "white womanhood" guarded so zealously in this system? Why is it a tragedy to the white community if a white woman has a mixed child but not if a black one does? It is miscegenation in either case, yet the ideology holds that the norms protecting white womanhood are to prevent the "mongrelization" of the races. Children stay with the mother, and it is not a violation of the system if a Negro mother has a mixed child; the ideology says the child is biologically inferior, and it is defined by law, the census-taker, and custom as a Negro. But if a white woman had a mixed child, what choices would there be? Force the mother to give the child to a Negro family, or to join the minority community herself? Surely not to accept the child as a member of a white family. The alternatives are too great a threat

---

[32] Lewis M. Killian and Charles M. Grigg, "Rank Orders of Discrimination of Negroes and Whites in a Southern City," *Social Forces*, 40 (March, 1961), 235–39; Edwin R. Edmunds, "The Myrdalian Thesis: Rank Order of Discriminations," *Phylon*, 15 (1954), 297–303.

[33] J. Allen Williams, Jr., and Paul L. Wienir, "A Reexamination of Myrdal's Rank Order of Discriminations," *Social Problems*, 14 (Spring, 1967), 443–54.

[34] W. S. M. Banks, II, "The Rank Order of Sensitivity to Discriminations of Negroes in Columbus, Ohio," *American Sociological Review*, 15 (August, 1950), 529–34; Killian and Grigg, *op. cit.*

to the white family and to the entire system of white superiority, so interracial liaisons with white females can never be allowed.

Selective Strategies of Change[35]

ECONOMIC EFFORTS. As the Southern system of discrimination was solidified at the turn of the century, efforts at change were aimed mainly at economic improvement. Chief among these was the gradual-istic program led by Booker T. Washington, the main feature of which was vocational education. Leaders of the minority community who promote gradualism and take pains to solicit white cooperation are often accused of furthering their personal interests, and of supporting the pattern of accommodation rather than protesting against it. Washington was criticized on this ground, but perhaps he managed almost the only gains possible for a time. The main concern of the Urban League, formed in 1911, has been the economic welfare of Negro migrants to Northern cities. Probably its most influential role has been as an employment agency, but it has also provided health, welfare, housing, recreational, and delinquency-prevention services. Its membership has been interracial and it has attempted to promote intergroup harmony.

EDUCATIONAL EFFORTS. Much of the outpouring of written and spoken words in twentieth-century America concerning intergroup relations has been designed to improve the lot of the Negro. Often the assumption has been that changes in beliefs and attitudes must precede changes in intergroup behavior, but much of the educational effort has accompanied economic, legal, or other strategies. The more formal research and teaching efforts have emphasized the changing knowledge about race and culture, along with historical and current intergroup conditions. Writers and speakers have made many strong emotional appeals. The mass media, churches, and many other or-organizations have combined information with persuasion. These activities have largely been interracial; even such Negro press efforts as publicizing the successes of outstanding Negro Americans have usually had white financial backing and encouragement.

Such educational efforts have by no means been limited to the

---

[35] Much of this section is based on Rose, *The Negro in America, op. cit.*, Chapter 15, "Negro Leadership and the Negro Protest," Chapter 16, "Popular Theories and Action Organizations," and Chapter 17, "Basic Protest Institutions: Church, School and Press."

North. An outstanding example was the Commission on Interracial Cooperation, another joint Negro-white effort, established in 1919 to work toward greater equality for the Negro in the South. It did not attack segregation as such, but opposed discrimination and called for racial justice. In 1944 it was replaced by the Southern Regional Council, which has played a key role in school desegregation. By sponsoring research and such activities as conferences and courses in the schools on race relations, it has attempted to foster interracial cooperation and orderly change.

The Association of Southern Women for the Prevention of Lynching, from 1930 to 1943, played a major role in sharply reducing the lynching of Southern Negroes. Many of the killings had been perpetrated in the name of white womanhood. The Association challenged the need for such a response and called for the protection of women of both races. Association members were mainly from rural communities, old families, and established churches, and most of their husbands were important state and local leaders. Thus they were influential, the very symbols of Southern white womanhood. Their approach was educational in the sense of reasoned persuasion, based on information and forthright logic. Their main tactic was publishing facts about lynchings and their consequences for the South; they sponsored research, lectures, discussions of all kinds, and they used petitions and direct persuasion of community leaders. They performed functions that moderates can do well—helped clarify the issue, provided much sound information, and kept channels of information and discussion open—and effectively persuaded.[36]

LEGAL CHALLENGES. Booker T. Washington's chief critic, W. E. B. DuBois, led the first strong public Negro protest against the Restoration. In 1909 he merged his Niagara movement with a white group to form the National Association for the Advancement of Colored People. The NAACP has continued to be interracial and to seek full equality for the Negro. Its chief strategy has been legal; it has provided legal counsel for Negroes in a great many situations, pursued appeals to the federal courts, and worked for civil rights legislation. In 1896 the United States Supreme Court established the separate-but-equal doctrine in the case of Plessy v. Ferguson, then followed this

[36] James H. Laue and Leon M. McCorkle, Jr., "The Association of Southern Women for the Prevention of Lynching: A Commentary on the Role of the Moderate," Sociological Inquiry, 35 (Winter, 1965), 80–93.

precedent and thereby gave federal support to the Jim Crow laws. The NAACP's continuing challenges of this doctrine and others have been based on the Thirteenth, Fourteenth, and Fifteenth Amendments, and other sections of the Constitution. It has won nearly all of several dozen appeals to the United States Supreme Court, a success attested to by the fact that the long-time chief legal counsel of the NAACP— Thurgood Marshall—in 1967 became the first Negro member of the nation's highest court.

These efforts have aimed at stopping discriminatory acts without waiting for educational processes to change beliefs and attitudes. In that sense they have been determined protest efforts, but they have been moderate in the sense of using legal processes to push for equal treatment under the Constitution. A basic assumption has been that the law is in conflict, reflecting a national dilemma rather than uniform sentiment behind systematic discrimination. Further, it has been assumed that federal interpreters and makers of the law would— when compelled to choose—prefer equal treatment for the Negro.[37]

The American Negro and World Wars I and II

Negro migration to cities and to the North first grew large during the World War I period, with resulting economic improvements and disappointments. Much of the increased contact was peaceful, but numerous (white) riots followed in the North; the threats to the Southern pattern met with strong resistance, with lynching as the ultimate sanction. This was a major period of growth and activity in the Ku Klux Klan. A major manifestation of the Negro unrest in the twenties was the separatist movement led by Marcus Garvey, the ultimate goal being a move back to Africa. Garvey denounced Negro leaders who worked in interracial organizations and he preached black superiority; he organized Negro business cooperatives, the failure of which ended his movement. Migration from the rural South slowed during the Great Depression, when American Negroes suffered severe economic setbacks, though many went North to have a better chance to get welfare funds and the few unskilled jobs available.

World War II initiated massive movements of the Negro population, and brought considerable economic gains, many of them under

---

[37] Jack Greenberg, *Race Relations and American Law* (New York: Columbia University Press, 1959), 1–78.

federal aegis, as we have noted. Some of the competition for jobs and housing resulted in riots, the largest being the pitched battle between the races in 1942 in Detroit. Yet the new kinds of contact in both civilian and military life gave a great many members of dominant and minority groups alike new visions of intergroup relations. The belief grew that tension and conflict can be avoided in interracial contacts when groups meet as equals. There is some research support for this hypothesis of equal-status contacts, but it evidently holds true in some situations and not in others.[38]

The American military forces were still markedly segregated during World War II, with Negroes generally performing unskilled tasks and being largely excluded from combat and from leadership. As a result of the widespread criticism, and the findings of studies of attitudes of soldiers and also of the outcomes of some carefully managed attempts at integration,[39] President Truman in 1948 ordered complete desegregation of the military. Combat was opened fully to Negroes, who were evaluated as successful fighters and leaders in the Korean War. The Army has become the most thoroughly integrated branch of the military, with whites very often serving under Negro command. Most of the adjustments took place before the civil rights drive began in the mid-fifties, and with relatively little tension and conflict.[40] Law can rarely bring about changes in civilian life as readily as in military life,[41] and much of the off-duty life of men in uniform remains racially separate.

Desegregation of the Schools

LEGAL ISSUES. Before the United States Supreme Court's 1954 decision in the five cases that included *Brown v. Board of Education*,[42]

---

[38] Barry S. Brown and George W. Albee, "The Effect of Integrated Hospital Experiences on Racial Attitudes—A Discordant Note," *Social Problems*, 13 (Winter, 1966), 324–33; Donald P. Irish, "Reactions of Caucasian Residents to Japanese-American Neighbors," *Journal of Social Issues*, 8 (January, 1952), 10–17; J. Allen Williams, Jr., "Reduction of Tension Through Intergroup Contact: A Social Psychological Interpretation," *Pacific Sociological Review*, 7 (Fall, 1964), 81–88; Bernard Meer and Edward Freedman, "The Impact of Negro Neighbors on White Home Owners," *Social Forces*, 45 (September, 1966), 11–19.
[39] Samuel A. Stouffer *et al.*, *The American Soldier*, Volume I (Princeton, N.J.: Princeton University Press, 1949), Chapter 10, "Negro Soldiers."
[40] Charles C. Moskos, Jr., "Racial Integration in the Armed Forces," *American Journal of Sociology*, 72 (September, 1966), 132–48.
[41] Greenbreg, *op. cit.*, 355–70.
[42] 347 U. S. 483. The other cases involved South Carolina, Virginia, Delaware, and Washington, D.C.

Negro schools had been improving and in the South they had been gaining on the white schools. The gap had been closing with respect to plant facilities and other capital outlays, teacher salaries and other instructional costs per pupil, and teaching loads.[43] For two decades the Supreme Court had handed down decisions requiring the admission of Negroes to graduate and professional schools, and some integration at this level had begun in twelve Southern and border states before May, 1954. Unequal training had usually been involved in the cases appealed to the high court, but in the written opinion in a 1950 case (*Sweatt v. Painter*),[44] there was *dictum* (gratuitous comment not directly relevant to the issue decided) to the effect that the separate-but-equal doctrine violated the Fourteenth Amendment. Seeing new visions of the possible, the NAACP posed the issue of whether or not segregated public schools were unequal by virtue of being separate, even if Negro facilities were as good as white ones.

The U.S. Supreme Court decided in favor of this view *that racially separate public schools are inherently unequal,* thus overruling the spirit of the separate-but-equal precedents. The *Plessy v. Ferguson* case is different both in regard to the facts (violation of a Jim Crow statute on seating in trains) and on the constitutional law issue (reasonableness of the use of state police power) from the school segregation cases. The constitutional issue in the latter was the use of race as a *legislative category* in statutes regarding public schools, and the decision was that this violates the *equal protection clause* of the Fourteenth Amendment. In short, it was held that racially separate public schools are *incapable* of providing equal educational opportunity.[45]

Opponents of integration have maintained that this decision was "unconstitutional." The argument that the Constitution leaves education to the states, which may "interpose" their sovereignty, ignores the obligation of the states to follow the Constitution in all they do. The notion that a court must follow its own precedents greatly oversimplifies how the law works. Courts normally follow precedents when there are any and unless they have compelling reasons not to, but

---

[43] Truman M. Pierce *et al., White and Negro Schools in the South* (Englewood Cliffs, N.J.: Prentice-Hall, 1955), 288–90.
[44] 339 U. S. 629 (1950). This case involved the law school at the University of Texas.
[45] Albert P. Blaustein and Clarence Clyde Ferguson, Jr., *Desegregation and the Law* (New Brunswick, N. J.: Rutgers University Press, 1957), 10–11, 95–125; Greenberg, *op. cit.,* 208–74.

typically there are only conflicting lines of *analogous* decisions.[46] Interpreting constitutions and statutes poses some special problems, but the judicial process is basically the same as without them.[47] The court had to choose between a line of analogous decisions in the *Plessy* tradition and another line that included the *Sweatt* case.[48] The citation by the NAACP of a brief prepared by 35 social scientists, documenting the finding that Negroes in segregated schools develop an inferior conception of self, followed the established constitutional law practice of using, "Brandeis Briefs." Courts often take judicial notice of scientific or professional beliefs of fact, or else use their own assumptions, and the material in this particular brief was directly relevant to the legal issue the court was deliberating.[49]

It is important to note that the decision of 1954 was unanimous. The implementation order issued a year later was also emphatic and unanimous, and it stated that desegregation of the schools was to proceed with "all deliberate speed." This was to allow for practical problems to be solved and for variations in school districts throughout the South, but the Court did intend for the boards to get on with integration. It continued to give high priority to matters concerning desegregation and in a 1969 Mississippi case it held unanimously that further delays in school desegregation were unconstitutional, regardless of administrative problems.

LEGAL EXTENSIONS OF DESEGREGATION. The Court's intention in the 1954 decision and in the implementation decree was quite clear—to hold all legislation based on racial classifications to be discriminatory, and therefore unconstitutional. In subsequent decisions the *Brown* case quickly became a precedent not only in school cases, but in those involving parks, golf courses, bathing beaches, transportation and other public facilities, and housing. In these decisions the Court continued to act with great unanimity; its course was clear.[50] After ex-

---

[46] F. James Davis and Henry H. Foster, Jr., "The Judicial Process and Social Change," Chapter 4, in F. James Davis et al., *Society and the Law* (New York: The Free Press, 1962).

[47] Foster, in Davis et al., *ibid.*, 149–73; Blaustein and Ferguson, *op. cit.*, 54–75.

[48] Foster, in Davis et al., *ibid.*, 173–92; Blaustein and Ferguson, *op. cit.*, 118.

[49] Blaustein and Ferguson, *op. cit.*, 126–37. Three of the seven works cited by the Court as part of the support for its opinion are: Kenneth B. Clark, *Effect of Prejudice and Discrimination on Personality Development* (Washington, D.C.: Midcentury White House Conference on Children and Youth, 1950), Frazier, *op. cit.*, and Myrdal, *op. cit.*

[50] Blaustein and Ferguson, *op. cit.*, 145–57, 180–209, 218–39; Vern Countryman (ed.), *Discrimination and the Law* (Chicago & London: University of Chicago Press, 1965).

tensions to numerous other situations, the Court in 1967 unanimously declared Virginia's statute against Negro-white marriage to be unconstitutional. Sixteen states still had such laws, and the Court indicated that their aim is to maintain white supremacy, and their effect is discriminatory.

PROGRESS AND RESISTANCE. By 1956–57 less than 4 per cent of the school districts in the South with both Negroes and whites had begun any desegregation, as compared with nearly three-fourths of such districts in the border states. The Deep South avoided it entirely for several years, but it came to Florida in 1959, Louisiana in 1960, Georgia in 1961, Alabama and South Carolina in 1963, and finally to Mississippi in 1964. In the South as a whole there was only token compliance for many years, but the amount increased considerably in the mid-sixties, with the results summarized in Table 12.1. It must be kept in mind that the proportion of students who are Negroes is much larger in the South than in the border states. By 1966–67, just under one-sixth of the Negro students in the South were attending schools with whites as compared with three-fourths in the border states, and for the region as a whole the figure was one-fourth. There has been considerable desegregation of colleges and universities in the South, and some of faculties at all levels of education.[51]

Most of the early integration was peaceful, the outstanding exception being at Little Rock High School, to which President Eisenhower ordered federal troops in 1957 to counter the defiance of the Governor of Arkansas, Orval Faubus.[52] Most of the districts in the border states have acted voluntarily; in the South there has usually been no action until ordered by a federal court. The admission of Autherine Lucy to the University of Alabama in 1956 precipitated a major riot, and in 1962 Governor George Wallace defiantly led the state's opposition to the first desegregation efforts at the elementary school level. When Governor Ross Barnett opposed the admission of James Meredith to the University of Mississippi in 1962, there was another white riot, and federal troops were ordered in to quell it. Whites reacted with demonstrations and some violence to the coming

[51] *Statistical Summary of School Segregation-Desegregation in the Southern and Border States, 1966–67* (Nashville, Tenn.: Southern Education Reporting Service, 1967), 1–4; Jim Leeson, "Desegregation: The Pace Quickens in the South," *Southern Education Report*, 2 (April, 1967), 33–37.
[52] Wilson Record and Jane Cassels Record, *Little Rock, U.S.A.* (San Francisco, Calif.: Chandler Publishing Co., 1960).

TABLE 12.1

PERCENTAGE OF NEGRO ELEMENTARY AND HIGH SCHOOL STUDENTS AT-
TENDING SCHOOLS WITH WHITES, AT FIVE-YEAR INTERVALS, IN THE SOUTH
AND THE BORDER STATES

| | *Percentage of Negro Students Attending with Whites* | | |
	1956–57	*1961–62*	*1966–67*
Alabama	o	o	4.4
Arkansas	.033	.139	15.1
Florida	o	.268	22.3
Georgia	o	.003	8.8
Louisiana	o	.004	3.4
Mississippi	o	o	2.5
North Carolina	o	.061	15.4
South Carolina	o	o	5.6
Tennessee	.078	.753	28.6
Texas	1.36	1.33	44.9
Virginia	o	.242	25.3
SOUTH	.144	.241	15.9
Delaware	28.5	53.7	100.0
Dist. of Columbia	97.0	85.6	86.3
Kentucky	20.9	51.2	90.1
Maryland	19.1	41.5	65.3
Missouri	—	41.4	77.7
Oklahoma	8.73	25.6	50.8
West Virginia	—	62.0	93.4
BORDER	—	52.5	75.7
REGION	—	7.6	25.8

SOURCE: Statistical Summary of School Segregation-Desegregation in the Southern and Border States, 1966–67 (*Nashville, Tenn.: Southern Education Reporting Service, 1967*), tables on pp. 1, 41–42.

of desegregation to some of the public schools of Mississippi, Louisiana, and Alabama in the mid-sixties.[53] The fact that schools were in most instances kept open, and desegregated without serious incidents, has been credited in part to white organizations such as HOPE, OASIS, SOS, COPE, and STOP. These have been predominantly white women's groups, following moderate but determined and timely tactics similar to those used earlier by the Association of Southern Women for the Prevention of Lynching.[54]

Much of the Southern resistance to school desegregation has been within the framework of law, at least in the sense that legal procedures have been followed. There have been (1) countless delays, using legal tactics; (2) pupil placement laws, enabling students to be put into given schools on the basis of individual criteria, race not being mentioned; (3) laws granting tuition to Negroes to study out of the state; (4) actions to close the public schools and substitute segregated private ones; and (5) legal actions to prevent the NAACP from operating in the Southern states.[55] Much of the South apparently intended to use such means to resist indefinitely, but they were whittled down with unexpected speed. The one considered to be the ultimate and unbeatable weapon, closing the public schools, had to be resorted to much sooner than anticipated; and it collapsed in 1959 when the U.S. Supreme Court ruled this action in Prince Edward County, Virginia, to be unconstitutional. Resistance continued, but few doubted the eventual outcome, especially after some very emphatic pronouncements during 1966–67 by the federal courts (and the Department of Health, Education and Welfare) that the period of "all deliberate speed" was over and school desegregation should not be further delayed.

Legal resistance has been supplemented by at least fifty Southern organizations using economic pressures, political pressures, and illegal force and intimidation to prevent integration in all areas of life. Most influential have been the White Citizens Councils and the re-

[53] Jim Leeson, "Desegregation: Violence, Intimidation and Protest," *Southern Education Report*, 2 (December, 1966), 29–32.
[54] Laue and McCorkle, *op. cit.*, 91–92. The initials of the organizations mentioned stand for, Help Our Public Education, Organizations Assisting Schools in September, Save Our Schools, Inc., Committee on Public Education, and Committee to Stop This Outrageous Purge.
[55] Blaustein and Ferguson, *op. cit.*, Chapter 15, "Avoidance, Evasion and Delay"; Greenberg, *op. cit.*, 221–45; Ernest Q. Campbell, *When a City Closes Its Schools* (Chapel Hill, North Carolina: Institute for Research in Social Science, University of North Carolina, 1961).

juvenated Ku Klux Klan. Much of the slow pace of desegregation, and much of the tension and violence attending it, must be attributed to these organizations.[56]

At least where school integration is concerned, Southern sympathy for resistance declined a good deal in the mid-sixties. In 1966, 74 per cent of a representative sample of Southern white parents said they would not object to sending their children to a school where a few children are colored, while only 38 per cent had agreed to this in 1963. As for the same question where half the children are colored, 44 per cent had no objection in 1966, as compared with only 17 per cent in 1963. And as for the situation where more than half the children are colored, 27 per cent did not object in 1966, but only 6 per cent in 1963.[57]

Research findings and reports of all kinds continue to receive attention in the still widely discussed issue of school desegregation. The U.S. Commission on Civil Rights has issued a two-volume report contending that any school that is as much as fifty per cent Negro is racially imbalanced, meaning that children in it are denied equal educational opportunity. By this yardstick, a great many children in both Southern and Northern cities are in racially unbalanced schools. The report also maintains that compensatory programs, such as "Head Start," do not have a lasting effect.[58] A major study of 600,000 students in schools in all 50 states, conducted for the U.S. Office of Education, lends support to these contentions and thus to the school integration movement. Evidently most schools do not offset the family and neighborhood influences Negro children bring to school with them, mainly their negative conception of self, but those in which more than half of the students are white can significantly improve the achievement of the Negro child. Achievement of the white child was not found to be associated very closely with racial balance.[59]

[56] Hodding Carter, III, *The South Strikes Back* (Garden City, New York: Doubleday & Co., 1959).

[57] *Gallup Political Index*, Report No. 12, May, 1966, 16.

[58] United States Commission on Civil Rights, *Racial Isolation in Public Schools* (Washington, D.C.: Government Printing Office, 1967); Jim Leeson, "The Attention Now Turns to 'Balance'," *Southern Education Report*, 2 (June, 1967), 12–15.

[59] James Coleman and Ernest Q. Campbell, with Carol J. Hobson, James McPartland, Alexander M. Mood, Frederick D. Weinfeld, and Robert L. York, *Equality of Educational Opportunity* (Washington, D.C.: U.S. Government Printing Office, 1966). The Civil Rights Act of 1964 directed the Commissioner of Education to have this study made.

There is evidence that Negroes and whites have continued to differ significantly in their outlooks on child rearing, the punishment of juvenile offenders, political identification, the role of the United Nations, the church, big business, and on minority groups.[60] The mass media evidently serve as a means for Negro adolescents to learn the white man's ways.[61] At least for middle-income Negroes, gradations of color continue to make a difference not only in life chances, but in the attitudes of the individual Negro toward his race, toward whites, and toward other matters.[62] One study, pertinent to the concern about how to prepare teachers to work with the disadvantaged student, suggests that family and neighborhood experiences are less crucial in the Negro's decision to attend college than nonfamily figures are, especially high school teachers.[63]

Teachers play key roles in the process of desegregation, and presumably their actions are related to their own attitudes toward the process and to their perception of the community's sentiments.[64] A study in North Carolina found that Negro teachers had been very much involved in the adjustments attending desegregation, but that their professional concerns had often made them cautious.[65] Another professional group, the clergy, have sometimes played a cautious, accommodating role, and at times a more militant one. A national sample of Negro adults found traditional religious involvement to be associated with a lack of militancy on civil rights matters, while involvement in the socially activist churches was associated with mili-

[60] Leonard Broom and Norval D. Glenn, "Negro-White Differences in Reported Attitudes and Behavior," *Sociology and Social Research,* 50 (January, 1966), 187–200.

[61] Walter M. Gerson, "Mass Media Socialization Behavior: Negro-White Differences," *Social Forces,* 45 (September, 1966), 40–50.

[62] Howard E. Freeman, J. Michael Ross, David Armor, and Thomas F. Pettigrew, "Color Gradation and Attitudes Among Middle-Income Negroes," *American Sociological Review,* 31 (June, 1966), 365–74.

[63] Patricia Gurin and Edgar Epps, "Some Characteristics of Students from Poverty Backgrounds Attending Predominantly Negro Colleges in the Deep South," *Social Forces,* 45 (September, 1966), 27–40. An exploratory study suggests that the self-concepts of Negro children can be changed both by teaching Negro history and by involving them in action programs; see David W. Johnson, "Racial Attitudes of Negro Freedom School Participants and Negro and White Civil Rights Participants," *Social Forces,* 45 (December, 1966), 266–73.

[64] Miriam Strouse Shirley and Helen Townsend Cropp, "Superintendents' Attitudes Toward Desegregation in the Public Schools," *Sociology and Social Research,* 41 (January-February, 1957), 181–86.

[65] Richard A. Lamanna, "The Negro Teacher and Desegregation: A Study of Strategic Decision-Makers and Their Vested Interests in Different Community Contexts," *Sociological Inquiry,* 35 (Winter, 1965), 26–40.

tancy.[66] The nation has seen white clergymen in both the accommo-dating[67] and the protest roles in the desegregation crises.

There have been many efforts to break up the *de facto* school segregation in the North associated with residential separateness of the races. In a study in a small city near New York it was found that lower class Negro mothers were more anxious than middle class ones to use a bus transfer system to enable their children to attend predominantly white schools. The (rejected) hypothesis was that middle class Negroes would be more motivated to transfer because they value education more, but evidently the lower class mothers saw the bus system as a way of breaking out of the ghetto.[68] In two other studies in the same general part of the country, upper middle class whites were more in favor of plans for racial desegregation of schools than were lower middle class whites. The interpretation was that families newly arrived in the lower middle class are anxious to keep lower class people from "spoiling" the areas to which they have moved, while upper class people feel less threatened and take a more cosmopolitan approach.[69] Segregated schooling and housing are indeed intertwined.

The Broader Protest, and Nonviolence

Coming on top of the changes occasioned by World War II, the desegregation decisions and their consequences had a great impact on the American Negro. Federal law was now on his side, and the discriminators were officially in the wrong. Great things were possible, yet desegregation seemed painfully slow. The sense of the rightness of their common cause grew, and new norms began to emerge that were consistent with the rising expectations and with collective means for combating the frustrating barriers to full equality.[70] As contrasted

---

[66] Gary T. Marx, "Religion: Opiate or Inspiration of Civil Rights Militancy Among Negroes," *American Sociological Review,* 32 (February, 1967), 64–72.
[67] Ernest Q. Campbell and Thomas F. Pettigrew, *Christians in Racial Crisis: A Study of Little Rock's Ministry* (Washington, D.C.: Public Affairs Press, 1959).
[68] Elmer Luchterhand and Leonard Weller, "Social Class and the Desegregation Movement: A Study of Parents' Decisions in a Negro Ghetto," *Social Problems,* 12 (Summer, 1965), 83–88.
[69] Kurt Lang and Gladys Lang, "Resistance to School Desegregation: A Case Study of Backlash Among Jews," *Sociological Inquiry,* 35 (Winter, 1965), 94–106; David Rogers and Bert Swanson, "White Citizen Response to the Same Integration Plan: Comparisons of Local School Districts in a Northern City," *Sociological Inquiry,* 35 (Winter, 1965), 107–22.
[70] Robin M. Williams, Jr., "Social Change and Social Conflict: Race Relations in the United States, 1944–64," *Sociological Inquiry,* 35 (Winter, 1965), 8–25.

with the limited, more selective, strategies long used by the NAACP and the Urban League, collective actions began to be taken that were broader in two senses: (1) they were all-out confrontations of the dominant community that might involve protest and/or negotiation on a number of fronts at once, and (2) they involved a higher proportion of the people in the Negro community.[71] Especially in the South, this meant that a growing number of Negroes were overcoming their fear of challenging the system. It meant new organizations and the rise to prominence of more militant Negro leaders—"race man" types in contrast both to the "Uncle Toms" and the "diplomats."[72] Only the more militant white liberals were welcome in these new organizations. The conference table and the legal strategies were increasingly seen as having only fed the Negro's frustration by producing token gains.[73]

THE MONTGOMERY BUS BOYCOTT. The Negro community of Montgomery, Alabama, began its boycott of segregated bus seating in December, 1955. It was so well supported that it dealt severe economic losses to the bus owners over a period of months. The NAACP supported the effort, and in 1966 the state law requiring segregation on public conveyances was held unconstitutional by the U.S. Supreme Court. The buses in the city were then desegregated. The boycott became a symbol of the success of organized collective Negro action against what widely came to be called the "white power structure." A Montgomery Negro minister, the Rev. Martin Luther King, Jr., led this boycott and immediately became widely known.[74] He was later to become head of the Southern Christian Leadership Conference, with headquarters in Atlanta, and to lead many demonstrations of Negro protest. The SCLC led an attempted boycott against the entire states of Mississippi and Alabama a decade later.

The fact that Dr. King was head of the Montgomery Improvement

---

[71] Lewis M. Killian, "Community Structure and the Role of the Negro Leader-Agent," *Sociological Inquiry*, 35 (Winter, 1965), 69–79.
[72] Daniel C. Thompson, *The Negro Leadership Class* (Englewood Cliffs, N.J.: Prentice-Hall, 1963), 164–71.
[73] Lewis Killian and Charles Grigg, *Racial Crisis in America* (Englewood Cliffs, N.J.: Prentice-Hall, 1964), 133; Louis E. Lomax, *The Negro Revolt* (New York: Signet Books, The New American Library, 1962), 78–111.
[74] Martin Luther King, Jr., *Stride Toward Freedom: The Montgomery Story* (New York: Harper & Row, 1958); L. D. Reddick, *Crusaders Without Violence: A Biography of Martin Luther King* (New York: Harper & Row, 1959), Chapters 8, 9, and 10; see also Charles U. Smith and Lewis M. Killian, *The Tallahassee Bus Protest* (New York: Anti-Defamation League of B'nai B'rith, 1958).

Association when the bus boycott was conducted pushed the new Negro militancy in the direction of a nonviolent approach, due to his training in the methods of passive resistance developed by Mahatma Ghandi in India. Dr. King was strongly convinced that the civil rights movement could succeed if Negroes and their allies appealed to the nation's Christian conscience and refused to return violence for violence.[75] He rejected racism and called for integration and brotherhood, and he led public demonstrations to coerce the conscience of the white power structure into accepting racial equality. He was jailed several times and he met some physical violence, yet he continued along the path of nonviolent protest. The Congress of Racial Equality (CORE) and the Student Nonviolent Coordinating Committee began as nonviolent organizations.

This disciplined kind of militancy is not easy to manage for large groups, especially in the absence of training programs. At every opportunity Dr. King used his access to the public to advocate and contribute to the mood of passive resistance, frequently insisting that the resort to violence would result in losses for the Negro rather than gains. His message had much support for several years, in contrast to the more limited success of a competing group known as the Black Muslims,[76] which appealed to black superiority and ultimate separation of the races. Dr. King was a determined "race man," one whose pacifism and calls for interracial respect and good will led to his winning the Nobel Peace Prize in 1964. In the late fifties his supporters became divided over his linking the drive for racial equality with the demand for ending the war in Viet Nam.

THE SIT-INS AND THE FREEDOM RIDES. Nonviolent resistance was adopted in 1960 by young Negroes who began sitting in the white sections of chain store lunch counters in the South,[77] and their discipline and orderliness in the face of arrests and harsh treatment impressed the nation. Student boycotts of chain stores in the North helped the protest in the South and resulted in management orders

[75] Lomax, op. cit., 93–111; Martin Oppenheimer, "Towards a Sociological Understanding of Non-Violence," Sociological Inquiry, 65 (Winter, 1965), 123–31; James W. Vander Zanden, "The Non-Violent Resistance Movement Against Segregation," American Journal of Sociology, 68 (March, 1963), 544–50.
[76] C. Eric Lincoln, The Black Muslims in America (Boston: The Beacon Press, 1961); E. U. Essien-Udom, Black Nationalism: A Search for Identity in America (Chicago: University of Chicago Press, 1962).
[77] Reddick, op. cit., 133–35; Lomax, op. cit., 133–59.

to desegregate their Southern facilities. A year later the Freedom Riders, an interracial group of Northerners who went South to test the extent to which interstate buses and trains were being desegregated, also followed nonviolent methods, under the tutelage of CORE. The purpose was to precipitate lawsuits and have them appealed to the federal courts in order to speed desegregation, a strategy that eventually was successful. Police officers aided the cause by arresting many of the Riders on charges of breach of the peace, inciting to riot, vagrancy, and other violations. Again the nation saw violence met with nonviolence, in several cities.

THE CIVIL RIGHTS ACTS OF 1964 AND 1965. The 1964 Civil Rights Act contains provisions against virtually the entire rank order of discriminations, with emphasis on schools and other public facilities, employment, union membership, and voting registration. It provides that federal funds be cut off for programs in which discrimination exists, a provision much resented in the South. The Civil Rights Acts of 1957 and 1960 had strengthened voting rights, but the Act of 1965 went much further, eliminating literacy tests and similar devices in all counties or states that had less than half the voting-age residents registered in November, 1964, and providing for federal examiners upon receipt of twenty or more complaints of voting discrimination in a county. The power of the long-standing coalition between Southern Democrats in Congress and Northern Republicans had been broken at least temporarily, and the Act of 1965 had the majority support of both parties. The same Congress voted for an investigation of alleged subversive activities on the part of the Ku Klux Klan.

Efforts by the SCLC and other groups had greatly increased the number of registered Negro voters before the passage of the Act in 1965, and this event spurred new efforts, doubling registration by a year later. The growing political power of Negroes was dramatized by the appearance of Negroes in public offices, including state legislatures, and by CORE's (unsuccessful) call for a separate Negro political party. Nationally, Negroes have voted heavily in recent Presidential elections; lower-class Negroes seem more politically active than lower class whites are.[78]

Extremist segregationists reacted violently to these gains, and

[78] Anthony M. Crum, "A Reappraisal of the Social and Political Participation of Negroes," *American Journal of Sociology*, 72 (July, 1966), 32–46.

many Negroes who were challenging the system were killed, including, in 1963, the head of the NAACP in Mississippi, Medgar Evers. There were acts of terrorism such as the bombing of homes and churches; four little girls died in the bombing of a church in Birmingham. Resentment against Northern volunteers helping mainly with voting registration resulted in the deaths of a number of them, including in 1965 the murder of a woman from Detroit, Mrs. Viola Liuzzo, and in the traditional failure of juries to return indictments or verdicts of guilty in the resulting trials. At Selma, Alabama, a white minister from Boston, the Rev. James Reeb, was beaten to death in 1965, and a group of marching protesters met a police assault near Selma with stunned nonviolence. Similar events took place in Mississippi, both over voting and desegregation of schools, and there was considerable tension in parts of Louisiana.

Following these events, and the urban Negro riots of 1965, there was much talk of a national "white backlash" against the civil rights movement. Considering the various antipoverty programs insufficient, the SCLC mounted a drive in 1966 to improve living conditions in the Negro areas of large cities. Concentrating on Chicago, Dr. King appealed to the white man's conscience as usual, and brought both economic and political pressures to bear, as well as publicity. By November of 1966, the national percentage saying that the Administration was pushing integration too fast reached a four-year high of 53 per cent. The percentage was 72 in the South, with 17 per cent saying "about right."[79]

Negro Mass Frustration, and Increased Militancy

TOKENISM AND SOUTHERN WHITE REACTION. The determined use of legal tactics had kept the pace of desegregation in the schools and in other areas of life slow, and much of it on a token basis. There had also been many threats and incidents of violence, including some against Negro children, so that by the mid-sixties there was much frustration and doubt among Negroes about the efficacy of federal court actions and decisions. The determined and frequently violent reactions to voter registration were especially jolting, and many Negroes doubted that the strong new civil rights laws were going to help them much. Legal strategy was not the only thing questioned;

---

[79] *Gallup Political Index,* Report No. 18, November-December, 1966, 6.

doubt grew about the wisdom of organized confrontations of the white power structure on a nonviolent basis.

HOUSING SEGREGATION. *De facto* segregation of housing has become an increasing issue as the Negro population has burgeoned in the cities.[80] Segregation has increased in many cities,[81] and has remained high in spite of a general decrease in the North and West during the fifties.[82] The marked residential segregation in Chicago cannot be explained by the low economic status of Negroes,[83] and in general residential differentiation is not closely related to variations in education, occupation, and income.[84] This suggests that the continued pattern of housing segregation is a matter of race, not just social class. When other city migrants have become able to afford better housing they have moved out of the ghettos, but racial visibility evidently retards this movement among Negroes. Newer cities in the South are more segregated than the older ones, where the "backyard" residence pattern of slave days has survived.[85]

The California Real Estate Association led a drive in 1964 to pass Proposition 14, an initiative to amend the state Constitution to nullify the state fair housing laws and to prevent future actions by the legislature and the courts to limit discriminatory actions of property owners in renting and selling. The passage of this amendment by a two-to-one margin of the state's voters attracted national attention and added to the growing frustration of urban Negroes. The chief argument for the Proposition had been that fair housing laws infringe on

---

[80] Don J. Hager, "Housing Discrimination, Social Conflict, and the Law," *Social Problems,* 7 (Summer, 1960).

[81] Albert J. Mayer and Thomas F. Hoult, *Race and Residence in Detroit* (Detroit, Mich.: Detroit Institute for Urban Studies, Wayne State University, 1962), 7; Donald O. Cowgill, "Trends in Residential Segregation of Non-Whites in American Cities," *American Sociological Review,* 21 (February, 1956), 43–47; Eunice and George Grier, *Discrimination in Housing* (New York: Anti-Defamation League of B'nai B'rith, 1960), 11; F. James Davis, "The Effects of a Freeway Displacement on Racial Housing in a Northern City," *Phylon,* 26 (Fall, 1965), 209–15.

[82] Karl E. Taeuber and Alma F. Taeuber, *Negroes in Cities: Residential Segregation and Neighborhood Change* (Chicago: Aldine Publishing Co., 1965).

[83] Karl E. Taeuber and Alma F. Taeuber, "The Negro as an Immigrant Group: Recent Trends in Racial and Ethnic Segregation in Chicago," *American Journal of Sociology,* 69 (January, 1964), 374–82.

[84] Howard M. Bahr and Jack P. Gibbs, "Racial Differentiation in American Metropolitan Areas," *Social Forces,* 46 (June, 1967), 521–32.

[85] Leo F. Schnore and Philip C. Evenson, "Segregation in Southern Cities," *American Journal of Sociology,* 72 (July, 1966), 58–67.

property rights, meaning those of a potential seller, who should be allowed to discriminate in selling or renting if he so desires. The courts did not consider this to be an absolute value when weighed against the right of the individual buyer to acquire property in a free market without regard to race or ethnicity. As discussion of fair housing laws continued, a national poll in 1967 found that 58 per cent knew what "open housing" is. Of these, 35 per cent favored national legislation to guarantee fair housing, but 54 per cent were against it and 11 per cent had no opinion.[86] In 1968 the United States Supreme Court rejected racial discrimination in the sale or rental of housing by individual owners. In general, Negroes apparently have seen this as but a token change in a grim and frustrating struggle.

ECONOMIC FRUSTRATIONS. Hopes ran high in the fifties as Negroes penetrated more new occupations, but white affluence increased much faster and the gap grew wider.[87] Then as poverty was rediscovered in the sixties, it was found that Negroes and other minority groups bore a heavily disproportionate share of it, as noted in Chapter 4. Moreover, Negroes were being paid less than whites for the same work, evidently about an average of $1,000 less per year.[88] Many whites evidently were still benefiting from the economic subordination of Negroes, notably middle class Southern housewives, white proprietors, managers, salesmen, and skilled workers;[89] and Negro professionals also apparently gain from it.[90]

For many Negroes, especially the poorest, there were some sharp economic setbacks in the fifties and sixties. Their unemployment rate grew to twice that of whites, and much higher in many of the urban ghettos. While weed control machines and other devices were replacing farm workers in the South at a rapid rate, automation was rendering obsolete one remaining unskilled job after another in the cities. Technological unemployment was not new, but its pace was great in these post-World War II decades, and frequent racial dis-

[86] *Gallup Opinion Index,* Report No. 22, April, 1967, 15.
[87] Nathan Hare, "Recent Trends in the Occupational Mobility of Negroes, 1930–1960: An Intracohort Analysis," *Social Forces,* 44 (December, 1965), 166–73.
[88] Paul M. Siegel, "On the Cost of Being a Negro," *Sociological Inquiry,* 35 (Winter, 1965), 41–57.
[89] Norval D. Glenn, "White Gains From Negro Subordination," *Social Problems,* 13 (Fall, 1966), 159–78.
[90] David H. Howard, "An Exploratory Study of Attitudes of Negro Professionals Toward Competition with Whites," *Social Forces,* 45 (September, 1966), 20–27.

crimination in hiring for the scarce marginal jobs engendered a feeling of desperation among Negroes—of being irrelevant and unwanted in a rich, expanding economy.[91] Federal efforts to improve the economic conditions of Negroes were varied and determined during the Kennedy and Johnson administrations, but the task was vast and not readily achieved.

Better educated Negroes have been less likely to be unemployable. However, they have very often had to take less demanding and less lucrative jobs than whites with the same training, a frustrating development for the typically upward mobile Negro student. And often when he does get the desired position he has trouble getting the housing he can afford in a convenient location. Thus the great increase in the proportion of Negroes attending high school and college has often produced frustration.[92] Negro migrants into cities after the mid-fifties were as a whole better educated than those already there, and they came increasingly from other cities seeking better opportunities.[93] Thus the better educated Negro very often experiences *relative deprivation*, so he hardly grows ecstatic upon learning that he has twice as good a chance to go to college as a European or that American Negroes as a whole have a higher level of consumption than the people of France. He compares himself with the white American, and apparently Negroes in general do. A national poll in 1966 found a much higher percentage of whites than of Negroes satisfied with their work (87 and 69 per cent), income (67 and 45 per cent), and housing (77 and 51 per cent).[94]

THE RIOTS OF 1965 AND 1967. The wave of major riots in the summer of 1965 was characterized by wholesale burning of buildings and looting in the urban Negro ghettos, and by some physical violence against "Whitey." Typically these outbursts were precipitated by an incident in which white police brutality was alleged to have occurred.

[91] Sidney M. Willhelm and Edwin H. Powell, "Who Needs the Negro?" *Trans-Action*, 1 (September/October, 1964), 3–6.
[92] Robert L. Derbyshire, "United States Negro Identity Conflict," *Sociology and Social Research*, 51 (October, 1966), 63–77; James A. Geschwender, "Desegregation, the Educated Negro and the Future Protest in the South," *Sociological Inquiry*, 35 (Winter, 1965), 58–68.
[93] Karl E. Taeuber and Alma F. Taeuber, "The Changing Character of Negro Migration," *American Journal of Sociology*, 70 (January, 1965), 429–41.
[94] *Gallup Political Index*, Report No. 18, November–December, 1966, 14. In 1966 Negroes expressed considerably more satisfaction in these areas and in education than they had in 1963 and 1965.

There were many charges that unnecessary force was used against Negroes to control the riots. Most of those killed or injured were Negroes, usually through police (and some national guard) efforts to stop the looting and to restore order.

News treatments probably contributed to the rapid spread of these outbursts, but there was evidently no organized nationwide plan of agitation. Investigations of the biggest riot in 1965, in the Watts area of Los Angeles, emphasized unemployment and other economic frustrations, including some confusion in the implementation of anti-poverty programs.[95] In an interview study of attitudes toward the riot, those Negroes who felt most deprived were most likely to feel leaderless, to approve of the riots, to be hostile toward whites and the police, and to be pessimistic about integration. These Negroes had the least contact with whites and, being most isolated from the institutions, programs, and channels of communication of the dominant community, were most prone to turn to violence to express and obtain redress for their grievances.[96] Just as the more rationally conceived confrontations such as boycotts, voter registration drives, and bloc voting have apparently enhanced Negro solidarity and personal identity,[97] so it seems that violent outbursts accomplish the same results for those who feel most deprived and alienated.

The series of riots in the summer of 1967 also followed the pattern of burning and looting in the black ghetto areas, although the most massive outburst involved a large part of the city of Detroit. This time there was more sniping and heavier counterattacks by the police and national guardsmen. Again there was evidence of spontaneous rioting primarily by young, deprived Negroes, pointing up economic frustration and bitter charges of police brutality. But this time more than the explosive expression of unrest by frustrated, alienated people seemed to be at work. There were charges by officials at all levels of government of political agitation to enlarge the riots and turn them into open rebellions. An all-black national conference on "black power," held in Newark, New Jersey, just after a major

---

[95] Report of the Governor's Commission on the Los Angeles Riots, December 2, 1965.
[96] H. Edward Ransford, "Attitudes of Negroes Toward the Los Angeles Riot," *Law in Transition Quarterly,* 3 (Summer, 1966), 191–96; *cf.* Stanley Lieberson and Arnold R. Silverman, "The Precipitants and Underlying Conditions of Race Riots," *American Sociological Review,* 30 (December, 1965), 887–98.
[97] Joseph S. Himes, "The Social Functions of Racial Conflict," *Social Forces,* 45 (September, 1966), 1–10.

riot in that city was brought under control, produced strong resolutions against integration with whites and in support of such separatist groups as the Black Muslims.[98]

BLACK POWER AND NEGRO LEADERSHIP. The concept of black power was publicized in 1966 by Stokely Carmichael, then head of the Student Nonviolent Coordinating Committee, in connection with the shotgun wounding of James Meredith as he marched in Mississippi to help Southern Negroes overcome their fear of voting. For a time the controversial concept seemed to be used chiefly as a reference to Negro voting power, but in 1967 it received far more radical interpretations, implying that Negro equality is impossible under the current political system. Two successive heads of CORE, James Farmer and Floyd McKissick, renounced housing integration in the cities and the drive for legal equality, and declared that nonviolence could not gain full equality for Negroes in Northern racial ghettos.[99] Charges spread that Carmichael was inciting riots, and his successor as head of SNCC, H. Rap Brown, was arrested for advocating and leading an outbreak in Cambridge, Maryland. Carmichael was banned from Great Britain for advocating racial violence, after having likened the riots in Newark and elsewhere to the American Revolution. He then attended a meeting in Cuba where he called for American Negroes to take up guerilla warfare as part of a hemispheric revolution.[100]

The long-time leaders of the NAACP and the Urban League, Roy Wilkins and Whitney Young, denounced such statements and the riots, dramatizing the fact that they had never had the support of the mass of less educated Negroes. Dr. King joined them in urging that the problems of the ghettos be solved; he saw the riots as tragedies, pleaded for nonviolent confrontation, and branded black power an unfortunate term. At this major junction in the drive for Negro equality the issues in the struggle for leadership were clearly drawn.[101] The leaders of CORE, speaking for the frustrated newly educated Negroes moving upward from the lower class,[102] in effect renounced the

---

[98] *Los Angeles Times*, July 24, 1967, I, 1, 14.
[99] *Ibid.*, July 3, 1967, I, 3, and August 1, 1967, I, 7.
[100] *Ibid.*, July 28, I, 18–19.
[101] Lewis Bowman, "Racial Discrimination and Negro Leadership Problems: The Case of Northern Community," *Social Forces*, 44 (December, 1965), 173–86.
[102] Seymour Leventman, "Class and Ethnic Tensions: Minority Group Leadership in Transition," *Sociology and Social Research*, 50 (April, 1966), 371–76.

norms of middle class restraint and the help of whites. Spokesmen for less restrained black power groups bid openly for the active support of the most deprived, alienated, violence-prone Negroes.

Support for the concept of black power was apparently accelerated by two national tragedies in April and June of 1968—the assassinations of Dr. King and Senator Robert F. Kennedy of New York, both symbols of hope to large numbers of Negroes. These and other events have dramatized the frustrated hopes of Negroes, thus contributing to their distrust of all whites, including civil rights activists. Growing black solidarity has been manifested in all-black meetings in many political and civil rights organizations, and in demands for separate schools, for separate housing, and for racial quotas in college admissions and in employment. Many middle class Negro leaders have embraced the concept of black power, as illustrated by Whitney Young's 1968 declarations that the Urban League will continue its traditional services but will make its main task the promotion of change for the black community.

The widening support for black power indicates the breadth and determination of the current phase of the drive for equality, but the interpretation of the concept varies all the way from the power of the vote to various forms of black national extremism.[103] *The dominant norms that seem to be emerging in the name of black power are those of pluralism, which means mutual respect among all racial and cultural groups and equality in all areas of life.* This implies integration into the society of a group that continues its identity rather than integration in the sense of complete assimilation. It implies the belief of fact that the black individual cannot "make it" by losing his group identity as white immigrants have done, and that blacks must unite and gain the power necessary to ensure their demands for equality as a group. The white community, slow to comprehend this position, continues to debate the changing and conflicting beliefs of value and fact in this dynamic but persistent American Dilemma.

PERSPECTIVE

Feelings run deep when racial and cultural groups meet and try to live together, and attendant beliefs have very often been racist.

---

[103] See *Southern Education Report*, 4 (July–August, 1968), 2–22, for four articles on "The New Mood of Blackness."

Rarely do racial and cultural groups meet or continue to live as equals, but only when a sizeable portion of the dominant group becomes anxious about this situation does it become an issue. Then it is a potential social problem as long as they remain distinct groups and stay in contact, unless (1) the inequality in status is eliminated, or (2) the dominant group can become satisfied with an ideology justifying its superordinate position. Change is a hallmark of intergroup relations but it often meets strong resistance, especially when racial visibility is involved.

The American Negro's drive for equality illustrates the involvement of the total structure of a society in major changes in intergroup relations[104] and dramatizes the conflicting beliefs of value and fact in this major American problem. Intergroup relations assume a variety of forms, and marked economic deprivation can be associated with everything from fatalistic resignation[105] to violent protest. The increased militancy and widened participation in the protest of the American Negro since the mid-fifties was at first largely nonviolent, yet it was a determined type of confrontation of the white community on a range of grievances, at first mainly in the South. This activity was encouraged by gains that had already been made by legal and other more limited means, gains that had inspired new visions of the possible. The second and more violent phase of the more militant protest evidently sprang from marked setbacks that occurred as aspirations soared.[106] In addition to much strong and often violent white resistance to Negro gains there were sharp economic reverses in the black ghettos, at a time of white affluence. The frustrated Negro masses responded to the more rebellious leaders' call for black power, a concept that has since been given wide support but varied meanings. Increasingly it seems to mean pluralism—mutual respect among equal groups.

[104] Ernest Works, "The Pattern Variables as a Framework for the Study of Negro-White Relations," *Pacific Sociological Review*, 10 (Spring, 1967), 25–33.
[105] Horacio Ulibarri, "Social and Attitudinal Characteristics of Spanish-Speaking Migrants and Ex-Migrant Workers in the Southwest," *Sociology and Social Research*, 50 (April, 1966), 361–70.
[106] James C. Davies, "Toward a Theory of Revolution," *American Sociological Review*, 27 (February, 1962), 5–19.

QUESTIONS FOR DISCUSSION AND STUDY

1. Do you believe there are many unprejudiced discriminators in your community? Many prejudiced nondiscriminators? On what evidence do you base your answers?
2. Why has much of the support of immigration control been called racist?
3. Why might there be a failure of communication, and what would it be like, if a Brazilian were told that one-tenth of the American population is Negro?
4. Do you believe the rank order of discriminations applies to minority groups other than the Negro?
5. Evaluate this statement: "Unless thorough education comes first, laws concerning minority groups can accomplish nothing."
6. How has law helped American minority groups? How has it worked against them?
7. What do you think has been the most effective Negro organization in this century? Why do you think so?
8. Why are fair housing laws so controversial? What are the main beliefs of value involved? Of fact?
9. Do you think the concept of "relative deprivation" applies to other minority groups as well as the American Negro?
10. How likely is it that the United States will soon solve its Negro problem? What about its Indian problem, and other minority problems?

SELECTED READING

Broom, Leonard, and Glenn, Norval D., *Transformation of the Negro-American* (New York: Harper and Row, 1965).

Campbell, Ernest Q. (ed.), "Analysis of Race Relations in Current Perspective," an issue of *Sociological Inquiry*, 35 (Winter, 1965).

Clark, Kenneth B., *Dark Ghetto: Dilemmas of Social Power* (New York: Harper and Row, 1965).

Killian, Lewis, and Grigg, Charles, *Racial Crisis in America.* (Englewood Cliffs, N.J.: Prentice-Hall, 1964).

Kramer, Judith, and Leventman, Seymour, *Children of the Gilded Ghetto: Conflict Resolutions of Three Generations of American Jews* (New Haven, Conn.: Yale University Press, 1961).

Mack, Raymond (ed.), *Race, Class and Power* (New York: American Book Co., 1963).

McEntire, Davis, *Residence and Race* (Berkeley and Los Angeles: University of California Press, 1960).

Rose, Arnold (ed.), "The Negro Protest," an issue of *The Annals*, (January, 1965).

Rose, Arnold M., and Rose, Caroline B., *Minority Problems: Textbook of Readings in Intergroup Relations* (New York: Harper and Row, 1965).

Rose, Peter I., *They and We* (New York: Random House, 1964).

Senior, Clarence, *The Puerto Ricans: Strangers—Then Neighbors* (Chicago: Quadrangle Books, 1965).

Thompson, Daniel C., *The Negro Leadership Class* (Englewood Cliffs, N.J.: Prentice-Hall, 1963).

Tumin, Melvin M., *Desegregation: Resistance and Readiness* (Princeton, N.J.: Princeton University Press, 1958).

Vander Zanden, James W., *Race Relations in Transition: The Segregation Crisis in the South* (New York: Random House, 1965).

Williams, Robin M., Jr., Dean, John P., and Suchman, Edward A., *Strangers Next Door: Ethnic Relations in American Communities* (Englewood Cliffs, N.J.: Prentice-Hall, 1964).

Yinger, J. Milton, *A Minority Group in American Society* (New York: McGraw-Hill, 1965).

Young, Whitney, *To Be Equal* (New York: McGraw-Hill, 1964).

V

Social Problems and Societal Development

A social problem arises when one kind of change is wanted but the things that it brings are not wanted.[1] . . . The father who wants his daughter to be educated may be pleased that she is able to get a job in an office but not so pleased when she wants greater freedom in deciding whom she shall marry.[2]

13. Social Problems in a World of Nations

THERE HAVE BEEN a number of references to other nations in the preceding parts of this book, but the social problems of the United States have been emphasized. In this chapter an attempt is made to provide some worldwide perspectives on the problem conditions discussed in Parts II and III, and on the additional problem of war. Though the treatment is brief and highly selective, it may both facilitate better understanding of our own social problems and provide suggestive leads for understanding some of the dilemmas of a changing world of nations. Comparative discussions of social problems must be made with care, especially within the framework employed in this book.

BELIEFS AND THE PROBLEMS OF NATIONS

Variations in Beliefs of Fact and Value

We have seen that a condition may be considered a serious problem in one time or place and desirable or harmless in another. What

---

[1] Morroe Berger, *The Arab World Today* (Garden City, N.Y.: Anchor Books, Doubleday & Co., 1964), 409.
[2] *Ibid.*, 412.

345

a society considers a problem depends on its hierarchy of values, as well as on its beliefs of fact about the threat posed by the condition, the ineffectiveness of preexisting norms, and the possibility of improvement through community discussion and action. If the condition is uniformly condemned it is a purely technical problem, unless there are value issues over the means to use. Societal change generates issues over the adoption of new norms, and some major value controversies over ends or means persist and become national dilemmas. The great variation in cultural patterns continues to be important, since the traditional norms of developing nations do not change readily or all at once. As a society struggles to incorporate new norms and practices into its social fabric, it may become greatly concerned about conditions other nations do not have at the time or do not consider major issues.

International comparisons of statistics on social problem conditions are of limited value, and not only because of differences in technical competence in gathering and reporting them. Nations count and collate those things they consider most important, if they are able to, and the definition of a condition affects the counting and the interpretation. And even if two nations do report with reasonable accuracy the incidence of such a condition as abortion or the use of marihuana, one may consider it a greater problem than the other does, and perhaps no problem at all. Comparative information on social problems must thus be interpreted in the light of the changing patterns of belief within each society.

International Convergences of Beliefs

While the world is far from being one community with a common culture, there have been significant developments toward international agreement regarding social problem conditions, especially since World War II. Discussions reflect a growing global consensus about the minimum standards of consumption and health, thus implying a common population policy.[3] Dozens of undeveloped nations have been jarred from a sacred to a secular outlook—from an "ethic of fatalism" to an "ethic of responsibility" toward various societal conditions.[4]

---

[3] Radhakamal Mukerjee, *The Oneness of Mankind* (London: Macmillan & Co., Ltd., 1965).

[4] Karl Mannheim, *Ideology and Utopia*, trans. by Louis Wirth and E. A. Shils (New York: Harcourt, Brace & Co., 1936), 170–71; Max Weber, *Essays in*

While usually preoccupied first with independence and then with the maintenance of stability and order, such nations have been urged to provide statistics on many domestic problems and to cooperate with international campaigns against them.

Especially after the emergence of the United Nations, the conviction grew in the more developed nations and among the most educated people around the globe that the world is increasingly one community even though separate nation-states remain. This implies that problem conditions anywhere in the world influence the lives of the people of all nations. In the words of one well-known sociologist:

> Social problems, in brief, are no longer viewed as local or national, but as international problems. Poverty in Indonesia or Chile or Timbuktu is coming to be seen as a social problem to the well-to-do nations of the world; malaria in Mexico, as a problem to all nations; inadequate nutrition anywhere, as the concern of the adequately fed everywhere. Housing, child labor, industrial exploitation, oppressive land tenure systems— these, in an increasingly integrated world, become social problems to the enlightened nations.[5]

This perspective was strongly reinforced in 1948 when the General Assembly of the United Nations adopted the thirty articles that comprise the Declaration of Human Rights. This declaration rests heavily on the American Bill of Rights, and also includes such rights as an adequate standard of living and equal treatment regardless of race, culture, class, or sex.[6]

The United Nations has taken considerable action to back this declaration, mainly through such specialized agencies as the International Labour Organization, the Food and Agriculture Organization, the United Nations Educational, Scientific and Cultural Organization (UNESCO), and the two health agencies mentioned in Chapter 5, WHO and UNICEF. United Nations publications have emphasized child welfare, housing, community development, displaced persons, the handicapped, and other concerns related to the increasing international consensus about social problems.[7] The UN has disseminated

---

Sociology, trans. and ed. by Hans H. Gerth and C. Wright Mills (New York: Oxford University Press, 1946), 120–25; Irving Louis Horowitz, *Three Worlds of Development* (New York: Oxford University Press, 1966), 291–363.

[5] Jessie Bernard, *Social Problems at Midcentury* (New York: The Dryden Press, 1957), 598.

[6] United Nations Department of Public Information, *These Rights and Freedoms* (New York: United Nations, 1950), 170–76.

[7] Bernard, *op. cit.,* 600–01.

many scientific and technological publications, fully aware that national development is based on beliefs of fact as well as of value. Its agencies have sponsored many coordinated attacks on problem conditions. For example, in 1966 UNESCO launched a large-scale attack on adult illiteracy as a means of facilitating economic development.

PUBLIC DISCUSSION OF NATIONAL CONDITIONS

The Political Context of Discussion

In the more democratic nations, open public discussion of issues is expected and encouraged. The more totalitarian a nation is the more its leaders seek indoctrination rather than enlightenment and critical discussion. Many nations are governed by dictators or by military or other oligarchies of the right or left, characterized by strict censorship of information and ideas and by rigid controls over public assembly and discussion. Because of the circulation of rumors and other undesired deviations from these norms, even the most totalitarian countries apparently have some measure of public discussion. However, both in these countries and in those more democratic ones where education and communications are severely lacking, only a few political elites have much opportunity to discuss public issues.

The Process of Discussion

The means of communication vary from one nation to another. Thousands of relatively isolated villages around the world now have at least one radio, so news of major political events has been greatly accelerated in the less developed countries. However, newspapers, magazines, books and background news treatments by radio, television, and film are rare in many nations, or available only to elites. The amount of education, the number and types of reference groups, the talking-over process, and feedback to provincial and national leaders, all vary from nation to nation. The extent to which the government is democratic affects the content and sources of communications, and the freedom of voluntary groups to discuss, communicate, and exercise influence. Thus the public discussion of problem conditions is quite varied around the world, and almost non-existent in many countries.

ECONOMIC INSECURITY

There is much international concern about hunger, housing,[8] and other aspects of economic insecurity. While much of the American support for economic aid programs has been prompted by the Cold War, there is also much humanitarian concern about food surpluses here while people in other countries are starving (see Table 4.5, Chapter 4). In discussions of the problems of developing nations, ill health and population growth are usually tied with economic insecurity. We have seen how the demand for medicine has often resulted in rapid population growth in areas lacking the capacity for the kind of economic development experienced by Western nations. We saw in Chapter 11 how United Nations agencies are appealing to the value of child welfare in attempts to sell programs of contraception.

The "have-not" nations in the post-World War II era have depended heavily on the "have" nations to bolster their economic security, but they have increasingly believed that something can and should be done about it through their own efforts. Besides attempting to promote economic development, national governments have adopted a variety of programs to help ensure a minimum level of living for their people. A summary of the "social" security programs of the 76 independent nations outside of Africa in 1960 showed that 71 had adopted work-injury programs, 58 had medical programs of some type, 56 had programs covering old-age, invalidism or death, 40 had family allowance plans, and 27 had unemployment insurance. The adoption of such programs was highly correlated with the level of economic development, and governments with more democratic participation tended to introduce them earlier than did the less democratic ones.[9]

ILL HEALTH

Despite the dramatic reductions of infectious diseases in the less developed nations since World War II, there are many more cam-

---

[8] Charles Abrams, *Man's Struggle for Shelter in an Urbanizing World* (Cambridge, Mass.: The M.I.T. Press, 1964).
[9] Phillips Cutright, "Political Structure, Economic Development, and National Social Security Programs," *American Journal of Sociology*, 70 (March, 1965), 537–50. The five major types of program form a Guttman scale pattern.

paigns to be waged before these mass killers will be as fully controlled as possible with present technology. The World Health Organization has emphasized continuing drives against malaria, cholera, smallpox, and other epidemic diseases, and has given considerable attention to leprosy and to cancer and other deteriorative disorders. Penicillin and DDT from outside nations are insufficient for the ongoing task of maintaining health in areas newly touched by the medical revolution. Nations attempting to develop their own medical facilities and personnel face many handicaps, including traditional beliefs and practices; lack of medical knowledge, skills, and materials; lack of economic resources; lack of sanitary facilities (both pure water supplies and waste disposal); and perplexing organizational difficulties.[10] There are endless challenges, frustrations, and issues involved in bringing the coveted wonders of modern medicine to the people.

MARRIAGE AND FAMILY ISSUES

Issues about marriage and family roles have become worldwide with the trend toward the equalitarian, nuclear family. There has been a great increase in the education of females, but in most countries equal educational opportunity has not meant immediate equality.[11] The adoption of Western dress, education, and other Western traits and institutions by non-Western countries does not necessarily indicate approval of our family life. The Middle Eastern students in America studied by the author were predominantly urbanites, and most of them approved of equal education for women and of open discussion within the family of problems, ideas, and activities. With these exceptions, however, they generally disapproved of the equalitarian trends in the American family. Two-thirds or so agreed that women are gaining too much authority, that they work away from home too much, that marriages are usually formed too young, and that families are loosely integrated. Three-fourths or so said that parents should approve of a marriage, that American children have too much freedom, and that families are too materialistic.[12] Similar results were obtained in Turkey in 1968–69 from returnees from study in the United States.

[10] Richard and Eva Blum, *Health and Healing in Rural Greece* (Stanford, Calif.: Stanford University Press, 1965). See also reports of the World Health Organization.
[11] Fuad Baali, "Educational Aspirations Among College Girls in Iraq," *Sociology and Social Research*, 51 (July, 1967), 485–93.
[12] F. James Davis, "Cultural Perspectives of Middle Eastern Students in Amer-

Parental arrangement of marriage has been losing its force as the occupation of the male has become less tied to the land under family control.[13] One recent study found the contractual marriage pattern still preferred to the romantic approach in Singapore, Burma, and India, but there was also some variation and uncertainty.[14] As for the termination of marriage, some countries such as Australia, with much lower rates of divorce than the United States,[15] consider it a problem. In many societies divorce has traditionally been frequent but not a threat to the economic or emotional security of the mate or the child in the extended family pattern, so divorce tends to become an issue as these patterns give way to the nuclear family.

The status of the child depends on marriage in the nuclear family system, and in Chapter 6 we noted the American dilemma concerning the status of the illegitimate child. Our rate of illegitimacy tripled from 1940 to 1963. In Great Britain, the rate of known illegitimate births tripled from 1937 to 1962, the greatest increase coming in the age group of mothers from 25 to 34 years of age. Several other nations in the British Commonwealth and in Northern Europe have experienced increases also, though not so great. One suggestion is that the family is becoming less important to personal status as government support of the welfare of the individual child increases.[16] In the Caribbean, where rates of illegitimacy remain high, the lower classes seem able to stretch their values to accommodate illegitimacy while those with higher status are more likely to consider it a deviation.[17]

Aging persons are losing their traditional places in the shifting family patterns of the urbanizing world, a change strongly resisted. Ancient family traditions are under strong pressures to change. A great deal of discussion and self-conscious personal adjustment ac-

---

ica," *The Middle East Journal* (Summer, 1960), 256–64; F. James Davis, "Perspectives of Turkish Students in the United States," *Sociology and Social Research,* 48 (October, 1963), 47–57.

[13] William J. Goode, *World Revolution and Family Patterns* (New York: The Free Press, 1963), 376.

[14] George A. Theodorson, "Romanticism and Motivation to Marry in the United States, Singapore, Burma, and India," *Social Forces,* 44 (September, 1965), 17–27.

[15] Lincoln H. Day, "Patterns of Divorce in Australia and the United States," *American Sociological Review,* 29 (August, 1964), 509–22.

[16] Shirley M. Hartley, "The Amazing Rise of Illegitimacy in Great Britain," *Social Forces,* 44 (June, 1966), 533–45.

[17] Hyman Rodman, "Illegitimacy in the Caribbean Social Structure: A Reconsideration," *American Sociological Review,* 31 (October, 1966), 673–83.

companies the working out of new patterns of family decision-making, child rearing, courtship, marriage, reproduction, and divorce. The acceptance of new norms means the discussion of a host of issues concerning the social status and role of the child, the mother, the father, and the grandparents.

PROBLEMS OF DEVIANCE

Mental Illness

Abnormal behavior has been defined in a great variety of ways in different cultures, often in terms of supernatural powers. Often it has meant the assignment of special roles in the society, and it has been met with everything from death to deification. Since traditional norms prescribe how abnormal behavior is to be treated, the responses are predictable and noncontroversial; but issues arise when the old norms are undermined by social changes. Abnormal behavior presumably varies from one society to another because the socially induced stresses vary, but comparative statistics are rare and unreliable because of the continuing relativity in definitions and responses.

We noted in Chapter 7 the traditional definition of mental illness in the Western world as shameful, dangerously deviant behavior. This has resulted in such reactions as banishment from the community, hiding the person at home, and confinement in jails and poorhouses, and later in isolated asylums. This labeling of abnormal behavior as deviance has been modified significantly by the rise of the view that abnormal behavior is illness (pathologies of the personality system) and that much of it is subject to treatment. However, the somewhat changed traditional view remains strong in current public discussions of treatment issues. Whether the deviant or the pathological perspective, or some combination, is now most appropriate for the United States for analytical purposes is hard to decide,[18] and the difficulty is much greater in cross-cultural comparisons.

As the health agencies of the United Nations sponsor discussions and distribute literature about mental illness, and request member nations to submit statistics, the responses around the world must be quite varied. Many of the world's people who have come to think of

---

[18] Shirley S. Angrist, "Mental Illness and Deviant Behavior: Unresolved Conceptual Problems," *Sociological Quarterly*, 7 (Autumn, 1966), 436–48.

physical health as improvable probably have great difficulty thinking of abnormal behavior in the same way. While representatives of the West seem to be attempting to present mental illness as a health problem, it seems likely that the deviance perspective comes through rather strongly in the discussions of community-centered treatment, the new drugs, and statistics on facilities. For example, many of those peoples who have not considered abnormal behavior to be dangerously deviant must wonder why we feel we must choose between hospital confinement and the use of tranquilizing and antidepressant drugs. There is little knowledge about comparative changes in the perception of abnormal behavior, and much room for research. Changes in perspective will probably be slower and more varied than for physical illness, unless a dramatically convincing demonstration of control such as the Germ Theory in action is forthcoming.

Crime and Delinquency

From within a nation one has some chance of checking on the factors that bias criminal statistics, yet we saw in Chapter 8 that all indexes of crime and delinquency are fallible. In cross-cultural comparisons the danger of misinterpreting statistics showing an increase in any type of deviant behavior is especially great, since such figures may reflect changing standards of conduct. A rising rate of physical assaults may indicate decreased tolerance of violence rather than more assaults, or higher rates of theft may measure an increase in the use of insurance and thus greater willingness to file a complaint rather than higher rates of stealing. The adoption of the juvenile court has resulted in changes in the method of handling and recording juvenile deviance in America and some other nations, and thus in great increases in officially reported delinquency.[19] While international criminal statistics must be used with great care, comparative studies of deviant behavior and of correctional ideologies and practices have contributed helpful perspectives.

Drug Use and Alcoholism

We saw in Chapter 10 that dilemmas in American efforts to control drug addiction and excessive drinking reflect the societal definitions of drug use (including nonnarcotics) as dangerous deviance

---

[19] Peter J. Lejins, "American Data on Juvenile Delinquency in an International Forum," *Federal Probation,* 25 (June, 1961), 18–21.

and of alcoholism as an illness. From comparisons with the experience of England and other European nations in which drug addiction is treated as a medical rather than a criminal law problem, it was possible to suggest that it evidently can be controlled without creating a large black market traffic by a combination of medical handling and effective limitation of the supply of narcotics. It was also suggested that where it is difficult (in the case of nonnarcotic drugs) or not considered desirable to limit the supply (alcoholic beverages), that a combination of the development of norms of moderation with a medical approach seems the most workable alternative.

Would these conclusions hold up and others emerge in further comparative analysis? For instance, it appears that in Puerto Rico—where American law is in force—that the pattern of drug use is similar to that which we have described for the United States.[20] But what about a country like Brazil, where schoolboys can buy maconha (marihuana) as easily as a comic book, for little more than the price of tobacco? It is asserted that the use of maconha and other drugs is not great among either teenagers or adults, and that the number of Brazilians treated for alcoholism is many times greater than it is for drug use. Or, why is the approach to alcoholism in the Soviet Union so similar to that taken in the United States? The Soviet Union also has a high rate (despite the Marxist dogma that alcoholism and other deviance signify capitalist decadence), considers it a medical problem, distinguishes between chronic and other alcoholism, has treatment centers, stresses psychological variables in rehabilitation, and promotes public health education against excessive drinking.[21] One wonders whether or not Alcoholics Anonymous and Synanon might work there, or would they wither in the absence of individualistic values and the Protestant ethic?

POPULATION PROBLEMS

The theory of population transition (see Chapter 11), which needs further comparative testing and qualification,[22] provides a focus for

---

[20] John C. Ball and Delia O. Pabon, "Locating and Interviewing Narcotic Addicts in Puerto Rico," *Sociology and Social Research,* 49 (July, 1965), 401–11.

[21] Vera Efron, "The Soviet Approach to Alcoholism," *Social Problems,* 7 (Spring, 1960), 307–15.

[22] Robert M. Marsh, *Comparative Sociology* (New York: Harcourt, Brace & World, 1967), 198–205.

an otherwise confusing mass of data and for the public debate about world-wide changes in human populations. We noted the shift in the mid-sixties both in the United States and the United Nations to a more determined attempt to encourage national programs of birth control. Motivation to limit family size is apparently increasing in country after country undergoing industrial-urban change,[23] and much is being learned about the conditions under which programs of birth control education succeed.[24] There are indications that many of the least educated women in many nations want to depart from traditional norms and use birth control. India, with its death rate reduced to a comparative low, has officially placed family planning on the same level of importance as national defense and agriculture. Even in communist countries, despite the Marxist dogma that overpopulation is a capitalist fallacy and birth control a capitalist plot, much use has been made of abortion and other birth control measures. Note the following summary from a 1966 news story:[25]

Here are some of the more notable recent events in world-wide population control:

1—Taiwan in less than two years has equipped one in every 12 women with an IUD device said to be 98% effective. . . .
2—Korea, . . . has done almost as well. . . . The nation's target for this year is to distribute 300,000 IUD's, perform 21,800 male sterilizations and provide free contraceptives to 150,000 persons.
3—India, which has budgeted $200 million for a five-year plan going into effect April 1, plans to distribute one million IUD's within the next year—20 million within five years.
The plan also anticipates five million male sterilizations and 10 million effective users of traditional contraceptives.
4—Pakistan last July began a family planning program with a per capita budget half again higher than India's. The official in charge has near-cabinet rank.
5—A pilot program in Thailand indicates that 70% of rural women want help with family planning. . . .
6—Turkey last year repealed old laws forbidding abortion, sterilization and the importation and sale of contraceptives. It also passed legislation to implement a national family planning program.
7—Tunisia began a government program on Jan. 1 with the objective of

---

23 Ronald Freedman, John Y. Takeshita, and T. H. Sun, "Fertility and Family Planning in Taiwan: A Case Study in the Demographic Transition," *American Journal of Sociology*, 70 (July, 1964), 6–27.
24 J. Mayonne Stycos and Kurt W. Back, *The Control of Human Fertility in Jamaica* (Ithaca, N.Y.: Cornell University Press, 1964).
25 *Los Angeles Times* (by Harry Nelson), March 6, 1966, C, 1–2.

distributing 60,000 IUD's a year, or one IUD a year for every 12 women in childbearing years. . . . The nation has also passed a new law that permits abortions for women with more than four children.

8—The United Arab Republic has extensive interest in family planning, and Kenya, the Philippines, Ghana, San Salvador, Columbia and Peru are beginning to show interest, according to the Population Council.

9—In Santiago, Chile, almost all public hospitals offer birth control supplies and the Catholic University Hospital carries on a careful project on oral contraceptives and the rhythm method.

10—Communist China is discouraging large families by encouraging women to remain single until 25 and men until 30 and by geographically separating couples for long periods. Party members reportedly receive no maternity leave or extra allowances after their second child.

All this birth control activity stands in sharp contrast to the view in such countries as Bulgaria, where there is great anxiety among its leaders about the falling birth rate. Bulgaria subsidizes children, taxes childless couples, discourages abortions, and promotes tolerance of illegitimacy—in the belief that the lowering rate of population growth threatens the nation's labor force, her military power position, and the whole social structure. The rate of growth in Bulgaria is now well under 1 per cent per year, a rate many countries are striving to get down to, or under. Whether a condition is a social problem or not indeed depends on the set of beliefs, of fact and value, subscribed to by those who behold it.

MINORITIES

Political changes, migrations, and other factors have continued in recent decades to create minority status groups. The resultant issues around the world have received much attention in the United Nations, with frequent references to the Declaration of Human Rights. The most discussed case is the *apartheid* (segregation) policies in the Union of South Africa, whereby the whites rigidly control the residence, movements, and occupations of the nonwhite four-fifths of the population. The repressive measures of a police state have been used, justified by an official ideology of racism, resulting in much tension, conflict, and the treatment of white dissenters as traitors.[26] The edu-

---

[26] William O. Brown, *Race Relations in the American South and in South Africa* (Boston: Boston University Press, 1959); Pierre L. Van Den Berghe, *South Africa, A Study in Conflict* (Middletown, Conn.: Wesleyan University Press, 1965); Austin F. Turk, "The Futures of South Africa," *Social Forces*, 45 (March, 1967), 402–12.

cated blacks have been caught in an especially painful squeeze, between the ambitions of Western man and the facts of their lowly
status.[27] In the face of the constant surveillance and the use of terrorism and police aggression to keep the blacks and coloureds in their
assigned statuses, nonviolent demonstrations have been unsuccessful.[28]

To attract more immigrant workers than were coming from Anglo
nations after World War II, Australia loosened its tight quotas somewhat and accepted people from Southern Europe, which was in an
earlier phase of explosive population growth than Northern Europe
was. The absorption of these people into Australian life has been much
discussed and carefully watched.[29] Great Britain has encouraged immigrants from Commonwealth areas in order to gain needed workers,
and has received many Negroes from the Caribbean, some from
Africa, and many dark caucasoids from India and Pakistan. Studies
of the resulting problem have shown the difference between acts of
discrimination and attitudes of prejudice, and have illuminated the
dilemma faced by Britons trying to choose between immigration controls and the tradition of treating all citizens of the Commonwealth
as if they were British citizens.[30] Three-fourth of the nearly one million
Negroes and "coloureds" have settled in London slums, and rising
tensions and incidents primarily over scarce housing have brought
increasing demands for the unprecedented step of immigration controls.

Political refugees have resulted from many international up-
heavals, creating minority issues in nations around the world and
adding to problems created by other migrations.[31] The establishment
of the State of Israel greatly lowered the numbers and status of Jews
in Arab countries, and made refugees of the Palestine Arabs who fled
and a minority group of those who remained.[32] Israel also initiated

---

[27] Leo Kuper, *An African Bourgeoisie* (New Haven, Conn., and London: Yale
University Press, 1965).
[28] *Ibid.*, 31; Leo Kuper, *Passive Resistance in South Africa* (New Haven, Conn.:
Yale University Press, 1960).
[29] F. Lancaster Jones, "Ethnic Concentration and Assimilation: An Australian
Case Study," *Social Forces*, 45 (March, 1967), 412–23.
[30] Michael Banton, *White and Coloured* (New Brunswick, N.J.: Rutgers University Press, 1960); Sheila Patterson, *Dark Strangers* (Bloomington: Indiana
University Press, 1964).
[31] W. D. Borrie *et al.*, *The Cultural Integration of Immigrants* (Paris: UNESCO,
1959).
[32] Walter Schwarz, *The Arabs in Israel* (London: Faber & Faber, Ltd., 1960).

attempts to assimilate immigrants from a great variety of cultural traditions, one result of which has been complaints by the Oriental Jews that they are dominated by the Jews from the West.[33] Meanwhile the Islamic countries have had to confront continuing issues over their religious minorities (such as the Coptic Christians of Egypt) and some political minorities (such as the Kurds of Iraq, Turkey, and Iran). The conflict between the black Christian minority constituting about one-fourth of the population of Sudan and the (white) Arab Muslim majority has taken on racial overtones in Africa. And the Cold War has aggravated the problems of Chinese minorities in the countries of Southeast Asia.[34]

WAR

Traditionally, far from being treated as a social problem, war has been glorified as the ultimate proving ground for bravery and national sacrifice. Nations of people have typically applied such ethical codes as the Ten Commandments only to the in-group, in the spirit of *tribal ethics;* you may cheat, enslave, or kill members of other groups, at least under provocations considered proper at the time and place. The teaching that one should treat all human beings according to the same ethical norms as those taught for the national in-group has long stood in opposition to the ideologies used to justify holy wars and national defense.

In the modern nation-state, to the degree that it is democratic, the use of war as an instrument of policy has been subject more to rational decision-making and less to the personal whims of rulers. The traditional belief of fact that wars are sooner or later inevitable lives on, though it has been questioned increasingly in this century. Wars and risks of wars have been justified in terms of potential as well as present dangers, and hoped-for improvements in the nation's military position, its diplomacy, and its economy. The costs have been much deplored, but held to be worth paying to gain greater national security.

[33] J. Isaac, "Israel—A New Melting Pot," Chapter 11 in Borrie *et al., ibid.,* 234–66; Judah Matras, *Social Change in Israel* (Chicago: Aldine Publishing Co., 1965).

[34] Richard J. Coughlin, *Double Identity: The Chinese in Modern Thailand* (New York: Oxford University Press, 1960); Donald Earl Willmott, *The Chinese of Semarang: A Changing Minority Community in Indonesia* (Ithaca, N.Y.: Cornell University Press, 1960).

For good measure it is often noted that wars contribute to technolog-ical progress and to other desired social changes.[35] War policies have received much support from theologians, including those "new ortho-dox" writers who count wartime killing a lesser sin than such things as giving in to a power-mad dictator and to genocide.

With the rise of humanitarian values, much attention has been focused on the human costs of war—the disease, starvation, family separations, blasted hopes, and the violent deaths of civilians as well as soldiers. This has coincided with the emergence of large-scale conflicts, world wars involving millions of people, and with the break-down of national isolation by new means of communication, trade, travel, and warfare. In the two decades after World War I the senti-ment was strong in America and many other countries that there should never be another war; but the threat of the expansionist dicta-tors in Germany, Italy, and Japan resulted in unprecedented support for World War II. Then came the United Nations as a more effective agency for keeping the peace, it was hoped, than the League of Nations had been. Instead it became the sounding board of the Cold War, and little support was accorded its peace-keeping function. How-ever, the presence of United Nations observers in trouble spots and the anxious discussions in the Security Council and the General Assembly have exercised considerable influence on member states and have symbolized the worldwide search for peace. In addition, United Nations agencies have publicized the view that social problem conditions anywhere in the world influence all countries, and also that a nuclear war is unthinkable because it would destroy so much of mankind.

The Korean War received fairly general public sympathy in the United States and in countries allied with it because of the fear of forceful international expansion by the Communist bloc, but also because many people supported the backing of strong resolutions by the United Nations against international aggression. The later inter-vention of the United States in Viet Nam, under somewhat parallel circumstances, became a major issue. The view that war is obsolete refers mainly to the big powers and their nuclear weapons rather than to guerrilla warfare, and the "war of liberation" in South Viet Nam became an issue in the United Nations. Much of the bitterness of the

---

[35] John U. Nef, *War and Human Progress* (Cambridge: Harvard University Press, 1950).

protest in the United States and elsewhere, apparently, stemmed from President Johnson's ordering a major escalation of American fighting only a few months after he assured voters in his 1964 campaign that this would be unnecessary and that he opposed it. Much of the opposition has been to involvement in this particular war, as it was in the Spanish-American and Mexican conflicts, not necessarily to war in general. Despite America's position as a great power, two beliefs of fact had wide support by 1968: (1) that the United States could not police the peace by itself everywhere in the world, and (2) that the policy of containment of Communist expansion was no longer a correct assessment of Communist strategy.

Some of the protest against American involvement in Viet Nam has apparently been against war itself, against its use as a political instrument. The daily portrayal of live warfare on television, for the first time in history, has probably had a considerable effect on public sentiment. Protests have usually emphasized humanitarian values, but also prominent have been the beliefs of fact that wars do not settle problems and that the speed of communications and weapons has rendered military defenses obsolete as a means of protecting the nation-state.[36] The more support this pacifistic orientation receives, the more of a public issue war in general becomes; but how much of the sentiment against involvement in Viet Nam is of this broader nature remains to be seen. In many of the new nation-states warfare has readily been resorted to as a legitimate means of achieving urgent objectives. If the resort to war in any and all situations does become a major public issue in the United States and in other national societies, it will certainly be one of our most complex, persistent dilemmas.

CONCLUSION

These glimpses of conditions in a rapidly changing world of nations, and the varied ways in which they are responded to, help throw our own social problems into some much needed perspective. Such comparative analysis is difficult within the analytical framework of public discussion, and the needed information is hard to find. In further comparative attempts we will need to remain alert to the different ways in which conditions are perceived and related to value priorities and beliefs of fact, as well as to the apparently growing

---

[36] Emery Reves, *The Anatomy of Peace* (New York: The Viking Press, 1963).

humanitarian and scientific consensus about many of the conditions of this changing world.

QUESTIONS FOR DISCUSSION AND STUDY

1. In what sense has UNESCO and other agencies been creating social problems as well as trying to help solve them?
2. How do you think the discussion of social problems differs now in India and China, or in East Germany and West Germany?
3. What are some of the growing similarities in outlook on economic problems around the world? Some of the major differences?
4. Why do you suppose the people of many nations have sought modern medicine so fervently, while resisting many other aspects of Western life?
5. Judging by American experience, how long will it be before the newly developing nations are willing to accept the equalitarian family? Is our experience necessarily a dependable indicator?
6. Using either illegitimacy or divorce as an example, explain why a social problem is more than a prevalent social condition.
7. In what type of cultural setting would you expect group counseling to be most acceptable? Least acceptable?
8. For what social problem condition do you think international statistics might be fairly reliable? Why do you think so?
9. Is the rise of the public definition of excessive drinking as a social problem an indication that heavy drinking is increasing? Explain. Would the same be true of drug use?
10. In what ways are population growth and issues regarding health, immigration, and minority groups interrelated in the modern world?
11. What developments are necessary in order to eliminate minority group problems completely? Do not oversimplify.
12. As a traditional society begins to make what seems to us to be progress in dealing with some of its problem conditions, why do the people concerned so often feel that life is becoming meaningless and futile?
13. Do you think that the resort to war under any and all circumstances will become a major public issue in the United States? in other countries? Explain.

SELECTED READING

Cavan, Ruth Shonle, and Cavan, Jordan T., *Delinquency and Crime: Cross-Cultural Perspectives* (Philadelphia: J. B. Lippincott Co., 1968).

Eisenstadt, S. N. (ed.), *Comparative Social Problems* (New York: The Free Press, 1964).

Goode, William J., *World Revolution and Family Patterns* (New York: The Free Press, 1963).

Jaffe, A. J., *People, Jobs and Economic Development: A Case History of Puerto Rico Supplemented by Recent Mexican Experiences* (New York: The Free Press, 1959).

Klein, Viola, *Women Workers* (Paris: Organization for Economic Cooperation and Development, 1965).

Laskin, Richard (ed.), *Social Problems: A Canadian Profile* (New York: McGraw-Hill, 1964).

Lerner, Daniel, *The Passing of Traditional Society: Modernizing the Middle East* (New York: The Free Press, 1958).

Pierson, Donald, *Negroes in Brazil* (Rev. ed.; Carbondale: Southern Illinois University Press, 1966).

Rose, Arnold M., "Hindu Values and Indian Social Problems," *Sociological Quarterly*, 8 (Summer, 1967), 329–39.

Sadoun, Roland, Lolli, Giorgi, and Silverman, Milton, *Drinking in French Culture* (New Haven, Conn.: College and University Press, 1965).

Schlesinger, Benjamin, *Poverty in Canada and the United States* (Toronto: University of Toronto Press, 1967).

Schramm, Wilbur, *Mass Media and National Development* (Stanford, Calif.: Stanford University Press; Paris: UNESCO, 1964).

Shibutani, Tomotsu, Kwan, Kian M., with contributions by Billigmeier, Robert H., *Ethnic Stratification: A Comparative Approach* (New York: The Macmillan Co., 1965).

Stephens, Richard W., *Population Pressures South of the Sahara* (Washington, D.C.: George Washington University, 1959).

Thompson, Warren S., *Population and Progress in the Far East* (Chicago: University of Chicago Press, 1959).

Tiryakian, Edward A., "Aftermath of a Thermonuclear Attack on the U.S.: Some Sociological Implications," *Social Problems*, 6 (1959), 291–303.

UNESCO, *Buddhism and the Race Question* (New York: International Documents Service, Columbia University Press, 1958).

Van Den Berghe, Pierre L., *Africa: Social Problems of Change and Conflict* (San Francisco, Calif.: Chandler Publishing Co., 1965).

Wagley, Charles, and Harris, Marvin, *Minorities in the New World* (New York: Columbia University Press, 1958).

Walker, Nigel, *Crime and Punishment in Britain* (Edinburgh: Edinburgh University Press, 1964).

Wright, Quincy, Evan, William M., and Deutsch, Morton (eds.), *Preventing World War III: Some Proposals* (New York: Simon & Schuster, 1962).

I have no objection to anyone as a human being and as a member of a community devoting himself to whatever movements of immediate or proximate social renovation that may interest him. I consider it equally defensible to devote oneself to the development of a science of such demonstrable reliability and predictive power that no regime will dare to ignore its spokesmen and practitioners. Which pursuit we follow, or the degree to which we follow each, is a matter of taste, interest, competence, and the compulsions of the situation in which we find ourselves. In short, I do not admit the assumed dichotomy between the pursuit of science on the one hand and "social action" on the other. The development of a reliable social science may be regarded as the most fundamental of all social action.[1]

14. Social Problems and Social Science

LIKE ALL SCIENCES, the social sciences are not primarily concerned with solving immediate, practical problems, but with the development of sound explanations of events. While a social problem is a dilemma about what action to take regarding some deplored condition, *a sociological problem involves explaining the conditions under which certain things happen in human society.* The same is true of scientific problems in economics, anthropology, and the other social sciences.[2] Yet the basic physical, biological, and social sciences have often produced knowledge that has resulted in great improvements in man's capacity to attain his changing goals. The resolution of one issue often results in the rise of unexpected new dilemmas, but with scientific knowledge and method it is possible to take a comprehensive, "clinical" approach that encompasses many variables and anticipates many outcomes.[3]

The sciences tend to be evaluated on the extent to which their knowledge has been successfully applied to problems of community concern.[4] Sometimes the drive for practical solutions has resulted in

---

[1] George A. Lundberg, *Foundations of Sociology* (New York: The Macmillan Co., 1939), 534.
[2] *Ibid.*, 29–31.
[3] Alvin W. Gouldner, "Explorations in Applied Social Science," *Social Problems*, 13 (January, 1956), 169–81.
[4] Marshall B. Clinard, "The Sociologist's Quest for Respectability," *Sociological Quarterly*, 7 (Autumn, 1966), 399–412.

major contributions to basic science, but an overriding preoccupation with immediate results can hamper the growth of fundamental knowledge. How can the most effective division of labor between basic and applied social science be brought about? How can social scientists best use their knowledge and skills in helping communities of people to cope with their social problems?

SCIENCE, TECHNOLOGY, AND PRACTICAL ACTION

A basic science is concerned with developing explanations of observable phenomena that are sound in terms of two criteria: (1) the explanations must be logically consistent, and (2) they must hold up when tested by appropriate factual observations.[5] Scientific knowledge facilitates predictions of the events studied, thus increasing the possibilities of controlling some phenomena and of making more effective adjustments to events beyond control.[6]

Technology is a systematic body of knowledge about how to attain specific goals. It is how-to-do-it knowledge, or organized "know-how." It rests on value judgments, since goals are derived from explicit and implicit priorities of value. The determination of goals is a different function from the steps taken to achieve them, but technologists may influence policy and in some areas of endeavor they are compelled to play a major role in the process of value integration. Judges must help in the never-ending task of integrating community values in order to make legal decisions.[7] The term "strict technology" is sometimes used to refer to exclusive preoccupation with the means, with no questioning or influencing of the ends.

The supporting ideology of an area of technology rests on beliefs of fact as well as on beliefs of value, and the beliefs of fact are not necessarily borrowed from the basic sciences. Some beliefs of fact in technologies are developed by the use of the scientific method in applied research, often without reference to more basic explanations.

---

[5] William J. Goode and Paul K. Hatt, *Methods in Social Research* (New York: McGraw-Hill, 1952), Chapter 2, "Science: Theory and Fact," 7–17; Bernard S. Phillips, *Social Research: Strategy and Tactics* (New York: The Macmillan Co., 1966), 37–42.
[6] Goode and Hatt, *op. cit.,* Chapter 4, "Science: Pure and Applied;" Phillips, *op. cit.,* 49–58.
[7] F. James Davis *et al., Society and the Law* (New York: The Free Press, 1962), 27–32, 66.

Some of the beliefs are traditional, and others are common-sense conclusions of the persons involved. Using legal reasoning again as an illustration, beliefs of fact about human behavior and social control have long been taken from folk traditions, philosophy and theology, and other sources. Judges and lawyers have begun to borrow knowledge from the social sciences, but the medical profession has developed much more effective ways of utilizing information from the several basic sciences, including sociology.[8] The relating of means to ends requires sound beliefs of fact, so technologies are improved by the incorporation of tested knowledge about cause-and-effect relationships. It is never assumed in the basic sciences that the current knowledge is complete and infallible, but explanations are constantly being tested and revised to improve them.

Bodies of how-to-do-it knowledge must be distinguished from the actions that put them into practice. *The term applied science often is used to refer both to science-based technology and to related practical action.* Both the practice of obstetrics and the organizing and communicating of the requisite knowledge are in considerable part applications of embryology and other biological knowledge. The professor of medicine whose research and teaching are limited to *how to* deal with problems of practice is playing only the technological role as defined here; if he has some patients he moves into the role of practitioner part of the time; and if he makes some contributions to biology or chemistry he plays the role of basic scientist in part. (Medical schools usually employ various basic scientists so that the physicians can concentrate on problems of professional practice.)

Let us consider briefly the profession of social work as technology and art (skilled practice). While pursuing the Master's Degree in Social Work (MSW), one studies such subjects as family case work, group work, community organization, interviewing, counseling, record keeping and report writing, and social work research. Attention is given throughout to the problems and methods of the various aspects of social work practice, and considerable time is devoted to gaining experience on supervised field placements. Professional technologies borrow from a variety of fields, and applications of economics, political science, biology, psychology, anthropology, sociology, and other disciplines are incorporated into the changing framework of social work know-how. Familiarity with the basic areas most utilized must

---

[8] *Ibid.,* 32–36.

be gained before the two years of concentrated study of professional matters begins. As for the goals and the supporting beliefs of value, child welfare, individual responsibility, minimum standards of living, and other community values figure prominently in the organized treatments of the philosophy of social work.

SOCIAL SCIENCE AND VALUES

Does the foregoing mean that social science has nothing to do with values? Social scientists continue to discuss issues about values, within as well as among the several disciplines. However, the consensus of most sociologists and a great many other social scientists and philosophers of science is that social science and values are related in the four ways discussed in the following.

1. *Science is Based on Certain Value Judgments*

The most basic value on which all science rests is that sound knowledge of observable events is superior to ignorance. From this are derived such values as intellectual honesty, readiness to admit error, and academic freedom.[9]

2. *Values are Part of the Data of the Social Sciences*

Much of the theory and research in the social sciences is concerned with the role of values in human society.[10] Considerable attention has been given in this book to the role of values in the rise and persistence of social problems. Basic analysis can contribute to community understanding of its value dilemmas, to the delineation of alternative means for coping with deplored conditions, and to the probable costs and consequences of different actions.[11] But whether the study of values is applied to the consideration of programs of action or not, it remains a central part of much of sociology and the other social

---

9 Goode and Hatt, *op. cit.*, 21–22; Roy G. Francis, "The Nature of Scientific Research," Chapter 1 in John T. Doby (ed.), *An Introduction to Social Research* (New York: Appleton-Century-Crofts, 1967), 8–9.
10 Goode and Hatt, *op. cit.*, 25–26; William R. Catton, Jr., "A Theory of Value," *American Sociological Review*, 24 (June, 1959), 310–17; Franz Adler, "On, 'A Theory of Value'," and a reply by Catton, *American Sociological Review*, 25 (February, 1960), 85–88; Robin M. Williams, Jr., *American Society* (2nd ed., Rev.; New York: Alfred A. Knopf, 1961), Chapter 11, "Values and Beliefs in American Society."
11 George A. Lundberg, Clarence C. Schrag, and Otto N. Larsen, *Sociology* (3rd ed.; New York: Harper & Row, 1963), 747.

sciences. This is a unique contribution to knowledge, not shared by the physical and biological sciences; but the other three ways in which social science and values are related are shared by all the sciences.

3. *Values are Involved in the Selection of Topics for Scientific Study*

While much scientific research, writing, and teaching is motivated by intellectual curiosity, the desire for recognition, and other considerations, much of it is altruistic. Many people become scientists because they want to contribute to the solution of the ills of society. The biologist who seeks grants to study the effects of tobacco very likely wants to help reduce the suffering and early death that evidently result from prolonged, heavy smoking. The economist who concentrates on the complexities of the business cycle likely wants to help alleviate and avoid the distress resulting from extreme upward and downward swings in the cycle, or to help prevent the destruction of the capitalist economy. Social scientists who choose to study such matters as race relations, international relations, and family relations are usually (but not necessarily) greatly concerned about such values as equal opportunity, individual dignity, peace, emotional health, and family stability.

However, once a study has been undertaken, the scientific norm is that no value judgments can be allowed to influence the research operations and the drawing of conclusions about the conditions under which things happen. Values may influence the selection of the topic to be researched, written, or taught about, but not the observations and the analysis. Some social scientists hold that they should confess their biases in all their work, so that others may note them and see what influence they have had.[12] A related view is that biases can at least be prevented from having an extreme influence if certain guidelines are followed.[13] Since sociologists and other social scientists study values, they are quite conscious of the need to be aware of their own biases and those of their colleagues, and to take them fully into account.

---

[12] Gunnar Myrdal, with the assistance of Richard Sterner and Arnold M. Rose, *An American Dilemma* (New York: Harper and Bros., 1944), "A Methodological Note on Facts and Valuations in Social Science," 1035–45.
[13] Howard S. Becker, "Whose Side Are We On?" *Social Problems*, 14 (Winter, 1967), 239–47.

American sociologists have been criticized for studying only American society, and for limiting themselves to theories and methods appropriate for that task.[14] It also has been suggested that sociologists (and presumably those in other disciplines) are affected by the interests and values of their clients, and thus by the functions they perform in a given society. For example, in the Union of South Africa the role of sociologists traditionally has been to study the plight of the poor whites and thereby to contribute to the training of social welfare workers, and to research on short-range economic problems.[15] In underdeveloped countries sociology is typically identified with social reform and social welfare, as it usually was in the United States early in this century. In short, the dominant value concerns of the society as well as of the individual scientist may heavily influence the selection of topics for scientific work. If the sciences are limited to work on certain currently pressing social problems, their progress toward more fundamental comprehensive knowledge is retarded.

4. *Values Operate in the Application of Scientific Knowledge to Human Problems*

Regardless of what motivates its development, knowledge in the basic sciences is neutral; it may be applied toward the attainment of different, even opposite, goals. Knowledge about the effects of an antibiotic drug may be used to combat diseases or to kill people. Knowledge about the growth and persistence of organized crime may be used to combat it, to avoid contact with it, or to build stronger rackets and syndicates. Reliable knowledge about the effects of certain kinds of mass media appeals may facilitate such varied ends as selling life insurance or beer, getting money for crippled children, getting the Germans during War II to accept the Nazi's wholesale slaughter of the Jews, or building support for churches. Clearly, some purposes must be designated and some value priorities have to become involved before scientific knowledge can be put to use. If the scientist is asked what to do, he must answer like the Cheshire Cat if he remains in the role of scientist—it depends on where you want to go. If the goal you seek is X, he may say, we will need to examine

---

[14] Everett C. Hughes, "Ethnocentric Sociology," *Social Forces*, 40 (October, 1961), 1–4.

[15] Richard C. Peterson, "Sociology and Society: The Case of South Africa, *Sociological Inquiry*, 36 (Winter, 1966), 31–38.

five alternative means of reaching it; if you seek Y, there are also a number of possible actions to consider, each with its costs and risks.

SOCIAL SCIENCE AND BELIEFS OF FACT

The expertise of any scientist is based on his knowledge of the ways certain things happen—on his judgments of fact. The social scientist's knowledge includes tentative conclusions about the functions of values in human activities and, despite such difficulties as those noted above, beliefs of fact about values may be tested and treated objectively. A basic assumption in science is that the key to objectivity in dealing with data of all kinds is *verifiability*. Full reporting of both findings and methods of research makes possible critical reviews and corroboration through replication by other investigators.[16] Hunches and insights are treated as potentially valuable leads for scientific work, but they do not become part of the tentatively accepted body of knowledge unless they stand up under test by appropriate observations.

The availability of increasingly dependable knowledge about man in society makes it more possible to anticipate the costs and the probable outcomes of alternative approaches to social problems, but working out these applications is no simple matter. In this book there have been many opportunities to note the current explanations of sociologists regarding social problem conditions and their associated dilemmas, and to compare them with beliefs of fact held in the community. How can society make use of basic explanations of fact that are relevant to social problems? Especially, what are the responsibilities and roles of the social scientists?

SOME ROLE ISSUES

Scientist versus Citizen

The scientist's personal values may lead him to prefer one means to another for reasons other than efficiency in reaching a goal, and he may likewise prefer the pursuit of one goal over another. If he takes action in accord with these preferences he departs from the role of scientist and adopts the role of citizen, or some more specific role such as parent, consumer, board member, or neighbor. Like other people

---

[16] Lundberg, *op. cit.*, 17–26; Goode and Hatt, *op. cit.*, 20.

in complex societies he has the problem of integrating his actions in his various roles into a reasonably unified personality, and it may not always be clear when he is speaking strictly as a scientist and when he is not. It often facilitates communication when he is addressing himself to policy matters if he prefaces his comments with phrases like, "speaking as an economist," or, "my view as a parent and member of this committee rather than as a psychologist, *etc.*" The social or other scientist who mixes his roles indiscriminately may succeed in persuading others to accept his value priorities, but the respect accorded to his role as a scientist is based on his command of explanations of fact.

This does not mean that the scientist cannot be an active participant in civic affairs. As a citizen he is free to participate in political activities, to discuss public issues, take stands on them, and to take action. Social scientists who become quite ardent in their espousal of causes often find it difficult for people to believe that they can be objective in their work, especially about the issues on which they are so active; yet a frequent argument is that those with the most specialized knowledge have a duty to society to see that it is used for the common good. The question, accepting the argument, is how. By direct action, by consulting with major decision-makers, by addressing oneself to general publics, by concentrating on making significant contributions to knowledge and trusting that others will find ways to apply them to community problems? A prevalent view at least in sociology is that the minimum responsibility is to point out the policy implications of research findings—in research reports, in textbooks, and in the classroom. Whatever the scientist does about public issues, however many roles he plays, scientific ethics require him to keep his scientific role as separate as he can from the citizen roles.

Researcher versus Social Engineer

Both basic and applied scientific researchers produce if-then statements, but the decision-makers and planners must make value judgments in their work.[17] If one remains in the role of scientist he contributes only to the technological beliefs of fact, but there are often pressures to make unqualified recommendations or in other

---

[17] Philip M. Hauser, "Social Science and Social Engineering," *Philosophy and Science*, 16 (July, 1949), 209–18; Philip M. Hauser and George C. Homans, "Schlesinger on Humanism and Empirical Research," *American Sociological Review*, 28 (February, 1963), 97–100.

ways to participate in the value judgments necessary for practical action. If he accepts a position as an administrator or planner he is no longer functioning as a scientist, basic or applied, though his background may be useful in the action role.

If a sociologist is asked by the Human Relations Commission of a city to direct a study of racial housing patterns and to prepare a written report of his findings, he is doing applied research whether he is paid or not. He may, if he is clever and diplomatic, manage to accomplish some of his own basic research along with obtaining the information desired by the Commission. When he writes his report he may devote a good deal of space to the probable costs and outcomes of alternative actions, specifying the supporting values of each and qualifying the beliefs of fact. If he is questioned in person about the report, he is still in the role of (applied) scientist if his explanations are of the if-then variety, concerned solely with beliefs of fact. The more he is drawn into involvement as a citizen, the more his responses are likely to reflect his personal value priorities on matters of race and housing. It may then be difficult, but not impossible, for him to keep the roles of researcher and social engineer separate.

Consultant and Public Educator versus Actionist

If a scientific consultant to any type of organization limits his contribution to if-then statements, he is performing a liaison function, helping to translate some of his special knowledge so that it can be used by decision-makers and planners. If a social scientist pushes a pet program that reflects his value preferences, or downgrades certain alternative means because they offend his values, he has entered the domain of the social engineer. Since the view that sociologists and other social scientists are qualified to tell society what it should want is generally rejected,[18] the consultant gives the most service for his fee if he concentrates on the relevant beliefs of fact in his discipline.

In speeches and in writings addressed to general publics the social scientist often treats social problems. One option is to adhere strictly to the role of scientist in such communications, the task being to make specialized knowledge available to the general reader or listener in understandable form—an exercise in public education. The oppo-

---

[18] Lundberg, Schrag, and Larsen, *op. cit.*, 743–46; Goode and Hatt, *op. cit.*, 27. However, some social scientists (including some sociologists) believe they can demonstrate the superiority of some values over others, at least as being more instrumental in achieving more ultimate goals.

site tack is to make an all-out case for a given program of action, which obviously requires the adoption of a certain value position along with some analysis. Social criticism also represents a departure from the role of social scientist, since it is of necessity based on certain values. The book, popular magazine article, or speech in which scientific knowledge about some issue is accompanied by a discussion of the pros and cons and supporting values of alternative actions is closer to the first option. It represents the assumption of civic responsibility, yet in the role of social scientist speaking to the community. Regardless of whether his public communications are education, exhortation, or some combination, the social scientist is obligated to make clear what role he is adopting at all times. This becomes complicated if he shifts roles often from one paragraph to the next.

Social Science and Publics

Specialists of all kinds discuss issues among themselves, and upon occasion they take action to get the community at large concerned about some condition. Scientific societies seldom make resolutions on public issues or agitate to enlarge publics, although they may if they believe their own survival is threatened. Social science documentation is often sought by professional or other groups that are seeking to influence a general public. Some well-known sociologists have been quite prominent in connection with some public causes—such as planned parenthood, school integration, and abolition of capital punishment—concerning which their data have produced overwhelming agreement on certain factual conclusions. Yet value priorities are also necessarily involved in programs of action on these matters, and are strongly urged, so the difficult task again is to separate the scientific and the citizen roles.[19] Such strong involvement is exceptional, and probably the major influence of the social sciences on the discussion of social problems is the dissemination to large numbers of students the ever-changing knowledge about how things happen in human society.

CONCLUSION

Values are a major part of the data of sociology and all the social sciences. Three other respects in which values are involved are shared

---

[19] Lundberg, Schrag, and Larsen, *op. cit.*, 747–50.

by the physical and biological sciences: certain value judgments underlie all science, values are involved in the selection of topics for scientific work, and in the application of findings to practical problems. In his scientific role, once his topic has been selected the social scientist attempts to avoid having his beliefs of value influence his observations and conclusions about questions of fact. He uses various means of checking on himself and his colleagues, relying on critical discussion of methods as well as conclusions, and on the ultimate check of verification by other observers.

Since value priorities must be established for making policy and taking action, the scientist who becomes involved in any way in the applications of his knowledge encounters problems in shifting from the role of scientist to citizen roles. Many social scientists with advanced degrees now are employed in technological and action roles, and others occupy a variety of applied research roles. The general guide suggested here for these problems of role identity is that it should always be clear whether the person is functioning in the role of social scientist or some other role, but no one should assume that this is an easy rule to follow.

Social scientists have had considerable influence on the discussion of public issues through a variety of channels, the major one probably being through teaching their subject matter to students. In this book we have seen many instances in which the changing knowledge in the various basic sciences has resulted in major shifts in the beliefs of fact accepted in the society—in visions of the possible and beliefs about patterns of causation—and often in the consequent rise, redefinition, or fall of major public issues. We have also seen instances where predominant public beliefs of fact are contrary to well established conclusions in the social sciences. As these young sciences develop more clearly demonstrated knowledge, and as it is successfully applied to technologies that are effective in coping with problems of major community concern, they probably will have increasing influence on the public discussion of issues. The hope is that the type of analysis pursued in this book can both contribute to sociological knowledge and to public understanding of the dilemmas of changing societies.

QUESTIONS FOR DISCUSSION AND STUDY

1. How can some condition such as divorce, alcoholism, or immigration be both a social problem and a sociological problem?
2. As discussed here, how would you classify knowledge about how to stop a prison riot: as basic science, technology, or professional practice? Explain.
3. In what ways is an area of technology an ideology?
4. Suppose a certain sociologist wants to remain in the scientific role in all his consulting, public speaking, writing, and applied research. On what basis can he indicate that one means of preventing juvenile delinquency is better than another?
5. Give an illustration of a systematic body of technology that is not based on science. Where do the supporting beliefs of fact come from?
6. Discuss the merit of this statement: "Social scientists are so obsessed with being objective that they are insensitive to the very existence of human values."
7. Does the fact that values influence the selection of a research topic mean that the results are of no scientific use? Explain.
8. What are some values the social scientist has a vested interest in from the standpoint of the survival of his craft?
9. Why do you think totalitarian governments either abolish the social sciences or restrict them to the study of particular problems?
10. How can the development of "pure" social science be regarded as "the most fundamental of all social action?"
11. Do you think social scientists can tell society what it should want? Explain.

SELECTED READING

Alpert, Harry, "The Government's Growing Recognition of Social Science," *The Annals*, 327 (January, 1960), 59–67.

Gouldner, Alvin, "Theoretical Requirements of the Applied Social Sciences," *American Sociological Review*, 22 (February, 1957), 92–102.

Lee, Elizabeth Briant, and Lee, Alfred McClung (eds.), *Social Problems in America*, (Rev. ed.; New York: Henry Holt & Co., 1955), Chapter 25, "Social Science and Social Policy."

Lundberg, George A., *Can Science Save Us?* (2nd ed.; New York: David McKay Co., 1961).

Lynd, Robert S., *Knowledge for What?* (Princeton, N.J.: Princeton University Press, 1939).

McDonagh, Edward C., and Simpson, Jon E. (eds.), *Social Problems: Persistent Challenges* (New York: Holt, Rinehart & Winston, 1965), Chapter 12, "Search for Solutions."

Neal, Sister Marie Augusta, *Values and Interests in Social Change* (Englewood Cliffs, N.J.: Prentice-Hall, 1965).

Rose, Arnold M., "The Social Responsibility of the Social Scientist," *Social Problems*, 1 (January, 1954), 85–90.

Valdes, Donald M., and Dean, Dwight G. (eds.), *Sociology in Use* (New York: The Macmillan Co., 1965).

Zetterberg, Hans L., *Social Theory and Social Practice* (New York: Bedminister Press, 1962).

Name Index

Subject Index

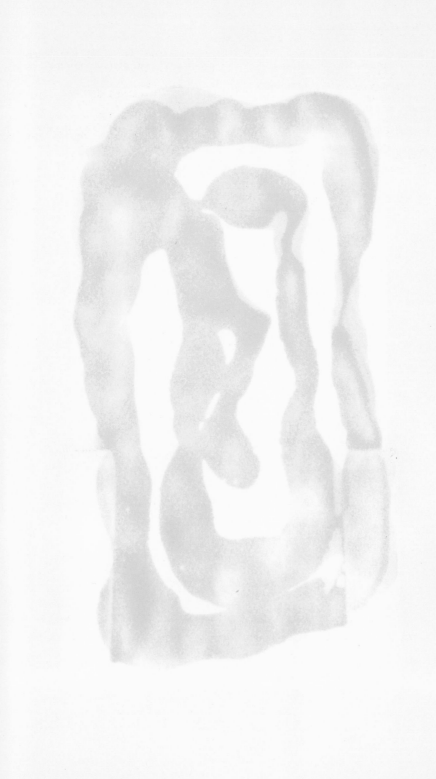

88868

DATE DUE

MAY 1 1 '78		
MAY 1 7 '78		
MAR. 0 8 1994		